The Presidency of
HERBERT C.
HOOVER

AMERICAN PRESIDENCY SERIES

Donald R. McCoy, Clifford S. Griffin, Homer E. Socolofsky
General Editors

The Presidency of
HERBERT C.
HOOVER

Martin L. Fausold

UNIVERSITY PRESS OF KANSAS

Published by the University Press of Kansas (Lawrence,
Kansas 66045), which was organized by the Kansas Board
of Regents and is operated and funded by Emporia State
University, Fort Hays State University, Kansas State
University, Pittsburg State University, the University
of Kansas, and Wichita State University

Library of Congress Cataloging in Publication Data

Fausold, Martin L., 1921–
The presidency of Herbert C. Hoover.
(American presidency series)
Bibliography: p.
Includes index.
1. United States—Politics and government—1929–1933.
2. Hoover, Herbert, 1874–1964. I. Title. II. Series.
E801.F25 1984   973.91′6′0924 [B]   84-17252
ISBN 0-7006-0259-3

Printed in the United States of America

To
Mac, Patsy, Alice
and
in memory of our brother, Sam

''To teach is to learn twice''
Joseph Joubert

CONTENTS

Foreword ix
Acknowledgments xi
1 The Education of Herbert Hoover 1
2 Victory 21
3 A New Beginning 39
4 The Crash 63
5 1930 83
6 The Corporatist Balance 105
7 1931: Things Get Worse 125
8 Depression and the Seventy-second Congress 147
9 Foreign Policy 167
10 Defeat 193
11 Rites of Passage 215
12 Epilogue 237
Notes 247
Bibliographical Essay 267
Index 279

FOREWORD

The aim of the American Presidency Series is to present historians and the general reading public with interesting, scholarly assessments of the various presidential administrations. These interpretive surveys are intended to cover the broad ground between biographies, specialized monographs, and journalistic accounts. As such, each will be a comprehensive, synthetic work which will draw upon the best in pertinent secondary literature, yet leave room for the author's own analysis and interpretation.

Volumes in the series will present the data essential to understanding the administration under consideration. Particularly, each book will treat the then current problems facing the United States and its people and how the president and his associates felt about, thought about, and worked to cope with these problems. Attention will be given to how the office developed and operated during the president's tenure. Equally important will be consideration of the vital relationships between the president, his staff, the executive officers, Congress, foreign representatives, the judiciary, state officials, the public, political parties, the press, and influential private citizens. The series will also be concerned with how this unique American institution—the presidency—was viewed by the presidents, and with what results.

All this will be set, insofar as possible, in the context not only of contemporary politics but also of economics, international relations, law, morals, public administration, religion, and thought. Such a broad approach is necessary to understanding, for a presidential administration is more than the elected and appointed officers composing it, since its work so often reflects the major problems, anxieties, and glories of the nation. In short, the authors in the series will strive to recount and evaluate the record of each administration and to identify its distinctiveness and relationships to the past, its own time, and the future.

The General Editors

ACKNOWLEDGMENTS

I will always be grateful to the fine colleagues who, without hesitation, talked with me about the manuscript and read and criticized portions of it: Selig Adler, Vaughn Davis Bornet, James Bowers, David Burner, Alexander De Conde, William Derby, J. William Frost, Frank Freidel, Jr., Louis P. Galambos, Ellis W. Hawley, Robert F. Himmelberg, Joan Hoff-Wilson, David A. Martin, Jordan A. Schwarz, Robert Sobel, and William Appleman Williams. Special thanks go to Donald R. McCoy and George H. Nash, for reading the entire manuscript, and to Mrs. Katherine H. Durand, of Washington, D.C., for reading the references to Quakerism. I trust that my work somewhat justified their time. Certainly any weaknesses in the book are mine, not theirs. As always, it is a pleasure to thank librarians, particularly the staff of the Milne Library here at Geneseo and, most especially, Richard Quick, the director; William Lane, the reference librarian; and David Parish, the documents librarian. The staff at the Herbert Hoover Presidential Library was of inestimable service—most noteworthy were Robert Wood, Mildred Mather, and Shirley Sondegard.

For financial assistance I thank the Research Foundation of the State University of New York, the Herbert Hoover Presidential Library Association, the Geneseo Foundation, and the SUNY Geneseo Faculty Senate, for several grants and fellowships; and Vice-President Thomas Colahan for a leave with salary (as I clutched my chest and explained to him my need, following heart surgery, to finish this book). Also, I was fortunate that the State University of New York gave me a grant to direct a conference on the Hoover presidency, which resulted in *The Hoover Presidency: A Reappraisal* (Albany: State University of New York Press, 1974), and that the National Endowment for the Humanities appointed me director of a summer seminar of fellows at the Herbert Hoover Presidential Library in West Branch, Iowa. Both experiences were rewarding and very helpful to my conceptualization of the Hoover presidency.

As always, I thank my family—("How's Hoover coming, Dad?"). Two people constantly encouraged me: my wonderful wife, Daryl; and my sister, Mrs. James W. Sheaffer, who put her considerable language skills to work criticizing the whole manuscript. I dedicate this book to my brothers and sisters who, with me, were raised in a home where Franklin D. Roosevelt was a demigod. I trust that their reading of the book will be as worthwhile a corrective exercise for them as it was for me to write it.

Martin L. Fausold

Geneseo, New York

1

★ ★ ★ ★ ★

THE EDUCATION OF
HERBERT HOOVER

Life is essentially a mixture of religion, family, education, and vocation. The mixture in Herbert Hoover's case appears to have been so increasingly joined and intensely reinforced as to explain, more than is usual, the fate of one who was to become president of the United States. This is not to say that, as Hoover progressed from the Quakerism of his youth to preeminence as a mining engineer and then as a public figure, his life did not change, as would be expected in so dramatic a transition from sectarianism to worldliness. Ideologically, however, the more Hoover's life changed, the more it seemed to stay the same.

"I come of Quaker stock," declared Herbert Hoover on the eve of his presidency.[1] These five words seemed to bespeak a lifetime of endless demands upon him. A Washington neighbor reported him as having said, prior to entering the White House: "A philosophy of rules telling you what to do in given circumstancs is a philosophy which you can sometimes escape from because, if circumstances arise which are not among the given circumstances, then there are no rules, and you can do as you like. But if your people make you believe that the 'Inner Light' would light everything, then you keep trying to expand that 'Light' to cover every new circumstance that happens and every new problem that arises, and you are never through. You keep getting new rules, from inside, all the time."[2]

Hoover's lifetime Quakerism belies his comment, "I never worked very hard at it."[3] If speaking spiritually about his Quakerism, he undoubtedly believed this comment about Quakerism. Although he sometimes wrote about the spirit, Hoover never seemed to be particularly spiritual. But viewing his Quakerism in secular terms, he could not deny what the world came to realize—that he did indeed work "very hard at it." The latter application of the tenets of Quakerism, although not divorced from spirituality, was so important that one must ask whence it came.

The intensity of Quakerism is frequently in proportion to the strengthening of the faith through generations of a Friends family. In Herbert Hoover's case, the family tradition of the religion was unusual. His ancestor Andrew Hoover (Huber) arrived in Philadelphia in 1738 and abandoned his Lutheran heritage in favor of William Penn's religion—the Society of Friends. Thus began a succession of very prominent Quaker leaders—first, Andrew's son Andrew, who, with his son David, founded and settled Richmond, Indiana, which became a national center of Quaker faith in the nation. More immediately, Hoover's father, Jesse, five times removed from Andrew's generation, was still practicing Quakerism when Herbert was born in 1874; and Jesse's Uncle John was a powerful Quaker preacher, writer, and a leading minister in West Branch, Iowa, during the 1870s and 1880s. Also on the paternal side, Herbert Hoover's great grandmother Rebecca was a recorded minister of the church.

The Quaker credentials on Hoover's maternal side are comparable. Although Jesse felt less the Friends' call than had his Uncle John, Jesse's wife, Huldah, Herbert's mother, more than made up for any religious deficiency on her husband's part. The Minthorns, Huldah's ancestors, who had arrived on the continent before Andrew Hoover, had founded a Quaker colony in Toronto, on what is known today as Quaker Street. Huldah, like two of her sisters and a brother, became a recorded Quaker minister. She did so in West Branch, where she and Jesse raised their young family. Huldah was moved beautifully by the "spirit" in the "meeting," frequently breaking forth into song. After Jesse Hoover, a successful business man, died of heart failure in the prime of life, when his son Herbert was only six years of age, Huldah frequently left her three children—Herbert, his older brother, Theodore, and his younger sister, Mary—in the care of Friends as she traveled to various meetings to proclaim the word of God. When Herbert was nine years of age, Huldah succumbed to pneumonia, and the children were then separated and cared for by Quaker kin in various places. Between this time and Herbert's entrance into Stanford University, he was raised by his uncle, Henry John Minthorn, a country doctor in a Quaker settlement in Newberg, Oregon.

2

Aside from the example of having had Quaker ministers and Quaker leaders in generations of Hoovers and Minthorns preceding young Hoover's introduction to the faith, numerous Quaker relatives within his lifetime pursued various Friends' vocations and avocations: medicine, education, Indian service, underground railroading, midwifery, and other activities that are generally of service to their fellow men, Quaker and non-Quaker alike. Of course Hoover's introduction to Quakerism came not only through Quaker tenets practiced by his family and neighbors but was also by the "meeting," the religious service that is frequently inseparable from family. At home, Hoover experienced what another young Quaker, Rufus M. Jones, came to call the "dew" of Quakerism: prayers, the silent grace before meals, the daily reading of the Bible, the simplicity of living. The Hoovers' white cottage in West Branch was probably typical of Friends' homes—plain and intimate: an unostentatious place for private conversation with friends and relatives, for quiet sociabilities, with limited and very select literature other than the Bible, with no musical instruments, with no playing cards, and certainly with no alcohol. Of most indelible influence on Hoover, as on all young Friends, was the Quaker silent worship at Fifth Day (Thursday) and First Day (Sunday) meetings where, as a young boy, Hoover sat for hours without squirming, daring only to "count his toes."[4]

Hoover frequently later chided his church for the severity of its customs. When he reminisced about his youth, he avoided mentioning the restraints of Quakerism and talked instead about sledding down Cook's Hill, swimming in the Wapsinonoc Creek, skinning rabbits, fishing for catfish, playing baseball, or exploring the woods. Even farm chores took on a romantic glow. Yet, the dew of Quakerism daily permeated the lives of young Quakers such as Herbert Hoover.

The most fundamental principle of Quakerism throughout its history has been the "Inner Light," which Hoover mentioned to that Washington neighbor. It probably makes Quakerism the most individualistic of all Christian religions, perhaps of all Western religions. Every man possesses the "Inner Light." Quakers particularly emphasize equality. The light of God, the unerring guide to Christian action, exists in every individual. In their "meeting," Quakers wait in silence for guidance. While young boys dare only to count their toes, their elders await the "Light" and speak God's words when they come. The Bible, when read daily, will support and inspire the "Light." God is immanent in all men. And to feel God and the inspiration of Christ, all attention must be directed to the voice of God and Christ. Thus there is no music, no stained glass, no pulpit, no leader—as there was not in the stark white meeting house that Hoover attended as a boy in West

Branch. True, his mother, Huldah, sang, and some Quakers went the way of more evangelistic Protestant form and service, but Herbert Hoover always preferred the plain meeting house and its silent service. He, as president, and his wife, Lou, were to a large degree responsible for the building of the plain and dignified meeting house on Florida Avenue in Washington.

It is important to be reminded that personal experience was the key to the "Inner Light," an individualism that made men equal (without denying, of course, a corporate unity). Friends so believed in individualism that they vigorously pursued the liberty and equality that were attached to it. Such a quest was accomplished by adhering to the tenets of the religion, which took the form of "Queries," read at the monthly meetings of Friends. The Queries—questions asked of Quakers over the centuries since George Fox had led his followers away from the formalities of Catholicism, Anglicanism, and Presbyterianism—were remarkably consistent, although changed to adjust to the times. By young Hoover's day and into the twentieth century, Friends were asked if they conscientiously opposed war, capital punishment, legal oaths, intemperance, gambling, secret societies, extravagance, discrimination, paid ministry, the double standard; and if they favored rights for laborers, education, social relief, temperance, proper treatment of Indians and Negroes, prison reform, the loving care of the insane, foreign missions, equality of the sexes, simplicity, religious tolerance, free ministry, civil liberty, and ecumenical cooperation?

The Queries, of course, were items of brotherly advice, repeated so often and so sternly that they implied a morality and will of God that demanded discipline and order among Quakers. Quakers, young Hoover apparently being no exception, practiced an "ordered liberty"— a seeming paradox. More than any other Christian denomination, Quakers stress the individual relationship of its members to God. Yet, Quakers are both consciously and unconsciously pressured to adhere to the tenets (Queries) that they believe Christ would have applied to their day, if not to His day—a "corporate individualism."[5] It seems safe to assume that such a fountainhead influenced Hoover to say, as he entered the presidency, "My concept of America is a land where men and women may walk in ordered-freedom." The transition from Quaker youth to president, however, was no sudden leap. The reader must realize that it came by stages of reinforcement. First, Hoover, in his Quaker moorings, learned that freedom, though essential, could never be absolute. His Quaker individualism required the discipline of self and cooperation with others. Only so could there be assured among men and women the equality of freedom and individualism. Thus was launched young Herbert Hoover's incremental march to high presidential belief and commitment.[6]

Hoover's education in life was composed of very distinctive stages, each uncannily drawing on the previous one and all leading to and strongly affecting his presidency. Following his youth came professionalism, beginning at Stanford. During part of Hoover's youth in Oregon he had lived with his brother, Theodore, at Friends' Pacific Academy. For a time thereafter he had helped his Uncle John Minthorn open up a real-estate office in Salem, Oregon, where young Hoover learned something of Quaker entrepreneurial style—diligence, honesty, consistent pricing, quality of product, financial success, and even a certain irascibility. Dr. Minthorn expected Hoover to attend a Quaker college—either Earlham or Haverford. However, a Quaker teacher of mathematics, who was recruiting students for the newly formed Stanford University, persuaded Hoover to enter the engineering program at that California institution.

There Hoover's world view expanded considerably beyond the confines of his youth. While he received a particularly secure grounding in geology in preparation for a career in mining engineering, his extracurricular activity was not sacrificed. He became treasurer of both his junior class and the Associated Students, helped to lead a movement of independent students against affluent Greek-letter fraternities, and made money on the side in various jobs. He had a shy, blunt manner, and at times he manifested a wry humor. He became quite influential, functioning, as David Burner, one of Hoover's biographers, has noted, "in some ways like the clerk of a Quaker meeting, always directing but never dictating."[7] Hoover's most recent biographer, George H. Nash, concludes that the Stanford years reinforced "in secular terms the lessons of his Quaker relatives: that one should live productively, that life is meant for accomplishment, that one ought to do a 'conscientious work.'" Nash notes that Hoover, after his Stanford days, gradually deviated from the "evangelical Quakerism of his youth" and that "his theological convictions were probably liberal or unorthodox." He drank, smoked, attended the theater, and for years after Stanford seldom attended the Quaker meeting. Still, the positive Stanford experience of Hoover's youth, with its emphasis on "conscientious work," democratic ethos, and antielitism, seems to have provided a strong bridge from his Quaker past to his professional and public future. None other than Stanford University's President David Starr Jordan best reflected the link from Hoover's Quaker wellspring to his professional affluence: "In helpfulness alone can wealth and power find consecration."[8]

Hoover succeeded at Stanford and was pushed forward by his geology professor and mentor, Dr. John C. Branner. The story of Hoover's incredibly successful mining career has been thoroughly told in several fine accounts. In short, the career began during his Stanford years with menial summer labor jobs at geological work in the Ozarks and the Sierras. After his graduation, it was, strangely enough, his typewriting skill that landed him in the office of a New Mexico–San Francisco mining firm, where his diligence and knowledge of mining were so impressive that the owner, Louis Janin, pushed him "on." The British firm of Bewick, Moreing and Company wanted just the right engineer to sample, survey, and evaluate gold mines in western Australia; and Janin recommended Hoover. There Hoover proved his mining brilliance by suggesting to the London firm that it develop the Sons of Gwalia Mine and by becoming the chief engineer of the eight gold mines of Kalgoorlie. Hoover's skill as an administrator matched his engineering prowess.

Of interest to our story of Hoover was his no-nonsense approach to the laborers in the mine—by offering them some of the best conditions in the world in regard to hours and wages, yet increasing hours and reducing wages when times required such action. Much of management, more than labor, came to appreciate Hoover. He was particularly valued for his intelligent yet firm direction.

Hoover's mining reputation, including his ability at hard bargaining, took him into many of the mines of China. Although his experience with the Chinese of all classes was frustrating, his successes were even greater than previously, perhaps, in part, because his marriage in 1899 to Lou Henry, a fellow geology student at Stanford, gave his life some needed equanimity. (Hoover's separation from the sectarian Quakerism of his youth allowed him to be not in the least concerned that a Catholic priest performed the wedding service in the home of Lou Henry's parents.) Soon he became heavily involved in and knowledgeable about large international economic forces, new financing techniques, the flow of international capital, world-wide economic organization, and the quickening pace of the technological revolution. Hoover's professional success and the broadening intellectual and cultural horizons in Australia and China were a natural outgrowth of his Quaker and Stanford habits and experiences: learning, hard work, sensible cooperation, commonsense decency, and good neighborliness.

During the first decade of the century, Hoover, on behalf of Bewick, Moreing, and Company, traveled around the world five times, intermittently living in London, first at 39 Hyde Park Gate, Kensington, and then at Red House in London's Campden Hill. The times in London were particularly happy for the young Hoover family, which included two sons, although the English, who were not familiar with Hoover's Quaker ways, often found his bluntness ungraceful. It was also during this period that the Hoovers built homes in California: first in Monterey and then a larger home in Palo Alto, near his increasingly beloved Stanford.

Herbert Hoover, now recognized as one of the world's foremost engineers, was engaged professionally—always hurriedly—in places as separated as China, Australia, Burma, Peru, Russia, and Mexico. After having terminated his tenure with Bewick, Moreing, and Company in 1908, he formed his own consulting firm and accumulated a vast fortune as a "doctor of sick mines," answering calls for mining advice from around the world.

By 1910 Hoover's professionalism, his mining intelligence, and his powers of engineering concentration seemed to have exhausted his frontiers. He began to talk about other vocations—academic life, partisan politics, newspaper journalism, public administration. Burner, in his biography *Herbert Hoover: A Public Life*, has an important chapter, "Engineer as Critic," which points up the distinction, yet the interdependence, of the stages in Hoover's life. Burner sees Hoover's engineering professionalism as manifesting what the great American sociologist Thorstein B. Veblen advocated for entrepreneurs at that time, an "instinct of workmanship"—an ingrained appreciation of the quality of workers and work—and not only a shrewdness of business. While there is little evidence that Hoover read Veblen, both of them agreed, coincidentally, about industrial precision, professional creativity, rational economics, moral imperatives, and public well-being. Veblen's concepts came from the world of academe; Hoover's came less from the academic world and more from a combination of Quaker tenets, corporate institutionalism, and world-wide practical experience. As Hoover might have read Veblen with pleasure, surely Veblen would have been pleased by Hoover's "workmanship," especially regarding industrial-labor relations. While Hoover changed his mind several times on the idea of compulsory arbitration between employers and employees, he always believed that labor unions were necessary antidotes to unlimited capital organization. And while unions, he felt, had a right to strike, he surely thought that such strikes were often too wasteful, an unnecessary condition if laborers were treated humanely with regard to wages and hours. He believed that it was incumbent upon employers to take a genuine interest in the general welfare of the workers. It was only professional to do so; Hoover insisted on this in his classic textbook, *Principles of Mining.*[9]

Hoover's ideas about capital, which largely emphasized order and what historians have come to call the "rationalization" of industry, were, of course, not peculiar to him. Many other business and professional leaders, for a variety of reasons, thought in the same way that Hoover did. They were institutionalists, the types of industrialists who sought to bring capital and labor together in the common cause of bringing order out of chaotic competition. Indeed, the ideas of such entrepreneurs were quite consistent with the new planning spirit of progressivism, whose hero, Theodore Roosevelt, was becoming Hoover's hero. Yet, few of the business and professional leaders were as committed as was Hoover to the abandonment of their large enterprises and to replacing them with a full-time devotion to a great movement that called forth many of the same tenets of Hoover's family Quakerism and his professionalism. Both experiences would be used in new ways during a new stage of his life.

In the few years before the outbreak of World War I in 1914 Hoover seems to have thrashed about for new directions to his life. In one important instance he and Lou translated into English the classic mining text of Georgius Agricola, the sixteenth-century German mineralogist. It was a long labor of love, consistent with both Quaker commitments to intellectualism and professionalism.

Some of Hoover's good work seemed almost aberrant—for example, his trying in 1912 to secure the cooperation of the British in a 1915 Panama-Pacific exposition, which was intended to publicize the resources and markets of the rapidly growing American West Coast. That effort, which gave Hoover his first important experience at public relations, was foiled by the United States Congress, which, by exempting United States ships from paying tolls to use the Panama Canal, enraged the British. The scale of Hoover's planning can be somewhat measured by his intention to have King George V attend the exposition, arriving at San Francisco via the Panama Canal. Hoover even visited government leaders in Paris and Berlin on behalf of the cause.

More Quakerly and professional than the effort for a Panama-Pacific exposition, although not more so than the intellectual exercise of translating Agricola's work, was the service that Hoover rendered to people in need at the outbreak of the great World War. Probably the best-known American in London when war broke out in August of 1914, Hoover headed the American Citizens' Relief Committee, which directed some 500 volunteers in aiding nearly 120,000 Americans to return to the United States. It was a performance par excellence of organized service, philanthropy, voluntarism, and administration.

More important but not unlike the experience of aiding Americans who were caught in the European war was the feeding and clothing of hundreds of thousands of Belgians who had been made destitute by the German invasion of their country. Hoover called it "the greatest job Americans have undertaken in the name of humanity."[10] The Commission for Relief in Belgium (CRB) was awesomely directed by Hoover, who often earned the enmity of people whose mission it interfered with. He, of course, cared little about British concern over the effect that food relief might have on their military strategies. Winston Churchill, first lord of the admiralty, called Hoover an S.O.B. Even some Americans accused Hoover of violating the Logan Act by working too closely with belligerents as he negotiated aid for Belgium. In due course, President Wilson supported Hoover's large efforts, as did Theodore Roosevelt.

President Wilson even approved congressional appropriations for the commission when sufficient philanthropic aid was not forthcoming. Prominent Americans, such as Henry L. Stimson, joined Hoover in his relief efforts for Belgium. And although the United States became a belligerent in the war and the CRB came under non-American administration, Hoover, from Washington, continued to make its policy decisions. He did the job magnificently, and although he personally shunned taking credit, he was widely applauded for it. This was Hoover as Quaker, professional, and public servant.

When the United States entered the war in 1917, Hoover was in a mood to continue to do public service on a large scale. He angled for the job as United States food administrator by describing his qualifications to prominent Wilson associates and by declaring publicly the importance of food to winning the war. For these reasons and because of Hoover's success in distributing food in Belgium, Wilson appointed him as food administrator. As such, Hoover served as a member of a small and influential war cabinet that continually advised the president on war matters. Under the Lever Act, Food Administrator Hoover had the power to regulate the distribution, exports, imports, purchases, and storage of food. He was virtually a food dictator. However, he had beguiled Wilson into using voluntarism rather than coercion to get food to "win the war." Waste became a favorite subject of Hoover's, and he persuaded most Americans, common folk and businessmen alike, to avoid hoarding, profiteering, and speculating with food. He had the power to coerce—mainly through withholding licenses to distribute food—but because of his massive public relations and his enlightened administration, he was able to accumulate extensive supplies of food stocks to feed military and civilian populations in America and Europe without the use of legal force.

It is important to note that Hoover's effort at the Food Administration was one of centralization and decentralization. From Washington he regulated many of the functions of federal corporations, national trade associations, and farm organizations. At the same time he decentralized many efforts of the Food Administration by seeking the cooperation of local buyers and sellers and small businessmen. At both levels, Hoover called for patriotism, sacrifice, hard work, and, most important, voluntarism and cooperation—elements that were generally consonant with his experiences as a youth, as a professional, and as a public servant.

It was little wonder that Hoover, at the end of the war, eagerly returned to the job of feeding destitute Europeans, the hungry of Allied and defeated nations alike. The postwar relief enabled Hoover to dispose of tremendous food surpluses that had accumulated in the United States during the war. While Hoover's prewar relief activity had largely been confined to Belgium, it now became multinational. Shiploads of food were rushed to European ports. Transportation routes—rivers and railroads—were cleared to move food inland. He boldly carried out many feeding operations, even when foreign governments would not assure repayment of American loans.

Although Hoover's role in 1919 as chairman of the Inter-Allied Food Council was his main responsibility, it was only one of many positions he held. He was also director general of the American Relief Administration, chairman of the European Coal Council, an economic advisor to the Supreme Economic Council, and a personal advisor to President Wilson. To a large degree, Hoover directed the economic reorganization of Europe while the peace negotiations dragged on in Paris. When the Treaty of Versailles was finally signed, the British economist John Maynard Keynes described Hoover as "the only man who emerged from the ordeal of Paris with an enhanced reputation. . . . This complex personality, with his habitual air of weary titan . . . , his eyes steadily fixed on the true and essential facts of the European situation, imported into the councils of Paris . . . precisely that atmosphere of reality, knowledge, magnanimity and disinterestedness which, if then had been found in other quarters would have given us a Good Peace."[11]

Hoover's growth of experiences importantly manifested themselves in his life upon his return home in 1919. Having, according to one scholar of the period, been at his best in providing relief for the principal former enemy, Germany, Hoover did not want such aid to end cruelly with the signing of the treaty in July. Therefore, he provided funds from various sources in order to enable the American Friends Service Committee to continue to provide relief aid. This action, quite by accident, brought together America's two outstanding Quakers of the century, Hoover and Rufus Jones, chairman of the Friends Service Committee. Each of these two Friends had an important influence on the other's life. When Hoover, on one occasion as president, became agitated in Jones's presence, only the eminent Quaker visitor could say such a thing as "Center down, Herbert." And Hoover accepted the Quaker admonition, normally an instruction to Quakers to prepare for their worship service.[12]

Many Americans thought that they had already done more than enough for the former enemy by the time the Treaty of Versailles was signed. But on 1 November 1919 Hoover wrote a lengthy letter to Rufus Jones, in which he insisted that "we have never fought with women and children and our desire must be to see the wounds of war healed through the world." Jones and his Quaker unit, with the aid of forty thousand Germans, fed over a million children a day in more than sixteen hundred German communities. Then Hoover extended American funds to Friends' relief work in Poland and Russia. Although Hoover was scornful of Bolshevism—and was displeased that Friend Jones would not accept all of his demands upon Russia as a condition for relief—the two saw to it that millions of Russian children were fed. Tension between Hoover and Jones flared up again when Hoover insisted that the American Friends Service Committee and other relief agencies in Russia work under the direction of the American Relief Administration and when the Field Service wanted to get out from under Hoover's direction. However, the differences between Hoover and Jones were quickly healed. "I have no reserves [sic] about the American Friends Service Committee. If there is anything in which I have implicit confidence, it is the right-mindedness of the people with whom I have been born and raised."[13]

In 1919, 1920, and 1921 Hoover was again immersed in the Washington scene. In 1919 he served as vice-chairman of the Industrial Conference to provide for postwar peace and prosperity for labor. In 1920 he announced his Republicanism and unsuccessfully sought the nomination for president. In 1921 he was appointed secretary of commerce. He tasted, not always to his liking, Washington bureaucratic and electoral politics: he was now engulfed in the political maelstrom. Years later he explained that as an engineer, he had understood cause-and-effect relationships and that political life was comparable, that politics caused criticism. "And, besides," he concluded, "I am a

Quaker. . . . We have a procedure in Quakerism known as 'cultivation of peace at the center,' and if you have peace at the center you drop hostility into this pool of inner quietness, and it is gradually absorbed.''[14]

Herbert Hoover's transition from his rather single-purpose career of food distribution—in Belgium before the United States became involved in the war, in the United States during the war, and in Europe after the war—to broad political activity in the 1919–21 period had significant repercussions. For Hoover to say that the political cause and effect of personal criticism of him would be dissipated by "peace at the center" was a gloss. His role as food administrator during the war had already demonstrated his aversion to political criticism. In a 1917 conversation with a dinner guest and admirer, Associate Justice of the Supreme Court Louis D. Brandeis, Hoover scornfully denounced Senator James A. Reed of Missouri for questioning the operations of the Food Administration. Brandeis discerned in Hoover a sensitivity and an ineptitude. "You are not giving expression to the common verities," he observed to Hoover. "I dare say you have not plumbed Reed to the depths." Brandeis, however, appreciated Hoover's role as the nonpolitical food administrator, describing him to a friend as "the biggest figure injected into Washington life by the war.''[15]

Now, by immersing himself in a wide range of Washington political activity, Hoover, more than ever before, would be confronted with a dilemma regarding political life, one that had some Quaker ramifications. The horns of the dilemma arose unconsciously from deciding whether one, in life, should be an absolutist or a relativist—should one stand "absolutely" on a principle and risk losing it, or should one compromise "relatively" on a principle and weaken it? Because the issue had always plagued Quakers and would burden Hoover throughout his long life, a mild digression seems to be warranted.

In William Penn's day, Quakers governed a whole commonwealth. Since the loss of that political power, however, they had largely resorted to the absolutist approach—or what Frederick B. Tolles suggests as a "Divine lobby" of example and persuasion. Friend Rufus Jones, in 1911, struggled with the issue thus:

> There has always been in the Society of Friends a group of persons pledged unswervingly to the ideal. To those who form this inner group compromise is under no circumstance allowable. If there comes a collision between allegiance to the ideal

and the holding of public office, then the office must be deserted. If obedience to the soul's vision involved eye or hand, houses or lands or life, they must be immediately surrendered. But there has always been as well another group who have held it to be equally imperative to work out their principles of life in the complex affairs of the community and the state, where to gain an end one must yield something; where to get on one must submit to existing conditions; and where to achieve ultimate triumph one must risk his ideals to the tender mercies of a world not yet ripe for them.[16]

In the political career that Hoover was entering, only time—a decade and beyond—would tell if he would "risk his ideals to the tender mercies of . . . [the] world."

The first of Hoover's excursions into Washington beyond the Food Administration was his role as vice-chairman of the Second Industrial Conference, which convened on 1 December 1919. (The first projected labor conference of leaders of labor, capital, and government had been aborted by a steel strike.) Because the conference chairman, Secretary of Labor William B. Wilson, was frequently absent, Hoover presided over a third of the sessions and was largely responsible for the final report, which was submitted on 6 March 1920. It endorsed many progressive measures, such as the forty-hour week, a minimum wage, the prevention of child labor, and equal pay for men and women. Of most importance was the fact that it recommended procedures for the settlement of industrial disputes and advocated the establishment of shop committees in factories to speak for employees. It also proposed procedures for the recognition of labor unions, although arbitration would be binding only if capital and labor agreed. Although little immediately came of the conference report, it clearly demonstrated Hoover's commitment to the principle of collective bargaining, earning him the gratitude of the president of the American Federation of Labor (A F of L), Samuel Gompers.

Hoover was well into the partisan political fray in 1920. Little wonder, for many Democrats and Republicans alike worked for his presidential nomination. "He is certainly a wonder," wrote Franklin D. Roosevelt to the United States ambassador to Belgium, Hugh S. Gibson, "and I wish we could make him president. There couldn't be a better one."[17] Other leading Democrats, including Ralph Pulitzer, Colonel Edward M. House, and Cyrus H. K. Curtis, publisher of the *Saturday Evening Post*, sought his nomination. There were, of course, many exceptions, such as Hoover's *bête noire*, Senator Reed, an Anglophobe who called Hoover a "recent acquisition to our population." Arthur S.

Link, a historian of the Wilson era, has concluded that Hoover could have had the Democratic nomination.

However, Hoover was really a Republican and had been so listed in *Who's Who;* in mid January 1920, at his suggestion, he was declared a "progressive Republican" by the president of the Chamber of Commerce, Julius H. Barnes. Hoover made it official on March 30, stating: "If the Republican party, with the independent element of which I naturally affiliated, adopts a forward-looking, liberal, constructive platform on the Treaty and on our economic issues, and if the party proposes measures for sound business administration of the country, and is neither reactionary nor radical in its approach to our great domestic questions, and is backed by men who undoubtedly assure the consummation of these policies and measures, I will give it my entire support. While I do not, and will not, myself, seek the nomination, if it is felt that the issues necessitate it and it is demanded of me, I can not refuse service."[18]

The year 1920 was neither a Democratic nor a progressive Republican one; it was a year for a conservative Republican nominee. Hoover made a stab at the nomination, losing the presidential primary in his home state to the isolationist former Bull Moose Senator Hiram W. Johnson. Although Warren G. Harding became the Republican nominee in 1920, the support that Hoover garnered in some primary races and from many newspapers and periodicals, as well as from many leading independent progressives, demonstrated that he was a political force of significance.

The Harding-Coolidge slate beat the Democrats, James Cox and Franklin Roosevelt, in November of 1920. In the race, Hoover campaigned for Harding, blamed the Wilson administration for being "in the main reactionary," and criticized the Democrats in the Senate for failing to accept the treaty of peace with reservations in regard to the League of Nations Covenant. Hoover, of course, was right about the reactionary aspects of the administration in the postwar period and about criticizing Democrats in the Senate for following Wilson's uncompromising stance on the Republican reservations about the League of Nations.

By election time, Hoover felt that he had had enough of public life, but he apparently succumbed quickly to the urging of Harding and Secretary of State-designate Charles Evans Hughes that he accept the post of secretary either of commerce or the interior. Conservative Republicans were aghast at the idea of a progressive Republican (and a former Wilsonian) in their midst, but Harding mollified them with the appointment of the very conservative Andrew W. Mellon of Pennsylvania as secretary of the Treasury. Hoover became secretary of commerce and immediately set for himself an ambitious program, mainly concerning departmental cooperation with industries, to standardize products and reduce waste, and work with the Labor Department to improve employer-employee relations.

Hoover's thought was as vigorous as his action, the processes seeming constantly to feed each other. As food administrator and as a member of the president's cabinet during the war, Hoover had observed and experienced, at firsthand, new forms of bureaucratism. He and leaders of other war agencies had employed means of scientific inquiry, professional management, expert administration, and agency coordination; and they were efficiently and inspirationally guided by President Wilson. Although the war administration in Washington had had its share of bureaucratic snarls, Hoover would never forget its efficient and orderly (corporatist) successes.

Now Hoover would transfer the processes of wartime productivity to peacetime stabilization. Many historians have come to agree that he was a leading, if not the dominant, figure in adapting the ordering ideas of the Progressive period and World War I to the corporatist formulas of the 1920s which were further refined by the New Deal.

There is no denying that Hoover, as secretary of commerce, used his war-administration experiences—especially the experiences of adaptation; the cooperation between and the coordination of groups and agencies; the federal tripartite balance; the balance of the societal segments of business, labor, and government; and the balance of liberty and order. Hoover, more than his fellow leaders of wartime agencies, always seemed to be thinking about and stressing a "middle way," especially to avoid coercion by government, as he believed he had been able to avoid it in the Food Administration.

President Harding was so eager to have the brilliant Hoover in his cabinet that he not only gave him a free hand to reorganize the Commerce Department but assured him a voice in financial, foreign, labor, and agriculture matters. Hoover, in the new administration, quickly staked out claims to many statistical, marketing, transportation, and developmental areas in other departments. Soon he was known as the secretary of commerce and "under secretary of everything else."

For all of Hoover's intrusions into other departments—where he frequently encountered the resistance of strong secretaries, such as State's Hughes, Justice's Harry M. Daugherty, and Agriculture's Henry C. Wallace—his largest efforts naturally revolved around the Commerce Department. There, Hoover quickly got up three legs in his rational order—the elimination of waste in the production and distribution of commodities, the expansion of American markets for the commodities, and the institution of countercyclical programs to ward off severe dips in the American economy. The Commerce Department's Industrial Waste Committee, under the direction of a once-radical Harvard student named Edward Eyre Hunt, led the way to a massive standardization and interchangeability of parts in most American industries, which was accomplished by inducing trade associations voluntarily to standardize their products. Market expansion at home and abroad came under the intelligent direction of Julius Klein of the Bureau of Foreign and Domestic Commerce. He, too, worked with trade associations to have industries exchange information regarding production and markets at home. In regard to foreign markets, the bureau investigated possibilities for and supported cooperative action by industries that were selling their products abroad. The Bureau of the Census, in the Commerce Department, disseminated statistical information to help industries to expand or contract their inventories so as to avoid drastic dips in the economy. It published the "Survey of Current Business," which systematized and made available the statistics that were provided by cooperating trade groups.

The range of specific activity in the Commerce Department under Hoover was demonstrated by its large and intricate involvement in such matters as transportation, communications, housing, the coal and railroad industries, agriculture, and unemployment. New controls over the fledgling aviation and radio industries were established under his tenure as secretary of commerce. The housing industry was aided by the new Housing Division, which worked closely with an industry trade association, the American Construction Council, which, in turn, disseminated data and advised the industry about various forms of home financing. Secretary Hoover gave much attention to attempting to "rationalize" the sick coal industry through modernization and regularization of the industry by coal associations and by federal fact-finding services in problem areas of employer-employee contracts. He tried desperately to persuade railroads to agree on rate revision and to have railroad operators assume an enlightened position in their relations with railroad unions.

The areas, external to his department, in which Hoover became most heavily involved were unemployment and agriculture. He had a compelling influence on the Department of Labor and was the principal force behind the Unemployment Conference of 1921. Edward Eyre Hunt, who was then serving Hoover in many capacities, became secretary of the conference, which recommended local action for most employment efforts; an increase in federal public-works programs; the expansion of the United States Employment Service; a refinement of the collection of unemployment satistics; and the establishment of a federal agency to plan future public works as a "balance wheel" in times of economic crisis. In sum, regulative programs for business were at the center of what was recommended. In the Agriculture Conference of 1922, which introduced several ideas of federal support programs for farmers in crop areas with large surpluses, Hoover successfully threw his weight against federal-government approaches to agricultural relief, particularly emphasizing voluntary farm-cooperative solutions to farm problems.

Hoover faced many obstacles to his wide-ranging efforts in the Commerce Department and the federal government—resistance from established federal agencies, from many private business and interest groups, and from certain labor unions. He had some difficulty in persuading Attorney General Harry Daugherty to accept trade associations, the key to Hoover's "cooperativism," as not being in violation of antitrust laws.

Stumbling blocks for many of Hoover's programs as secretary of commerce were occasionally marks of success. Anyone as dynamic and as wide ranging as Hoover would naturally make enemies. On balance, however, he was strikingly successful in his tenure at the Commerce Department; a half-century later the mammoth new Commerce Department building would appropriately be named in his honor.

What explains Hoover's modes of thought and action during his political service in the decade prior to his presidency—principally his commitments to a variety of balances that were implemented by such means as cooperation, voluntarism, mutual self-help, philanthropy, and individualism? One view has stressed his managerial ability, which operated beside his aversion to intrusion by the federal government and his seeking to create order in the private sector. Another suggests his familial heritage as applied to the problem of securing an ordered freedom for his countrymen as a whole. In truth, the solutions associated with the ideology of his familial Quakerism and his professional and public services were remarkably similar and reinforcing. The governmental form that Hoover embraced also called for a "new individualism" to be achieved through institution building rather than laissez faire.

One way to understand Hoover's political philosophy in the 1920s is to look closely at his most important written work during the period, *American Individualism*, published in 1922.[19] The little book was in germination from 1917, or thereabouts, and reflected much of his thought, if not his day-to-day actions, throughout the decade and his presidency. While historians can readily see in *American Individualism* a plea for the kind of order that many enlightened business and political leaders of the day were seeking, a close reading seems also to reveal the influence of his religious heritage, though it was far more secular than sectarian.

In the booklet, Hoover calls upon Americans to ponder the several great social philosophies of the Western world—individualism, communism, socialism, syndicalism, capitalism, autocracy—in order to determine the nation's direction. He favors unabashedly "American individualism," a philosophy, however, to be tempered by assurance to all citizens of an "equality of opportunity" and of freedom from "frozen strata of classes." Hoover's philosophy is not capitalism, which he views scornfully as a philosophy of laissez faire and "rugged individualism." His is a philosophy of individualism through the coordination of capital, government, and labor. Of course, the other philosophies, which are largely European, are to be dreaded even more than capitalism.[20]

Concerning the properties of American individualism and the ideals of the American people from whom Hoover sees the properties emanating, his family and professional background is quite apparent! The properties: intelligence, character, courage, and divine spark are, of course, American, but in combination, they appear to be uniquely Quakerish; and the ideals seem to be even more so: "pity, fealty to family and race, the love of liberty; the mystical yearnings for spiritual things; the desire for fuller expression of the creative faculties; the impulses of service to community and nation. . . ." In listing Hoover's properties and ideals of individualism, one is almost reminded of "Quaker Queries." And, as in the Quaker meeting, the emphasis is on the individual, not on coercive institutions. In both church and state, Hoover expected institutions to free individuals and to make them responsible, not to coerce them. "All we can hope to assure to the individual," he wrote, "is liberty, justice, intellectual welfare, equality of opportunity, and stimulation to service."[21]

The third chapter in Hoover's *American Individualism*, "Spiritual Phases," naturally enough emphasizes the prime influence of religion on the individual in America, as opposed to the influence of social and economic systems. Indeed, he sees that the last two are "inspired" by the first. In so writing, Hoover seems to be discussing the "Inner Light" of Friends. "The divine spark," he writes, "does not lie in agreements, in organizations, in institutions, in masses or in groups. Spirituality with its faith, its hopes, its charity, can be increased by each individual's own effort. And, in proportion as each individual increases his own store of spirituality, in that proportion increases the idealism of democracy." Hoover goes on to discuss the divine inspiration that rests with all individuals, and maintains that "the divine spark can be awakened in every heart." Such a belief brought our forefathers to these shores.[22]

Hoover recognizes the existence and the importance of the organization of individuals, but he does so differently from the way in which institutional economics or sociology does. Rather than such collectivities directing the aspirations of individuals, they, in the form of vast Tocquevillean associations, should voluntarily represent the aspirations of individuals for mutual advancement, self-expression, and neighborly helpfulness. Hoover wrote that "many men came to believe that salvation lay in mass and group action. . . . They conceived that this leadership could be continued without tyranny; they have forgotten that permanent spiritual progress lies with the individual."[23]

In the subsequent three chapters of Hoover's little book, which deal with "Economic Phases," "Political Phases," and "The Future," Hoover addresses the pragmatic efforts of institutionalists, their desire to build a better America of individuals through an advance of "greater invention," "elimination of waste," "creative production," and "better distribution and services." What is important, warns Hoover, is that Americans guard against the radical "demagogues" on the left and the "stand-patters" on the right. Politically, capital must be curbed and regulated, yet the initiative of individualism must be maintained. Obviously, Hoover, as he does so often, calls for a "balance of perspective." He concludes by noting that "our individualism" is not just the middle ground between autocracy and socialism; it is also an individualism of "responsibility" and "service." Hoover is certain that "American individualism" will be assured only if America preserves its distinctiveness, equalizes opportunity, glorifies service, and holds to its faith in intelligence, character, courage, initiative, and "divine spark"— ideas that emanated from and were reinforced in his stages of familial upbringing, engineering professionalism, Progressive service, and the political life during his years at the Commerce Department.

2

★ ★ ★ ★ ★

VICTORY

As 1928 dawned in the United States, the nation had never been more Republican. Since its founding, the Grand Old Party had usually been closely contested in presidential elections by the Democrats and, at times, only less so by other party advocates, such as Greenbackers, Populists, and Bull Moosers. Even the scandals of the Harding era, so close in time, had had little effect on Americans as they surveyed the field of Republican candidates for the American presidency in 1928. Although viewed as lesser figures in the perspective of history, they were then powerful and attractive leaders—Charles Gates Dawes, the rugged, aristocratic "Hell and Maria" vice-president; Frank Orren Lowden, the former governor of Illinois; Charles Evans Hughes, Supreme Court justice and recent secretary of state; Gen. John Joseph Pershing, the military hero; George William Norris of Nebraska, the inheritor of the Bull Moose insurgency; Senators James E. Watson of Indiana, Charles Curtis of Kansas, and Guy D. Goff of West Virginia; and Herbert Clark Hoover, the brilliant secretary of commerce. The irony was that the last on the list of many, and the least political, should eventually come first.

Few national political leaders ever warmed to Herbert Hoover in 1928. President Coolidge probably reflected Republican exasperation, when he explained in May of 1928, "That man has offered me unsolicited advice for six years, all of it bad."[1] The remark, of course, was outrageous. In fact, the opposite was true.

Hoover's advice during the Coolidge administration was indeed taken seriously on such matters as the government's encouragement of the use of farm cooperatives rather than the federal bureaucracy to resolve the problems of agriculture; the development of electrical power by private parties where possible (but by government where necessary); government "persuasion" that speculative banking practices be curbed; the use of the Labor Department's "good offices" to conciliate labor-employer disputes; the sponsoring by government of conferences, commissions, and studies to plan antidepression efforts; and numerous others. Hoover's plentiful advice had been given with dispatch and confidence, and invariably, it fitted his ideas of balances, which had been so long in germination. Governmental and political leaders expressed a begrudging admiration for the superactive secretary of commerce, and the American people almost always admired him.

Herbert Hoover had a good press. The public-relations apparatus that he had honed for years to proselytize his various administrative endeavors—his Food Administration during World War I, his various overseas relief efforts, and his recent administration of the Commerce Department—was now turned loose on making him his party's choice for president and subsequently the nation's choice. Yet, it was not gimmickry that pushed Hoover forward. His agents had a good subject, and they understandably and effectively emphasized Hoover's traits that had been attractive for so long: his seemingly low-key, behind-the-scene efforts for good, his scorn for the "political approach," his many administrative talents, his humanitarian propensity, his articulation of the rational approach by government, an ordered freedom. A coterie of newsmen, and others who had long been loyal to "the Chief," came forward to do their share. George E. Akerson, Hoover's publicity assistant in the Commerce Department, and particularly Walter F. Brown, his assistant secretary of commerce, were well prepared to launch the nomination effort on the day that Calvin Coolidge said, "I do not choose to run for president in 1928." Eminent and eager though many other contenders were for the presidential nomination, none could match Hoover in money, organization, and image. Weak spots in his drive for the nomination, such as some primary defeats and Coolidge's reluctance to enlist in the cause, were brushed aside as the secretary of commerce entered the Republican National Convention in Kansas City, Missouri, as the front runner.

The Republican Convention convened on June 12, in a great hall built nearly three decades earlier, just prior to the Democratic nomination of William Jennings Bryan. Hoover was more akin to the Great Commoner's rural interests than most observers supposed, both then and now. Nevertheless, denim-clad farmers, bearing hoes and rakes, milled about outside the hall to protest the front runner's plan for farm cooperatives to resolve the problem of crop surpluses. At the same time, inside the hall, leaders of farm blocs tried to get a strong government-action farm plank and a nominee other than Hoover—someone who, as president, would implement their plank. But the convention was over almost before it had started. Party patriarchs, as conservative as the farmers were radical, resignedly proceeded to confirm the foregone conclusions of platform and slate. Yet, some among the patriarchs actually showed enthusiasm. While the keynoter, Simeon D. Fess, and the chairman of the Resolutions Committee, Reed Smoot, were terribly tedious, the permanent chairman, George H. Moses, did not fail his audience. An original Hoover-for-president man who, like many patriarchs, had been bought off by Hoover with vague promises, Moses eulogized his party and took on the enemy in the Democratic camp, whoever he might be, shouting: "Whether he emerges from another spectacle like the 103-round battle . . . [of 1924] or whether he comes from an overpowered convention held spell-bound by the glare of the Tammany Tiger, we are ready for him. Bring him on and we will bury him. We welcome him with hospitable hands to a bloody grave."[2]

Although Hoover's nomination was assured, his managers were little involved in the building of the platform. It would have been unlike the Iowan to intrude too obtrusively and too publicly on the convention's will, especially when this was not necessary. The platform—with its planks on efficiency in government, reduced federal expenditures, tariff protection, support of labor, and good international relations—was quite acceptable and was flexible enough for him to use it as a base for his New Day, a term that was occasionally used to designate what his presidency would be. Especially was Hoover satisfied with the principal planks on the Eighteenth Amendment and the cooperative approach to the great farm problems. The first was quite consistent with his Quaker sobriety, and the second was based on the Coolidge farm program, which Hoover himself had, to a large extent, designed.

With the platform built, the convention proceeded, on June 14, with the roll call of states for the purpose of nomination. Alabama yielded to California, and John L. McNab, a well-known lawyer from the latter state, in the first three sentences of his speech, blurted out the name of his nominee, his good friend Herbert Hoover, thus triggering the first of two planned demonstrations. McNab's address, which was more believable than most of the subsequent nominations, was viewed by the public as being superior to the others. He presented his nominee as the universal man that he was: "engineer, practical scientist, minister of mercy to the hungry, administrator, executive, statesman, beneficent American, kindly neighbor, wholesome human being."[3] Then there followed the nomination of lesser lights in the party: James Watson, Charles Curtis, George Norris, and Guy Goff. Hoover's stronger opponents, such as Dawes, Lowden, Hughes, and Pershing, had long since bowed to his inevitable nomination. Attempts made by Watson, Curtis, Norris, and Goff to block Hoover's nomination were futile. The secretary of commerce was nominated on the first ballot by a near-unanimous vote. Curtis probably reflected the attitude of most professional politicians when, before the voting, he had questioned the legitimacy of Hoover's Republicanism and strongly suspected that Hoover would put the party "on the defensive from the day he is named."[4] But after the voting, Curtis and the professionals changed their minds and congratulated the nominee; Curtis gladly accepted second place on the ticket. Hoover preferred others for the second place, but he left the selection up to the convention, and Curtis seemed to be most available.

What enthusiasm the professional Republicans in Kansas City lacked for their candidate, others across the land compensated for. Throngs in the District of Columbia applauded as candidate Hoover dutifully rode to and from his Commerce Department office. Of course, within the department, old friends hailed the chief. Great newspapers praised him in ways that are usually not experienced, even at nomination time, with such accolades as "superb capacity," "most useful American citizen now alive," "a new force in economic and social life," more "knowledgeable of world conditions" than any other president, "irresistible appeal . . . to the rank and file," "a technological man," a new departure in politics, undoubted "integrity," "the cast of a scientist . . . a genius."[5] The candidate reacted modestly to the praise, not being unaware that crowds and their spokesmen frequently had mindless qualities. Yet, as if to respond, Hoover wired to the convention his intentions of attacking grave moral and spiritual problems and of giving his best to advance the welfare of all the people.

Two weeks after the convention in Kansas City the Democrats met in Houston, Texas, and there, as the Republicans had done, chose their front runner on the first ballot. And like the Republican professional politicians, the Democratic leaders also lacked enthusiasm for their candidate. The partially paralyzed New Yorker Franklin Roosevelt seemed to be an exception, as he again nominated his state's "Happy Warrior," Governor Alfred E. Smith. This time Roosevelt's man was not to be denied the nomination, as he had been in 1924. Although others in the party were placed in nomination—Senators James A. Reed and

Walter F. George, of Missouri and Georgia respectively; Congressmen William A. Ayers and Cordell Hull, of Indiana and Tennessee; Jesse H. Jones, of Texas; Huston Thompson, of Colorado; Atlee Pomerene, of Ohio; and Evans Woollen, of Indiana—Smith quickly received the nominations. And as at the Republican Convention, prohibition and relief for agriculture were the large issues, at least on the surface.

Whereas Hoover had accepted the Republican planks, Smith took exception to those of his party. The New Yorker telegraphed the Democratic Convention his refusal to accept the Eighteenth Amendment; and because of his completely urban stance—brown derby and all—he could not convince westerners of his knowledge and sincerity regarding agriculture, especially on such measures as the Farm Bureau's "equalization fee" to support the government's purchase of surplus commodities. Smith's defiance of the dry plank was particularly repugnant to the heartland of the party, the South; in addition to his antiprohibition position on the Eighteenth Amendment and his total urban breeding, he was a loyal son of the Roman Catholic Church. Otherwise, the South would have found his political conservatism quite congenial. In fact, the patriarch of the Southern Democracy, Senator Carter Glass, found Smith credible on most domestic issues, such as the tariff, labor, and even agriculture. But Glass thought it "a great pity that these other things will be over-shadowed by the revolutionary proposal" to repeal the Eighteenth Amendment. The courtly Glass even matched Smith's profanity by telling him literally that "it was a piece of 'damn folly' to risk a national election on a proposition [the repeal of the Eighteenth Amendment] impossible of accomplishment; . . . it could not be done in a century." The Virginian confided to his governor that Smith was directing his campaign at the "wringing wet eastern states" and was assuming that "he already has the support of the ignorant and plebian [southern] elements."[6]

As Walter Lippmann noted then, and as David Burner has noted since, Smith displayed a very conservative side in 1928, which was manifested by his history of opposing woman suffrage, the proliferation of governmental agencies, the rising cost of government, and governmental interference with business. In many respects, Hoover was the more liberal and progressive candidate in 1928.[7]

With nomination in hand, Hoover, using the bureaucratic tools that he had accumulated during a lifetime of business and governmental management, launched a superb campaign. Inexperience in electoral politics would bode ill in his dealing with members of Congress after the election and in facing future elections, but adept organization and a very fine public image sufficed for this campaign.[8] With almost embarrassing dispatch, Hoover removed the chairman of the National Committee, William M. Butler, and replaced him with a fellow cabinet member, Secretary of the Interior Hubert Work. Other confidants were placed in key positions. Hoover was sure enough of his control of the campaign to tolerate some of the Old Guard pros, such as George H. Moses, to head the eastern campaign, and Charles D. Hilles, to serve on the Executive Committee. Close associates were placed in the more important positions: James W. Good, as director of the western campaign, with offices in Chicago; and Walter H. Newton, as head of the Speaker's Bureau. Both of them had acted for Hoover on the floor of the convention. Hoover and Work, and many insiders who by then knew their chief's ways, set to work, constantly conferring with and directing Republicans from various states, as if they expected a close campaign. When state situations became doubtful, the conferences sometimes became strained, as when Governor John S. Fisher and Edward Martin of Pennsylvania and Theodore Roosevelt, Jr., and Ogden L. Mills of New York were closeted for lengthy sessions about the Republican condition of their respective states. Of course, young Roosevelt and Mills had much to tell their candidate about the ways of Alfred Smith, since both of them had been resoundingly defeated by the Tammanyite in gubernatorial campaigns.

No little part of Hoover's planning efforts in midsummer was directed toward the grand launching of the campaign on the day of notification and acceptance, August 11. Then, some seventy thousand Americans crowded into the stadium at Stanford University and watched as a committee from the Republican National Convention notified Hoover that he was their candidate. Their man was ready, having spent weeks on his speech of acceptance. After renditions by four brass bands, the leading of cheers by Stanford students, and the appropriate notification ceremonies, the nominee stepped forward and, by the miracle of a public-address system, stolidly spoke to the vast throng and, by the even-greater miracle of the wireless radio, addressed some thirty million Americans across the nation. To Hoover's advantage, his unmoving and determined stance before the microphones caused his words, as one historian reports, to "come out better than they went in."[9] Thus, his lengthy and seemingly ponderous message was acceptable, and to those who listened, he offered important considerations.

Hoover discoursed on prohibition, calling it, not a "noble experiment," as some historians have scornfully reported, but a "social and economic experiment, noble in motive." He explored the problems of agriculture, calling for great expenditures of money to reorganize the farm marketing system along more sound, economic, and cooperative ways. He vigorously endorsed collective bargaining for labor and the curtailment of the use of the injunction against labor. He called for the development of water power in the nation's great drainage basins. He pledged himself to find ways to end destructive boom-and-bust cycles in the American economy. He articulated concepts, but most essential of all, he addressed the relationship of the government to the people.

The relationship of government to people, which Hoover so frequently addressed, has come to be described by some historians by a term that is not familiar to many people, American corporatism. This was Hoover's belief in a voluntary interaction of segments which would avoid an excess of government regulation that might "extinguish the enterprise and initiative which had been the glory of America." Yet, Hoover believed, government should regulate and compete when necessary to provide an "equal opportunity to all citizens." He pleaded for a new spirit of cooperation between the government and the people, which was more possible than ever in 1928 because of the new growth of great organizations to represent "workers, farmers, business men, and professional men with a desire to cure their own abuses and a purpose to serve public interest."[10] The effect that Hoover's sentiments had then is impossible to measure now. While many Americans had faith in the man who spoke to them, others did not comprehend the true meaning of his words, and of course, still others viewed his speech as being the usual campaign rhetoric.

In addition to lining up state leaders, Hoover and his organization were always conscious of the great interest groups of the nation. He rallied the support of the powerful trade associations in the business community. Of course, Smith also curried industrial favor, especially with the appointment of John Raskob of General Motors as his national chairman. Franklin Roosevelt tried to bring the chairman of the board of the Chamber of Commerce, Julius Barnes, into the Smith camp by telling him that Hoover had gone back on the Wilsonian dreams to which both Roosevelt and Barnes had been committed. That most of the business community was committed to Hoover, not to Smith, was evident when Barnes expressed rage at Roosevelt's ploy.[11]

Organized labor was divided in its support of Hoover and Smith. In retrospect, both candidates seem to have enjoyed labor's respect. It is not difficult to understand their respect for Hoover, given his consistent prolabor record, ranging from his work with the industrial conferences in the Wilson and Harding administrations to his opposition to the wrongful use of the injunction to restrain labor. During the campaign, John L. Lewis, the head of the United Mine Workers (UMW), acclaimed Hoover as "one of the greatest statesmen of modern times";[12] and although the American Federation of Labor was chary about endorsing presidential candidates after it had supported the losing third-party candidate, Robert M. La Follette, in 1924, it was reported that "no one around [A F of L's President William] Green doubts for one minute that he cast his vote for [Hoover]."[13]

Farmers did not easily come into Hoover's camp. After a decade of low prices, they preferred a more definite federal action than Hoover's cooperative solutions to their problems. But farm leaders fell into line. "I am as much interested in your election," wrote Grange Master Louis J. Taber to Hoover, "as any candidate . . . since Theodore Roosevelt"; he added: "We go a bit further [than the Republican cooperative plank] and believe that the Export Debenture idea . . . is essential, . . . but this matter can be worked out when we approach it."[14]

Louis J. Taber was only one of the many old supporters of Theodore Roosevelt who stumped for Hoover in 1928. Senator William E. Borah represented the values of western progressivism—especially on prohibition and farm aid—in his support of the Republican slate. Jane Addams represented the urban progressives of the West in her backing; she commented at length about how alike were Hoover and Sidney Hillman, president of the Amalgamated Clothing Workers, in their hopes for urban workers. "Mr. Hoover," she wrote, "has proposed to do on a large scale what Mr. Hillman has already achieved in at least one great clothing establishment in Chicago, securing to the workers themselves the profits resulting from technological improvements as well as a tenure of work elsewhere in the establishment, for the displaced man."[15] Of course, not all former Bull Moosers flocked to Hoover's support. Many saw him as being in "the big business interest" camp. Hiram W. Johnson and Harold L. Ickes commiserated with each other. "Borah is making a holy show of himself [in supporting Hoover]," wrote Ickes; "my . . . contempt of him [has] grown measureably every day"[16]—a sample of western vengeance that would rub off on Hoover in future years. Johnson told Ickes that as Hoover's political strength grew, his character weakened.[17]

But many businessmen, farmers, laborers, and Bull Moosers were for Hoover. The Hoover organization had a knack for gathering its support as well as endorsement from others, even from among some Irish and other groups of new immigrants. Memoranda pertaining to strategy in the file on the Hoover presidential campaign attest to the organizing skill of his campaign managers.

In six major addresses between August 11 and November 2, Hoover's campaign largely turned on the issues that he had raised in his acceptance speech. These issues, in turn, frequently related to special geographic sections and interest groups in the nation. In West Branch, Iowa, he addressed the agricultural issue and the importance of family life. At Newark, New Jersey, he talked about the need to use public works to offset unemployment and the need to create machinery to mediate the labor-management disputes and to restrain the use of the injunction. In Tennessee he discussed several points, such as the enforcement of prohibition, tariff protection, the expansion of foreign trade, the building of farm cooperatives, and very important, "fair play" in the campaign. In Boston he noted that the tariff was a dominant issue between the Democratic candidate and himself—that Republicans would protect the nation's property from unfair competition. In New York City he took his most aggressive, nearly demagogic, stance, accusing Smith of espousing state socialism, especially because the New Yorker seemed to favor federal-government solutions to agriculture and to the problem of electric power. Also Hoover criticized Smith for choosing to modify the Eighteenth Amendment, which would be a gross interference with constitutional government. Hoover capped his campaign in St. Louis by appealing to farmers and by reiterating his view in regard to cooperation between labor and capital.

Unfortunately, one issue of the campaign—that of Smith's Catholicism—hung over the election process in ways that would reflect badly on the Republican side for decades. The issue was not important as far as the outcome of the campaign was concerned. Almost any Republican, and especially Hoover, would have won under almost any circumstances in 1928. The issue was, however, revealing about the United States and had implications for the future. Many Americans debased themselves on the issue. Even the almost always clean editor of the *Emporia* (Kans.) *Gazette*, William Allen White, stooped to write: "There is a fundamental reason, based on the law of Causation in morals, why the Catholic so-called Religion should not secure a dominant influence over the nation's life. Everywhere and always it represents the downward slant of moral principles."[18] And Assistant Attorney General Mabel Walker Willebrandt ranted before Methodist ministers in Ohio about the evils of Catholicism. When the public resented such tactics, the Republican organization sheepishly denied its own well-laid plans for Mabel Willebrandt's diatribes. Even Hoover became involved, writing in his own hand a press release describing her activity as "free lance," when, in fact, the Speaker's Bureau had sent her to Ohio and then had dispatched her to Tennessee to continue to deliver her invectives.[19] While Hoover had sincerely called for "fair play" in the campaign, the fact was that he did not protest strongly against his organization's deprecating use of Smith's Catholicism.

The religious issue, of course, was compounded by the Democratic candidate's overt urbanism and his strong antiprohibition stance, issues that were equally irrelevant to the outcome of the campaign. Smith's "foreign" ways spurred a whispered campaign of snobbery against the New Yorker. Hiram Johnson complained to Harold Ickes that the Borahs "could not tolerate such common people [Al Smith and his wife, Kate] in such a high position." Ickes responded, noting that "if the country could stand Mrs. Harding . . . they ought to be able to stand Mrs. Smith."[20]

Of course, Smith's loyalty to his church, his Eastside brogue, his brown derby, and his defense of alcohol were as much resented by southern Democrats as by northern Republicans. It was little wonder that the Republican organization sent Mrs. Willebrandt south. Many southerners were ready to defect to her party. "Who could have prophesied a year ago," wrote a Virginian, "that the upright, unimpeachable Democratic party would, . . . by some evil magic, find itself transformed into an organization in which the whiskey-soaked and the corrupt Gotham politician would feel quite at home . . . [and] by a promise [to bring back the saloon and] destroy the fruits of decades of progress towards national sobriety?" The southern Democracy would support no ticket "so alien to the spirit and genius of democracy."[21]

On 6 November 1928 more Americans thronged to the polls to elect a president than ever before in history—nearly eight million more than only four years previously—for a total of 67.5 percent of those who were eligible to vote. Never had the electorate given so many popular and electoral votes to one candidate. Herbert Hoover gathered in 21,392,190 of the former and 444 of the latter, as compared to 15,016,443 and 87 garnered for Smith. (Norman M. Thomas, the Socialist candidate, received 267,420 popular votes and no electoral votes.) In his home on the campus of Stanford University, Hoover, at 7:30 P.M., learned that he had won handily his only election to public office.

Across the nation, in New York, Alfred Smith graciously accepted his defeat. Political poignancy filled the air. While Hoover and his followers faced the New Day with an understandable confidence, given the chief's unprecedented vote, the Smith camp was as understandably sullen. Where their leader only commented that "one could not say his beads in the White House," a follower, four days after the election, let loose his pent-up rage in a letter to Smith's friend Robert F. Wagner. "As an American citizen, Catholic by religion," he wrote, "I most . . .

vehemently protest . . . the unfair, unwarranted and un-American attacks upon my . . . church and religion, and appeal to you, in the name of justice and fair play, that steps be taken to banish forever . . . the spreading of venom and hate against the millions of our citizens professing the Catholic religion, to the end that we may be a united Brotherhood of Man."[22] Wagner's correspondent was, of course, wrong in his implication that religion explained the Democratic defeat. Herbert Hoover won because of a favorable public image, a superbly organized campaign, and the good fortune of Republican prosperity.

Most historians have cut through the veneer of the election results—of Hoover's having won all but six southern states and Massachusetts and Rhode Island—and have attributed to Smith the Democratic party's inroads into urban America. The Democratic candidate captured cities where Republicans had usually dominated, such as St. Louis, Cleveland, San Francisco, New York, Boston, New Haven; and he made strong inroads in Philadelphia, Pittsburgh, Chicago, Detroit, and Omaha. He won fifty of the nation's largest urban counties and took 122 counties across the nation that were normally safe for the Republicans. Also of weighty importance was the fact that Smith cracked the solid Northeast for his party.

Thus, Smith's Catholicism, although it was not related to the results of the election, was symbolically important in the campaign as part of the great urban mix—with its polyglot new immigration, its "foreign ways," its consumption of alcohol—that set the stage for making the Democratic party, during the next decade, the urban party in America. The frustration of Wagner's Catholic correspondent was such that he and many other urbanities would not leave the party of Al Smith, at least r.ot for half a century. The Bourbon Democrats who left the party in the South to vote for Herbert Hoover would return to their traditional party when a Protestant would again lead their ticket. In the meantime, the president-elect, treasuring his mandate, prepared to accept the mantle of the great office.

Elihu Root—the wise man from Clinton, New York, who knew so well the pressures of Washington, including presidential interregnums—urged the president-elect to get into the background and to get out of the capital until Inauguration Day. Very few men have experienced such Republican divisiveness as Root had when he had watched insurgents and standpatters embroil President Taft only a decade and a half previously. Perhaps Root feared a similar fate for the nation's new leader. Hoover knew the possibility of such a replay. William E. Borah, from the old insurgency, worked feverishly hard for Hoover in the campaign, and Borah would want his price: a special session of the Congress to provide relief for farmers.[23] And the conservative George H. Moses, who headed Hoover's New York headquarters and had irreverently called Borah and other insurgents "the wild jackasses of the desert," was ominous in exacting his price. "As I told you," he wrote to Hoover only three days after the election, "there are but few things I shall . . . ask of you. These things I will present in due time—and . . . if they are granted, I will give you receipt in full."[24] Borah reported to Mark Sullivan—a publicist who was one of Hoover's handymen—that to make sure he got his "few things," Moses "tried to organize a little group of ten or twelve Republican Senators [to] . . . 'compel the president to play ball.'" Sullivan cautioned Hoover not to "take on the faintest atmosphere of suspicion or of interpreting hostility . . .—[that] Moses has an impish turn of mind."[25]

The press appeared to give inordinate attention to the president-elect. Hoover thought that they seemed to "have a Divine mandate to invent something sensational each day." The president-elect, sensitive to the power of the press, had things to tell them, but he was afraid of moving too rapidly on Coolidge's preserves. It was not surprising that he agreed with Root on the need to get out of Washington. "It was partially with this in mind," he wrote to Root, "that I have undertaken the South American journey, and I am proposing to stay in Florida or somewhere away from Washington until March 4th."[26]

Besides giving Hoover a respite from political trials in Washington, the South American trip was important as the real beginning of the United States' good-neighbor policy—a policy that reached fruition in the New Deal. On November 19 Hoover left the United States on the USS *Maryland*, and he returned on January 6 on the USS *Utah*, both of which were battleships. Coolidge wanted him to go by cruisers, which "would not cost so much." However, Hoover needed room. He wanted to take Mrs. Hoover, who spoke Spanish, a diplomatic staff, and a press contingent. The last did him more harm than good. Press relations on the trip deteriorated because of George Akerson's censorship—a portent of future press relations.

Associations were, however, very good with Central and South American countries that were visited: Honduras, Salvador, Nicaragua, Costa Rica, Equador, Peru, Chile, Argentina, and Brazil. There were minor problems—some demonstrations against the "Colossus of the North"—but generally Hoover furthered the possibility of becoming good neighbors by calling for more contacts, cooperation to upgrade prosperity, and the common pursuit of freedom and democracy. In fact,

Hoover became so enamored with the possibilities of establishing better permanent relations that he returned home determined to disavow in his Inaugural Address any unnecessary intervention by the United States in the affairs of the hemisphere, only to be discouraged by former Secretary of State Charles Evans Hughes, who advised: "Nothing that you could properly say [on unnecessary intervention] would satisfy them." The president-elect was learning that his every word—especially in the forthcoming Inaugural Address—would be "searched for some hidden meaning." Nevertheless, he generated good will for his country by saying in many capitals of South America: "I wish to symbolize the friendly visit of one good neighbor to another."[27] The commitment during his administration to any form of nonintervention in South America would bear out the sincerity of his remarks.

The sojourn in Central and South America did give the president-elect an opportunity to reflect on policy in regard to intervention in the hemisphere and elsewhere, such as in the Philippine Islands. Henry L. Stimson, the United States governor general in the islands, wanted Hoover to squash ideas of independence that had been spread by vested-interest groups that were seeking protection against Philippine exports to the United States.[28] Other foreign affairs, such as the Geneva Disarmament Conference, were examined by Hoover, as were a gamut of domestic policies.

One important internal policy, unemployment, was aired in New Orleans during Hoover's absence. Before a conference of governors, Governor Ralph Owen Brewster of Maine outlined Hoover's plan for a $3-billion prosperity reserve fund, to be used to relieve unemployment in times of depression. The cylical problem of unemployment had bothered and fascinated Hoover for a decade, and in response to warnings from friends that it was again surfacing, he, through Brewster, sounded out the governors. They responded favorably to the idea of a reserve fund, and labor leaders reacted even more favorably. However, uppermost on his own mind and in the thoughts of the new "president watchers" everywhere was the cabinet, which would administer the great departments and advise the president for four years.

Upon Hoover's return on 6 January 1929, he, against his previous better judgment, spent two weeks in Washington attending a steady stream of conferences with the president, congressional leaders, and numerous delegations that had recommendations for appointments to high office. He concluded his business in Washington on Saturday January 19, and he rested on the Sabbath, attending the Friends' meeting house on Irving Street and entertaining associates at dinner. On Monday he headed south for Belle Isle, the beautiful Florida villa of

J. C. Penney on Biscayne Bay, where he intended to fish for a week before he finished making his cabinet appointments and refining his Inaugural Address.

Hugh Gibson, ambassador to Belgium and an old associate from European-relief days, advised his chief to avoid the "appointments curse of every incoming president" and to let the congressmen have their way in making the lesser federal appointments, leaving to the president the "full liberty" to make the important policy appointments.[29] On the lesser appointments, Hoover generally left the Coolidge appointees on the job. The retention of Coolidge's public servants was painless and made sense, although it denied the new president a source of patronage pressure which might have been applied to wayward members of Congress. (Hoover's successor, Franklin Roosevelt, would wait for one hundred days, until after he had obtained his program from a special session of Congress, before he would make his lesser appointments.) In regard to the cabinet and subcabinet appointments, Hoover solicited advice from important leaders, many of whom were outside of the party structure, such as elder statesman Elihu Root and Hoover's young devotee Christian A. Herter. Mark Sullivan made many contacts around the country for the president-elect, as did William R. Castle, Jr. Much advice was unsolicited, such as that of the vice-chairman of the Republican National Committee, Ralph Williams, who felt that Hoover should have one politically wise cabinet member, namely Williams himself.

Not surprisingly, the cabinet that Hoover selected was revealing of the incoming administration. In general it was composed of men of business, wealth, loyalty, conservativism, and Protestantism. Also, cabinet designees were nonsoutherners, men of integrity, impersonal administrators, and as Learned Hand commented, "on average very good." And many of them had subcabinet members who were Hoover's intimates of long standing who particularly understood and represented his administrative vision.

As is the case with any president, the path to selection of the cabinet was strewn with problems of ideology, geographical balance, political representation, reward for service, administrative talent, and, very important during the process, the problems of dealing with the press. One cabinet position emerged from all the others as a problem for the press, that of the attorney general. William J. Donovan, the colorful colonel of the famous Sixty-ninth Fighting Division in World War I and the powerful head of the antitrust division in Coolidge's Justice Department, wanted to be attorney general. With such credentials and because he had come out for Hoover when the country was still in doubt about what Coolidge meant by his "I do not choose to run" statement, the president-elect was favorably disposed toward Donovan. Then the pressure on Hoover to renege became too intense—because Donovan was antiprohibitionist and Catholic, or so said the press. Donovan's stand on prohibition did pose a problem. Mabel Willebrandt, when sounded out by Hoover's aide Lawrence Richey, pointed to an avalanche of protest from prohibitionists. Borah and the labor leader William N. Doak anticipated organized Senate resistance, largely due to Donovan's antiprohibition stand. They thought that the president might lose the fight, a bad way to launch a new administration. Hoover pondered whether Donovan, as attorney general, would be able to enforce the Eighteenth Amendment if it were to come under the Justice Department. Of more importance were the president-elect's doubts about Donovan's ability to enforce the antitrust laws, given his bad record as head of that division. An attorney general who was weak on two significant points would be particularly susceptible to attack by Senate insurgents.

As inauguration time approached, Hoover became particularly annoyed at the press's criticism that religious intolerance was blocking Donovan's appointment to the cabinet. The president-elect came to believe that Donovan had "developed . . . a vast capacity for intrigue which resulted in starting the press campaign." Furthermore, Hoover felt that such intrigue marked an immaturity that would make for bad administration, although he finally offered Donovan the governor generalship of the Philippine Islands—"a position greater than any cabinet position." Donovan did not want or take the Philippine Islands post; and Hoover scratched off a handwritten note, explaining for posterity what had happened.[30] The bad press on the Donovan affair was another portent of press-relations problems to come to the new administration.

For attorney general the president-elect really wanted his old friend and Supreme Court Justice Harlan F. Stone; but Stone refused the office. Hoover finally elevated to the position a competent solicitor general, William D. Mitchell. William R. Castle, who was charged with reporting on Mitchell, wrote that he was "a man of the finest intellectual caliber and in any position there could never be [a] question of his integrity."[31]

Charles Francis Adams, a naval officer from the distinguished family of presidents, was selected to be secretary of the navy. Hoover appreciated his high cultivation and his frequent disinterested public view. Besides, Adams favored disarmament, which fact pleased Hoover's

Quaker and economy sensibilities. And the secretary-designate, unlike Stimson, would seldom question the president's judgments.

Dr. Ray Lyman Wilbur, president of Stanford University and a lifelong friend of the president-elect, was persuaded to accept the position as secretary of the interior. Hoover considered it a premium appointment, for as will be noted, it was in the Interior Department that Hoover planned to carry out many of his studies and reforms to aid important segments of American society, such as children, the sick, the aged, the ill-housed, and Indians.

Andrew W. Mellon's retention as secretary of the Treasury was the president's nod to the Old Guard of the party and to those citizens who considered him to be the "greatest secretary of the Treasury since Alexander Hamilton." That Hoover did not concur in the latters' opinion was evidenced by his reliance on Undersecretary Ogden Mills for advice on fiscal and monetary matters.

It is a tribute to Hoover that he wanted Senator Charles L. McNary to be secretary of agriculture. McNary had coauthored the famous McNary-Haugen bill, a congressional measure to control farm prices, which had been anathema to Hoover. Perhaps evidence that Hoover all along intended to run the Agriculture Department by way of farm cooperatives, which he had always favored, is found in his ultimate selection of Arthur Hyde for the agriculture post. Hyde had been a Ford car dealer and governor of Missouri; he knew very little about agriculture.

The appointment of an engineer and businessman, Robert P. Lamont, to the Commerce Department secretaryship, around which Hoover had built his own public career, might not be explicable except that the president's men were already in every nook and cranny of the department. Hoover came to regret the appointment.

As undistinguished as the appointments of Hyde and Lamont were those of James W. Good and James J. Davis, respectively, to head the War and Labor departments. Good, a fellow Iowan, was rewarded for faithful political services to Hoover. His belief in the regulation of public utilities made him something of a liberal. Because Hoover had influenced Secretary of Labor James J. Davis during the Harding and Coolidge administrations, he was sure that he would continue to do so as president. Walter F. Brown, a master Ohio politician, became a strong head of the Post Office Department. He had given much political advice to Hoover when Brown had served as one of Hoover's assistant secretaries in the Commerce Department and would, of course, give even more political advice as postmaster general.

36

In sum, Learned Hand was probably right about the cabinet. While Hyde, Lamont, Good, and Davis were rather average, they were compensated for by the others. And many of the Hoover underlings in the departments, the "New Patriots," generally added strength to the departments—Ogden Mills, in Treasury; F. Trubee Davison, in war; Julius Klein, in commerce; Ernest Lee Jahncke, in navy; David S. Ingalls, in navy; William R. Castle, in state; and Charles E. Hughes, Jr., in justice.

As important as the president's cabinet—or more so—were the issues to be addressed by the new administration. The most pressing of them constituted a collision course for the president. Borah, who was so important to Hoover, and the senior senator from Iowa, Smith W. Brookhart, had called on the president-elect when Hoover returned to the capital from his trip abroad and had received from Hoover a pledge to support farm legislation in a specially convened session of Congress. Eastern interests, such as those of du Pont and Union Carbide, with a considerable assist from Joseph R. Grundy of the Pennsylvania Association of Manufacturers and John Q. Tilson, the House majority leader, were as much for tariff revision as westerners were for agricultural legislation. The farm interests also wanted tariff revisions, although confined only to farm schedules. But powerful industrialists would not hear of that. Therefore, both farm and tariff legislation would be in the congressional hopper after March 4, an incongruity, for while farm and industrial representatives would engage in logrolling early in the special session of the Congress, their interests were antithetical and would spell trouble for the president. The president-elect, however, more innocently than not, was oblivious to the forthcoming struggle. So was Tilson. He thought that Congress could work its will quickly and have the farm and tariff legislation on the White House desk before July 4.[32]

In the meantime, Hoover, assuming that agricultural and tariff legislation would be tidied up in short order, addressed a range of other issues: enforcement of prohibition, regulation of aviation, legislation on national origins, flood control of the Mississippi, the development of inland and St. Lawrence waterways, and reorganization of the government. Yet, Hoover feared confronting Coolidge with a stance that in comparison might appear more vigorous than that of the outgoing president; thus, the president-elect prepared his Inaugural Address, conscious that his predecessor would be nearby.

3

★ ★ ★ ★ ★

A NEW BEGINNING

At 1:10 on the rain-soaked afternoon of 4 March 1929, Chief Justice William Howard Taft stepped to the inaugural stand on the east side of the Capitol and administered the presidential oath to Herbert Hoover. Americans, some fifty thousand in number, remained in place to listen, with the help of "cleverly-arranged amplifiers," to the Inaugural Address that followed; and by the most ambitious radio-broadcasting arrangement up to that date, people halfway around the world tuned in. The new president first addressed the twin goals of prosperity and freedom, stressing that the former should continue, but never to the detriment of the latter. Both were extremely important to Herbert Hoover: evening out the cycles of unemployment and protecting American freedom. Little did he or his fellow Americans realize that, in time, full employment and individual freedom would seem to be incompatible; that four years hence, the nation, if necessary, would willingly sacrifice freedom for employment. That conflict of a far-off day was, however, remote as on this day Hoover reminded the nation of how deeply indebted it was to Calvin Coolidge "for wise guidance in this great process of recovery" from war and its aftermath. Reform was also on Hoover's mind: he reminded his countrymen and fellow citizens of the world that the nation was building "a new economic system, a new social system, a new political system." To assure economic prosperity, for example, government and business would cooperate, manifesting the "highest conception of self-government." Such cooperation, however, would not preclude governmental regulation to assure fair business competition and the fair treatment of customers by monopolies such as public utilities. The administration's commitment to the "new social system" would be evidenced by such actions as the encouragement of education and of public health, to assure its incorporation "into our governmental system as is public education." The new political system would always eschew "intolerant partisanship" and would, among other things, reestablish a criminal-justice system in order to safeguard the nation's order. This would be done by the redistribution of function, the simplification of procedure, the establishment of special tribunals, and, of course, the enforcement of the Eighteenth Amendment. The new president also declared his intention to address seriously the foreign policy of the United States.

In his concluding paragraphs, which were always important in Hoover's addresses, the president reiterated the important theme, the metaphor of Scylla and Charybdis—the need for government to steer a course between its own lust for bureaucratic power and the greed of private economic agencies. Then he fell very naturally into enunciating the precepts of his American Individualism. Just after "self-government" and "justice," next among his American ideals and aspirations was "the maintenance of ordered liberty." These were followed by "the denial of domination by any group or class; the building up and preservation of equality of opportunity; the stimulation of initiative and individuality; absolute integrity in public affairs; . . . the freedom of public opinion; . . . the growth of religious spirit . . . ; the strengthening of the home; the advancement of peace."[1]

The people applauded the Inaugural Address, but as was frequently the case when they listened to Herbert Hoover, they were not inspired. The same words from an animated spokesman might have brought a more enthusiastic response. The new president's words were well thought-out and well phrased, which was somewhat rare, because in this case they were succinct, and they lacked a certain cumbersomeness that was normal in many of his speeches. Probably no president's Inaugural Address had come from a heart as sensitive and a mind as honed on the great issues as was Herbert Hoover's. It has been said that the Hoover presidency, by the standards of the Progressive generation, "should have been one of the high points of the Century." In the tradition of Quakerism and Progressivism, the new president believed that words speak for themselves and that the people wanted logic, not rhetoric or charisma. It was odd to suppose that people wanted only analysis, not inspiration; but Hoover and many Progressives—and engineers—accepted such thinking. Besides, such a view coincided with Hoover's shyness and general dislike of public speaking. So, the people's enthusiasm seemed to be reserved for another on this day—for the outgoing president.[2]

The press appeared to warm to Herbert Hoover more readily than did the people. The *New York Times*, which had supported Smith, reflected press reaction generally. On Inauguration Day it described the president-elect's "versatile ability and sterling character." Two weeks later it spoke of his able use of executive power and of his "Progressive leaning," and two weeks after that it noted how he had impressed his personality on the country. Almost biweekly the *Times* praised the new chief executive. By May 12 his presidency was being called "the dawn of the Hoover Era." And for the first time, the *Times* noted that "the man elected has the feel of the people." Nevertheless, in fact, Hoover was still an enigma. The people were still experiencing little devotion for their president. Much of the public that had communicated with the taciturn Coolidge seemed to be perplexed by President Hoover. They generally agreed with the press that he was efficient, hard-working, nonpolitical, and concerned; however, they did not know him. They did not respond unkindly, but they did not react with the warm feeling that is usually accorded to newly elected presidents.[3]

Those who were close to the president have revealed, both then and since, their affection for the new chief executive. Of course, his own official family would always sympathetically describe his demeanor. His White House staff would be particularly effusive later in recalling those days. They were so zealously loyal at the time that political author Robert Allen unkindly called them the Vestal Virgins. The staff included Walter H. Newton, who was in effect the senior secretary by nature of his substantial duties regarding executive appointments, government reorganization, and presidential contacts with the executive and congressional branches; Larry Richey, the president's confidant, who was in charge of personal affairs, correspondence, and office management; George E. Akerson, who was in charge of the press, public relations, and the daily schedule of the president's visitors; and French Strother, an administrative assistant who was in charge of research and social reform. In addition the president used his military aides for substantive defense matters. The president had two clerical secretaries, Ann Shankey and Myra McGrath, both of whom were functionaries. All were devoted, loyal, competent, and very supportive of the president.

The new president busied himself immediately. He did most of the in-depth analyses. And he became rather the office detailist. He held the reigns tightly—and uncomplainingly. Because the staff respected their chief so much, they worked harder and harder by his rules to provide details and facts for his arrangement and analysis, unaware that his rules tended to isolate him from ideas, if not from people. Because he worked so hard and never prodded unseemingly, Hoover's staff forever adulated him. Theodore G. Joslin, who in 1931 succeeded George Akerson as press secretary, would write an especially moving memoir about his White House experiences under Hoover. Others who were outside the secretariat but were more important in the advisory role, such as Ogden Mills, Walter E. Hope, Henry M. Robinson, Edward Eyre Hunt, Mark Sullivan, Henry J. Allen, and Henry L. Stimson, were comparably attracted to the president and remained so in afteryears.[4]

Henry L. Stimson, the eminent secretary of state, provides an important key to understanding Hoover's personality throughout his White House years, particularly because of the vivid contrast between the two of them. Far more than others among Hoover's counselors, Stimson dared, then and later, to make a franker appraisal of the president. He assiduously recorded his assessments. Because Stimson had wanted properly to wind up his affairs as governor general of the Philippine Islands, he arrived on his job in the capital some weeks after the inauguration. To become more quickly oriented to his job as the president's first minister, Stimson spent his first ten days in the White House. He wrote about the president's kindness and about how he had come to have a great apprecation for Hoover's high intelligence. The two ranged over great issues of foreign policy, such as the possibility of independence for the Philippine Islands, tariff revision, disarmament, the World Court, and foreign debts.

Stimson swung somewhat uneasily into the White House routine. He joined the "medicine-ball cabinet"—close friends of the president who worked out with him each morning from 7:00 to 7:45. Revealing differences in life style and temperament between Hoover and Stimson soon became evident. "The President dressed," reported Stimson to his diary, "with marvelous rapidity, quicker than anybody I ever met in or out of the Army, and he practically always beat me to [and through] breakfast. Breakfast was a rather disorganized affair because the president had two big dogs in the room and allowed them to climb all around and over him and eat off his plate and fork." Stimson usually dressed deliberately and ate leisurely. Hoover worked in the same way that he played and ate—hard and hurriedly. Stimson worked in the same way that he played and ate—leisurely and deliberately. More important than the difference in tastes between the two was their demeanors. Hoover's harried pace inclined toward impatience and pessimism. When things did not go his way, he was readily discouraged. He frequently saw the enemy who was there to stop his progress. Or as Stimson came to observe, "He always saw the dark side first." Stimson's calmness

42

inclined toward patience and a positive conduct. His personal life style seemed to say: ''The job will get done, particularly if you don't look for conspiracy.'' The potential enemy could be a friend if treated like one, if treated without suspicion. Hoover's potential enemies, in fact, more frequently than not, became adversaries, increasingly so as his presidency evolved. Stimson observed with increasing regularity the deepening of White House gloom as the president's term advanced and his problems deepened. Nevertheless, although Stimson was more objective and critical in his observations of the president than were most of Hoover's other intimate advisers, he saw Hoover's superior qualities and spoke kindly of him.[5]

Stimson's counterpart in the lower echelons of the White House—Irwin Hood (''Ike'') Hoover, the chief usher—also saw Hoover's gloom. In his memoirs, *Forty-two Years in the White House,* he describes the Hoover presidency as ''the hardest one to work for.'' ''He [the president] would go about never speaking to any of the help. Never a good-morning or even a nod of the head. Never a Merry Christmas or a Happy New Year. All days were alike to him. Sunday was no exception, for he worked just as hard on that day if not harder than on any of the others. There was always a frown on his face and a look of worry.''[6] While most of the chief usher's implied criticisms of the president and the first lady were trivial, Ike Hoover captured much of the same spirit that Stimson did. Both observed that the president seemed to see ''the dark side first.'' But where Stimson made allowances for personality traits and the difficulties of high office and was only saddened, Ike Hoover, sophisticated though he was, made few allowances and reacted negatively. In retrospect, observers a half-century later understood better than did either Ike Hoover or Secretary Stimson. The dourness that both saw, and that the former never forgave, is explained by the clash of the man and the office. The new president had a Quaker commitment to the duties of the ''awed'' office that shut out extraneous matters. At best, social amenities came hard to Hoover, let alone exchanging pleasantries with White House servants, especially as the depression deepened and the days grew longer.

Hoover's White House days were very long indeed. He rose shortly after 6:00, worked out at medicine ball, and had breakfast by 8:30. From then to 11:00 he worked on speeches and messages, dictated letters, made heavy use of the telephone, read many daily newspapers, conferred with his staff, and addressed administrative minutia, never wasting energy as he moved from item to item. (Although a detailist, he had superb abilities for grasping the large picture.) From 12:30 to 1:30 P.M. he met the public, with whom pleasantries were about as hard to exchange as with servants, not because he cared less for people and servants than did other presidents, but because he felt he had more important things to do on their behalf. Afternoons were reserved for the whole gamut of administrative functions, such as consultation with commissions, cabinet members, congressmen, and callers. He left the office between 6:00 and 7:00 P.M. and dined at 8:00, usually having as guests persons who were concerned with some important policy matter. Evenings were devoted either to more conferences in the Lincoln study or to state dinners. One of the few privileges of office that Hoover did thoroughly enjoy was taking leave of his company when he chose to retire, usually to read sundry government reports into the night. The president frequently departed abruptly, although civilly, especially from counselors such as Stimson. Hoover was seldom gregarious with cabinet members, servants, or the public in general.

Beyond Hoover's circle of intimate advisers and close observers was the world that, in the long run, would count most to him. The intimate advisers would always remain loyal and supportive. Observers such as Ike Hoover would never really matter. The cabinet, politicos, reporters, and congressmen represented the great constituencies that mattered most to Hoover, as they do to all presidents.

The cabinet served the president well, and Hoover, in his *Memoirs*, could point with pride to their integrity as well as to their loyalty. He might have added those additional criteria for appointment—administrative experience and minimal partisanship—that had been to a great extent evidenced. Although efficient, the cabinet was quite unspectacular. One member described it as ''a body of operating vice presidents in charge of administering departments . . . which meets for purposes of coordinating administrative action.''[7] This was not completely true. Stimson and Ogden Mills, the undersecretary of the Treasury, advised the president on great policy matters, the former on foreign affairs and the latter on domestic matters. Andrew Mellon, the ''Old Guardist'' of the cabinet, had little regard or affection for Hoover; and Hoover distrusted his ideology almost from the beginning and particularly with the coming of the depression, when the secretary of the Treasury saw ''liquidation'' of capital, labor, and the farmer as the only real solution. (By ''liquidation'' Mellon meant the process of culling out weaklings and misfits.) Almost from the start, Hoover relied on Ogden Mills, a blue blood from New York, for advice on fiscal and monetary matters. Mills's ability, integrity, and independence—traits not unlike Stimson's—quickly earned him the esteem of the new president. Up to a point the president appreciated an independence of mind, certainly when minds were as keen and educated as those of Mills and Stimson. Hoover especially valued Mills's hard work—the lack of which in Stimson he never quite understood. (Hoover frequently attributed Stimson's lassitude to poor health.) Like Stimson, Mills pleased the president by keeping his position in the cabinet relatively free from partisan politics. Eventually the president would replace Mellon with Mills, appointing the former to the post of ambassador to England.

Hoover took his new cabinet seriously, and others besides Stimson and Mills carried weight. But they were less important as advisers. Ray Lyman Wilbur, secretary of the interior, had been close to Hoover since their Stanford days and, as much as any one person, served as the president's alter ego. It was natural that in Wilbur's department the president effected much of his governmental reorganization by concentrating there broad and substantive policies that had long been germinating in his mind: policies regarding conservation of natural resources, the welfare of children, the public utilities system, the treatment of Indians, housing, and public education. William D. Mitchell, the attorney general, lived up to his reputation as being an intelligent man of integrity and also as being a cautious, "conservative Democrat." Charles Francis Adams, another eastern aristocrat, showed enough independence to appeal to the president but not too much to offend him. When Hoover desired more cuts in the navy than Adams wanted, the secretary obeyed orders and concurred. As earlier noted, Hoover came to wish that he had made Adams secretary of state. (Stimson responded to the president's demands far more hesitatingly than did Adams.) James W. Good, Robert P. Lamont, and James J. Davis, in comparison with other cabinet members, appeared to be innocuous in their roles in the War, Commerce, and Labor departments. James Good's death in November 1929, however, denied to Hoover a much-needed political adviser. Walter F. Brown, the postmaster general, was the president's principal liaison with the partisan political constituency.

Hoover was a largely nonpartisan president—in that tradition of the prewar Progressivism that deprecated partisan politics. It is ironic that for nearly half a century after his presidency, Democrats seemed to run against him every four years, for he was far from being the partisan Republican that they described. Herbert Hoover disliked the partisan political life. He disliked crowds and hobnobbing with the politicos, and especially did he disfavor appointing partisans to office. He firmly believed that the government should efficiently serve the people and not be a public trough for partisan followers. It was one thing to use and order partisans during a campaign, as Hoover had done very well, but it was another thing to reward the followers with public offices. Their rewards would have to come from someone other than the president of the United States. They frequently came from Postmaster General Walter Brown, who directed party matters throughout Hoover's presidency.

During Hoover's years at the Commerce Department, he had made Brown assistant secretary, appointing him for much-needed political advice and direction. Apparently, Hoover named Brown to the cabinet for the same purpose. Brown, who had been raised in the tough school of Ohio politics, was intelligent and level-headed, and he tried to keep the president's political house in order. This was not easy. For one thing, the retention of a large number of holdovers from the Coolidge presidency left little patronage for the administration to work with. Also, the president was reluctant to squander important positions on patronage appointments. Henry J. Allen and William Allen White, who were loyal Kansas supporters of the president, pleaded with Hoover to appoint one Richard J. Hopkins as a federal judge, lest their political organization suffer in Kansas. Hoover procrastinated. Was Hopkins the best man, he wondered. Hoover eventually appointed Hopkins, but only after much soul-searching.[8] Frequently, the president did not become involved at all in patronage matters; Brown took care of them. When Hoover asked him to "clean up" a southern political situation and afterwards nervously wondered how he had managed, Brown replied calmly, "Everything is all right." Brown, however, could not do it all. If the administration were to sustain the political support that it had enjoyed on Inauguration Day, the president would have to lead his partisan troops.

Hoover's rather pristine politics precluded much of what could have been his presidential leadership. Within two months of his inauguration, some of his close friends feared for him. "As I see it," wrote Mark L. Requa, a California associate of long standing, "the great weakness of the president is that he is over the heads of most of the people, that he has no time for small talk and petty politics; that he has not the ability to slap people on the back and tell them that they have done a good job. I hear it on every hand and it is giving me a great deal of concern . . . . Not withstanding the president's marvelous ideals there seems to be abroad a feeling that he is too much of a machine."[9] The same administrative machine that shunned public audiences and White House servants and, to some degree, peers like Stimson eschewed partisans. One historian, Barry Karl, sees Hoover's nonpartisanship as another of those Progressive myths that the president accepted as a tenet to live by, along with the assertion of an independent, noncharismatic leadership.[10] It should be noted that while Hoover's politics was frequently nonpartisan, it was just as frequently very personal, perhaps more dangerous.

The partisan arena is only one part of the political design of the presidency. Other constituencies are as important politically, not the least of which being the press. As has already been noted, the editorial pages of great newspapers gave the president an impressive send-off. The Washington reporters of most papers were as eager as were their chiefs back home to report favorably and interestingly on the new president. Having used Hoover as the best source of the capital's news during his days at the Commerce Department, they were quick to forget both his reticence to meet them during the campaign and his imposition of near-censorship during the South American trip. They were heartened by news that he would meet with them semiweekly and would permit more direct quoting, eliminating the "spokesman" routine for handing out White House news. The president would speak for himself and directly to the press corps. Reporters were pleased that he quickly reaffirmed his interest in openness and good press relations. However, they were soon to be disappointed. Within three weeks the president seemed to belie his intention to develop good press relations. He insisted on having questions written in advance, questions that Akerson frequently culled in order to "protect" his chief. The president's technique of resorting to handouts as a form of direct quotation had a dampening effect on press conferences. Hoover's presence before reporters produced less and less news. On March 26 he said, "Well, I have no question lodged in advance which gave me time for cooperation with you and little mature thought." On March 29: "There is no use getting out your paper because the only questions I have today relate to matters I am unable to make any announcement about." On April 9: "I am afraid this is going to be a famine morning." On April 12: "There is a partial famine today." On April 16: "Well, I am afraid there is a famine today." April 23: "There is a famine today again." April 30: "I haven't a single question from the Press this morning." May 3: "I have a better supply of questions today. However, so many came in just ten minutes ago that I am not going to deal with them until next time." May 10: "Well, I have one question today, and I am not quite in a position to make an adequate reply to it, so this is a famine day."[11]

Discouragement and then frustration soon infected the Washington press corps. When reporters approached Akerson for relief, little was forthcoming. Worst of all, in the eyes of many reporters, Hoover played favorites, inviting as guests to his Maryland retreat, Rapidan, such "dependable" reporters as Mark Sullivan, a syndicated columnist; Richard V. Oulahan of the *New York Times;* William Hall of the *Chicago Tribune;* Gene Wilson of the *Washington Star;* Leroy T. Vernon of the *Chicago Daily News;* Frank R. Kent of the *Baltimore Sun;* and David Lawrence of the *United States Daily News.* As reporters had turned to Hoover as a Washington source during his cabinet days, now they frequently turned to Stimson in this administration, although Stimson's news was largely limited to foreign affairs. Stimson did meet with reporters frequently, although he, too, often sought out the senior reporters for favorite treatment. But because he exposed himself in fairly good humor to the open and freewheeling press conferences and frequently to obstreperous questioning, he seemed to be justified in occasionally meeting separately with the more responsible reporters. It was revealing that Hoover, as compared to Stimson, incurred considerable wrath for following the same pattern, but this was understandable in view of the president's comportment.

While party leaders and reporters were limited in their search for an answer to the president's lack of cooperation, the Congress was not so limited. It had a constitutional right and duty to act independently of the president. And when he didn't "play ball," as was frequently the case, their independence was loudly enunciated. Some historians are justified in sympathizing with the president, who was caught somewhere between the western insurgent Republicans, the eastern Old Guard of his party, and the Democrats from other sections, mostly the South. However, strained relations between Congress and the president were not peculiar to the Hoover presidency. As Edgar E. Robinson and Vaughn D. Bornet have pointed out, there was a classic twentieth-century conflict between the provincialism of congressional constituencies and the president, whose constituents—the whole citizenry—sought a modern leader. James MacGregor Burns has called such a crisis "the deadlock of democracy."

What Robinson and Bornet imply, but hesitate to enunciate, is that presidents are political leaders who must deal with the inevitable conflict, if they are activist presidents with programs to be mobilized. Hoover's fertile mind was full of programs that were consonant with his well-thought-out ideology of balances. What observers of the Hoover presidency usually do not recognize is that Hoover's balances were frequently inimical. For example, the president believed so much in the federal tripartite arrangement that time and again he refused to use the necessary executive power to thwart Congress's measures that might upset the balance of industry, labor, and government. This built-in problem of contradiction was compounded by Hoover's reluctance to

wield partisan political power. During its first six months the administration was frequently stymied on such measures as the agriculture and
tariff bills. No activist president in this century has kept his distance
from the Congress as did Hoover, and in the congressional wings of
1929 stood the western insurgent Republicans—"sons of the wild
jackass"—as suspicious of the new president as were their flouters, the
Old Guard of the East.

By the fall of 1929 many congressmen were scorning the president's
condescendingly educational and apolitical approach. Strangely
enough, Hoover frequently felt more at home with congressional
Democratic leaders, John Nance Garner and Joseph T. Robinson, who
were as partisan and provincial as the eastern and western Republicans.
What Garner and Robinson wanted was Democratic victory in the
election of 1930 and a triumph in the next presidential election.

No situation during Hoover's administration better illustrated the
sensitivity to the "proper" relationship of government to industry—and
of the executive to the legislative branch—than the passage of the
Agriculture Marketing Act of 1929. The poor condition of agriculture
pervaded the 1920s and the Hoover administration. Agriculture's weak
state is examined in detail in subsequent chapters. It suffices to say here
that low farm income made agriculture the sickest of American industries and that Hoover promised William E. Borah and other western
senators that he would convene a special session of the Congress to
enact corrective measures. The measure that Hoover favored called for a
farm board to aid the agricultural industry by loaning vast sums of
money to support layers of farm cooperatives, which in turn would help
farmers to control their production of crops so as to avoid costly
surpluses and low prices. In so doing, the government would extend its
helping hand to the nation's farmers, but not in a domineering way.
Farmers, through their local, state, and regional cooperatives, would
determine their own fate. As the Federal Farm Board would avoid
bureaucratic control, so the agricultural industry, through the individual
farmers in the cooperative movement, would avoid a bureaucratic
control of farmers. Yet Hoover's desire to balance the agricultural
industry and government was in conflict with his commitment to
balance the executive and legislative branches of government. To
achieve the former balance by adhering to the latter balance would
prove to be very difficult.

For over a decade, Hoover had thought long and hard about the
problems of farmers and had been instrumental in guiding agricultural

policy during the Harding and Coolidge administrations along cooperative lines. The great farm organizations and their representatives in
Congress, however, were interested in more-direct governmental solutions to the farm problems of overproduction and low prices. The
McNary-Haugen bills, the export-debenture plans, and the cost-of-
production proposals—all called, in various ways, for federal farm
subsidies in order to help farmers to compensate for their burden of the
high cost of taxes, land, transportation, and farm implements and
particularly to enable farmers to share the relief that manufacturers
derived from the high protective tariff. In short, the agricultural industry
wanted parity with industry in general in the nation. Hoover, though,
feared the statist solutions.

The president viewed his recent election as a mandate to carry out
his own farm policy. He thought that he had been explicit enough in
calling for a "Federal Farm Board . . . to assist . . . the [agricultural]
industry to meet . . . the varied problems." Since he had outlined his
"fundamental concept of agriculture . . . [as] one controlled by its own
members, organized to fight its own economic battles and to determine
its own destinies," he thought that Congress should have known that
he would avoid, at all costs, governmental control and domination of
agriculture. Especially should it have understood the mandate since he
had declared that his proposals were not "to put the government into
the control of the business of agriculture, nor to subsidize the prices of
farm products and pay the losses thereon, either by the federal treasury
or by a tax or a fee on the farmers."[12] Through a $500-million revolving
fund, a Federal Farm Board would loan the farm community money to
organize and strengthen cooperatives, which in turn would help farmers to produce and market their crops more efficiently and at less cost.
The control of industry by the farmers would not be unlike the bankers'
control of currency by means of the Federal Reserve System.

Farmers who had powerful spokesmen in their great interest
groups, and especially in the Congress, were suspicious of Hoover's
cooperative approach to their problems. They did not understand the
mandate. They had not been "educated." Even Borah and Smith
Brookhart, who had exerted the most pressure for the special session,
saw the mandate quite differently. Brookhart believed that the president
would support the direct federal control of surpluses; therefore
Brookhart called for a $1.5-billion stabilization fund to guarantee crop
prices as Hoover "did while head of the Food Administration during the
War." Senator Arthur Capper, the president's friend from Kansas,
believed that Hoover favored setting up "stabilization corporations and
other agencies to deal at once with the problems of seasonal and annual

surpluses of farm products.''[13] Confusion reigned in the Senate, and the farm bloc, which was not usually given to seeking presidential direction, did so in this case. But the possibility of intrusion by the president offended his sense of the necessary independence of the branches of the government. He would not draft the legislation, even though the Congress had been convened at his behest to secure relief for the farmers.

When the president did send his special message to Congress on April 12, he did little to lessen the confusion about the government's role on the stabilization of production. Finally, Hoover wrote to Senator McNary, chairman of the Senate Agriculture Committee, opposing the idea of any kind of direct subsidy to farmers who were exporting commodities at a price lower than the domestic market price.[14] The president's letter was not enough to stop the Senate from putting an export-subsidy provision into the agriculture marketing bill. Thirteen Republicans, including Hoover's staunch supporter William Borah, joined thirty-four Democrats to defeat the president. The Republicans who voted for the provision were, almost to a man, western insur-gents—Moses's ''wild jackasses.'' At dinner on May 13, Simeon D. Fess, the assistant Republican whip, commiserated with the president and described the insurgents, including Borah, as pseudo-Republicans.

The *New York Times*, in an editorial, wondered why, after only two months in office, the president faced such a ''formidable party revolt'' in the Senate.[15] Much of the answer involved Hoover's belief in the executive branch's hands-off approach to the Congress—his unwilling-ness to work things out with the insurgent Republicans. It was too much to ask westerners, who for a decade had clamored for a strong support program, to exclude such a program from the bill, at least without some political persuasion on the president's part. In addition, the president would not play the patronage political game with Congress. Republican leaders pointed out to the president that had he placated Senators William B. Pine of Oklahoma and Thomas D. Schall of Minnesota with some patronage and assurance, the export-debenture plan would never have been included in the bill. But the president was not in the habit of ''trading.'' He felt that he represented the welfare of the people and that Congress represented the politicians. Former Secretary of Agriculture William M. Jardine complained that there ''is some very bad leadership from the bottom of 16th Street''—the White House.[16]

For weeks the two houses of Congress were deadlocked on the agriculture measure. House Speaker Nicholas Longworth held the line for the agriculture marketing bill without the export-debenture plan; but the Senate was determined to stand by the plan. When leaders held a breakfast meeting on the matter at the White House, the president made no suggestions. While the House-Senate Conference accepted the House bill, the Senate turned it down. At long last, on June 12, a successful strategy was worked out, but with little direction from the White House. The House again lined up with the president in support of the bill. The Senate, rather than carry the onus of refusing aid to farmers, also passed the bill.

For all of the president's unassertiveness in the passage of the bill, he made the signing of the act an event. "We have at last made a constructive start at agricultural relief with the most important measure ever passed by Congress in aid of a single industry." He alluded to how the Farm Board, like the Federal Reserve System, would control the "currency" of the industry. Through the board, farmers' cooperatives would control the flow of the nations basic crops.[17]

Westerners, for whom the act had primarily been passed, were far less enthusiastic than was the president about the Agricultural Marketing Act. Along with its lack of the strong governmental role that they wanted, the act was vaguely drawn. In short, it provided for the Federal Farm Board to administer loans, from a revolving fund of $500 million, to agricultural cooperatives to aid farmers in the production and marketing of their crops. Hoover was anxious to implement his balanced government-industry solution to agricultural distress. Persuading Alexander Legge—who had been assistant to Bernard Baruch on the War Industries Board during World War I—to chair the Farm Board, the president made sure that Legge and other appointees were safely opposed to the export-debenture program, which provided "excessive" governmental support. Furthermore, the president made it clear to the board that its duty was to organize the integral marketing cooperatives on a commodity basis, not to stabilize farm prices by making governmental purchases of commodities. He suggested that the board should first attack the problem of wheat, that a midwestern conference of farm leaders should form a national "company" to lend money (which would be allotted by the Farm Board) to cooperatives for the construction or lease of facilities and for marketing advances to the members of the cooperatives. The board did as the president suggested. Throughout the summer and fall of 1929, it valiantly set up its divisions and initiated the implementation of the act. Central marketing facilities and services were established; educational work on the value of cooperative marketing was conducted; funds were allotted to cooperatives for advance payments to farmers; and national commodity organizations were set up. Hoover's balances of informal corporatism seemed at last to have been launched.[18]

In addition to the strong governmental legislation that farmers had pleaded for, but to no avail, they wanted increased tariff schedules on farm imports that competed with their basic crops. Hoover reluctantly acceded to their wishes. Although the president was no advocate of high tariffs, he did believe in a schedule of protective tariffs, especially for the stricken farmers. But alas, the president fell into the same trap that many other presidents have fallen into. Once the hearings had opened, Congress, particularly the Senate, proceeded to logroll increases in tariffs on nonfarm as well as farm commodities. Speaker Longworth restricted the House to increases in tariffs on farm imports. The Senate, however, was a far-different body. Logrolling there was a common occurrence. Eastern Senators demanded protection for industrial interests, which outraged western insurgents.

The Senate's preeminent advocate of high tariff protection was Senator Joseph Grundy, president of the Pennsylvania Manufacturers' Association. Hoover thought that he had convinced Grundy of the need for decreases on industrial products, but by midsummer the proposed schedules were obviously far higher than any schedules that the president had campaigned for. While Hoover expressed some concern, the insurgents complained loudly, and again Borah led the way. As was the case with the passage of the Agricultural Marketing Act, the president maintained his silence, his executive unobtrusiveness. He somewhat eased his conscience with the belief that the flexibility provision in the tariff measure, which would authorize a scientifically administered Tariff Commission to raise or lower tariffs, would be its saving grace—that after the passage of the bill, the administration could lower any inordinately high schedules. However, insurgents, who should have appreciated such a progressive approach to whittling down unnecessarily high tariffs, refused to give the president that authority.

The president was silent on the flexibility provision, thus inviting adamant criticism from Democrats and the press. He hoped that his supposed friend Grundy would support the flexibility provision. Grundy at first agreed to this, but then, with no concern for the president's feelings, arrogantly changed his mind. So the president was without support in any quarter: from the Old Guard, the insurgents, or the Democrats.

During the fall, when the president had hoped to be finished with the tariff, Borah and his insurgent colleagues joined the Democrats to defeat those Republicans who supported the commission's authority to "fix" the schedules. Democrats were gleeful. A White House summary of editorial comment noted that "the present situation clearly demonstrates the collapse of Republican leadership in the Senate and . . . is seriously jeopardizing the very existence of the Republican Party."[19] So, while the president achieved from Congress his coveted Agricultural Marketing Act, such was not the case with the tariff legislation.

The tariff fight, although in many respects it paralleled the president's problems with Congress over the passage of the Agricultural Marketing Act, was far more debilitating and prolonged. Tariff bills seem to bring out profound tensions—so much so in this case that the burden of passage was carried by the president throughout the remaining months of the special session and far into the next congressional session. A discussion of it more properly belongs in chapter 5, "1930."

While Herbert Hoover seemed at times to be out of his element in the world of congressional and partisan politics—both of which were manifestations of an electoral politics that was disdained by and sometimes unfamiliar to the president—he was in his element in the world of administration. The Hoover presidency would accommodate twentieth-century ideas of executive reorganization and the managerial presidency. One need only glance at the development of the executive branch to sense the opportune timing of Hoover's entrance into the presidency. In the late nineteenth century a joint committee of Congress had tried, with little success, to give some order to executive management. In 1906 Theodore Roosevelt had appointed the Keep Commission, composed of executive-branch insiders, to suggest administrative changes; but Congress had thought that the president was asserting too much executive power and therefore had prohibited him from continuing the study. Then William Howard Taft had succeeded in establishing the President's Commisison on Economy and Efficiency, which at least demonstrated the general need for a "whole" conception of executive administration. It was to study such specific areas as budget, organization, personnel, revenue, and business practices. Wilson had demanded enough administrative changes to win the war, but the Joint Committee on Reorganization, 1920–24, representing Congress and the administration, was the first real beginning of executive reorganization. Hoover was the foremost administrator to speak out for the recommendations of the committee, which ranged from the reorganization of departments according to function, on the one hand, to making them all more efficient and less costly. But Hoover's interest was not just in saving money. "Whatever these reductions of expenditures may be," he reported to the committee, "they are not . . . as important as the . . . ability of Congress to handle . . . expenditures with better comprehension and long view policies." But executive reorganization came hard to the jealous Congress, and as prosperity enveloped the second half of the decade, Congress saw increasingly less need for economy and efficiency in government. Herbert Hoover would have to accomplish it on his own.[20]

The new president, having reorganized much of his Commerce Department, was confident that he could bring much of his vast experience to bear on revision of the executive branch. He would build his administration "brick on brick, stone on stone, by which, in the end, great institutions are created."[21] To men like Hoover, great institutions such as the United States government are not built on the shifting sands of electoral politics. And the cement of his administration would be cooperation between loyal administrators, expert consultants, and himself. In the executive branch, he could deal with men who would see the logic of his programs of service and act accordingly. With his branch, if not with the others, he could do a better job of managing the balance between government and citizenry—providing the services of the former without jeopardizing the initiative and independence of the latter. Hoover viewed all departments as being great instruments for serving the citizens, each in a specific way: Treasury with the taxpayers, War and Navy with servicemen, Justice with lawbreakers, Commerce with businessmen, Labor with laborers, and so forth. As for the Department of the Interior, the president thought of it as being the service department *par excellence* for serving citizens.

The president explained his administrative procedures to French Strother and to others early in the administration. Little was to be left to chance. All was to be planned assiduously and implemented by design. Hoover knew that any real strategies would have to be his responsibility. And he was acutely aware that there frequently would be resistance in many departments—that bureau chiefs were often more selfishly partisan than partisan politicians. The president would frequently use conferences, committees, or commissions to plan the resolution of great problems. Theodore Roosevelt had used such organizations extensively, and Hoover had encouraged their use during the Wilson, Harding, and Coolidge administrations. They could be "managed": the appointment, the charges, even the recommendations, and, of course, the implementation. They would be no financial burden to the government, for they could be supported by philanthropy. They would not add to the governmental bureaucracy, for they would convene, digest facts, draw conclusions, report findings, adjourn, and educate the public about great issues and solutions. The federal departments would use their "good offices" to initiate the studies and to implement the solutions. It was an administrative system of expected efficiency. And while Hoover moved with dispatch to implement the system, it was to be a continuous system of factual study and scientifically cautious implementation, not one to adjust its "sails to the breeze of the day; [but] to ripen with the slow progress of the years."[22] This was right out of the administrative tradition of Progressivism—a Progressive myth (of expert administration) that Hoover sought to make real.

No president in a hundred years, excepting Woodrow Wilson, had moved his administration so quickly and so extensively into domestic reform. Through Andrew W. Mellon, a strong secretary of the Treasury who represented Old Guard interests in the cabinet, the president ordered that department to publish all large governmental refunds of gift, estate, and income taxes; this was an important repudiation of the secretary's earlier policies. Also, contrary to Mellon's previous tax policies, the president announced that he would ask Congress to place taxes on a more graduated scale, by reducing them by two-thirds on lower incomes, one-third on middle incomes, and only one-fifth on higher incomes. To federal prohibition officers in the Treasury Department, Hoover issued orders that they adhere strictly to legal search-and-seizure efforts in their enforcement of prohibition. In time, Hoover placed the whole enforcement machinery in the Justice Department, where it belonged.

William D. Mitchell, the conservative attorney general, was instructed to publish the list of backers of all judicial appointments so as to expose any undue partisan pressure. When Hull House's Jane Addams expressed concern that political prisoners had been incarcerated, Hoover became similarly concerned and received assurances from the attorney general that such was not the case. Assistant Attorney General Mabel W. Willebrandt was eased out of the Justice Department, lest her overzealous methods in regard to prohibition would dominate when the responsibility for enforcement of the Eighteenth Amendment would be transferred to that department. Also very important by way of reform was the Justice Department's appointment of the eminent prison authority Sanford Bates to undertake massive corrective measures in the system of federal prisons. Numerous prison-reform measures were prepared during the early months of the new administration. Probably the most startling of the president's instructions to the attorney general was that there be no "Red scare" during his administration, that if Communists wanted to picket peacefully in front of the White House, they should be permitted to do so.

As noted, the Interior Department, headed by the president's friend Ray Lyman Wilbur, was the service department in which Hoover carried out his most extensive changes—many of which were in the conference format, a planning method that sometimes required time to launch. Almost instantly, however, the plight of the Indian was addressed. Hoover's fellow Quaker Charles J. Rhoads was appointed commissioner of Indian affairs. Rhoads had been treasurer of the Indian Rights Association and had brought into the department a policy of an enlightened treatment of Indians. He immediately eliminated the practice of having segregated Indian boarding schools and attempted to assimilate the Indians without impairing their culture. It was a difficult task that was only partially achieved. Hoover agonized over the conflict. In the attempt to better the service to Indians, federal expenditures on their behalf were doubled, with most of the additional funds going to education and health.

In policy matters pertaining to natural resources, most of which came under the jurisdiction of the Interior Department, Hoover has been called "the first conservationist president since Theodore Roosevelt." Partial testimony to the fact was borne out by the following efforts. He constantly urged the oil industry to avoid using wasteful measures. He appointed Horace M. Albright, a recognized conservationist, as commissioner of the National Park Service. Hoover effected the transfer of some two million acres of federal land into the national forest reserve. He denied to Insull power interests the rights to construct a dam in the naturally beautiful Cumberland Valley. He requested Congress to extend the Federal Power Commission's jurisdiction over interstate power companies, thus saving for posterity vast redwood areas of the West Coast. And within three months of taking office, the president had successfully urged Congress to pass the Boulder Canyon Project Act, which caused the *New Republic* to editorialize that "advocates of public ownership may well congratulate [Secretary Wilbur for his plans] . . . for the distribution of Boulder Dam power." Seventy-five percent of the dam's water power was to go to publicly owned corporations in California. In August the department began to make its survey of the needs for water power and waterways in the upper Mississippi Valley, and in September, Hoover called for a St. Lawrence seaway and a Great Lakes waterway. The president also gave early attention to the possible development of the basins of the Allegheny, Illinois, Missouri, Tennessee, and Columbia rivers. His conflict with George Norris over the development of public power in the Tennessee Valley came considerably later during the administration.[23]

The State Department was the scene of vigorous action. There it was really a matter of enlightened attitude as much as action. Hoover was better equipped than any of his twentieth-century predecessors to address issues of foreign policy. His massive food-distribution programs before and after World War I, as well as his participation in the Versailles Conference of 1919, had gained for him valuable foreign experience. And while he was secretary of commerce, his interests in American and world commerce had constantly brought foreign issues into his purview. His trip to Latin America after the election had laid the groundwork for much of the hemispheric policy of his administration.

Henry L. Stimson, as secretary of state, would greatly enhance Hoover's foreign policy. Their ten days together in the White House had determined much of the spirit, if not the unforeseen outline, of the policy for the ensuing four years. Both wanted naval disarmament, and together they laid the groundwork for the London Naval Conference of 1930: Stimson wanted for the administration the success that Charles Evans Hughes had achieved in the Washington Arms Conference of 1922, and Hoover wanted to divert military expenditures to social needs, "to convert swords into plowshares." Both gave important consideration, in 1929, to ways in which the administration could make the Nine Power Treaty and the recent Kellogg Peace Pact work. Stimson, in particular, thought of methods by which the latter pact could be supplemented: for example, by United States participation in the World Court. The president vigorously supported Stimson's plan for Senate ratification of a treaty to establish United States membership.

There were other considerations of United States foreign policy, such as vigorous discussions regarding the recognition of Russia, ways for the administration to implement a "good neighbor" policy in South America, and independence for the Philippine Islands. Together, Hoover and Stimson determined upon the withdrawal of United States marines from Central America and the Caribbean. The withdrawal took place in Nicaragua in 1933 and was initiated in Haiti in the same year. Having just returned from the Philippines, Stimson was much concerned about the independence movement, which would end the islands' tariff advantage for the United States. He persuaded Hoover that such a course would be too damaging to the islands to justify independence. So, a policy that appeared to be expansionist was actually one of active and enlightened interest in another nation, not unlike the new administration's policies regarding many nations of the world. In sum, the first eight months of the Hoover administration were "dazzling" in foreign affairs.

Some of the president's actions cut across departmental lines. Those regarding the condition of Negroes were particularly noteworthy. Consistent with his Quaker scorn of prejudice, Hoover had refused to sign any agreement to restrict Negroes or Jews from moving into his neighborhood on S Street. During his presidency, Negroes were entertained in the White House. The White House invitation to Mrs. Oscar DePriest, wife of the black congressman from Chicago, created a furor among southerners at some cost to the administration's southern support. The first prison sentence that Hoover commuted was that of a Negro who had been convicted of the murder of a white woman, though no one had witnessed it. Also, the president demanded increased appropriations for Freedman's Hospital and Howard University. Frequently, Hoover went outside of the government to aid Negroes, as when he attempted to persuade foundations to support his plan of some years to loan money to Negro tenants and sharecroppers so that they could purchase the land that they worked. Nevertheless, many bureaucrats in the administration continued the old ways of discrimination against Negroes, as when the secretary of war placed Negro and white Gold Star Mothers on separate ships on a pilgrimage that they made to Europe. However, when the bureaucrats and the secretary of war behaved thus, they were not following the example of the president.

Perhaps most of Hoover's administrative changes emanated from the conferences or commissions that he appointed to address large areas of policy. The larger departments could offer the services of government to the conferences. The recommendations made by a conference would invariably call forth voluntary action by citizens and, when necessary, legislative action, with care being taken that federal involvement be limited. Perhaps no conference received more attention or better typified the administration's approach than the White House Conference on Health and the Protection of Children, which convened on 2 July 1929. It called together twenty-five hundred delegates to study all aspects of child welfare. Its thirty-five volumes of findings became the source books for social workers for years to come. Hoover and Wilbur worked in tandem in generating the conference, as they did for conferences on waste, housing, public-land policy, oil conservation, and federal involvement in public education.

As important as these conferences were, perhaps the more profound problems were addressed by committees or commissions that were much more heavily staffed and more expertly oriented. Of such bodies the most important were the President's Committee on Recent Social Trends and the Wickersham Commission on Law Enforcement. The former would not issue its report until the end of Hoover's term; the latter would report within a year.

From the perspective of a half-century, the President's Committee on Recent Social Trends was in many respects exciting, regarding both its past and future. It epitomized much of the tradition of the new reform in social science, which had first been suggested with the formation in the late nineteenth century of the Civil Service Reform League and the American Economics Association. The concern that such organizations had for the national welfare had been further and substantially expressed in Theodore Roosevelt's great Conservation Conference of 1908 and by the federal agencies of World War I, such as the War Industries Board and the Food Administration. By the time of the Hoover presidency, the methodology of assessing great national problems had been well honed: the survey of the problem, the organizing of the research, the interpretation of findings, and the implementation by education—all at the hands of social-science experts. Hoover knew the methodology firsthand from his days in Food Administration and the Commerce Department. In both agencies he had learned—in fact, had largely been responsible for—the value of tying the philanthropy-industrial-banking network into problem solving. In addition to Hoover's experience during World War I and in the Commerce Department, his numerous contacts with the analytical experts of his profession of engineering had added to his reserve of ideas and talent.

Hoover's problem-solving approach dovetailed with his Progressive beliefs in a noncharismatic, nonpartisan, and independent administration. His problem-solving approach came early in the administration with the idea of making a vast survey of the whole national scene—its "trends"—a survey to be made by the nation's leading authorities in the social sciences, such as Charles E. Merriam, Howard W. Odum, William F. Ogburn, Wesley C. Mitchell, and Edward Eyre Hunt.

It is not difficult to believe that the idea of such a vast social-science survey was largely Hoover's, since it is so obviously a composite of his ideas and practices. Nor is it difficult to understand that he gave it a priority comparable to the reorganization of the executive branch and particularly the large actions centered in the Interior Department. The president was anxious to expedite the gathering of social-science data for the solution of social problems. French Strother was put to work on the project. Strother and William Ogburn—an important sociologist who was in the process of moving from Columbia University to the University of Chicago—conferred in Washington on September 6. Although the meeting was inconclusive, Ogburn understood and sympathized with the president's emphasis on a two-pronged approach to the nation's social ills—by the Interior Department and by a social-science survey. On September 26 the president met with several social scientists—Ogburn; Wesley C. Mitchell, a Columbia University economist; Charles Merriam, a University of Chicago political scientist—and French Strother, Secretary of the Interior Wilbur, and Shelby Harrison of the Russell Sage Foundation. Hoover invited those present to give him a ten-minute statement on their views about such a survey. The president then summarized the group's favorable reaction and announced his own approval. On October 21 the committee submitted to the president the plan to survey twenty-four fields, from population, food, and natural resources to public administration. Largely on the advice of the organizing committee, the president, on December 21, announced the appointment of the President's Committee on Recent Social Trends. The *New York Times* exclaimed editorially that "all possible information should be made utilizable by the central government, but that action upon it should be left in the hands of self-governing communities." In short, the *Times* concluded, the study would bring together facts upon which the imagination might plan "and around which patriotic impulses and something of the 'prophetic strain' as regards the future of the country [might] be rallied."[24]

The President's Committee on Recent Social Trends, which had the potential of doing long-range social planning, made a report at the end of Hoover's term. One issue that was crying for immediate attention was the breakdown of law enforcement in regard to the Eighteenth Amendment. No issue was so emotionally charged in the early months of the new administration, and none so plagued the president. It was grist for an immediate objective and deliberative analysis by a committee or commission that would have the staff and the time to consider effective methods of enforcement. In his acceptance speech, Hoover had promised that, if elected, he would appoint such a commission. After the election he went beyond that promise by broadening the charge to the prospective commission to address law enforcement generally. Because of this broadened charge, antiprohibitionists thought that the president was putting violation of the Eighteenth Amendment on a level with murder and rape; prohibitionists thought that the president was obscuring the issue. The issue had been given prominence not only in the president's Inaugural Address but also in his first address as president to the people in late March. On May 20 the commission was appointed. Hoover tried to get the most eminent of Americans to serve, and in part he succeeded. Then, the president charged them to consider the entire federal machinery of justice: the reconstruction of its function, the simplification of its procedures, the provision of additional special tribunals, better selection of juries, and the more effective organization of agencies that dealt with investigation and prosecution. "It will," concluded the president, "also naturally include the consideration of the enforcement of the Eighteenth Amendment."[25]

The nation applauded the staff and the charge of the Commission on Law Enforcement. Besides George W. Wickersham—its chairman, who had been Taft's attorney general—the able and forthright members of the commission included Newton D. Baker, Wilson's secretary of war; William S. Kenyon, a United States circuit judge; and Roscoe Pound, the distinguished dean of Harvard Law School. None was recommended by the Anti-Saloon League of America or the Woman's Christian Temperance Union. Mabel Willebrandt complained to Walter Newton that she had not been consulted. The president wanted a much higher quality than he could expect from a Willebrandt nominee. "I agree with you," William Gibbs McAdoo wrote to a friend about the new administration, "that Hoover has made a good start."[26]

Just as all seemed to be going well with the prohibition study, trouble surfaced. Chairman Wickersham suggested in a letter to Governor Franklin Roosevelt of New York that the nation's governors might well consider the enforcement of the prohibition law within the states, leaving to the federal government the preventing of the importation, manufacture, and shipment of alcohol in interstate commerce. The chairman was implying, correctly, that federal enforcement of the illegal sale of alcohol was not feasible. The reaction across the nation was mixed. Drys felt that Wickersham had prejudiced the case. Many thought the president should dismiss the chairman. Wets admired the chairman for his forthright stand. The president was silent and must have pondered the volatile reactions that he encountered in the sheaf of editorials and letters that the White House staff placed before him.

After eight months into the presidency, Hoover seemed to be living up to expectations. His competency as the nation's chief executive, if uninspiring, was largely unquestioned. Changes were occurring as they had not for a decade. "Hoover is making enemies right and left—especially right," reported Mark Sullivan. "Higher tariff barons, jingoes, brass hats, big Navyites, Prohibition fanatics, patronage hounds, and in general, those who dread change" oppose the president, said Sullivan. The *New York Times* editorialized that Mr. Hoover was "at his best" as he addressed the great problems of American life. Criticism of the president was muted. The Republican good fortunes apparently were assured. The real presidential test, however, was yet to come. The crisis of affairs had not yet been met. It came sooner than was expected.

4

★ ★ ★ ★ ★

THE CRASH

Before the great stock-market crash of October 1929, the *New York Times* industrial index had risen from 83 points in 1921, to 181 by mid decade, to 443 just prior to the crash.[1] It then dropped astoundingly over the next three years to a low of 85 in 1932.[2] Because the stock-market slide from 1929 to 1933 was accompanied by at least a 25 percent reduction in employment during the same period, many observers have concluded that the slide was related to the unemployment and that the Hoover presidency was largely responsible for both. Before addressing the charges that the administration unfavorably affected the stock market and the economy, it is essential to first explain the general nature of the United States economy in the decade prior to the crash and the Great Depression.

The United States emerged from World War I as a creditor nation, a position that presumed a role as international stabilizer in the Western world. With victory at hand—a victory that was in large part due to the nation's phenomenal productive capacity—prosperity seemed to be assured. (At least the prosperity seemed to be assured once the severe problems that had been tied to the conversion from war to a peacetime economy had subsided.) Much of the economic life of the nation during the 1920s appeared to confirm the prospect. The nation's standard of living was much enhanced, particularly because wages of industrial workers increased by nearly 20 percent between 1923 and 1929,[3] and because of a vast expansion in the construction industry and such new enterprises as the production of electricity (and their appliances) and, of course, automobiles. The gross national product (GNP) increased from $128 billion in 1921 to $204 billion in 1929.[4] Also the nation had become conscious of unusual improvement in such social services as playgrounds, parks, public libraries, and public-health facilities. The education of young Americans reached unheard-of proportions in the country. The number of college students in the 1920s alone doubled, to nearly one million. And cities burgeoned, bustling with cultural as well as economic activity. To most of its citizens, the nation seemed to be on a permanent economic plateau, initiated a decade before and elevated by the war. Indeed, the rise in the stock market appeared to them to be a natural phenomenon.[5]

The citizenry was not alone in seeing the prosperity of the 1920s as reason for confidence in the future. Just six months prior to the crash a committee of experts, under the chairmanship of Herbert Hoover, released a report on the decade's economic condition, *Recent Economic Changes in the United States*. The committee showed, according to economic historian Broadus Mitchell, ''a nearly complete infatuation with prosperity and the promise of its continuation.''[6]

Still another irony of history is that Hoover, who more than any other public figure addressed the stresses of economic cycles and the consequent problems of unemployment, would chair a committee on economic changes which seemed to misconstrue the present and the future. The *Recent Economic Changes* report and its predecessor studies, *Business Cycles and Unemployment* (1923) and *Seasonal Operation in the Construction Industries* (1924), by Hoover's direction, had searched for economic tools to eliminate cycles and to stabilize the economy. Hoover believed, from his own experience and observation, that prewar national organizations (such as the National Civic Federation, the Chamber of Commerce, and the American Federation of Labor), the war agencies (such as the Council of National Defense and his own Food Administration), and the postwar groups (such as the National Bureau of Economic Research, which undertook the *Recent Economic Changes* study) were close to finding such tools. All the organizations and the studies suggested to Hoover that industrialists, investors, laborers, consumers, and the public could coordinate their activities regarding production and inventories so as to even out the economic cycles. Through various forms of associationalism, they could control production and the accumulation of inventories during periods of prosperity in order to be able to increase production during periods of recession. By so doing, they would also pursue the replacement of adversary relations between capital and labor with coordinated action that would be productive yet protective of individualism, manifesting both order and liberty. Hoover, as secretary of commerce, had increased trade associations to over two thousand in number so as to effect cooperation and mutual self-help on the parts of business, labor, and government. The *Recent Economic Changes* report was the latest and most voluminous of Hoover's suggested studies.

Broadus Mitchell's criticism of the *Recent Economic Changes* report must, of course, be understood in the context of the times. He formed his criticism of the report during the last years of the New Deal; this reflected his own infatuation with what appeared as Keynesian aspects of the Roosevelt era. He gleefully quotes the charge to the Committee on Recent Economic Changes "to make critical appraisal of the factors of . . . instability" and to recommend changes of the same, and then he suggests that the charge hardly squares with the opening sentence of the report: "Acceleration rather than structural change is the key to understanding our recent economic developments."[7] Thus, to Mitchell, the report appears to be simplistic, if not naïve. In fact, however, the study, over which Hoover presided, reflected as much economic sophistication for the 1920s as Mitchell did for his time at the close of the New Deal. Worse yet, Mitchell's bias in his analysis fails to quote the conclusion of the *Recent Economic Changes* report, by Wesley C. Mitchell, which warns the nation of the very kind of cyclical problem that had disturbed Hoover for a decade. Mitchell must have been aware of the gross inconsistencies that are found in the report. While one specialist has noted that the mass production and consumption of those years would have the "object of reducing the price and extending the market,"[8] another expert saw "a more or less conscious policy [on the part of manufacturers] to shut down the plant . . . rather than to offer their products at greatly reduced prices."[9] Mitchell concluded:

> The incomes disbursed to consumers, and to wage earners in particular, must be increased on a scale sufficient to pay for the swelling volume of consumers' goods sent to market. The credit structure must be kept in due adjustment to the earnings of business enterprises. Security prices must not outrun prospective profits capitalized at the going rate of interest. Commodity stocks must be held in line with current sales. Overcommitments of all sorts must be avoided. The building of new industrial equipment must not be overrapid.[10]

But even Wesley Mitchell did not see how structurally flawed the American economy really was in the 1920s, nor did any leaders and observers of consequence. Very shortly after World War I a glut of agricultural goods on the world market reduced American exports of them to Europe by 80 percent during the decade and a half after the war.[11] The loss of so much of the foreign agricultural market was accompanied by a myriad of other problems for farmers: the indebtedness that they had incurred so as to capitalize on the war market; the reduction of the domestic market during the 1920s, which was largely caused by dietary changes and a decrease in population growth; the overproduction of farm commodities, as a result of the vast mechanization of agriculture; the tilling of additional land by farmers in a feverish attempt to make up for their economic losses; the reluctance of farm families to withdraw from the overcrowded agriculture field; and the drastic drop in farm prices, especially at the end of the decade. The sickness of agriculture had more impact than we have generally supposed. Historians have frequently glossed over the fact that by 1930 nearly half of the population was still living on farms or in rural communities (those with less than five thousand people) whose institutions were adversely affected by the agriculture plight.[12]

Although the international situation was a constant problem for agriculture throughout the decade, the nation was blinded to it by America's fervor for its overall favorable balance of trade. Ultimately, however, worsening world economic conditions would affect the total American economy as it did the economies of all nations. Among the important sources of such international problems were depreciation in currency exchange, the speculative economic fevers, inadequate lending mechanisms, rampant bank failures, and intense competition for national economic advantage. Illustrative of the competition were high tariffs, trade quotas, cartel arrangements, and export subsidies. Most European nations, to be sure, had never really recovered from the war. Yet, much of the weaknesses of their economies was due to America's unwillingness to import European products and thus to provide European countries with dollars so that they could pay off American loans.

While technological changes in industrial America gave the nation a sense of prosperity during the 1920s, they also had an injurious effect. For example, the rapidly developing automobile, electrical, fuel-oil, and synthetic-fiber industries hurt badly the older railroad, coal, and textile industries. Employment in the railroad and coal industries had decreased, respectively, by 11 and 24 percent by the time of the crash; and while employment in the textile industry remained fairly constant, approximately one-fifth of its workers were earning 30 percent less at the end of the decade. Paradoxically, growth industries, such as automobile, construction, and electricity, had a negative as well as a positive impact on the economy. Of course, such industries at times spurred the economy. Millions of Americans were employed in the automobile, electrical-utilities, construction, and allied industries, such as rubber (for automobile tires), appliances (to use electricity), and glass (for buildings and residences). Yet, for whatever reason, durable products such as automobiles, electrical appliances, and residences seemed to have reached a saturation point in the late 1920s; and when they did so, they affected not only the production of the commodities themselves but the allied industries as well. Furthermore, automobiles, houses, and some electrical appliances usually required a long-term indebtedness, which posed severe financial burdens for buyers during recession and depression times.

The economy of the 1920s was further blemished by a one-third decrease in organized labor. Labor unions made no inroads into many manufacturing concerns, such as steel, and none in such sick industries as mines and railroads. Membership during the decade decreased from 5,047,800 to 3,442,600. Without union organization, labor could not demand its share of the profits of the 1920s. While the hourly earnings of workers in manufacturing increased by 8 percent in the 1923–29 period, the total profits of corporations during the same period increased by 62 percent.[13] With a disproportionate share of profits going to capital, there was in effect a hidden inflation. Employers, little realizing that higher wages were necessary to assure the continued purchasing of the increased commodities that they were manufacturing, unwittingly helped to accelerate the saturation of their own market by not increasing wages. In addition, the market for goods was being affected by technological unemployment, which reached a total of 1.5 million employees by 1928.

To worsen the problem of saturation, the profits of business were being plowed back into industry, spurring all the more overproduction and underconsumption. Such action was frequently precluded by mergers, which limited competition and concentrated control of prices in the leadership of fewer and fewer firms. Manufacturing and mining mergers increased from 67 in 1922 to 221 in 1928, and the number of concerns that disappeared increased from 309 in 1922 to 1,245 in 1929.[14] The concentration of industrial power was in large part due to weak enforcement by the federal government of the Federal Trade Act and antitrust laws. While Herbert Hoover, as secretary of commerce, had favored having industries share their market and price information, he opposed abuse of that sharing of information, and he strongly supported regulation by the Federal Trade Commission (FTC) and enforcement of antitrust laws as much as he opposed the manipulation of prices.

So, the economic flaws of the nation in 1929 went largely unrecognized. In the stock market, which is often viewed as a barometer of prosperity, the nation witnessed the increase in the number of shares of stock being traded on the security market, from 236 million in 1923 to 1,125 million in 1929. This unprecedented increase provided a sense of security, which was made false by the lack of required prospectuses behind the issuance of stock, by the low margin requirement on loans to purchase stock, by little control over investment money by private and public agencies, and by the general speculative fever.

The fulcrum of Hoover's presidency would be the great stock-market crash of October 1929, which preceded the Great Depression. Franklin Roosevelt, as he sought the presidency in 1932, would blame Hoover for the crash. One of Roosevelt's eager correspondents confirmed this contention with a story about Hoover's involvement in the speculative fever that had caused the crash. This story went back to 1925 and 1927, when, by most popular accounts, the Wall Street fever began with Federal Reserve action to allow an increase in the money supply by lowering the discount rate (from 4 to 3.5 percent) and by purchasing government securities. The purpose was not to spur buying on the American stock markets but to aid England's economy as it returned to the pre–World War I gold standard. As the correspondent's account went, in 1927 the important New York bankers George F. Baker and Paul M. Warburg had warned Coolidge and Hoover that, while lowering the interest rates in the United States as compared to those in England might make the latter a better place to invest money, it would fan a speculative fever in America, which had been started by a similar 1925 easy-money policy. When they took their leave of the president, Hoover had closeted himself with the gentlemen, expressing disagreement with them and insisting that the rise in stock purchases and prices was a reflection of confidence in the American banking system. Banker Baker vehemently disagreed, declaring to the secretary of commerce that if loans for speculative purposes were to continue, within six months "we will witness one of the greatest financial catastrophies that this country has ever seen."[15]

In his *Memoirs*, Hoover insists that he voiced protests against the Federal Reserve Board's easy speculative-money policies of the 1925–27 period to the governor of the Federal Reserve Board, Daniel R. Crissinger, and to United States Senator Irvine Lenroot. In fact, Hoover noted, he had drafted a letter that Senator Lenroot sent to the Senate Banking and Currency Committee, protesting the Federal Reserve policy and stating specifically that "there is [a] connection between the credit released by the Federal Reserve System and this great increase . . . in street loans . . . because advances from the Federal Reserve are capable of great pyramiding."[16]

The accounts of Roosevelt's correspondent and Hoover's *Memoirs* are not contradictory, despite the views that John Kenneth Galbraith expresses in his book *The Great Crash*. Galbraith comments that if Hoover had protested the Federal Reserve's actions, he had made his objection a "well-kept secret."[17] In fact, he did keep it a secret. It was like Hoover, although he was wary of bankers like Baker and Warburg, to avoid criticizing their institution and to proclaim confidence in the American system. When he acted to constrain bankers, Hoover usually did so behind the scenes—for example, before a Republican senator like Lenroot, in whom he had some faith. Hoover's wariness of bankers, paired with his endeavors to show confidence, had particularly manifested themselves many times during his presidency.

By inauguration time, more Americans than ever were conscious of the stock exchanges and their appeal for investments. Approximately two million Americans had invested in the market. Although this number seems to be a small proportion of the population, it undoubtedly included a substantial share of the professional, manufacturing, and business leadership in cities and villages across America. And even when leaders were not investing in the New York market, its rise encouraged them to participate vigorously in the economic activities of their communities.

In March 1928 the *New York Times'* average price of industrial stocks rose 25 points, and in the whole year of 1928, it gained 129 points, rising from 331 to 460. In January of the new year it had gained 30 points. The president-elect and some members of the banking community were becoming particularly alarmed at the bullish nature of the market.

The Federal Reserve System in 1929, with Hoover's blessing, before and after his inauguration, pursued a "direct action" policy of trying to persuade the New York Federal Reserve Bank to refuse to grant discounts to banks that were suspected of lending largely for purposes of stock speculation. George L. Harrison, governor of the New York Reserve Bank, still feared an orgy of speculation, and through Christian A. Herter, Hoover's faithful aide of World War I relief days, on 5 April 1929 Harrison asked if he might give the president his views on the Federal Reserve and the Stock Market situation in general.[18] Presidential Secretary George Akerson replied: "The situation in the . . . market is making it impossible . . . [for Harrison to see the President]. the

President has not even seen members of the Federal Reserve Board down here for fear of the effect on the general situation in New York."[19]

In due course, Hoover did accept a memorandum from George Harrison under the condition that the submission "be held in strictest confidence, however."[20] Harrison undoubtedly pleaded that the president urge the Federal Reserve Board to permit the New York Federal Reserve Bank to discourage speculative loans by raising the interest rate from 5 to 6 percent. Hoover and the Federal Reserve Board in Washington refused, feeling that such tightening of money might precipitate a run on the market. Hoover ironically believed that authority to regulate the New York Stock Exchange "rested only in the Governor of New York, Franklin D. Roosevelt," who, according to Galbraith, was "following a laissez-faire policy . . . on the matter of the stock market."[21]

Franklin Roosevelt was not the only prominent Democrat who was taking a laissez-faire position on the market. Bernard Baruch, Hoover's erstwhile Wilsonian coadministrator during World War I, complained to such important columnists as Herbert B. Swope and Frank R. Kent and the father of the Federal Reserve System, Senator Carter Glass, that the "direct [persuasive] action" of the Federal Reserve Board represented a perversion of its power.[22] Wilson's own former secretary of the Treasury, William G. McAdoo, took the same position. Hoover and Glass, however, were as one in support of continuing at least the policy of persuasion.[23] The "direct action" persuasion seemed to be halting the feverish rise in stock prices until the president of New York City Bank (who was a board member of the New York Federal Reserve Bank), Charles E. Mitchell, defied the Federal Reserve System and announced the availability of money for purposes of purchasing stock. The market rose sharply again. While Glass thought that Mitchell should have been fired from the New York board for his deed,[24] Baruch congratulated the bullish bank president, saying, "The Federal Reserve System is itself a wonderful thing and so are all of the inventions which have come from the trials and tribulations and the genius of our people, but they become nuisances when they are handled by blundering fingers." Baruch then, as in almost all of his correspondence on the subject, proceeded to chastise President Hoover for having helped raise this "Frankenstein" of easy money in the first place.[25]

Baruch's charge was a dubious assertion. The fact was that nobody seemed to know where the responsibility of the Federal Reserve System rested in relation to the borrowing of money for speculative purposes in the 1925–29 period. For one thing, the Federal Reserve System had no statutory authority over the currency reserves of banks or over the margin requirements on loans to the stock markets. And there were varying views on the extent to which the ''Fed'' should use the control of the discount rate and open-market purchases to influence the supply of money. In 1931 the board's principal staff aide, Charles S. Hamlin, surveyed divergent views on the subject for Senator Glass, ''merely to point out that the whole problem is in a state of transition, and that even economists are not clear in their own minds just what sort of influence they would like to have exercised.'' Hamlin concluded, ''I cite it also to show how difficult it is at any time to obtain satisfactory expert advice as to what should be done in the way of control of speculative activities.'' In such a context, Hoover and Glass seemed to be at least as much on the side of the angels as did the financial adviser Bernard Baruch and the governor of New York, Franklin Roosevelt. The whole speculative process was searing both the president and the father of the Federal Reserve System. Hoover, by 1929, thought that bankers were generally ''iniquitous''; Glass specifically thought that Charles Mitchell was a lawbreaker.[26] Financial advisers, such as Baruch, and Democratic leaders, such as Franklin Roosevelt, seemed, in fact, to feel much less compunction about speculation in the stock market.

Compunction among Hoover and his advisers spread, as a result of the rise in sales of common stock, decreases in the bond and government-securities market, and the condition of the economy in general. Eugene Meyer, an administration insider, reporting to Hoover on the New York financial situation, said that ''three out of four financial people express the opinion that there is no bond market.'' Ogden Mills's office in the Treasury, where Hoover's confidence in the department continued to repose, knew that economic conditions for ''our current offering of certificates . . . could hardly have been less favorable.''[27] Meyer and Mills, like Hoover, were concerned that bonds and government securities were being eschewed for more-lucrative Wall Street securities. The files of the Bureau of the Budget for June 1929 reported an increase in unemployment and bank failures in various parts of the country, particularly in the South and the West. Although Secretary of Commerce Lamont played down such reports, Secretary of Labor James J. Davis urged that the president call a conference of organization executives to consider ''the stabilization of employment . . . [as] the first step to be taken to get rid of the fear of unemployment.''[28]

But as fears of a run on the stock markets and consequent unemployment appeared on the horizon, President Hoover thought he would be able to draw on his vast experiences in and knowledge of industry and government to avoid any serious economic dislocations.

Indeed, he had reason to be pleased with his presidency thus far; the result was a catalogue of actions that had seldom been achieved by an incoming president, ranging from the mammoth appropriations to aid agriculture to a gamut of actions affecting such important matters as conservation of natural resources, public construction, child welfare, prohibition, and conditions of Indians, as well as a wide range of foreign affairs. Hoover expected the actions to have a salutary and stabilizing effect on the nation.

Hoover's supreme self-confidence on economic matters stemmed even more from the prior decade than from the first months of his presidency. No American public leader had so addressed possible solutions of anticyclical problems that had occurred in the decade since World War I. As the frequent presiding officer of Woodrow Wilson's second Industrial Conference in 1919, he had become aware of labor's justified fears for the postwar period. As the member of Harding's cabinet who was most charged with antidepression measures during the 1921–22 recession, he had backed the letting of public-works contracts to boost employment. He had conceived of and directed the Unemployment Conference of 1921, from which had come numerous anticyclical studies, including the later study *Report on Recent Economic Changes.* He had supported the Kenyon bill of 1921, which had called for public works during future depressions. In 1928 he had urged Senator Ralph Brewster of Maine to ask state governors to support a plan to establish a $3-billion reserve fund for public-works purposes. And in the same year he had looked with favor upon Senator Wesley L. Jones's bill, which was a stronger version of the earlier Kenyon bill.

As important as Hoover's administrative preparation for economic crisis was the ideological foundation, which was rooted in the unusual interaction of family, religion, education, and vocationalism in his life. The reader need only be reminded of Hoover's early exposure to the tenets of noncoercion, self-help, and mutual cooperation, of liberty and order; of his education during adolescence, in school and life, which stressed a combination of knowledge and equality of opportunity; and of the attitudes that he had acquired as a professional in regard to hard work, intellectualism, profit, rationalization of industry, and an empathy for fellow men, whether they were the victims of war, the producers of war material, or skilled and unskilled employees. Indeed, Hoover surely thought that his firm ideology—as expressed in *American Individualism*—could lay to rest any evil that his presidency might face.

The story of the great stock-market crash has been told so many times and in so many places that a description of these horrendous days is perhaps unnecessary. The September 13 drop in public utilities from 259.3 to 250.4 was known as the Babson Break (for Roger W. Babson, who had warned about the coming crash). The average of industrial stocks dropped twelve points on October 19, a day that was described as one of "technical correction" (so portrayed by the press, which suggested that the worst was now over). October 23, which brought the exchange of 12,894,650 issues, for an average drop in the price of industrials of $30.97 per share, was known as Black Thursday. The selling of 23.5 million shares on Tuesday October 28 at a price drop of $49.12 in industrials has come to be known as "the day the bubble burst."[29]

The enormity of the drop in the stock market can be more clearly appreciated when it is placed into the context of decreases in the price of securities over a period of months and years. The high September 1929 price of industrial common stocks of 469.5 dropped to 247.6 in October, to 220.1 in November, and rose slightly in December. Although the market rose to a new high of 257.3 in April 1930, it descended to 196.1 by the end of that year and, respectively, to 116.6 and 84.81 by the end of 1931 and 1932.[30] The figures about the slide that began in October 1929 do not tell of the strenuous efforts that had been made earlier by the leaders of the New York Stock Exchange and by bankers to save the market by bidding up shares, mainly in United States Steel, in order to bolster confidence. Soon, however, the same leaders retreated to making minimal purchases in order to effect an orderly liquidation before abandoning any organized effort to stem the vast slide.

It is a sad quirk of history that during the days of the slide, which was so ominous for Hoover's future, the president was enjoying the height of his power. Having accomplished much during the previous months and, during the week preceding the crash, having engaged Britain's prime minister, Ramsay MacDonald, in a satisfying dialogue on the subject of disarmament, Hoover now enjoyed his first lengthy respite from the White House. On October 21 in Detroit, he participated in Henry Ford's celebration of the fiftieth anniversary of Thomas Edison's invention of the electric light bulb. Then he returned east through Cincinnati, Ohio, and Louisville, Kentucky, where to some one hundred and fifty thousand people in the former place and considerably fewer in the latter, he spoke of his engineer's dream to "gird America with dredged and modernized waterways, such as the Ohio, the Mississippi, the Tennessee Rivers, and thousands of miles of other rivers and canals."

In the periods between speeches, Hoover was railroad-bound for Washington, relaxing, but doing less well because of the news of Black

Thursday and even less well after he had read a long memorandum from Thomas W. Lamont, a senior partner in the House of Morgan, in response to a report from Henry Robinson, Hoover's recent emissary to Wall Street. To Hoover's chagrin, the memorandum argued, neo-classically, that "nature will effect necessary cures" caused by Wall Street disturbances. That Lamont's letter was a tortured view is evident in early drafts, in which he described his brethren in the market as gamblers who "have passed all bounds." But Lamont's Darwinistic version of the market that Hoover read must have made the president wonder what his friend Henry Robinson would think of this outcome of his mission.[31]

While Lamont was wont to allow nature to cure the Wall Street problem, another respondent to a Hoover query believed that the crash in the first instance was caused by the Federal Reserve System's interference by raising in August the New York discount rates, thus causing "a typical money panic of the kind that the Federal Bank was created to avoid."[32] From another quarter the Senate's Democratic leader, Joseph T. Robinson, offered a more rhetorical criticism, one that Democrats such as Franklin Roosevelt would emphasize in the 1932 presidential campaign—that the triumvirate of Coolidge, Mellon, and Hoover all along had given "little if any warning . . . to the helpless to seek shelter from the wrath of the Great Crash." They did it, implied Robinson, to create the illusion of prosperity in order to elect Hoover as president of the United States.[33] Hoover's recent respite on the water-ways and railways of the Midwest would be his last for some time.

The president's first public reaction to the crash was to put the best possible face on it, saying what Democrats for years would not forgive him for—namely, that "the fundamental business of the country, that is, production and distribution, is on a sound and prosperous basis."[34] After Hoover's brief statement, Julius Klein, assistant secretary of commerce and probably Hoover's closest associate of long standing in the department, spent hours on a radio address to put flesh on the president's short statement. Klein's statement was as revealing of White House fears as it was of the president's pronounced confidence. Many of Klein's points were so positive as to be suspect: There had been no appreciable increases in the stock of manufactured goods; there had been a tendency for wages and output per worker to increase; the decline in security prices did not greatly affect the buying power of the community, on which buying power rested the activity of production, the earnings of corporations, and the employment of labor; the export trade was not being affected by the speculation; the crash would have little effect on the overwhelming majority of families; the nation had abundant savings for better equipment and productivity; production had increased by 25 to 35 percent since 1919; the buying power of citizens who had been affected by the decline in securities was not very large; 95 percent of the population did not need to cut purchases of commodities; employment and freight-car requirements were up over the fall of 1928; and the farmer was in a relatively strong position. Candor surfaced only once throughout the address. Having presented a catalog of America's reasons for confidence in its economic future, Klein quietly offered a caveat: "Just what relation should exist between that confidence and his present attitude toward the stock market is something for each individual to decide for himself."[35]

Behind the rhetoric of Hoover's and Klein's confidence, the president worked, indeed, as if a crisis were at hand. Both of their confident statements on business conditions belied their understanding of the crash's potential to cause a depression. Secretaries Davis and Lamont confirmed the fears of Hoover and Klein: Davis foresaw "an epidemic of fear and extreme caution, causing a retrenchment and curtailment of buying, which . . . will make itself felt in increased unemployment"; Lamont thought that "the purchasing power of many of our people has been reduced." A Federal Reserve report, shared with the president, was even more alarming: "The situation is far from liquidated . . . it is honeycombed with weak spots."[36]

By mid November, Hoover had moved with dispatch to try to avert a possible depression. By then he had formulated various devices on the part of the federal government to stimulate the economy—for example, increases in public-works expenditures; the release of credit by the Federal Reserve System through purchases of securities and decreases in the discount rates; and reductions in federal income and corporation taxes. Although not described publicly as such, all were anticyclical proposals that were consistent with Hoover's considerations over the decade; and in due course, all were implemented. In post–New Deal economic terms, they lent a fiscal and monetary aspect to Hoover's ideas, although time came to tell, by the end of his term, that the president had backed away from vigorous fiscal policy, as had the Federal Reserve System from the active monetary policy.

In a more public fashion the president called leaders of the nation's railroads, major industries, labor organizations, and the construction industry to the Cabinet Room of the White House for a series of economic-stabilization conferences. Then he called upon the nation's governors and mayors to cooperate in expanding their public works to ease the unemployment problem.

Of the stream of callers that Hoover received in the Oval Office and of the succession of conferences that he conducted in the Cabinet Room, his meeting with industrial and business leaders on November 21 was, for the president, most crucial. Appropriate cabinet members and the elite of industry, including Henry Ford, Owen D. Young (General Electric), Myron C. Taylor (U.S. Steel), Pierre Samuel Du Pont, and Julius Barnes (Chamber of Commerce), shared confidences with the president regarding their concerns about the economy. While varying in regard to their suggestions for warding off an economic crisis, some adhered to Andrew Mellon's philosophy of liquidation, while most thought that the president should lead in suggesting cooperative efforts between government and industry to meet any economic crisis.

Herbert Hoover, of course, was an expert at orchestrating such stabilization meetings; he knew exactly what he wanted said, how it would be said, and what conclusions would be adopted. After the recital of expected views, the president efficiently and confidentially outlined his opinions: that the depths of the depression were not known; that the depression would last for some time; "that there were two or three millions unemployed by the sudden suspension of many activities"; that there must be liquidation of inflated values and prices; and that the depression was world-wide, an aftermath of World War I. The president then, just as efficiently, detailed the duties of all conferees: the problem of unemployment must be handled humanely; social order and industrial peace must be maintained; inflated values must be liquidated in an orderly fashion; the nation must readjust to new concepts of living.[37]

To influence the industrialists who were present, Hoover noted especially that there must be no liquidation of labor, that labor was not a commodity. Unmitigated unemployment, he warned, would harm families, would deepen the depression by reducing purchasing power, and would cause industrial strife. Industrialists heard the president say that the first shock of depression must be absorbed by them. Still stolidly reciting his outline, Hoover ticked off specific aims that would aid the employment of workers: the maintenance of wages; the initiation of new construction; the shortening of the work day; and again, the care for employees. In return for their cooperation the president assured the industrialists that labor would withhold and, in some cases, withdraw wage demands. The industrialists agreed to the president's program and agreed to carry it out (which they, in great part, did do throughout the following year). The president then adjourned the conference and proceeded to receive labor leaders in the same place on the same afternoon.[38]

Conferences continued. On the next day the president met with the leaders of the building and construction industries. And on the subsequent day he sent telegrams to the nation's governors, requesting them to cooperate with him in increasing public works. On the day after that, he directed the secretary of commerce to set up an organization specifically to coordinate federal, state, and local public works for purposes of implementing his anticylical program. As the president expected, the governors replied positively, including the governor of New York, who expected "to recommend to [the] legislature . . . much needed construction work program . . . limited only by estimated receipts from revenues without increasing taxes."[39]

The more the president addressed the possibility that a depression would result from the crash, the more determinedly he pursued his anticyclical efforts—in ways that were unprecedented in American history. He requested his secretary of labor to provide him with more-precise figures on employment. He urged the cabinet to speed up construction in their respective departments. He suggested to Secretary of Commerce Lamont that the latter announce an expected increase in forthcoming Christmas purchases. ("Of course, it cannot be done unless you feel that is the situation.")[40] He urged the president of the Chamber of Commerce, Julius Barnes, to encourage business to spend funds on necessary repairs over the winter months.

However, bad omens began to appear. Commerce Secretary Lamont became increasingly pessimistic about conditions. Labor Secretary Davis could not get a handle on the numbers of unemployed. The *New York Times* said that the president was losing in popularity. Secretary Davis came in with news that, during a ten-day period before Christmas, one million Americans had become unemployed.[41]

To say that Herbert Hoover as president caused the crash and the depression that would follow, as Roosevelt and the Democrats suggested in 1932, is ludicrous. The crash was probably inevitable—a matter of time. But why October of 1929? There are many possible explanations: the late-summer downturn in economic indexes may have awakened enough smart traders in the stock market to sell; the September collapse of Clarence Hatry Enterprises in England may have called home some foreign investments; Roger Babson's September warning that the New York crash was coming may have had an effect on some people; the refusal of the Massachusetts Public Utilities Department to let Boston Edison split its stock—an unheard of prohibition— may have alerted Americans to get out of the vast utilities market. It is more likely that there was no one particular cause; rather, the selling prices for securities were manifesting an unstable investment process, which had ballooned to a breaking point.

The unprecedented depression that was about to descend upon the United States might well have been as inevitable as the crash; almost surely, it was beyond resolution during Hoover's presidency, especially given the state of economic literacy and the conservative institutions and ideology of the times. The president, in his *Memoirs*, which were published more than two decades after the event, came to blame the depression on "The Great Storm Center . . . in Europe." "At that moment, the enormous war destruction, the economic consequences of the Treaty of Versailles, revolutions, unbalanced budgets, hugely increased armaments, inflation, the gigantic overproduction of rubber, coffee, and other commodities, through overstimulation from artificial controls, and a score of other aftermaths of the war . . . finally broke through all efforts to fend off their explosive forces."[42] Charles P. Kindleberger, in his important book *The World in Depression, 1929–1933*, rather agrees with Hoover that unstable international economic conditions largely explain the world-wide depression, which affected so adversely the United States economy. He mainly holds that the asymmetry of world economics was responsible for the depression. (By "asymmetry" he means perverse private practices in the market, such as cartels, and erratic loans and destabilizing government actions, such as tariffs and export subsidies.) But Kindleberger differs with Hoover in delineating those nations that were most responsible for the unstable international economic conditions. Unlike Hoover, he blames the United States particularly for not replacing Great Britain as the world's economic leader. He tellingly notes the three kinds of essential leadership that the United States shunned: (1) to purchase distressed commodities from abroad; (2) to provide needed liquidity to distressed areas in the world; and (3) to sustain the flow of long-term capital. Contrarywise, the United States respectively created immense tariffs, spent its liquid assets on its own productivity, and ultimately cut its loans to foreign governments and institutions. Kindleberger is especially unhappy because the United States did not devalue its currencies when England went off the gold standard in 1931. Had it done so, he argues, we might have provided liquidity to purchase distressed commodities, to continue to grant loans abroad, and in various ways to sustain the flow of long-term capital.[43] Lester V. Chandler, an important historian of the depression, puts it more succinctly: "The United States, the world's greatest power, certainly contributed strongly to the decline abroad, . . .

[for it] took no effective action to stem the decline of economic activity at home or to lessen its impact on other countries."[44]

Another important approach to understanding the Great Depression is to place it in the cyclical sweep of United States history. Such a historical view demonstrates that the nation's modern economic system began during the post–Civil War period, when the founders of American capitalism were concerned with creating "the condition necessary for economic development [under which] . . . free competition . . . would be given ample opportunity for unhampered performance."[45] Ideally, such a system would ensure productivity, economic growth, full employment, and price stability. Each generation of laissez-faire economists thereafter believed in perpetuating the system by minimizing public interference with it. But as the "liberal idealization" became entrenched by the end of the nineteenth century, the concurrent development of the industrial revolution, with its technological and organizational changes, brought the system increasingly under the control of individuals or groups of individuals. As Gunnar Myrdal has noted, "Instead of obediently adjusting themselves to a given framework of society and accepting the burdens and rewards as they come out from the working of the forces within this framework, the individuals begin to cooperate in order to influence this process and, going even further, to adjust the framework itself according to their own interest."[46]

So, according to Myrdal, capitalism became imperfectly competitive—at first through various forms of private economic concentrations in the post–Civil War period, then with countervailing governmental power at the turn of the century. By the 1920s some business and governmental leaders were attempting to work together in a way that would eliminate both destructive competition and inordinate governmental control. Many of Hoover's beliefs reflected such a rationalization. But while the capitalist structure was changing, the image of that structure for most Americans did not change. Competition, as Arnold Toynbee has explained, "came to be believed in as a gospel . . . from which it was regarded as little short of immoral to depart."[47] Thus, systems of laissez-faire and quasi-concentrated capitalism were on a collision course.

As expected, an integral part of the American capitalist system had been its periodic crises: the period of overproduction, followed by a liquidation of surplus, followed by a renewal of demand and of production. One important school of history notes that the cyclical crises inherent in such a system were reasonably brief in the century prior to the 1920s, as a result of the dynamics of population growth, geographic expansion, wars, and industrialization. It further notes that by the decade of the twenties the old dynamics was not as applicable. To a large degree the accumulation of business capital during the 1920s outran the development of opportunities for profitable employment in the private sector. There was far too little of the population growth and geographical expansion that had so dramatically affected the United States for half a century. There was no war, such as World War I, to absorb vast industrial production. And the new industries that had started up during the 1920s were not comparable to those of the post-Civil War period, which came to be recognized as America's Industrial Revolution.[48]

The above explanation of the Great Depression is something of a modification of the "trade cycle" interpretations. It argues that there are four cycles, of which the scenario described above is the longest—that of fifty years—and is known as the Kondratieff cycle. Such a cycle encompasses three shorter cycles: the minor ("Kitchin") cycle, which has an average duration of forty months; the major ("Juglar") cycle, with an average length of nine to ten years; and the building ("Kuznets") cycle, which averages twenty years. The cyclical interpretation becomes particularly impressive for our purposes when it explains that the four cycles coincided on their down-side point during the 1929-33 period, which, if this is really true, goes a long way towards explaining the Great Depression.[49]

For some economists, especially Milton Friedman, "the monetary hypothesis" is most important in explaining the Great Depression. It contends that a decline in the stock of money almost always foreshadows a depression and that failure to increase the stock of money during any depression will very likely prolong it. In short, rising prices caused by a reduced supply of money preclude the necessary stimulation of economic growth. There apparently was confidence in the nation's banks in 1930, but in the year following the crash, bills bought by the Federal Reserve System fell by $110 million, and discounted bills fell by $390 million. Such action, according to Friedman, did not provide the 3 to 5 percent annual increase in the money supply that would have been necessary in order to attain a comparable rate of economic growth. Proof of the impact of monetary policy on the economy was evidenced by the October 1931 rise in the discount rate from 1.5 to 3.5 percent; this caused a 24 percent fall in industrial production over the ensuing twelve months. Thus, Milton Friedman and Anna J. Schwartz entitle their story of the Great Depression *The Great Contraction*. Many historians of the period believe that had Benjamin Strong, head of the New York Federal Reserve Bank, not died in 1928, the Federal Reserve System would have manipulated the currency in the way that Friedman has suggested and thus would have made the stock of money sufficiently high throughout the years of the Hoover presidency so as to avoid the tight-money policy, which precluded investment, productivity, and consumption.[50]

Probably the most popular interpretation of the Great Depression, which dominated much of the New Deal and post–New Deal thought, is the "stagnation" or "spending" hypothesis. It maintains that Franklin Roosevelt in 1932 came close to agreeing that the nation had overbuilt its productivity, thus exhausting investment opportunities. Stagnation was the result of many causes, such as a decline in population growth, the "closing" of the frontier, a lack of revolutionary innovation to replace the rise of the automobile and electrical industries, technological over-production, the loss of need for a capital market (a result of the self-sufficiency of corporate capital), and the need of investment only for repairs and replacement. As a consequence of the "stagnation" condition, New Deal fiscal policy (government spending and taxation) was seen as a necessary antidote. The American economist Alvin H. Hansen and John Maynard Keynes, his British contemporary, were the apostles of such fiscal planning to resolve the depression.[51]

Other observers of the Great Depression have viewed its principal cause as being what Jim Potter has referred to as a "sectoral imbalance." This school contends that the terms for the export trade of primary production were unfavorable, particularly among agriculture producers. During the 1920s farm prices fell between 30 and 60 percent, and farm incomes fell accordingly. The decline in farm income not only greatly reduced the purchasing power of the rural community but also very importantly reduced the demand for the products of the industrial community. Potter submits that in terms of the growth rate that is necessary in a healthy economy, the "non-agricultural sector of the American economy needs to expand at three times the rate of the agricultural sector." We shall see that agriculture, the sickest of America's industries during the 1920s, continued to suffer its unenviable fate during the years of Hoover's presidency.[52]

In the ensuing chapters we shall note that Hoover's emphasis on international efforts to resolve the world economic crisis intensified as the depression deepened, right down to the moment when he took leave of his office. The cyclical nature of depressions had always been and would continue to be a matter of grave concern to the president. Indeed, the *Recent Economic Changes* report had been largely motivated by Hoover's anticyclical considerations very early in the decade.

Other explanations for the depression—monetary, fiscal (stagnation), and sectoral—were similarly addressed by the president. We shall observe Hoover's continual efforts to so approach them: first, to urge the Federal Reserve System to loosen credit, as Friedman was to suggest some three decades later; second, to effect governmental expenditures so as to unbalance the federal budget (Hoover did this to such an extent that Herbert Stein, chairman of the Nixon presidency's Council of Economic Advisers, would describe Hoover as more of a fiscalist than his successor, Roosevelt); third, to struggle with the sector of greatest need, agriculture, by launching his presidency with the Agriculture Marketing Act, the largest peacetime relief effort in United States history. One must describe as uncanny Hoover's antidepression efforts in those areas that historians have singled out as being the principal causes for the economic plight that came on the heels of the great stock-market crash of 1929. Why, then, did the president fail to bring an end to the depression? If it was because he lacked time during his first term, why did the nation deny him another four years in which to finish the job? The time remaining in the first term will provide an answer.

5

★ ★ ★ ★ ★

1930

On New Year's Day 1930, Herbert Hoover's first in office as president, he shook hands with six thousand of his fellow Americans. The feat demonstrated the seriousness with which he took the ceremonial role of the presidency, as he did when once a week he opened wide the White House doors to those who wanted to shake the hand of their president. In later years, Hoover gave up the New Year's Day handshaking event, especially when the depression had descended, and the public's coolness had come to dominate the White House atmosphere. But for 1930 and for most of 1931 the president was as effusive as his Quaker reticence would permit. In his own way, Hoover actually enjoyed some of the public roles of his high office, especially those of informal and personal contact. For example, when dawn broke on that first New Year's Day of his presidency and two citizens appeared in line hours in advance of the presidential hand shaking, Hoover gladly invited them to share a White House breakfest of bacon, eggs, and muffins with him and two of his medicine-ball teammates, Ray Lyman Wilbur and Harlan F. Stone. It was not uncommon for the president quietly to perform such warm deeds. When Henry L. Stimson took his friend Allen Klots and Klots's son Binkie to meet their president, the secretary of state was moved by Hoover's treatment of the boy; he thought that the president was at his best, "very nice and kindly."[1] Few presidents strived as hard as did Hoover to do their duty as president, and if his relations with the public, like those with party men and congressmen, faltered, more often than not he had at least tried in his inimitable way.

By early 1930 Hoover had settled into his White House routine and was attacking his job with relish, confident that he was successfully resolving the great issues, such as those centering around the great crash. Everything proceeded according to the prodigious schedule that he had organized upon assuming office. The president moved effortlessly from subject to subject, making himself available to his staff, seldom prodding or showing irritation at errors. He continued to waste little time on trivia. The number of conferences seemed to increase: on one day he conducted twenty-six! Conferees viewed him as being always alert, sometimes cryptic, and usually very compelling. As presidential burdens increased in number, so did dinner guests, almost always for purposes of conducting increasingly urgent presidential business. Stimson marveled at the machinelike routine. In fact, he worried about it, thinking that the president needed far more relaxation than was afforded by the early morning medicine-ball workout and his occasional brief fishing expeditions at Rapidan, his retreat in the Maryland mountains. Stimson seemed to take more seriously his own affluent sports, such as golf, squash, duck hunting, tennis, bowling on the green, and horseback riding. Hoover continued to ponder the possibility that his secretary of state's physical weakness required him to engage in many forms of recreation.

Stimson also enjoyed much more of the social life in Washington than did Hoover. Actually, Stimson gave the president and the first lady high marks for providing "dazzling" entertainment at the White House. Speaker Nicholas Longworth and his wife, Alice Roosevelt Longworth, continued to be impressed with the White House entertainment, rating the presidential dinner table the best she had ever known to have been set by the White House. For a while in early 1930, White House social life was marred by a "society feud" between Vice-President Curtis's sister, Mrs. Dolly Gann, who served as official hostess for the bachelor vice-president, and Alice Longworth. The contention was over seating precedence at White House dinners, the vice-president believing that his sister should be seated closer to the president than were the wives of foreign diplomats. Protocol-conscious Speaker Longworth and his out-spoken wife resented Dolly Gann's seeming intrusion. Feuds between the Longworths and the vice-president and Mrs. Gann erupted time and again. The press made more of them than did the Longworths, if not the vice-president and his sister, who fretted continually about the issue. The president was perplexed and upset by the whole matter. Stimson, whose department was responsible for diplomatic protocol in the capital, came to the rescue, placing Mrs. Gann after the dean of the diplomatic corps and his wife but before other diplomatic wives. The president and Mrs. Hoover were glad to have the matter resolved. Everyone seemed to be satisfied, at least for the time being, especially Alice Longworth, who not only thought that Dolly had been put in her place but also appreciated the president's according herself and her husband special status on the social calendar by dining with them before accepting invitations from cabinet officers, contrary to the customary order during the social year. In short, the Hoovers tended to their ceremonial (and social) business as diligently as the president did to his official affairs.[2]

Assessments of Hoover's first year as president have confirmed his administrative talents, which observers have stressed almost exclusively. Journalist Anne O'Hare McCormick called him a fact-finder, who in his first year had established half as many investigating commissions as Wilson had in two terms. She noted that where Woodrow Wilson or Theodore Roosevelt would have warned or preached, Hoover had planned—not only with conferences and commissions but also with individuals. "Next to work, he wants people to talk to."[3] In fact, because he talked to so many people, she called him our most gregarious president next to Theodore Roosevelt. Will Durant declared, before the University of Virginia Institute of Public Affairs, that the president would emerge "as one of the most capable executives in history," despite the ranting of third-rate politicians.[4] Mark Sullivan agreed, describing Hoover as a "combination of practical ability with ideas of benevolence; sufficiently familiar with economic forces and sufficiently experienced in directing them to be able to deal competently with interrelated mechanisms upon which . . . civilization rests."[5] William Starr Myers, a professor of political science at Princeton, concurred. To him Hoover manifested a blueprint presidency, which demanded facts before it would proceed. Stimson seemed to be the one exception among those who praised Hoover as a planner. He believed that the president planned too much—that running the government from the White House "was not like building a bridge where you had to calculate the stress of every portion. Human affairs don't work that way," he wrote in his diary; "by planning and waiting for results [the president] gave the appearance of timidity."[6]

Partisans were little heard from in their assessment of the president's first year. Senator Simeon D. Fess and Congressman John Q. Tilson expressed innocuous praise, which was recorded in the press. Charles Michelson, the new publicity director for the Democratic party, issued his daily statements, which at first dealt more with the high-tariff evils of Republicans in Congress than with the president per se. Senator Robert M. La Follette, Jr., in his very limited edition of *Progressive Magazine*, represented Republican insurgent opposition to the president's actions that allegedly favored monopolization, patronage appointments, high tariffs, and imperialistic foreign policy—charges that were far more alleged than real.

Walter Lippmann, the dean of the nation's commentators, was more perceptive than most analysts who looked back on Hoover's first year. He saw presidential indecision regarding stock-market speculation, price fixing by the Farm Board, and tariff revision. In these cases, he commented, the president had been afraid to confront, respectively, the Federal Reserve Board, the Farm Board, and Congress. Lippmann believed that Hoover lacked Theodore Roosevelt's or Woodrow Wilson's ability to fight "fire with fire, passion with passion, slogans with slogans." He attributed Hoover's political weaknesses to political inexperience. By 1930 Lippmann perceived a history of such weaknesses. He might have remembered how, a decade earlier, the tough Democratic Senator James A. Reed had been able to rattle Hoover for days. As Louis Brandeis at that time had worried about Hoover's inability to plumb Reed's depths, so now Lippmann seemed to be reaching the same conclusion. Where Brandeis had quickly seen Hoover's weakness, Lippmann came more slowly to discern it. When Professor Felix Frankfurter of Harvard Law School helped his friend Lippmann come to recognize Hoover's weaknesses, Lippmann responded, "I think it may be that I continue to look at his past glories through the glasses of the Hoover legend." Lippmann agreed with Frankfurter's criticism that Hoover had a "promotion" tendency. Such a change in attitude had, Lippmann added, "a somewhat disparaging implication which I shouldn't want to make without qualification. Hoover, in spite of everything, is a very considerable fellow."[7]

Of all of Hoover's presidential wrongs that Frankfurter pointed out to Lippmann, none distressed the Harvard professor more than Hoover's not having named Harlan Fiske Stone as chief justice of the United States Supreme Court. Frankfurter's disappointment is only of symbolic importance to our story. Important is what the selection of the chief justice tells us about Hoover as president. For example, it is significant that President Franklin Roosevelt later, rather than Herbert Hoover now, elevated the latter's close friend Stone to the highest judicial position in the land. Hoover's denial of the appointment to Stone was the last straw to Frankfurter, who wrote to Lippmann:

"Whatever I shall get hereafter from Hoover I shall regard as bounty of the gods. I expect nothing from him through reliance upon courageous conviction." He added that anything from the new chief justice, Charles Evans Hughes, would also be a "gift of the gods."[8] Frankfurter had mightily appreciated how, on the high bench, Stone had frequently allied himself with Justices Louis Brandeis and Oliver Wendell Holmes in relating the law more to the social and economic crises that affected society. He believed that Stone's elevation to the Court's first position would have replaced the more property-oriented ideology of the retiring chief justice, William Howard Taft, with a liberal ideology that would be more attuned to changes in society. Taft himself fearfully expected the president to appoint Stone to his place.

It was little wonder that Frankfurter and Taft expected Hoover to appoint Stone as chief justice. Hoover and Stone had become fast friends as members of Coolidge's cabinet. Stone had been a fearless attorney general. Both had come from rural communities, and both were "self-made" men. Each appreciated the other's intelligence and commitment to public service. Both preferred an evening of intellectual conversation to Washington's nighttime society. Since the mid twenties their families had been increasingly in each other's company. Among other attractions, deep-sea fishing occasionally brought them together. And when Hoover had become president, Stone had been the first and most faithful member of the medicine-ball cabinet. They were big, rugged men, and Stone did not hesitate to "give a [strong toss of the ball] . . . to the president."[9]

Stone had been ecstatic about the idea of Hoover's becoming president, and although Stone's judicial position precluded any speaking on the stump, he unashamedly told his friends of his enthusiasm about Hoover's election. He seemed to be most impressed by Hoover's "co-operative" approach to government, a liberal approach that avoided both drastic reform and stifling regulation. Stone appreciated Hoover's influence on business practices, which he thought had been accomplished by "inducing cooperation through personal leadership." After the election, Hoover and Stone talked for hours about how their mutual beliefs in new and higher political leadership could be launched in the new administration. It could be accomplished, in general, by efficiency and, specifically, by appointing to federal office " 'the best available man' for the job regardless of his politics." "That is the Chief's idea," wrote Stone, "—and a noble one it is."[10]

The president had wanted Stone to be his first cabinet officer— secretary of state—or to claim almost any position of his choosing, but Stone refused. Then Hoover tried to get him to take over what became the Wickersham Commission, and again Stone refused. Stone wanted to be chief justice, although his judicial propriety barred him from whispering any such ambition—especially to the president. There were conflicting stories regarding Hoover's selection of Hughes over Stone for chief justice. One was that Assistant Secretary of State Joseph P. Cotton, a political adviser to Hoover, had suggested that Hughes deserved to be offered the appointment because of the valuable support he had given to Hoover during the presidential campaign and that Hughes should be offered the position with the expectation that he would refuse, because Charles Evans Hughes, Jr., would then have to resign as solicitor general. (The son would not be able to argue the government's cases before his father.) Then, or so Cotton is alleged to have contended, Hoover could appoint his friend Stone. The president supposedly called Hughes, to offer him the appointment; and to Hoover's dismay, the New Yorker accepted. A more plausible story was told by Stone to his confidant and mentor, John Bassett Moore—namely, that Hoover had asked Stone for advice about Taft's successor without indicating that Stone himself was being considered. Stone urged Hoover to appoint Benjamin Cardozo. Hoover then apparently asked about Hughes; to this suggestion, Stone reacted unfavorably, on the grounds of age and "continual professional employment." A little later, Attorney General Mitchell indicated to Stone that the president was interested in appointing Hughes. Moore, in his memorandum about his conversation with Stone immediately after the appointment of Hughes, reported: "It seems . . . clear that the president did not want a man of 'liberal tendencies.' " Moore believed that the appointment of Hughes contributed mightily to the disenchantment of the nation's liberals with the new president.[11]

Liberal criticism of Hughes as chief justice of the Supreme Court—such as that expressed by Felix Frankfurter—was muted. Liberal brethren on the Court, in fact, appeared to be supportive. Brandeis said: "Confirmation ought to be made at once and ought to be unanimous." Benjamin Cardozo, of the New York Court of Appeals, called the appointment "a great choice of a great man for a great office." Frankfurter, however, was not alone in voicing criticism. Such inexorable Senate insurgents as Borah linked Hughes to the Court's recent conservative decisions, even though Hughes had not been on the bench since 1916. George Norris feared that Hughes, on the high bench, would represent both a politico who recently had run for president and the influence of "untold wealth." Some senators hinted darkly at a presidential conspiracy to perpetuate the conservative Taft philosophy. But the liberal Senator Robert F. Wagner, a fellow New Yorker, favored confirmation, which was forthcoming on February 13 by a Senate vote of fifty-two to twenty-six. Although the Senate's sensitivity to the president's appointment of the chief justice was quiet and latent, a more experienced president might have learned from it.[12]

Almost on the heels of the concerns over the nomination of Hughes, the president was called upon to fill a high-court position made vacant by the death of Justice Edward T. Sanford. This appointment, not unlike that of Hughes, was revealing about Hoover: it manifested the president's seeming unawareness of the current demands for judicial appointments of highly qualified persons. For that reason and because it was a cause célèbre of the year, the story of the appointment is told in detail here.

That the president had not learned from the Hughes affair was seemingly evidenced by his nomination of John J. Parker, a judge on the Fourth Circuit Court of Appeals in Richmond, Virginia, whose confirmation was denied by the Senate of the United States, the first such situation since the last century. It was an omen suggestive of the administration's ill fortunes.

John J. Parker, who was forty-four years of age, was a man of intelligence and high integrity. Attorney General Mitchell reportedly studied more than one hundred of his decisions before assuring the president about Parker's judicial soundness. As in the case of Hughes, the announcement of Parker's nomination was initially applauded by the press, the bar, and many public officials. Southerners, Democrats and Republicans alike, took pride in the president's having turned to their section in making such an important appointment. But Senate insurgents, who were forever probing the president's actions, found things regarding Parker that the president, his attorney general, and John Parker himself had not dreamt of.[13]

William Borah, by now Hoover's *bête noire*, was a member of the judiciary subcommittee that was deciding whether Parker should or should not be confirmed. Borah's antennae were not necessarily sharper than those of Attorney General Mitchell, but by the time the subcommittee had gotten down to business on the Parker appointment, the *New Republic*, the American Federation of Labor (A F of L), and the National Association for the Advancement of Colored People (NAACP) had informed key Senate insurgents of their serious reservations about Parker. The *New Republic* was not precise about its doubts. It wondered whether Hoover had picked ''a great judge or a conspicuous southerner.'' It also wondered about Parker's Fourth Circuit Court of Appeals decision, in a 1927 Red Jacket case, to sustain an injunction of the federal district court that enjoined employees of 316 coal companies in southern

West Virginia from breaking their yellow-dog contracts in order to join the United Mine Workers (UMW). William Green, president of the A F of L, thought along the same lines, only much more precisely. By the time he appeared before the Senate subcommittee, he was sure that Parker had had a judicial opportunity to deny the sweeping injunction that Federal District Court Judge George W. McClintic had served against the nonunionized mine workers—an injunction that prohibited using even peaceful persuasion on mine workers to get them to join the UMW. Parker had based his decision largely on the decision in the *Hitchman Coal and Coke* case of 1917. Green thought that Parker should have relied on the *Tri-City* case of 1919, in which Chief Justice Taft, in the majority opinion, had supported peaceful picketing as a way of persuading workers to break yellow-dog contracts. Even Taft thought that such action was legal as long as unions did not use "deception . . . and misrepresentation with non-union employees by seeking to induce such employees to [secretly] become members of the union" contrary to their yellow-dog contracts. Borah learned from Green's testimony and forever after agreed that Parker had relied too heavily on the *Hitchman* precedent.

The Green-Borah argument about judicial precedent was suspect, however. The Supreme Court, on writ of certiorari, refused to hear the UMW's appeal of Parker's Red Jacket opinion and thus sustained Parker's use of the *Hitchman* precedent. And Green himself, in testimony before the subcommittee, said that his concern was not so much that Parker had used the *Hitchman* case as precedent but "that he has shown in the opinion he wrote and through his judicial attitude that he [Parker] was in entire sympathy and accord with the legal and economic policy embodied in the injunction issued by Judge McClintic." Green rather eloquently added: "Believing that these conclusions are correct, Labor is of the opinion that . . . another injunction judge will become a member of the Supreme Court of the United States. As a result, the power of reaction will be strengthened, and the broad-minded, humane, progressive influence so courageously and patriotically exercised by the minority members of the highest judicial tribunal in the land conspicuously weakened."[14]

White House consternation over the opposition to the Parker appointment was understandable. Parker was no "injunction judge"; he had no such record. And President Hoover had a history of fighting injunctions that seemed to quell unions; indeed, he had a well-known history of encouraging labor organizations. Labor unions were an important part of Hoover's balance of government, labor, and industry in America. It was reputed, probably truthfully, that Green had supported Hoover's very election to the presidency less than two years previously. And his friend Harlan Stone, of the Supreme Court's liberal triumvirate of Brandeis, Holmes, and Stone, had spoken well of Parker in a memorandum to the president—not, however, without a caveat or two regarding Parker's "range of legal knowledge" and "political experience and contacts."[15] The fact was, however, that Parker appeared to be supporting labor injunctions at just the time when the nation, for a decade, had gradually questioned the high court's pro-property decisions and when the nation, just two years hence, would pass the Norris–La Guardia Anti-injunction Act, which would make yellow-dog contracts illegal.

The effort to confirm Parker as a justice was compounded by a charge from the NAACP that he was anti-Negro. It documented the fact that in his 1920 campaign for governor of North Carolina, he had said: "The Negro as a class does not desire to enter politics. The Republican party of North Carolina does not desire him to do so."[16] The statement was typical of southern office seekers in 1920, but in 1930 the NAACP wondered how such a person could approach the Fourteenth Amendment questions regarding Negro rights with "dispassionate, unprejudiced and judicial frame of mind which would enable him to make a decision according to the Constitution." Parker was no racist. In fact, subsequent decisions in his Fourth Circuit Court manifested the reverse. But as the A F of L was accelerating the move to collective bargaining, the NAACP was seeking to end the curse of racial prejudice. What was detrimental was Parker's "appearance" of having an antilabor bias and racial prejudice.

As the Republican insurgents in the Senate picked up the cry of labor and Negroes, some regular Republican senators feared for their political lives; so much so that they had their leader, James Watson, urge the president to withdraw the nomination. Some Democrats who were inclined to give Hoover his nominee were persuaded to do otherwise when Senator Kenneth D. McKellar of Tennessee discovered a letter from Assistant Secretary of the Interior Joseph M. Dixon to Walter H. Newton, which had urged the appointment of a southerner like Parker as "a master political stroke at this time." But the president, very typically, became adamant. He would not withdraw the nomination. The growing opposition in the Senate became just as adamant. Hoover, of course, resented senators like Watson who put political consideration before the principle of defending a man of Parker's intelligence and integrity. Few senators came to the administration's defense on the issue.[17]

Parker might have saved the administration from embarrassment and himself for the Court had he appeared before the judiciary committee to explain his actions in the 1920 election and the 1927 Red Jacket decision. Even though he had done so in writing to the committee, his personal appearance and commitment to high judicial standards would probably have gained him at least the support of one more senator. He was, after all, an intelligent and attractive public figure. But the president's advisers felt they could hold out, that when the "chips were down," the party regulars would come through. On Wednesday 7 May 1930, with the galleries packed to witness one of the Hoover presidency's first great tests, ten regular Republicans defected. The last "coffin nail" was a charge made by Democratic Senator Henry F. Ashurst of Arizona that Republican Senator Clarence C. Dill of Washington had been offered a judgeship in exchange for a pro-Parker vote. Dill's denial—that he did not want to be a judge—was plausible, but in the emotion of the moment, the charge reflected adversely on the administration. Following the dramatic countdown, the Parker nomination lost, by a vote of 41 to 39. One more vote for the administration would have produced a tie, which Vice-President Curtis would have broken in the president's favor. Hoover took the defeat in dignified Quaker silence. Perhaps, as Stimson would come to learn, the president did not understand the "psychology of combat." Instead of "toughing" it out, he might have fought more openly, sending Parker to the Hill to say what he and his president believed—that labor has a right to organize and that Negroes are Americans entitled to an "equality of opportunity."[18]

Hoover apparently learned from the experiences of the Hughes and Parker appointments. His next appointments were winners for the administration and the nation. Owen Roberts, of Pennsylvania, who had served as one of President Coolidge's Teapot Dome and Elks Hills prosecutors in the recent oil scandals, was nominated and quickly confirmed—to the approval of Frankfurter and Borah. Although regarded as conservative, at least his judicial soundness was not to be questioned. Frankfurter wrote to Stone: "I do not believe that there are any skeletons in his mental closet. Facts will have ready access to his mind." Hoover, who seemed to be contrite about his conservative appointment, told Henry Allen that he would yet prove to the Kansas progressives that he, the president, was one of them. He reflected to Allen that Hughes more often than not would line up with Stone, Holmes, and Brandeis. And, of course, Roberts had prosecuted the Republican secretary of the interior, Albert Fall. Yet, almost as if to compensate for the conservatism of his first two appointees to the

Court, his next and last appointee, two years hence, would be Benjamin Cardozo. William Allen White appreciated Allen's report of the president's feelings but remonstrated again that the president might better come to terms with westerners like Borah and Norris than with easterners like Simeon Fess—that the former were "far nearer the heart and thought of the whole country."[19]

While the Senate was rejecting the president's appointment of John J. Parker to the Supreme Court, both houses of Congress were attacking the administration's tariff program. It will be recalled that late in 1928 Hoover had been persuaded that once he had been inaugurated as president, he should convene a special session of Congress to afford farmers some relief legislation: the increase of tariffs on foreign agricultural commodities was to be one form of relief. But the attitude of Congress toward tariff measures is always volatile. The fight for this one was particularly debilitating to the president and, even after it had passed, would haunt him throughout his term, and seemingly forever thereafter.

Just as William E. Borah had led the opposition to the nomination of Parker, so he did on the tariff bill. The Idahoan and the president, who had been most mutually supportive during the fall of 1928—Borah backing Hoover for president, and Hoover being for a special congressional session on agriculture—were now drifting far apart. Not surprisingly! Both were strong and independent public men. Each, in quite different ways, manifested political iconoclasm: Borah, by being extremely unpredictable; Hoover, by being just the opposite, unalterably committed to his well-laid plans for American government. One would have expected Borah to accept Hoover's idea of a provision for flexibility in the tariff law so as to enable a newly formed Tariff Commission to scientifically study tariffs for the purpose of recommending decreases or increases to the president. But Borah came to oppose the provision intensely, because it would give too much power to the president.

Hoover, still committed to the idea of congressional independence, gave little executive direction to the construction and passage of the Smoot-Hawley Tariff Act, thus allowing the measure to become fair game for legislative logrolling and for attacks by the Old Guard, the Democrats, and particularly by Borah and other "sons of the wild jackasses." The president, although outwardly calm, was seething about Borah's opposition. He expressed his feelings to White House intimates, especially to Senator Henry Allen, who in turn informed his friend William Allen White. White again became unhappy with the way in which the president and Allen were continually "jumping on Borah and westerners"; White still hoped that the president would lead western progressives, not fight them. The president, wrote White, "has every instinct that is common to the progressive masses." But as it had with President Taft, the tariff issue seemed to drive Hoover into conservative arms.[20]

Hoover and Borah had started out together on the tariff trek in the special session of the Congress that had been convened on 15 April 1929. Both had wanted to fulfill their campaign commitments to aid agriculture by substantially increasing tariffs on agricultural commodities and by instituting only "limited revision" of other schedules. Borah, as was true with most westerners who had lived more closely than had Hoover with a decade of agricultural distress, was more visceral about the tariff solution to the farm problem. Westerners had long sought ways to equalize the tariff, to give farmers the same protective benefit that industrialists got from it. Their McNary-Haugenism and their export-debenture efforts were, basically, attempts to equalize tariff benefits. Hoover had taken "the cooperative approach" to the problems of the farmers' surpluses. The president was as willing as Borah and westerners to increase tariffs on farm commodities in order to protect the farmers' domestic markets. Frequently he could defend the protective tariff better than they could. To the critics of protection who argued that foreign retaliation would affect the overseas markets of American farmers, Hoover responded that foreign trade was no longer a barter between two nations. Rather, the president argued that world trade had become a common pool into which all nations poured goods and credit and from which they extracted goods and credit as needed. Thus, high tariffs on agricultural commodities would not affect the volume of American exports. Hoover pointed to the increase in American trade overseas that had come on the heels of the higher schedules of the Fordney-McCumber Tariff Act of 1922.

It will be remembered that, when the special session had convened a year earlier, it had not been expected that the tariff measure would be particularly troublesome. House Speaker Longworth and Senator Reed Smoot had expected to make quick work of it—to have a bill on the president's desk "in a month or two," with substantial increases on farm commodities and only "limited revision" of nonfarm schedules. But Hoover should have known the history of wrangles over tariffs. As he watched hundreds of witnesses plead for tariff increases on nearly every imaginable manufactured commodity during the House committee hearings, he should have anticipated the avalanche of increases that came when the House as a whole convened on 15 April 1929. He justifiably became fearful that the House would go beyond the suggestion of only "limited revision" of nonagriculture schedules. But typically, he kept his fears largely to himself and made it clear that he would not dictate to the Congress. Besides, he believed that party leaders in Congress would recall what he had said many times about "limited revision" of many schedules. However, in the absence of presidential restraint, the avalanche came.

Although the president was unhappy about the high tariffs, low-tariff Democrats, such as Cordell Hull of Tennessee, were vitriolic in their reaction: "The hog has returned to his wallow, and the dog to his vomit." The average farm schedules in the House of Representatives rose from approximately 25 percent, and the average of manufacturing schedules climbed nearly 10 percent. Because of industry's long history of receiving tariff protection and because of its other advantages over agriculture, such as its monopolistic tendencies, Borah revolted in the Senate. He and his fellow western insurgents attacked the House measure on three fronts, two of which were particularly offensive to the president. One of Borah's resolutions, which called for excluding any revision of industrial schedules, lost by a close vote of 38 to 39. The other two fronts were the bruising ones to the president. By a 54 to 33 vote the Senate inserted an export-debenture provision into the legislation. The provision was a complicated bounty whereby farmers would be subsidized for losses that they might incur by selling agricultural surpluses overseas. (For such losses, farmers would receive certificates, which they either could apply against import tariffs or could sell to general importers, who would use them for that purpose.) Hoover had always opposed the export-debenture measure, which the Grange had long recommended; he thought it was too much of a government-oriented solution to agriculture's problems. But the president would not now publicly indicate his feeling about it, and so the Senate passed the measure. Hoover became particularly concerned in the fall of 1929 when Borah and his western colleagues moved to exclude the "flexibility provision" of the law. Such a provision was essential to the president, for with it he would be able to increase or decrease particular schedules by 50 percent, thus correcting abuses that might be perpetrated by Congress. At last, on September 24, the president spoke: "No tariff bill ever enacted has been or ever will be perfect. . . . Furthermore, if a perfect bill were enacted the rapidity of our changing economic conditions and constant shifting of our relations with economic life around the world would render such items in an act imperfect in some particular within a year. . . . The flexible provision is one of the most progressive steps taken in tariff making in all of our history." With that, time ran out and the special session, which had lasted for more than half a year, adjourned; and the tariff legislation was as much in doubt as ever.[21]

The regular session of the Seventy-first Congress convened on 2 December 1929. Although the new Congress was buried in the minutia of routine legislation and other programs that the president was interested in, such as ratification of the recent London Naval Conference Treaty, which commanded the nation's headlines, the great tariff debate continued. Three groups took shape on the issue: insurgent Republicans, led by Borah and George Norris of Nebraska, whose vociferous opposition to increased industrial schedules grew steadily; Democrats, whose opposition contained more partisan rhetoric than fact (over a thousand recent Democratic votes were either supportive of increases in schedules or against any decreases); and those congressmen who were not definitely committed one way or the other. In the Senate the principals who got the lion's share of press coverage were Borah and Norris, who fought against Reed Smoot of Idaho, David A. Reed of Pennsylvania, and James Watson of Indiana. The debate continued for more than six months, as both houses returned again and again to bounty provisions, such as the insertion of export debentures, and the elimination of the flexibility provision, the former of which the president finally opposed publicly and the latter of which he publicly insisted upon. In the Senate the flexibility provision was, in the end, included in the measure only because of Vice-President Curtis's vote, which broke a 42 to 42 deadlock on the issue.

Out of conference deliberations and final congressional action, on 13 June 1930, 3,293 tariff items had been considered, with 2,171 remaining unchanged and 1,122 being changed (with 887 increases and 235 decreases). Agricultural schedules were increased, according to the average Fordney-McCumber schedules, from 38.10 to 48.92 percent and, according to the average of manufacturer's schedules, from 31.02 to 34.31 percent.

The most important tariff provision, at least the one that was most debated in Congress, was the flexibility provision. The president had insisted that the Tariff Commission be empowered to move more quickly in making recommendations to the president about changes in tariff schedules.[22] Frank W. Taussig, the eminent authority on tariff history, noted, however, that little change from the previous act was really effected in the flexibility provision, although the administration, in a study published at the end of its term, made much of the provision. Taussig also believed that tariff increases were futile, in that industry already had its protection and agricultural surpluses were such that the lessening of foreign competition would be of little aid.[23]

The tariff did the president and his party far more harm than good. Few people were satisfied, except for the president's more-conservative cabinet members, such as Andrew W. Mellon and Robert P. Lamont, and the Old Guard leadership in the Congress, such as Reed Smoot, who viewed the rising tariff barriers all over the world as inevitable nationalism. Little wonder that William Allen White warned Henry Allen to prepare the president for the "progressive demonstration" that the country was "steaming up."[24]

The administration's antidepression efforts made little news during the first half of 1930, attracting far less attention than the ratification of the London Naval Conference Treaty; the appointment of Hughes, Parker, and Roberts to the Supreme Court; and the great tariff debate. The paucity of economic headlines reflected, rather, the nation's confidence that the president had the economic situation in hand. On the third day of 1930 Secretary of Commerce Lamont had told the president that twenty-nine governors had planned, cumulatively, $1.3 billion worth of public-works construction, far more than during the previous year, and that public utilities, railroads, and the American Telephone and Telegraph Company planned, respectively, to spend on public employment $14 billion, $1 billion, and $700 million.[25] The federal government itself expedited and increased its public-works construction on federal highways, veterans' hospitals, federal buildings, waterway improvements, and military facilities by $19 million, although such expenditures were miniscule in comparison to the outlays made by state and local governments and industry. By March the Departments of Commerce and Labor had reported to the president that the nation had indeed responded to his request for increased construction, that unemployment was largely concentrated in only twelve states, that employment generally had reached its low point in December and early January, that wage lines were being held, that credit was being made available at lower interest rates, and that "all the evidence indicates that the worst effects of the crash . . . will have passed during the next sixty days." The president readily made public the good news from the Commerce and Labor departments.[26]

Nevertheless, the president's confidence in the economy did not square with the restlessness that was being felt by keen observers inside and outside of the administration. The president went far out of his way to assuage Congresswoman Ruth Hanna McCormick, by assuring her that all they had done would successfully overcome the "industrial depression." At the same time, Edward Dana Durand, a statistician in the Commerce Department, cautioned Secretary Lamont about being overly optimistic regarding the economy, saying that "it is impossible to make any approximately correct estimate of the total number unemployed at this or any other time."[27] Felix Frankfurter, repeatedly warning Walter Lippmann about Hoover, reported that the president's optimistic reports were incorrect.[28] William Green, who did not believe the president's confident reports, wrote to Hoover to inquire if he could see his "way clear to sponsor a provision for an adequate employment service" in the administration. The president responded to this communication by asking if Green would "approve the setting up of some sort of body to exhaustively examine the [unemployment] situation."[29] The Federal Reserve Board went so far as to question publicly the administration's encouraging statements, causing the president to have Secretary Lamont try to quiet the governor of the board, Roy Young: "It is very discouraging in the face of all we are trying to do."[30] The president's encouragement did not lessen any of his strenuous efforts to stem any possible continued slide in the economy. He tried to bring Governor Young and the Federal Reserve Board into more-constructive exercises, such as loosening credit by discounting far more bills than the Federal Reserve System was inclined to do, so that the housing industry might be buoyed up because of the ready absorption of first and second mortgages on homes. One of Governor Young's researchers studied the credit situation and reported that "in so far as obtaining Federal Reserve Bank credit is concerned, the channels with the reserve banks are adequate for all present and prospective needs of the country." It was suggested that nationally chartered home-mortgage banks might be set up to encourage and direct the distribution of mortgage money. Shortly the president would sponsor legislation to provide such an institution.[31]

Without question the administration was making valiant efforts to increase its public expenditures and to line up congressional support for bills involving increased construction on rivers and harbors. Yet the president pressured his departments to reduce their expenditures in order to keep governmental deficits at a minimum. At that, Hoover anticipated a budget deficit of between $20 and $30 million. He urged the chairmen of the Senate and House appropriations committees, Wesley L. Jones and Will R. Wood, respectively, to stop radical new bills which could well add up to $300 million of additional expenditures.[32]

Most members of Congress and the president were of one mind about limiting federal expenditures in the spring of 1930. Both opposed the bill to permit veterans to borrow up to 50 percent of the face value of their bonus certificates. The *New York Times* praised the president for having "his whip in hand." Yet the president also wanted to have purchasing power in the hands of the people. He again urged the Federal Reserve Board to increase the amount of currency by having the government purchase securities on the open market. Eugene Meyer represented the president in trying to effect such a program. While the New York Federal Reserve Bank was ready to purchase such securities, the Federal Reserve Board in Washington and the Open Market Committee, which consisted of the governors of the twelve Federal Reserve Banks, were not willing to do so.[33] Eventually, Meyer would replace Young as governor of the Federal Reserve Board; but during the summer of 1930, the president was not able to achieve any credit for the people.

By the summer of 1930, Hoover had hidden well the administration's internal anxieties brought on by the, as yet, generally unrecognized depression. Rather, he took increasing satisfaction in the precedent-breaking antidepression efforts that the administration had accomplished: its stabilization conferences; its loosening of credit; its reduction of taxes; its increase in federal public works and stimulation of state public works; and the fact that the Federal Farm Board, which had been in existence before the crash, had aided agriculture with large purchases of surpluses. The massive relief bills that were being called for by some congressmen were viewed by the president and by much of the public as examples of midterm election-eve politics.

In much the same way that the president had ignored the radical solutions that some congressmen proposed in regard to the depression, so did he oppose the radical solutions proposed outside of Congress. He was particularly offended by an idea put forth on 2 October 1930 by Gerard Swope, president of General Electric, that the president call a special session of the Congress to "request it to issue a billion dollars of bonds . . . [the proceeds from which] should then be offered to various communities to allay the tragic circumstances of unemployment." Instead, Hoover appointed a cabinet committee on unemployment and the President's Emergency Committee on Employment, PECE, for short. Col. Arthur Woods, an old friend of the president's from World War I days, chaired the latter and watched over its eight sections, which were to work with executive departments, state and local officials, industry, social-welfare agencies, public-works bodies, statistical organizations, women's groups, and public agencies. Drawing on Hoover's successful bureaucratic experiences during World War I, PECE would offer centralized direction to decentralized bodies to aid, voluntarily and cooperatively, the increasingly distressful unemployment situation. The president and the American people were hopeful of its success.

By the end of the year, factory unemployment had increased by 8.3 percent, according to the *Federal Reserve Bulletin*. PECE's Chairman

Woods knew that more than exhortation would be necessary. Like administration insiders who previously had expressed fear of a very unhealthy economy, he sounded a note of high pessimism when he proposed a national shock treatment—that the president advise Congress that "our fellow citizens are facing a desperate emergency." Woods suggested that the president say: "In short, our industrial system finds itself in a grave, tragic, stupid and anomalous situation." Specifically, he suggested that the president ask Congress for $375 million for public employment. But consistent with his show of confidence in the system and with his recent plea to Congress to constrain spending, the president quietly dismissed Woods's suggestion.[34]

On 21 May 1929 Franklin Delano Roosevelt wrote to Louis M. Howe, saying that he was very "keen" to hear about how his confidant would politically size up Herbert Hoover, with whom Howe had just had a "confab" in the White House.[35] Hoover's stature as being the president who had received the greatest popular and electoral vote ever was large as compared to that of the governor of New York, who in 1928 had just experienced the narrowest of victories, with a plurality of 25,000 votes. Yet, the mercurial nature of American politics was seldom more manifested than when, just seventeen months later, the president's party would suffer a devastating defeat as Roosevelt's plurality would increase to 750,000 votes.

The Democratic landslide of 1930, which accompanied Roosevelt's reelection as governor, was all the more surprising because of the apparent strength of the Republican president during the previous summer. Many newspapers thought that Hoover's stature had gained as Congress adjourned in July. Although he had frequently differed with the Congress—a constitutional expectation—he had achieved his major legislative measures: the farm and tariff acts; the establishment of many important commissions, particularly the Wickersham Commission and the President's Committee on Recent Social Trends; key federal appointments; and most important, Senate ratification of the London Naval Conference Treaty. Also it was argued that forceful direction was being given to various consequences of the great crash. William Green of the A F of L praised Hoover heartily for effecting cooperation between employers and workers and for keeping up the wages of labor.

Herbert Hoover was a strong president on the eve of the midterm elections. If an economic crisis were perceived by the public, it in many respects accrued to the president's advantage—at least in the summer of

1930. As the midterm campaign heated up, however, the rhetoric of the "out" party became more telling. Democratic luminaries—such as former presidential candidate Alfred E. Smith; the minority leader of the House of Representatives, John Nance Garner; and New York's Governor Franklin D. Roosevelt—reached for issues and began, even though cautiously, to blame Hoover for the unemployment in the nation. The potential Democratic presidential candidates, such as Garner and Roosevelt, attacked the Hoover presidency where Charles Michelson, the publicity director for the Democratic National Committee, had left off on September 1.

For thirteen months, from July 1929 to August 1930, Michelson had ground out 406 almost-daily caustic statements, three-fourths of which he drew from Democratic congressmen. Among the fifty-two congressmen whose congressional speeches Michelson used were several of George Moses's "wild jackasses," such as Robert M. La Follette, Jr., George W. Norris, Gerald P. Nye, and Smith Brookhart. However, Michelson got most of his material from such articulate Democrats as Senators Joseph T. Robinson, Alben W. Barkley, Pat Harrison, Thomas T. Connally, and David I. Walsh and Congressmen John Nance Garner, Joseph W. Byrns, John McDuffie, Charles R. Crisp, and James W. Collier. Michelson assiduously fed his statements to all of the Washington correspondents and to many papers in the nation that had no reporters in Washington. Interestingly, the Hoover economic "slump" was not an important issue with Michelson. The Smoot-Hawley Tariff was the important issue, being the subject of 280 of the 406 statements. However, when the midterm campaign began in earnest on September 1, the groundwork for the Democratic candidates for the House of Representatives and the Senate had been well laid.[36]

The appearance of Hoover's political strength during the summer of 1930 belied the facts. Although the president could say that he had achieved his program in the Congress, he revealed to Stimson a lack of combat psychology—an unwillingness to constantly press the opposition. Hoover was reluctant to join the political battle, and he frequently refused to fight Congress. So, Democrats and insurgents had carte blanche to oppose the president inside and outside of Congress. The nation little realized how sensitive the president was to the growing opposition during the autumn. When Stimson offered him "affectionate good wishes" regarding a forthcoming October campaign speech in Cleveland, Hoover was touched. Not good at fighting politically, he was at the same time unable to show the public his attractive humanity. "Underneath his shyness," wrote Stimson in his diary, "he is so sensitive and really human that it is a tragedy that he cannot, apparently, make that side of his nature felt in his public contacts."[37]

The issues that developed during September and October, some of which were conspicuous, some in early maturation, and others latent, were all foreboding. High tariffs were always grist for the Democrats' grinding, even though the Smoot-Hawley Tariff had been just about as much their doing as it had been the Republicans' responsibility. The agricultural depression, which had been around for a decade, and an emergency, a great drought in the West, were conspicuous concerns. Issues that had not fully matured, but nevertheless penetrated political sensibilities, were the economic conditions and the administration's probusiness ties. A latent issue was isolationism, which was appearing because of the administration's unsuccessful defense both of the London Naval Conference Treaty and of United States participation in the World Court. The issue of prohibition was still more dormant than not, for while some Democratic politicians, especially in New York, were very wet, most across the nation, especially in the South, were particularly dry. A weakness that might have rubbed off on Republican candidates was the president's image, more real than not, as being a party leader who had no followers. If voters were not aware that many Republicans in Congress did not defend the president on issues such as the export-debenture farm amendment, the tariff-flexibility provision, and the nomination of John Parker, they were conscious of those insurgent Republicans who not only refused to defend their Republican president but also more often than not fought him. It mattered not that they had no programs of their own, but rather had nostrums, such as the equalization fees, export-debenture amendments, and government subsidies. The fact that William E. Borah, who so loudly campaigned for the president in 1928, was usually just as loud in opposing him in 1930, did not help the Republican party or the president.

Although midterm elections usually help the "out" party, the party that achieves a presidential victory, as the Republicans did in 1928, does not usually lose the Congress two years later. The Republicans lost over fifty-two seats in the House of Representatives, eventually giving the Democrats control by one vote. And the Republicans nearly lost the Senate, holding control of it by only one vote. The president listened to the election returns and was saddened. Stimson, perhaps remembering the last presidency that he had served—Taft's—feared for Republican divisiveness. The secretary of state, who believed that Hoover had more leadership qualities than Taft had, gave the president his loyalty. "This is a time," he told him, "when you will know your friends." Hoover, who frequently warmed to Stimson's solicitude, almost "pathetically" expressed his appreciation.[38]

In retrospect, Republican losses were inevitable in 1930. Latent or not, the issues favored the Democrats, especially given the agricultural depression, the western drought, the general economic conditions, the probusiness stance of the administration, the president's internationalism, prohibition, and the president-without-supporters syndrome (as in the defeat of the John J. Parker nomination). And the Democratic timing seemed to be right. The issues grew louder in late October.

Hoover blamed the defeat of many Republicans on their own failure to support him. Coolidge's former secretary, Edward T. Clark, reported to him that White House political strategy was to leave such defeated Republicans to their fate, that the president would now reform the party according to his own blueprints. Among the plans was one to isolate the insurgent Republicans in the Senate by allowing the Democrats to organize it. Then, presumably, wayward Republicans would either have to go with the Democrats or return to the fold.[39] It was just such pussyfooting by Hoover that William Allen White had feared. He thought, as history would show, that the wave of the nation, and thus of the Republicans, would be more with the ideology of national insurgents than with his party's conservatives.[40]

6
★ ★ ★ ★ ★

THE CORPORATIST BALANCE

As the nation approached the centennial of Herbert Hoover's birth, scholars of diverse schools gathered in Geneseo, New York, in April 1973 to discuss the Hoover presidency. The occasion marked what Arthur M. Schlesinger, Jr., later described as the beginning of "the collective phase . . . of the Hoover rehabilitation."[1] "Herbert Hoover and American Corporatism, 1929–1933," a paper by Ellis W. Hawley, was the most representative and the most poignant of the presentations; it provoked discussion there and elsewhere for the following decade.[2] Professor Hawley's important research had been particularly influenced by a New Left historian, William Appleman Williams, who, in a 1970 review article in the *New York Review of Books*, encapsulated his long and hard thinking that Hoover had uniquely understood America's need for balancing the society's three functional units—capital, labor, and the public—lest perversions accrue if one group should dominate. Williams said: "If the corporations took over—fascism. If job-oriented labor leaders took over—a mutant, mundane, and elitist corruption of socialism. If government *per se* took over—an elitist, bureaucratic and community-destroying hell-on-earth." Hoover's presidency provided an alternative that attempted to create a balanced tripartism that acted so as to advance community interests, a system that Hawley has dubbed American corporatism.[3]

The word "corporatism" actually was foreign to Hoover's terminology. One prominent historian thinks that the application of the word and concept to the thirty-first president is "a thin reed" and is contrary to Hoover's "immense pragmatism."[4] Williams was asked why he had attributed to Hoover's booklet *American Individualism* (1922) the idea that the three units of government needed to cooperate. Williams reported that while the concept of corporatist balance is only suggested in *American Individualism*, he knew, from all of his reading in the Hoover sources, that it was there. (Williams insists that corporatism is not a concept of today that is being applied back to Hoover's era but, rather, was a concept in time that was moving forward to Hoover from the intellectual thought of Napoleon Bonaparte, Abraham Lincoln, and Karl Marx.)[5] Hawley was very specific in outlining examples of Hoover's attempt to achieve a properly harmonious relationship among the great units, a relationship that Hawley called variously "corporatism" and "associationalism." An analysis of the Hoover administration's relationship to capital and labor requires an examination of the president's belief in a balance of power that allows government, capital, and labor to develop into a larger cooperative unit through which the society as a whole can be organized and improved. Hoover's view went considerably beyond that view of corporatism which only equalized the units.

The purpose of this chapter, therefore, is to discuss in some detail the relationship of the Hoover presidency to capital and labor and, in the process, to try to determine the applicability of the term "corporatism" to the administration. Essentially the questions asked are: Did the Hoover presidency strive for balance among society's three functional units? Did it succeed? Even more important, did the president go beyond trying to equalize the units and attempt to direct their development into a larger cooperative unit through which the society as a whole would be improved?

Hoover's farm policies probably provide the best illustration of his presidency's use of corporatist formulas—the relationship of government to farmers as businessmen—and their blending with liberal traditions. As noted, his policies took form in the Agriculture Marketing Act, signed on 15 June 1929. The array of classical liberal themes that are included in the concept of corporatism—such as decentralization, voluntarism, cooperativism, and individualism—are aspects of an agricultural sector that is envisioned as being prosperous, free, orderly, self-disciplined, and also capable of acting as a responsible partner in community undertakings. By the fall of 1929 the president was buoyant about the beginnings of his concept.

In the Agriculture Department's 1930 annual report to the president, Secretary of Agriculture Arthur M. Hyde, though he was intensely jealous of the independent Farm Board set up by the Agricultural Marketing Act, contemplated its ability to provide multifaceted farm relief. Secretary Hyde emphasized particularly the following functions of the Farm Board, which had a revolving fund of $500 million: "Strengthening the bargaining power of producers and increasing the efficiency of their marketing operations through the development of effective cooperative-selling associations, stabilization corporations, and clearing houses." Next came a call for "stabilizing the supply of agriculture products and minimizing fluctuations in prices by preventing surplus production in so far as possible, and by effective distribution of surpluses once produced." The secretary anticipated other forms of farm relief, such as "the broadening of markets" at home and abroad, the correcting of "maladjustments in transportation" of agricultural commodities, and the agricultural reform closest to the secretary's heart, the development of "a national agricultural policy with reference to land utilization, marginal lands, and, in general, the control of the farm-land area." Vague as the law was, it was clearly designed to improve the farmers' bargaining power and to stabilize their production: it was not Secretary Hyde's idea to reduce land acreage. Specifically, the report continued, the act "contemplates that where conditions require such action, the board will assist in the organization of stabilization corporations and clearing houses to assist in tempering the influence of abnormal surpluses upon prices."[6]

Hoover had visions of the Farm Board's doing for the flow of agricultural commodities what the Federal Reserve System was to do by way of controlling emergency surpluses and contractions of currency. The emphasis was, of course, on emergency situations, not on continual intrusions by government. While loans to farmers and governmental purchase of commodity surpluses would enable farmers to meet glutted market conditions, the president was really more interested in helping the farmers to help themselves—as individual entrepreneurs working in great cooperatives to control their own production, eliminate waste in their production, produce their own commodities more efficiently, bypass expensive middlemen, and finally, market their production more profitably. The president took satisfaction in having, for a decade, aided the farm cooperative movement, which would be enhanced by the Farm Board, and in having warded off government controls as a way of improving the farmer's lot.

The White House argued that farmers had enjoyed a gradual economic recovery over the decade. Although we have seen that agriculture was the sickest of industries during the 1920s, some selected data supported his contention. Whereas the gaps between farm prices and industrial prices had been at 85 percent of parity in 1921 (as compared to 100 in 1914), the yearly average from 1925 to 1929 rose above 90 percent. Then more than ever, Hoover believed that the cooperative approach had been correct all along. Farm conditions seemed to be constantly improving. Even with an ominous drought condition in the West, "it is probable," wrote Secretary Hyde in a report to the president, "that the total income from agriculture production for the 1929–1930 crop year will equal, if it does not exceed, that of the 1928–29 season."[7] Given better agricultural conditions, the Farm Board, with its expertise and massive revolving fund, was expected to place the individual farmer at least on a par with all American producers, a place that the farmer had long sought and had held only briefly, shortly before and during World War I.

It is ironic that as Secretary Hyde was writing his encouraging report to the president, the stock market collapsed. After the crash had had its immediate impact on investors, it next adversely affected the farmers. They probably constituted the largest body of Americans with the highest potential for economic suffering. Farm mechanization, depressed markets, increased indebtedness, and high nonfarm prices could more easily tip economic scales against the farmer than against other economic segments, with the possible exception of laborers in low-skill jobs.

Although just after the market crash the president feverishly conducted White House conferences with representatives of important economic segments, he did not need any large agricultural conferences, since the Farm Board machinery was already in place. Farm Board Chairman Alexander Legge immediately advanced loan funds to several existing cooperatives in order to cushion any fall of farm prices, and he specifically authorized loans by national wheat and cotton cooperatives to shore up the prices of the commodities. It was felt that federal support of these two very basic commodities would aid other farm markets. For the time being the action seemed to work. Almost unnoticed was the precedent of price fixing by the federal government.

When the price of wheat dropped dangerously close to a dollar a bushel ($1.01) in February 1930, a low point that had seldom been reached during the decade, the Farm Board established a wheat-stabilization corporation to stem the drop in price by making direct purchases on the market. Hoover disapproved and suggested that such direct action was not intended by the law. When, however, the price took an upturn, he prodded the chief of the Bureau of Agriculture Economics to give the Farm Board public credit for what it had done. The president also suffered considerable criticism from private purchasers of large supplies of wheat on the market, who resented the Farm Board's acquisitions. His long-time friend Julius Barnes, who was chairman of the board of the Chamber of Commerce and was a large wheat exporter, began a darkly veiled correspondence with the president, chastising the Farm Board for making "government a dominant price factor," for creating "hazard instead of a trade security," for stifling the "forwarding trades," for frightening private "investors and speculators," for creating "alarm, resentment and resistance in foreign consuming countries," and for "the disorganization of the entire marketing facilities which touch the grain country through twenty thousand country stations."[8] Hoover must have been stung by the charges. Farm Board Chairman Legge initiated a correspondence with the president, defending the Farm Board's purchases and insisting that wheat prices, with two exceptions, had reached the lowest point in fifteen years and that the board's action did not constitute price fixing. Rather, he argued that the Farm Board's purchases were intended to prevent "excessively high prices as well as extremely low prices."[9]

Because of the weak underlying condition of American agriculture, many of its crop areas became quickly depressed. The Farm Board, through cooperatives, made loans to farmers to protect the price of other commodities and, as in the case of wheat, engaged in direct purchases of cotton. Wheat and cotton were of course the dominant commodities of their respective agricultural areas, the West and the South. The wheat problem seemed to be the most severe commodity problem. In late spring, wheat prices began to take another slide; by midsummer they had dropped to 70.6 cents a bushel. Such a low price was little to show for the Farm Board's purchases of more than one-fourth of the nation's wheat supply. So, on July 12, the board ceased to make purchases of wheat but agreed, for the present, not to sell its holdings. The threat, however, to dump the massive wheat holdings on the market at some future date made farmers and commission buyers, like Julius Barnes, feel more insecure than ever.

By midsummer 1930 it seemed apparent that until general recovery should take place, farm production would have to be reduced. Both Secretary Hyde and Chairman Legge traveled west to try to induce farmers voluntarily to effect a 10 to 25 percent reduction in acreage. The farmers were unhappy with the emissaries and their mission. Wheat farmers viewed reductions in acreage as a further reduction in their gross income. Even Hoover's good Kansas friend Henry Allen could not believe that the administration was serious about the voluntary reductions.[10] Legge became testy with critical Kansas farmers, telling them to solve their own problems, that it was not his job: "Do as you please . . .

I don't care what you do." He then told the editors of a Wichita newspaper, who complained about the government's ideas about voluntary crop reduction, "to go to hell."[11]

The administration failed to induce voluntary crop reduction so as to raise wheat prices. It had no way of releasing its massive wheat holdings. Foreign markets for wheat were flooded with heavy shipments from Danubian countries and Australia. With the foreign market what it was, with the domestic market's being increasingly depressed by general economic conditions, and with the threat of liquidation of Stabilization Corporation holdings, wheat prices continued their descent. In February 1931 the Stabilization Corporation desperately renewed its purchases, but to no avail. The price per bushel dropped from 58.3 in February to 51.9 cents in June, when the government permanently terminated its program of buying wheat.

By midsummer 1931 the board held 257 million bushels of wheat, which it proceeded to sell on the open market. Within one month it drove the price down to 36.3 cents a bushel. Chairman Legge resigned. So desperately low was the price that it would drop only 3 cents more by the time of Hoover's defeat in November of the following year. The price had almost hit rock bottom.

Wheat was only one of Hoover's farm problems. The attempt to stabilize cotton prices took essentially the same course. That effort failed also, as did more modest efforts to shore up the prices of other farm commodities. Carter Glass was appalled at the Hoover administration's failure to stabilize farm prices. He harked back to the Grange's export-debenture plan as "the only reasonable measure of relief, aside from a reduction of the tariff." He wrote to a fellow southerner that it was "the only thing proposed that would have given the wheat and cotton farmers a moderate draw-back from excessive tariff rates. Coolidge and Hoover had frantically opposed this proposition and Hoover forced his abominable Farm Board with its consequent disastrous experience."[12]

Although it is hard to imagine that Hoover's farm policy could come to more grief, it did so with his handling of the great drought of 1930 and 1931. The drought struck the Ohio and Mississippi river valleys during the summer of 1930, ruining crops, livestock, and water sources and, what was most dreadful, threatening famine. The drought, to Hoover, was a more tangible and logical problem than that of the nationwide descent of farm prices. He attacked the drought problem with almost a sense of eagerness, not unlike his behavior in the great European relief effort during World War I and, later, the Mississippi flood-relief challenge. Here he could make corporatism work. He canceled a planned vacation, ordered investigations, convened the drought-states governors, asked railroads to reduce transportation costs, emphasized the need for credit expansion, and called upon the Red Cross to relieve suffering—all in the cooperative spirit of advancing community interest. Hoover, or so Louisiana Congressman James B. Aswell reported, promised to support a $60-million program for crop seed and animal feed, with some resources being set aside for human consumption. But then the administration apparently backed down to $25 million, excluding the provision for human-food support. The president appeared to be heartless.

It is interesting that the drought files of Hoover's Presidential Papers contain copies of Grover Cleveland's veto message regarding congressional aid to drought-stricken counties in Texas. Hoover might have been impressed by the Cleveland declaration that there was no such "warrant . . . in the Constitution, and I do not believe that the power and duty of the General Government ought to be extended to the relief of individual suffering. The lesson should be constantly enforced that though the people support the government, the government should not support the people."[13] Hoover seemed to be haggling with the Red Cross to feed the people, rather than to have the federal government do it. When the Red Cross balked, an Arkansas congressman charged the administration with willingness to feed "jackasses but . . . not starving babies." It was a sorry spectacle: the president standing on a perceived constitutional prohibition, and Congress pleading for human relief.

An investigator from the Department of Agriculture reported the tragic farm conditions to the president. Another said that "probably one-third of the families are living on starvation rations." Even the Society of Friends, which was devoted to the Quaker president, was unable to do much for the drought-stricken farmers. Farm Board Chairman Legge announced his willingness to sell cheaply, or on credit, surplus wheat for hungry farmers. The president demurred, personally fearing the creation of a patronizing government. Hoover, one recent historian has reported, wanted to save the farmers from government. William Allen White, who was always a Hoover confidant, attributed the president's opposition to direct federal relief for drought victims to "his passionate, almost bigoted, belief in America." Finally, the president accepted a $65-million relief package, which, although it was silent about its being used for feeding humans, was used for such a purpose. Obviously, Hoover derived no political credit for at least feeding the victims.[14]

Nevertheless, in agriculture, more than in any other policy area, Hoover's corporatist ideology was a shaping force. The Agricultural Marketing Act had been well planned: it provided a powerful board that would extend federal expertise and revolving loans to individual farmers (entrepreneurs), who would voluntarily cooperate in more efficiently producing and more profitably marketing their commodities so as to stabilize their economic condition and put them on a par with other American producers. But the economic reality foiled the ideal. Starting with a weak farm economy, the Farm Board was forced to turn almost immediately to the economic relief of farmers rather than to the organization of individual self-help operations. With the deepening of the depression, the possibility of the American farm family's surviving through individual initiative, cooperative marketing, or voluntary crop reduction became increasingly remote. And when they became hungry, as was the case particularly in the great drought areas, Will Rogers warned: "They are going to eat, no matter what happens to budgets, income taxes, or Wall Street values. Washington mustn't forget who rules when it comes to a show down."[15]

As the farm situation became more emotionally charged, the president almost masochistically stayed on his "ordered freedom" course. He could and did, in the 1932 presidential campaign, list a dozen contributions that his administration had made and would make to agriculture, including farm credit and land-use programs; nevertheless, the Hoover program lacked the governmental thrust that was increasingly being demanded to effect relief. Not that solutions, governmental or otherwise, abounded. Governor Roosevelt of New York urged a farm constituent "not to yield to counsels of despair, because depressions always come to an end and business also eventually adjusts."[16] Old plans, such as the export-debenture and McNary-Haugen ones, were suggested but generally rejected.

Deep in the research offices of the nearly defunct Farm Board, Joseph S. Davis, Mordecai Ezekiel, and John D. Black worked to refine a domestic-allotment system that would attack the problem of depressed farm prices by rewarding farmers with benefit payments for reducing their production. It is interesting to note that the Farm Board, as the Hoover administration came to an end, supported what would be the basis for the New Deal's farm policy. But Hoover himself did not. Roosevelt's only request of Hoover, during the lame-duck session of Congress after the Republicans' defeat in 1932, was support for the Christgau domestic-allotment bill to pay farmers for reducing acreage. Hoover thought that such a vast governmental approach would upset the corporatist balance.

Regarding the relationship of the Hoover administration to corporations, trade associations, and other forms of aggregate capital, folklore identifies the thirty-first president with capital's inequities. Revisionist history has largely acquitted both Hoover and capital of much of that traditional guilt. The particular school of revisionism, called variously "organizational synthesis" and "neo-institutional," describes modern corporations as having undergone decisive changes of a "reform" nature during the 1890–1915 period—a reform in stabilizing industrial productivity and marketing. In such a view, the notion that business-men at the turn of the century were monopolistic "robber barons" is simplistic and contrary to emerging evidence that business emphasized, not divisive competition, but "efficiency, continuity, systematic controls and group action."[17]

Herbert Hoover, during the 1920s, was so committed to bringing efficiency and the elimination of waste to American industry that to effect this, he brought to bear the full weight of his good offices as secretary of commerce and president. Indeed, Hoover's prepresidency role in using the government to rationalize and stabilize business was immense and warrants analysis for understanding his role during the presidency. More than any single American, he had encouraged organi-zations, principally trade associations and farm organizations, to intro-duce orderly, rational, and bureaucratic procedures to entire industries. Such associations came into existence in the late nineteenth century but became important only after 1900 and particularly during the early 1920s under the drive and inspiration of Hoover as secretary of commerce. He invited industries to establish trade associations, which could then accept his department's expertise in reordering their respective indus-tries through new efforts at standardizing, increasing efficiency, elim-inating waste, engaging in research, and gathering and sharing statis-tics. As food administrator during World War I, he had presided over such a cooperative effort, and he intended to do the same during the peace that followed. His portfolio in the Harding cabinet was premised on that design.

But in such a design, Hoover, in the perspective of that day (and this) frequently emerges as particularly favoring aggregate capital. At first blush, it seems so. Both Woodrow Wilson's and Warren Harding's attorney general protested that the trade associations in Hoover's great plan were in violation of the antitrust laws. In a test case in 1921, *American Column and Lumber Company* v. *United States*, the Justice Department prosecuted the American Hardwood Manufacture Associa-tion and won a Supreme Court decision. The Court agreed with the Justice Department that the association's exchange of statistics, includ-ing prices, amounted to price fixing and the control of production. Certainly it appeared so. The American Hardwood Manufacture Association, comprising 361 lumber concerns, required monthly reports on pricing and marketing data, which the Court viewed as the pursuit of a uniform policy of pricing and production.[18]

The *Hardwood* decision (as the *American Column* case was called) frightened trade associations away from what they did best—namely, sharing valuable data, which they viewed as bringing order to their industries but which government prosecutors might see as a pursuit of price fixing. Two years later the Court reaffirmed its position on price listing and certain other data exchange by trade associations, in an important case, the *United States* v. *American Linseed Oil Company.* Hoover saw his design slipping. He succeeded somewhat in getting Justice Department support for the exchange of data between trade associations, if processed through the Commerce Department so as to minimize the possibility of price fixing. Trade associations, however, sensed Attorney General Daugherty's reticence about supporting data exchange that the Court might disapprove. Time, nevertheless, was on Hoover's side. When Daugherty's scandals in the Justice Department drove him from office, his successor, Harlan Fiske Stone, was more amenable to the Hoover Commerce Department's procedure for receiving and transmitting trade-association data. Stone was particularly helpful a year later when, as a new member of the Supreme Court, he joined a new majority in overturning the *Hardwood* and *Linseed Oil* decisions in a landmark case of 1925, *Maple Flooring Association* v. *the United States.*[19]

While liberal historians might see Hoover's adamant support of antitrust relief for trade associations as typical of the 1920s conservatism, closer analysis argues to the contrary. Liberals must take seriously the lead of Justices Oliver Wendell Holmes and Louis Brandeis in supporting the trade-associational activity in their *Hardwood* dissent, and in the *Maple Flooring* majority, in which they were joined by the third liberal on the bench, Harlan Stone. Their opinions give credence to the organizational synthesis of American history and its view of what might be called Hoover's Trade Association Movement. Oliver Wendell Holmes, in his short 1921 *Hardwood* dissent, declared that the "ideal of commerce was an intelligent interchange made with full knowledge of the facts as a basis for a forecast of the future on both sides." Besides, he wryly noted that if the interchange were to be prohibited, the big companies would get trade information anyway, and the smaller ones in the back country would suffer. In addition, Holmes thought that antitrust laws were frequently a denial of freedom of expression. By the early 1920s Brandeis, the New Freedom apostle of antitrust enforcement, was thinking rather like Hoover—that companies should cooperate rather than combine. If business could not organize into trade associations, Brandeis asked, how could labor organize into unions? And he wondered if problems of misbehavior by business and labor should not be handled at the state and local level. He feared that antitrust legislation might enhance too much the power of the federal government. Specifically, in the *Hardwood* dissent, Brandeis argued that the Hardwood Association, rather than creating a monopoly, replaced blind competition with stable and orderly business procedures. Like Holmes, he felt that trade associations actually thwarted the consolidation of business into large trusts and that freedom of speech required an interchange of information among traders. It is important to note, however, that although Hoover and Brandeis both supported trade associationalism, there were differences between them in their attitudes toward large corporations and the protection of small businesses. Hoover's ideal was "ordered liberty" and social efficiency; Brandeis's was more the preservation of small property than efficiency.[20]

In the *Maple Flooring* case of 1925, the Court upheld trade associations and their exchange of data, in part because the lumber association had eliminated penalties imposed on violators of the listed prices and because new minimum prices had reduced profits from 10 to 5 percent. Stone, like Holmes and Brandeis and the majority, felt that under new associational procedures the exchange of data on prices and production did not fix prices and production. Stone, who was to become, in the next decade, Franklin Roosevelt's chief justice, applauded Hoover for the great economic value of trade associations, whose exchange of information could help to avoid economic crisis.

So, from 1925 to his presidency, Hoover made the most of judicial approval of his brand of trade associationalism. Frequently he succeeded with his design, but not always. For one thing, those were the years of numerous mergers, which, in theory, trade-associational action was meant to prevent. Also, while trade associations were cooperating with the Commerce Department in bringing order to various industries through standardization and simplification of products, it became a tiring process and did not result in the sharing of approximately $600 million in savings with labor and consumers, as Hoover had hoped. The lumber industry, the center of many of the court cases, experienced more internal conflict than cooperation, which resulted in destabilization. Still, Edward Eyre Hunt, secretary of the committee that in 1929 issued the *Report on Recent Economic Changes*, spoke glowingly of "America's increasing economic stability," which he largely attributed to the communication of a gamut of economic factors within trade associations and between such associations and the government.[21] This seemed to vindicate the ideas that had been articulated from the beginning of the decade by Hoover, Holmes, and Brandeis, and later by Stone.

While his presidency encouraged corporations to cooperate and share information with their industry, Hoover did not favor price fixing, and he made sure that his Justice Department enforced the antitrust laws. He knew that businesses could be greedy and that their bankers could be iniquitous. Such greed and iniquity should be reined in by antitrust prosecution. He did not believe that exploitation by businesses in modern commercial life was unimportant or, as Holmes called it, "drivelling cant."[22] Hoover, during his presidency, refused to appoint William J. Donovan as his attorney general because, as head of Coolidge's antitrust division, Donovan had been very weak on antitrust prosecution. Here Hoover agreed with Holmes's devoted friend Felix Frankfurter, who charged Donovan with having given "advance dispensations to combinations, mergers [and] trade associations."[23]

Hoover's new attorney general, William D. Mitchell, told the American Bar Association that his department would no longer give advance approval to association plans, a habit that Donovan had gotten into. When the counsel of the National Electrical Manufacture Association tested the new policy by asking John Lord O'Brian, the new head of the Antitrust Division, for approval of a data-exchange plan, Counselor Charles Neagle concluded from the meeting: "Any extensions of trade association activities beyond the limits of the decision in the *Maple Flooring* case involved the willingness of those concerned to stand prosecution, either by indictment or by suit in equity."[24]

O'Brian meant what he said. Trade-association plans that appeared to be price agreements in violation of the Supreme Court's landmark trade-association decisions of the 1920s were red flags and brought vigorous prosecution. Even as the depression deepened, cases were initiated against the Wool Institute, California Petroleum Refiners, the Bolt and Nut Association, and the Sugar Institute. The four cases were settled by the defendants' signing consent decrees. The Sugar Institute, feeling aggrieved because Donovan had approved their plan in 1927, struck back with an expensive propaganda effort. O'Brian had less success in prosecuting Appalachian coal agreements—the Court permitted agreements in that beleagured industry. He rebounded, however, by bringing pressure on the Federal Trade Commission to stop supporting price fixing and customer-allocation codes.

Ironically, the administration's efforts at antitrust enforcement in the Justice Department stymied the Commerce Department's efforts to push further the trade-association movement. The corporatist approach of balancing government and business—of the government's encouraging trade associations but not to the point of allowing them to capture and use government power for narrow business interests—seemed increasingly to be ineffective in the face of depression conditions.

Hoover had often deplored the excesses of capital. Unfortunately, his accusations were usually viewed as being more rhetoric than policy—by contemporaries and historians alike. "Any practice of business which would dominate the country by its own selfish interests is a destruction of equality of opportunity," said President Hoover in his Kings Mountain speech of 7 October 1930. In the next sentence he invoked the balance: "Government in business, except in emergency, is also a destruction of equal opportunity and the incarnation of tyranny through bureaucracy."[25] At Valley Forge, on 30 May 1931, Hoover had called forth the proper balance of government and capital: "Amid the scene of vastly growing complexity of our economic life, we must preserve the independence of the individual from the deadening restraints of government, yet by the strong arm of government equally protect his individual freedom, assure his fair chance, his equality of opportunity from the encroachments of special privileges and greed or domination by any group or class."[26]

A far-stronger test of Hoover's restraint-of-capital commitment, enunciated at Kings Mountain and Valley Forge, came on 17 September 1931, when Gerard Swope, president of General Electric Company, suggested a massive economic plan whereby trade associations would stabilize production and consumption, minimize unemployment, and solve problems "of security for the worker and his family in illness, disability, involuntary idleness, old age, and death." The plan, which was to be formulated by rules that would be free from antitrust restraint and under federal supervision, deeply offended Hoover on both scores. However, the setting aside of antitrust enforcement was more offensive. Specifically, Hoover told his attorney general:

> This plan provides for the mobilization of each variety of industry and business into trade associations, to be legalized by the government and authorized to "stabilize prices and control distribution." There is no stabilization of prices without price fixing and control of distribution. This feature at once becomes the organization of gigantic trusts such as have never been dreamed of in the history of the world. This is the creation of a series of complete monopolies over the American people. It means the repeal of the entire Sherman and Clayton Acts, and all other restrictions on combinations and monopoly. In fact, if such a thing were ever done, it means the decay of American

industry from the day this scheme is born, because one cannot stabilize prices without restricting production and protecting obsolete plants and inferior managements. It is the most gigantic proposal of monopoly ever made in history.[27]

In December of 1931 the Chamber of Commerce took up the defense of much of the Swope plan and emphasized particularly that part which called for the revision of the antitrust laws. Hoover's response to the Chamber of Commerce's President Henry Harriman was similar to what he had said about the Swope plan. He would not support alteration of antitrust laws except possibly as they related to the sick natural-resource industries. Harriman, Julius Barnes, and substantial numbers of other large businessmen did not understand that Hoover's corporatist balance precluded the revision of antitrust laws. Barnes patronizingly told the president that "if you could meet and talk with men in various lines of industry as I do, you would feel that anti-trust revision is a question of major importance."[28] But Hoover was adamant. He became increasingly concerned that revision of the antitrust laws would lessen competition, would lead to waste and inefficiency among corporations, and would enhance the narrow, rather than the broad, social interests of capital.

A footnote to Hoover's insistence on balance recalls that, in 1922, the head of the American Construction Council had urgently asked Secretary of Commerce Hoover to enlarge the role of government in organizing the construction industry's statistical program. Hoover had agreed, suggesting that the head of the council, Franklin Roosevelt, appoint a committee of experts on construction that would voluntarily meet with both Roosevelt and Hoover on such a statistical program. But in due course, when Roosevelt asked Hoover to "intervene" with two large firms that were reluctant to cooperate with the American Construction Council on stabilizing construction (presumably on a basis of gathered statistics), Hoover refused. According to Peri Arnold, who has studied this facet of the Hoover-Roosevelt relationship, Roosevelt had "no such strong inhibition to a little shove by government." The National Recovery Administration, a hallmark of the first New Deal, Arnold continues, "was to show all the earmarks of Hoover's commitment to voluntary cooperation with industrialists blessed with the gift of government authority." Roosevelt, as president, would use the authority to mandate industry-wide agreements on prices and wages, which move meant setting aside antitrust prosecutions and evidenced two profound differences from his former leader.[29]

Hoover, as president, espoused a trade associationalism that intended to bring capital to a high level of productivity and profit. However, he embraced with equal fervor a corporatist balance that constrained capital in order to equalize it with government and labor.

The relationship between the Hoover presidency and capital has traditionally been viewed as being an unusually warm one; conversely, his administration's association with labor has been regarded as being lukewarm at best. Such interpretations are now being refuted by revisionist historians. Still, little attention has been given to government-labor relations during the Hoover presidency. As with government-capital relations, a brief examination of Hoover's ties to labor, both prior to and during his presidency, is necessary to an understanding of the corporatist balance.

In the decade preceding his presidency, Hoover proved to be a generous friend of organized labor. In fact, historians agree that seldom in American history has an important public figure worked so hard on labor's behalf only to suffer its deepest opprobrium a little more than a decade later. Hoover had known Samuel Gompers during the war years and had served with him on the American delegation to the Peace Conference in Paris. Aside from what he perceived to be Gomper's enlightened position on nonviolent labor organization, Hoover esteemed equally the labor chief's fervent opposition to the then-emerging communism. Gompers, in turn, appreciated Hoover's strong support of those businessmen who desired to cooperate with labor through such vehicles as the National Civic Federation. By the end of the war, Hoover had fairly well in mind a government-capital-labor scheme for Americans, and those who heard him out recognized the fact. In 1919 Wilson appointed Hoover as vice-chairman of the Second Industrial Conference, from which he emerged as the leading figure.

The report of the Second Industrial Conference, which, it was hoped, would resolve the problems of postwar industrial conflict, strongly supported collective bargaining based on secret elections. While the report was vague, what Hoover really articulated marked the peak in his support of labor. He believed both in collective bargaining for unions and in shop councils for all workers. The shop councils would give a voice in labor-management relations to the mass of unskilled workers who were ignored by craft unions such as the A F of L. Most labor leaders applauded Hoover's work on their behalf. In commenting to the Senate Education and Labor Committee on the action report of the Second Conference, specifically, and on America's industrial strife generally, Hoover insisted that the labor discord could not "be settled by any form of legal expression, whether it is by [court] injunction or compulsory arbitration." Then his corporatism surfaced. With management consolidated into large business units, he concluded to the committee, government should encourage the organization of employees similarly in large entities "in order that they may expect an equality of bargaining power."[30]

More important, Hoover believed that organized labor, like organized capital, should assume a responsible place in community endeavors. Labor was understandably suspicious of Hoover's "shop council" approach, with its intricate plan for mediation. The well-established craft unions recognized that shop councils would represent both union and nonunion workers and would lack the force of law. Organized labor, of course, was little interested in sharing the bargaining table with the mass of unskilled workers for whose individual rights Hoover cared. As labor's most forceful cabinet member, Hoover had carried his message far and wide, through his Commerce Department and his engineering profession, with which he usually had very friendly relations.

The story of Hoover's defense of labor's rights during the early 1920s has been told in other places. It suffices here only to illustrate his specific aid to labor. In the second half of 1921 he conceived the President's Conference on Unemployment and convened therein a spectacular array of labor, business, academic, and engineering experts, from whom evolved a wealth of suggestions to reduce economic slumps by eliminating waste, extravagances, speculation, overexpansion, and inefficiency in production. Most important, in a foreword to one of the conference's reports, Hoover applauded "constructive suggestions as to the deferment of public work and construction work of large public-service corporations to periods of depression and unemployment."[31] Such control of business cycles would aid both labor and business.

Well known were Hoover's successful efforts in 1922 and 1923 to persuade the steel industry to adopt the eight-hour day. Less well known, also in 1922, was his rage, directed at Attorney General Daugherty, for the most sweeping injunction in American labor history. The infamous Wilkerson injunction enjoined railroad shopmen from communicating strike strategy in any form. One can visualize Hoover eagerly soliciting Charles Evan Hughes's support as the two walked to the cabinet meeting, where the secretary of state quickly lined up Hoover, and others whom he as the secretary of commerce had surely influenced to oppose the injunction: Albert B. Fall, Will H. Hays, James J. Davis, and Theodore Roosevelt, Jr. The fact that such pressure caused the injunction to be altered very mildly demonstrates the sharp contrast between the views of Hoover and President Harding toward labor. The injunction as a strike-breaking device would be eliminated once and for all only when, as president, Hoover, ten years later, signed the Norris–La Guardia Anti-injunction Act, a logical culmination of his 1922 protest.[32]

As Hoover's opposition to labor injunctions was a portent of organized labor's late influence, so also was his role in the 1925 railway labor bill, which guaranteed railroad workers the right to choose union leaders "without interference, influence or coercion." It was little wonder that the new leader of the A F of L, William Green, a Democrat, probably voted for Herbert Hoover in 1928 and that United Mine Workers' chief, John L. Lewis, at the time acclaimed candidate Hoover as "one of the greatest statesmen of the age."[33]

Many historians have assumed that Hoover was an antilabor candidate in 1928. Reasons for such interpretation are so numerous as to almost defy a contrary interpretation. For one, only recently has revisionism pointed up Hoover's many prolabor efforts during the decade before the election. Second, labor did not, in fact, formally support Hoover, just as it also did not support Al Smith. Third, Hoover made no special appeal to labor in 1928, as he disavowed any class appeal as being foreign to the United States. Fourth, Smith, an urban politician, showed more interest in anti-injunction legislation than did Hoover, whose party turned down a strong anti-injunction minority plank, suggesting rather feebly: "We believe that injunctions in labor disputes have in some instances been abused and have given rise to serious question for legislation." Fifth, the New Deal subsequently became such a haven for prolabor legislation that Hoover's support of labor in the 1928 campaign has been discounted. Vaughn Davis Bornet, the definitive historian of labor and its role in the election of 1928, concludes his commentary on the relationship between labor and Hoover during the campaign by quoting the teamsters' president, Daniel J. Tobin, a partisan Democrat and ardent Smith supporter. Stating that Wall Street's great unhappiness about Hoover's nomination was a good omen for labor, Tobin said to his union members: "Hoover may change his attitude towards labor upon becoming president, but we hardly think at the age of fifty-six he will change and become different from what he had been in the past, because a man of his age who had always insisted on a square deal for the down-trodden surely cannot, on becoming robed in the regalia of the president, change his nature and his attitude."[34]

Dan Tobin was right in thinking that Hoover, as president, would not be apt to change his attitude toward labor. Just as after the Great Depression observers looked back upon Hoover as the antilabor presidential candidate in 1928, they labeled him, in the presidency, as antilabor in even harsher terms. Harsher because laborers, especially the unskilled, felt so deeply the ravages of the depression and were frequently little aided by Hoover's relief efforts. Although those efforts marked unprecedented federal fiscal expenditures—a vast increase in federal expenditures for public works in 1930 and 1931—such relief fell short of the jobs that laborers needed and wanted. And Hoover's guiding philosophy of exhorting philanthropic, state, and local relief supplements also fell far short of the need for relief. Hoover finally signed a massive relief bill in 1932, but, as will be noted, it was inadequate for the nation's needs at a time when over 20 percent of the labor force was unemployed. It should be understood that labor's suggestions for organizing employment and relief were meager throughout the Hoover presidency.

The relief problem and Hoover's hesitation over Senator Robert Wagner's three bills (for public-works planning, unemployment-statistics gathering, and unemployment-agency services), which are also discussed elsewhere, are not as germane to understanding Tobin's prophecy of 1928 and the government's relationship to labor as is the president's reaction to the Norris–La Guardia Anti-injunction Act of 1932. While the president struggled over various means to relieve unemployed workers, he saw the institutional importance of eliminating, once and for all, the curse of judicial injunctions, which for decades, from the famous Pullman-strike injunction of 1894 to the Wilkerson injunction of 1922, denied labor its ultimate weapon, the right to organize, to bargain collectively, and to strike.

On 23 March 1932, Hoover signed the Norris–La Guardia Anti-injunction Act, which provided that the worker shall ''have full freedom of association, self-organization, and designation of representation of his own choosing to negotiate terms . . . of his employment.'' Furthermore, the bill drastically limited the issuance of federal injunctions to restrain strikers, practically eliminated the use of ''yellow-dog contracts,'' and even provided for the replacement of ''prejudiced'' judges in contempt cases. From such legislation all important subsequent refinements of labor law flowed—including the very important National Labor Relations Act of 1935.[35]

What is puzzling about the view that Hoover sought a balance of government, capital, and labor is the proponderant view of Hoover, then and now, as being a foe of labor. It is such that one must question whether Hoover was even-handed in his treatment of labor and industry and, if not, why not? Even if one discounts the political rhetoric of Hoover's contemporaries such as Norris and La Guardia, who were convinced that the president signed the bill only because he had no choice, and the political rhetoric of future decades, suspicion is still raised by documents on the issue in the Hoover Presidential Library. To illustrate, do Walter H. Newton's many reservations about the Norris–La Guardia bill, which he expressed to House Republican leader Bertrand H. Snell, reflect Hoover's reservations? Newton, the president's liaison with Congress, questioned the bill's liberal provisions regarding potential strikers' violence, boycotts, demonstrations, and picketing. And when Attorney General Mitchell, in an official memorandum, advised the president to sign the bill, one wonders why he sent simultaneously a confidential memorandum raising questions similar to those of Newton, particularly one about the bill's possible conflict with antitrust legislation. And most ominous was Mitchell's warning to Hoover that if he did not sign it, the bill would be so overwhelmingly overridden that the Court might construe the act even more liberally than Congress had intended.[36]

Hoover's belief in ordered freedom—which was rooted in the thought and habit of his youth and had been reaffirmed by both the industrialists' new concern for order (''rationalization'') at the turn of the century and the Progressives' dual ideology of regulation and freedom during the first two decades of the century—explains much of the corporatist balance of his presidency. By the early 1920s Hoover had become a resolute advocate of governmental influence to bring stability to capital and labor, but only if the liberty of both were unimpaired. As a result, the agricultural policy of the Hoover presidency was meant to create a great farm board to aid farmers as individual entrepreneurs to help themselves voluntarily through the use of cooperatives, and not through the use of governmental programs that might jeopardize their freedom. And large business enterprises were encouraged by government to stabilize their industries through cooperative efforts in their trade associations, the development of which Hoover, as secretary of commerce and as president, had fostered so persistently. Yet, Hoover's trade associationalism in no way meant collaboration among corporations in an unethical and illegal sense. He resented greed and deceit among businessmen and vigorously enforced the law when corporations were in violation of antitrust acts or the Federal Trade Act. Certainly, Hoover as president would not support a revision of antitrust laws that might permit corporations to cross the line between cooperation and a collusion—a line that would give an unfair advantage to certain corporations or would be harmful to the public. And just as Hoover encouraged the organization of farmers into agricultural cooperatives and industries into trade associations, so he encouraged labor to organize trade unions, or shop councils (which were to give laborers some voice in management decisions). It becomes obvious that Hoover defined government's role as one of supporting the organization of farmers, industrialists, and laborers but never to a point of tipping the balance in favor of government, capital, or labor. He strove to maintain what we have come to call the corporatist balance.

Hoover's political ideology was not as refined as his engineering and administrative career led many observers over the years to believe. Nor was it as profound as many revisionist historians concluded fifty years later. And to some historians, "corporatism"—as a term applied in the late twentieth century to Hoover's political thought—was as much a misnomer as it was an inexact application of it during his Department of Commerce and presidency years. Yet, Hoover, often more intuitively than intentionally, did strive to balance societal units so as to have each one assume its proper role to better its condition and the society as a whole. If he lacked precision in articulating the corporatist balance and its conversion into a larger cooperative unit—the society—his actions frequently did not.

Edward Eyre Hunt, perhaps the person of most influence on Hoover's planning ideas in 1929, saw the promise and problems of corporatism when he summed up the findings of committees that he and Hoover had shepherded over the decade, such as the Committee on Business Cycles and the Committee on Recent Economic Changes. Hunt concluded that "research and study, the orderly classification of knowledge, joined to increasing skill, well may make complete control of the economic system a possibility." Hunt warned, however, that the nation must consciously and deliberately develop a "technique of balance" if society as a whole were to benefit.[37]

7

★ ★ ★ ★ ★

1931: THINGS GET WORSE

The president anticipated the Wickersham Commission's report of mid January 1931 with foreboding, and justifiably so. It would greatly compound his problems, unreal as that would seem a half-century later when the economic affairs of the Hoover presidency were viewed as having been so catastrophic. To many Americans in early 1931, however, it was not the economy that was viewed as diastrous; it was the complete breakdown in the enforcement of prohibition. Even when Hoover had assumed office two years before, enforcement of the Eighteenth Amendment had become chaotic. Citizens of Michigan had been receiving life sentences for a fourth conviction for selling alcohol. The Maryland House of Delegates had voted down prohibition-enforcement legislation. The Massachusetts State Senate had asked Congress to repeal the amendment. The United States Congress, out of frustration, had passed the Jones Act to impose a five-year sentence or a $10,000 fine, or both, on first offenders—this at a time when New York City Police Commissioner Grover A. Whalen was claiming that he had thirty-two thousand "speak-easies" to contend with.

The president dealt conscientiously with the issue of prohibition. He increased the number of federal enforcement personnel and upgraded their qualifications. He transferred the federal supervision of prohibition from the Treasury to the Justice Department. He implored states to assume their proper concurrent enforcement responsibility. Most important, however, was the president's appointing the Wickersham Commission of distinguished Americans to critically consider the entire federal machinery of justice, the redistribution of its functions, the simplification of its procedure, the provision of additional special tribunals, the better selection of juries, the more effective organization of our agencies of investigation and prosecution.[1]

Although Hoover's charge to the Wickersham Commission was a broad one, there can be little doubt that his particular interest was the enforcement of prohibition and that he expected the commission strongly to recommend the continuance of prohibition. He had reason for confidence. Even before Wickersham was appointed, he had suggested that most violators of prohibition be tried without juries—a telling position, especially for a former attorney general of the United States. (It is revealing that Supreme Court Justice Harlan Stone refused the chairmanship, fearing that his friend the president would expect a "political" report, meaning one that would be supportive of enforcement.) Now, however, Hoover feared that the commission would suggest that the nation abandon the whole cause, which, upon his nomination, he had described as "noble in motive and far-reaching in purpose."[2]

Why did the president fear the possibility and reality of the repeal of prohibition? He knew that it was not working, and at times he had even asked Henry L. Stimson and others about the possibility of a serious revision of the amendment. And while he saw the evils of alcohol, he personally had long ago left the "dry" attachments of his youth. In his London home he had a fine wine cellar. In his prepresidency days, he had drunk two cocktails daily, frequently at the Belgian embassy. He had appointed two "wets," Secretary of Commerce Robert P. Lamont and Secretary of the Navy Charles Francis Adams, to his cabinet. After his presidency, he came to enjoy the cocktail hour as a favorite time of the day.

Hoover's explanation of his commitment to prohibition, even as it failed during his administration, was his constitutional responsibility as president. The great lawyer Elihu Root told him that the president's mere suggestion of repeal would undermine the enforcement of the amendment in those places where it had been successful. More important, the Constitution provided no role for the president in the amendment process. (Root, however, was so "wet" that one wonders if the president, in his *Memoirs*, might not have embellished the lawyer's comments to him.)

Yet, why would such constraints cause the president to fear a Wickersham report that might and, in fact, did reflect rapidly declining public support and national division on the issue—a division that called for some revision of the amendment? (The president was so fearful of the report that he threatened to create a smoke screen on the day of its release by announcing news of naval disarmament.) When the commission did report that seven of its eleven members favored some form of revision of the amendment, why did the president transmit the report to Congress with a half-truth, "The Commission . . . does not favor the repeal of the Eighteenth Amendment as a method of aim."[3] And when the commission's report demonstrated that there was no effective enforcement of the amendment, why did the president assert that there had been improvement in the enforcement of the amendment during his administration? The commission's report bitterly disappointed the president. It barely addressed the many missions that he had assigned to it. All that it accomplished was to spell out vast national differences of feeling about the amendment, ranging from its retention, to its revision, to its repeal.

An authoritative interpretation of Hoover's continuing opposition to revision or repeal during his presidency is contained in Norman Clark's study of prohibition, *Deliver Us from Evil*. Clark concludes that in the 1928 presidential campaign, Hoover had been entrapped by the important political support of the arch "drys" Senator William E. Borah and Methodist Bishop James Cannon, Jr.; that "having allowed them to pilot his campaign train, Hoover had to go where . . . [they] were determined to take him."[4] Their "pound of flesh" was enforcement of the Eighteenth Amendment. Clark's point has some merit. In 1928 the nation had not started its rapid decline in support of the amendment. It seemed good politics to Hoover in 1928, particularly because of his disposition to make enforcement succeed. But to contend, as Clark does, that Borah, Cannon, and the "drys" forced Hoover to stay with the failing amendment two years later because of his election commitment does not ring true. Hoover was not easily frightened, nor did he possess anything like Borah and Cannon's narrow view of prohibition. Nevertheless, the political motivation, like Root's legalistic reasoning, is part of the mosaic of Hoover's determination to keep the nation dry. But is there a centerpiece to the mosaic?

Central to understanding the president's adamant opposition to repeal or revision of prohibition may well be an escalation of Hoover's behavior and thought in succeeding stages of his life. In fact, Hoover's support of prohibition during his presidency appears to be a prime example of that reinforcement process. We have noted that Hoover's developing "education" through various stages of his life leading to the presidency was frequently an escalation of tenets of his early familial years. It will be remembered that Quaker Queries, which were so much a part of Hoover's early life, were brotherly advices, which, at such times as when prohibition was prescribed, were demanding admonitions. Quakerism was very constraining, for all of its stress on individualism. Prohibition is an important case in point. To Quakers, it ranked in importance with their antislavery movement and, like it, was rooted in the era of the nation's founding. By the time of Hoover's youth a century later, it reflected an evangelistic fervor that manifested the narrowest of confines, especially in the rural Quaker settings of Iowa and Oregon. Quakers there inquired not only about who made and sold alcohol but about who of their brethren drank it. Queries, such as those regarding the use of alcohol, impressed upon Hoover the necessity for both order and freedom, or, as Friends historian J. William Frost describes the essence of Quakerism, "a corporate individualism."[5] The call to avoid alcohol aptly illustrated the disciplined order that limited individualism among Friends.

Although Hoover, from his Stanford days on, moved from sectarian to secular Quakerism, he seems to have internalized the moral inhibitions of his youth, especially when these were reinforced during succeeding periods of his life. While the entrepreneurial and public-service stages of Hoover's life in the two decades following his Stanford days do not particularly reveal his attitude toward the consumption of alcohol by others, they do manifest reaffirming influences that may well explain his adamant support of prohibition during his presidency. His notable mining ventures and experiences at the turn of the century put him in a class of capitalist gentry who sought rationalization and order in industry. One avenue to such a condition, which was certainly adhered to by Hoover, was a considerate treatment of labor. Hoover came to see the elimination of "waste" as being essential to both the payment of adequate wages to employees and the assurance of profit to the employer. As an engineer working with thousands of employees, Hoover feared conditions that were wasteful to employees and employers. Drink, as a wasteful habit, could well have threatened Hoover's quest for order. In short, Hoover's early and adolescent life was one of order and prohibition; his professional career was one of order, with a fear of waste to which drink could well contribute. If one adds to these stages his ensuing public service during the Progressive movement, to which he subscribed, then his resolute support of the Eighteenth Amendment takes on particular meaning. Progressivism espoused an ordering of society and a fervor for prohibition—both causes that were akin to the tenets of Hoover's youth.

Prohibition logically suited Hoover's ideas of a society's rational ordering of individual freedom, especially when done so democratically by a vote of two-thirds of the Congress and by the legislatures of three-fourths of the states. In a perverse way, it provided the best of both worlds to Hoover—the right of a society to maintain moral order; the right of individuals to their liberty excepting where individuals together constrain that liberty for moral reasons. And as president, Hoover felt strongly his ultimate responsibility for enforcing that amendment, which he had described as "so noble in motive." He paced the office, expressing to Henry L. Stimson and Ogden Mills his chagrin that their state, New York, had abandoned the concurrent enforcement of the prohibition amendment. It is little wonder that the president came very slowly to accept the idea of repealing the amendment. His stance on prohibition, as in the case of his obdurateness on many other issues, was rooted in his youth and was so strengthened in stages of his life down to his presidency that he declared the wish of his administration to be that America be "a land where men and women walk in ordered-freedom."[6] The prohibition amendment manifested for Hoover such a strong mixture of societal ordering and individual behavior that it was one of the most compelling of his commitments as president. Thus he staunchly stood by prohibition until late in his presidency, and then would forsake it only out of dire political necessity.

Presidential politics was low-keyed immediately following the midterm elections and into the first half of 1931—the calm before the storm of depression which a year and a half later would reach such proportions that it would have an important effect on the nation for a half-century. Senate Democratic leader Joseph T. Robinson assured Republican Majority Leader James Watson and President Hoover that Democrats would cooperate in passing appropriations bills for fiscal year 1932. Leaders of the important southern wing of Senate Democrats, Carter Glass and James F. Byrnes, publicly supported their Senate leader's truce—not without caveats about Democrats having a solid front when the Seventy-second Congress convened in the following December. Cooperative Democrats were not without ambitions regarding the next Congress and the presidential election of 1932.

The White House particularly appreciated the way in which Joseph Robinson answered the president's plea for cooperation in late 1930. Robinson also had reservations, telling the Gridiron Club that Democrats could not be expected entirely to submerge their party identity. Edward T. Clark wrote to Coolidge about how Robinson had endangered his leadership by "bravely" assuring the president of his cooperation. I wonder what "our own peerless leader in the Senate [James Watson] . . . would have done under similar circumstances?" he further wrote. Clark's letter, which was typically full of political chitchat, went on to describe how Hoover had agreed that Democrats should not become "Hoovercrats." Clark concluded by implying that the president might fare better with congressional Democrats than with Republicans for "he . . . has been greatly hurt by the failure of anyone [of his own party] to defend him on the floor of the Senate."[7] So, given the fact that Democrats would eventually turn partisan, that Republican leaders like Watson were lukewarm about their president, and that the insurgent Republicans were even then planning federal production and distribution of electrical power at Muscle Shoals (TVA), the calm was ominous.

Politics beyond the presidential circles seemed to be more mercurial. When Al Smith and John W. Davis pledged "cooperation" to stem the depression, columnist David Lawrence called it the "luckiest break" and suggested to Hoover that he call them in on Armistice Day, "a truce day," to "commit" them to a nonpartisan approach to the depression. The president would have "everything to gain."[8] But while Smith and Davis were pledging to cooperate, Franklin Roosevelt was listening to Bernard Baruch, who privately wrote: "The Republican party has on its back hard times. . . . Don't you help them."[9] The busy mails reflected the charged political situation. William Allen White, the Republican counterpart of Baruch as adviser to presidents, also wrote to Roosevelt that "these are great days for you Democrats . . . if the old ship [of state] rights herself" and stays afloat. But White feared that after the calm "the [nation's] crew will come storming out of the fo'c's'le, and throw the whole quarter deck crowd into the sea, Democrats and all."[10]

Another of Franklin Roosevelt's correspondents, Col. Edward M. House, Woodrow Wilson's old alter ego, wrote on 1 January 1931 that the eyes of the nation would be on Roosevelt during his second inaugural as governor of New York, that he should "strike a high and progressive note in [his] . . . inauguration speech," and that he should look at Wilson's 1913 presidential Inaugural Address.[11] If Roosevelt did scrutinize Wilson's address, he only partially took it to heart. Unlike Wilson, Roosevelt avoided the great issues of the day: unemployment, agricultural distress, prohibition. He did learn from Wilson what Hoover also had gleaned as a public servant in that same administration—the evils of centralized government. While Herbert Hoover felt little solace from the overwhelming reelection in 1930 of a state governor who would likely be his opponent for the presidency two years hence, he must have drawn some comfort from the New Yorker's espousal of a doctrine that he, Hoover, had been writing and speaking about for a decade. On 1 January 1931 Roosevelt could not have been more Hooverian as he said to his New York and national audience: "If we [take the easy road of centralization], we may discover too late some day that our liberties have disappeared. Let us pause in our pursuit of materialism and pleasure, and devote greater efforts to retain these liberties within the communities in which we dwell."[12] Hoover's only reservations might have been the governor's unwillingness to have New York assume more of its share of antidepression responsibility. Roosevelt, in truth, had done little by 1931 to ease his state's economic problems and, in fact, criticized the federal government for being too radical in its efforts. He was especially hesitant in commending the president's public-works spending to ease unemployment.

The storm soon appeared on the political horizon. Republicans, albeit insurgent Republicans, were behind much of it, and with particularly good cause. In late December of 1930 it was revealed that Robert H. Lucas, the executive director of the Republican National Committee, had employed "dirty tricks" to try to stymie the reelection of insurgent George Norris as Republican senator from Nebraska. Most alarming was the distribution of cartoons of a barroom scene depicting a poorly clad child trying to drag a drunken father home. It was entitled "The Al Smith-Raskob Idea of Happiness" and carried an alleged Democratic communication linking Norris to the Democratic wet cause. The attempt was ludicrous, for few politicians in Washington were as dry as George Norris. In January of 1931 a Senate investigating committee brought before the public all the charges of secret and illegal expenditures of money, fictitious printing orders, and the identification of the cartoon's publishing house as being the same one that printed *The Fellowship Forum*, the official organ of the Ku Klux Klan. To make matters worse, Congressman Will R. Wood walked out of the White House after conferring with the president and defended Lucas's behavior. And Hoover did not disavow Wood's defense. "I hunched the facts in the Lucas-Norris-Hoover situation, knowing all three boys," wrote William Allen White to the president's good friend David Hinshaw. White repeated an old refrain: "It was the dream of my life to be a sort of liaison person between the Norris–Borah–La Follette group and the White House, but things have drifted so far and got so bitter and unreasonable on the side of progressives that I suppose there is no hope of reconciliation. Yet there was no good reason and no good sense in letting the thing drift that far. These fellows were the only solid force in the Senate. They can always be depended on, and the Republican crowd cannot, and the middle of the road crowd cannot. . . . [It] is all just too rotten bad."[13]

When the third (and short) session of the Seventy-first Congress convened on 2 December 1930, the nation was not in a radical mood. To most Americans the president's second annual message to Congress in late 1930 seemed plausible enough. Its new view was that the "major forces of . . . depression now lie outside of the United States." Yet, internal efforts in the United States—stabilization of wages, cooperation between government and industries to maximize employment, the extension of private and public construction, the organizing of committees to "effect relief of the distressed"—allowed Hoover and most of the nation to be optimistic about the future. The president emphasized particularly his aid to agriculture through the federal Farm Board and to the unemployed through the President's Emergency Committee on Employment. And although various federal public works in the current fiscal year exceeded $500 million, the president asked for nearly $100 million more to "provide further employment in this emergency"—a sum that was far short, however, of what Arthur Woods, chairman of the President's Committee on Employment, had suggested. The president concluded that although the short session did not permit "extensive legislative programs," a number of important items should be placed under consideration—electrical-power regulation, railroad consolidation, antitrust revision, various veterans' affairs, and social services.[14]

The president, indeed, seemed to be asking for more than enough. The Democratic governor of New York asked for no more. In fact, he continued to worry about what radical Republicans in Washington might try to do. He urged New York victims of the depression "not to yield to the counsel of discouragement," insisting that depressions do come to an end.[15] Democratic leaders in the Congress, such as Congressman John Nance Garner and Senator Thaddeus H. Caraway, also had reservations about Washington radicalism, such as overappropriating. They were fearful of how bureaucrats would spend the extra money that the president was requesting. Senate Majority Leader Joseph T. Robinson, of course, had already pledged his cooperation to the president.

Some in the nation began demanding more of presidential relief efforts. "Where is there a program offered us?" asked a modestly important political scientist, the president of the Southeastern Political Science Association. He concluded sarcastically: "Observe this chief agent of the business man, this efficiency engineer in government, this expert in administration.''[16] Liberal Democrats, who were few in number, and insurgent Republicans, who were increasing in number, prodded the president and Congress to take seriously the appropriation of at least $50 million for direct relief to drought-stricken farmers—legislation that the president worrisomely viewed as being precedent shattering.

When, however, insurgent congressmen awoke to the nationwide nature of the depression problem, they put into the congressional hopper bills totaling nearly $4 billion for relief. Nevertheless the president, with the aid of the leaders of both parties, kept Congress on its "economy course," which they felt was essential to national confidence and recovery. It was ominous that some moderates defected. Even David I. Walsh, the generally cautious Democratic senator from Massachusetts, called the administration's construction bills inadequate. Said Walsh on the Senate floor: "I am sick and tired of the absence in high places of sympathy and appreciation of this [relief] problem. . . . I protest in the name of millions of people who look to their government in this hour of distress for sympathy, aid, and relief." Hoover, however, prevailed. He was more assertive in lobbying Congress than he had been during the previous year. The *New York Times* thought it unfortunate that the president had not shown such leadership earlier.[17]

When members of Congress returned in early 1931 from a Christmas season made harsh for unemployed constituents, an increasing number among these legislators were more prone to hear out the insurgent Republicans and liberal Democrats. While the president successfully continued to hold the line on direct relief, except for the $45-million drought bill, more and more types of Americans were becoming noticeably weary of the president's continued emphasis on mutual self-help, local government's responsibility, "growth of character," and the avoidance of "opiates of government charity." It was significant that on the same day that Socialist Morris Hillquit assailed the president on his solutions for relief, the usually conservative *New York Times* editorialized that the president was too insistent in calling upon the "people to work out their solutions in the midst of misery."[18]

In addition to the relief bills, congressional dissidents honed their relief arguments on the particular issues of electrical power, veterans affairs, and Senator Wagner's bills on employment services and planning. Although Hoover had suspected that the short term would not make possible legislative action prior to the *sine die* adjournment on

March 3, calls for a special session were now being more clearly heard. The storm was coming closer.

In addition to calls from increasing numbers of congressmen for more spending for relief, Hoover had to accept a near-unanimous congressional action to pay World War I servicemen a bonus that would average between $225 and $500 per veteran. When in his December 1930 "Message" he had asked Congress to study "the inequalities in services and allowances" to veterans, he did not mean for it to pass a bonus that would increase the loan value of compensation certificates from 22½ percent to 50 percent. Just a few months previously he had talked the American Legion out of endorsing such a bonus. But the temptation to tap the Treasury was too much for veterans and congressmen alike. On February 16 the House approved the "cash" bonus by a vote of 363 to 39. Nothing that the president could say would dissuade them. Three days later the Senate forced one of Hoover's few friends in the Senate, Chairman Reed Smoot of the Finance Committee, to give up the bill so that they could pass it 72 to 12. Although the bonus had more than twelve foes in the Senate, the House vote had set the tide against them. As expected, the president vetoed the measure, warning Congress of the bill's class nature and of the grave injury it would do to the government's financial structure. The House's override of the veto came on the same day, 328 to 79—after only forty-three minutes of debate. The Senate overrode the veto, 76 to 17, on the following day. Only a few Republican stalwarts stood by the president. An exception was William Borah, who was always unpredictable.

If Hoover's foes had conspired to introduce in Congress measures on which to solidify western insurgents and eastern Democrats, nothing would have succeeded better than George Norris's Muscle Shoals bill and Robert Wagner's so-called three bills to aid unemployed laborers. The first, a bill to establish government production and distribution of electrical power in the Tennessee Valley, would become a hallmark of the next administration. The president's treatment of Wagner's various bills to decrease unemployment would earn him pronounced condemnation of the A F of L's President William Green, heretofore a frequent supporter of the Hoover administration; and it further fanned the flame of western insurgency as well as the increasingly dissident labor force.

Senator Robert Wagner of New York was one of the very few Democrats who matched the insurgent Republicans in their fight for "relief." He sided with them in their demands for direct aid to farm victims of the drought. Although he was at first opposed to any direct federal support of the people, his conscience would not permit him to vote against the appropriation. He came to see that the "rare emergency" justified the drought-relief appropriation, and he found a precedent for direct relief in the American aid to people in Belgium, Russia, China, and Puerto Rico—the precedents that Hoover himself was largely responsible for. Wagner's reputation as a leader of congressional relief forces, however, was based on his labor legislation. It was not unnoticed that as Wagner correctly saw a precedent for direct relief to farmers in Hoover's drive for funds for Belgium and Russia, he also found precedent for relief of labor in the Unemployment Conference of 1921, which Herbert Hoover had chaired.

In 1928 Senator Wagner had introduced his three bills for labor—a bill to plan public works as a "balance wheel" to even out economic cycles, a bill to improve the government's statistics-gathering functions, and a bill to create an effective system of public-employment agencies. The bills languished in committee throughout 1928 and 1929. The New York Senator again introduced the bills in January of 1930, this time making sure that they went to a friendly committee, Commerce, which was chaired by a Republican insurgent, Hiram Johnson of California. Two of the bills—on gathering statistics and on planning public works— passed, the first in July of 1930 and the second in February of 1931. Although the two bills escaped presidential veto, the administration procrastinated in carrying them out, fearing an unnecessary expenditure to implement the former and the vast long-term financial commitment required by the latter. The third of Wagner's bills, that for the establishment of an effective system of employment agencies, passed in Congress. It was vetoed by the president. The director of the President's Emergency Committee on Employment (PECE), Arthur Woods; former Secretary of Labor James J. Davis; and William Green pleaded with the president to sign the employment-agency bill, but he vetoed it on the grounds that the Employment Service then existing in the Department of Labor would thus be abolished—and that months would elapse before the new service could be implemented, thus leaving the nation without any employment service. The president's rationale, according to his *Memoirs,* was that by transferring control of the federal employment office to state and local governments, political machines would control the jobs of workers, a "Tammany Hall" operation.[19] While the president's action seemed to be inconsistent with his commitment to decentralization, one must accept at face value his fears of political machinations of local political workers. It was, however, a perplexing move to many Republicans who were becoming increasingly reluctant to defend their president.

Wagner's three bills marked the New York senator as labor's apostle; and George Norris's Muscle Shoals bill made him the farmer's counterpart. For years the Nebraskan had wanted to have the federal government operate the Wilson Dam on the Muscle Shoals of the Tennessee River and to sell electricity to the people in that valley. Since the completion of the Wilson Dam in 1925, private power had purchased the dam's electricity and had distributed it to the people in the valley at a considerable profit. Not surprisingly, private power groups became apoplectic at the thought of governmental operation and distribution of the electrical power. They carefully launched a massive campaign to point up the "socialistic" aspect of Norris's proposal. At the height of Republican prosperity in the mid twenties, Norris had made little headway with his proposal; but when that prosperity had been shattered by December 1931, Norris got the votes to support his bill. On 3 March 1932 the president vetoed the measure. On the next day, most southern Democrats, along with liberal northern Democrats such as Wagner, and insurgent Republicans attempted to override the president's veto but failed by only six votes. While the president's claim that the plan was impractical had little force, his objection on the basis of his principle of opposing governmental competition with business is understandable, although at the time his actions were frequently condemned as being a payoff to the power industry.

The president's veto of Norris's bill was not a payoff to the power industry. The fact was that few congressional bills flew so much in the face of the president's beliefs about balancing government and industry. That Hoover was capable of supporting the federal development of public power was evidenced by his strong support of the dam on the Colorado River. The Colorado dam project, a massive engineering feat that was undertaken by the federal government, was begun in July of 1930 after the lengthy and tedious negotiation of a six-state compact which provided for the municipal and private generating and distribution of power. Furthermore, the compact provided for reimbursing the federal government for the construction of the dam. Critics of the administration chose to ignore the "Hoover" dam project when the president vetoed the Muscle Shoals project. William Allen White mused that Hoover, who had spoken so eloquently about developing America's great river basins, had broken faith when he vetoed Norris's bill. But unlike most proponents of Muscle Shoals, White stayed with the president. "There is enough good left to be worth salvaging," he wrote to Judson King, the famous conservationist.[20]

So, the short Congressional session, which the president thought would have time only to study some of the great issues of the day, put on his desk legislation that sorely tested his veto power, at a high political price. Little wonder that the president welcomed its adjournment until the next December. The administration then entered the executive phase of depression relief, one that was better suited to Hoover's administrative talents.

The president was indeed relieved that Congress had adjourned on 3 March 1931. The *Kiplinger Washington Letter* reported to its select clientele that the president would move the administration to the resolution of unemployment problems. The *Kiplinger Washington Letter* shared the feeling of many during the early spring of 1931 that Hoover's administrative talents would be addressed to economic solutions since congressional interference would be removed. But adjournment afforded the president little relief. Even before congressmen left Washington, their constitutents began blaming the administration for the economic depression with increasing intensity.

An important example of that intensity is a galley proof of an article that was sent to the president, which condemned him for vetoing the Wagner National Employment Service bill. The author, Miss Mary Van Kleeck, had been a member of the president's Unemployment Conference of 1921 and currently was head of the Department of Industrial Studies of the Russell Sage Foundation. She articulately refuted the president's notions that the Wagner bill would eliminate the valuable elements in the present federal employment program, particularly employment coverage for farmers and veterans. She insisted that all segments of America should be covered by the law and that the law would provide for the transition to it from the previous act. Most telling was Miss Van Kleeck's argument that the Wagner bill's concept of state agencies and federal coordination had an important history, including Hoover's own 1921 Conference on Unemployment. Typical of the academic community's reaction was a cogent point made by Harvard's Simon Slichter: "It is simply not true that the bill would have destroyed a going concern." He described the president's veto message as "one of the most dishonest documents I have ever read."[21] The *Kiplinger Washington Letter*, however, thought that the president had "pulled the teeth" of the Employment Service criticism by appointing an assistant secretary of labor to coordinate functions of the Employment Service. A week later the *Letter* noted that there was even "more wild, irresponsible thought being expressed than when Congress was in session."[22] Adjournment did not afford Hoover the personal relief he had anticipated.

The president only momentarily got away from it all in mid March by boarding the battleship *Arizona* for the West Indies, where he could combine some official calls and deep-sea fishing. It was a stag affair, with Secretaries Ray Lyman Wilbur and Patrick Jay Hurley (who had become secretary of war when James Good died), Larry Richey, and Mark Sullivan as the president's principal companions. It was Hoover's only extended vacation leave from the White House during his term. He had gotten away a year previously for some deep-sea fishing off the coast of Florida, and he would get away later, but only at short distances, usually to Rapidan, and only for brief periods of time. Soon the depression would set in so hard as to preclude any real vacationing by the president. At the moment, the president was in a light-hearted mood and was relaxing with his most intimate friends. Once they were south of Cape Hatteras, the ocean swells were quiet and rolling. Between stints of medicine ball and deck tennis, the president napped, two hours on some mornings and even longer in the afternoons. The navy band provided dinner music in the ward rooms, and in the evenings, sound motion pictures were the principal entertainment. The nation was interested in the apparatus that allowed the president to maintain radio contact with his son, who was recuperating from tuberculosis in Asheville, North Carolina. Interspersed in the radio conversations with Herbert, Jr., were tales by Hoover's granddaughter Peggy Ann about snow in North Carolina. Once in the Caribbean, the president did his duty by making calls in Puerto Rico and the Virgin Islands. Hoover liked the turnout of holiday throngs and particularly enjoyed being greeted by children. He always seemed to be touched by little ones. Their sickliness in the islands bothered him. He favored continued federal aid to Puerto Rico and the Virgin Islands, but he made it clear that the retention of them by the United States was only for purposes of defense.

All too infrequent were such holidays, given the benefit that they gave the president. "He was in fine shape, looked ruddy and well, and had an entirely different 'psychology' from when he went away," wrote Stimson in his diary upon his return. "I never saw the effects of a vacation on anybody in . . . [such a] short time."[23]

Thus, it was in a salutary frame of mind that the president invited a boy hero, Bryan Untiedt, of Colorado, to the White House. It was like Hoover to be impressed by the heroic deed of the young boy, who had saved his schoolmate from almost certain death in a Rocky Mountain blizzard. It was also like the president to spare the lad the trials of national attention that are attendant upon such an invitation. The Secret Service ensconced the young guest in the White House while the press was held at bay. The boy warmed his way into the hearts of the Hoovers and the staff alike.

Bryan Untiedt was unaffected by the presidential attention. He seemed to possess a "beautiful . . . innocence." For several days he had the run of the White House, including the Lincoln Study, where he and the president talked at length. In Herbert Hoover's customary way with children, he said just enough to keep the boy talking interestingly, indifferently, and with "sublime . . . calmness." Upon leaving, Bryan was given an affectionate good-by from the president, and Mrs. Hoover seemed to offer some tearful motherly advice. Even the head usher, Ike Hoover, who seldom complimented the Hoovers, did so in his description of the boy's visit with them in the White House.[24]

The touching story of Bryan Untiedt's visit coincided with the appointment of Theodore Joslin as White House press secretary to succeed George Akerson, who had left Washington for a job with Paramount Films. Shortly after the visit, Senator Robinson accused the new press secretary of trying to humanize the president. Joslin was, in fact, interested in reporting "humanizing" news, such as the boy-hero's visit; but he gained little cooperation from the reticent president—so little cooperation that when such stories as that of the boy's visit did come out, politicos like Robinson were suspicious. The Democratic leader announced that the American people were more interested in palliative measures that the president might administer to the depression, although his own single suggestion for relieving the economic distress was the lowering of the tariff.

Comments like Robinson's, which became frequent during the late spring, seemingly brought to an end, for the duration of the president's term, vacations and White House moments of joyful sentimentality. They jolted the chief executive into even-harder working habits, which seemed to earn for him the motto "work is life." Joslin's memoirs of the latter half of the presidential term are threaded with illustrations of Hoover's desperate efforts to end the increasing economic depression. Accompanying such toil was an increasing gloom. Within forty-five days of Stimson's comment on Hoover's "fine shape" following the vacation, the secretary of state wrote that "it was like sitting in a bottle of ink to sit in his room."[25] Yet the president did have some refreshing moments in spite of increasing bleakness. Young people continued to serve as a tonic to him. When Stimson again took the children of his special assistant Allen Klots up to Rapidan, "no sooner had the president spotted them than he went to them and began to talk with them and he was at his best as usual with children."[26]

While Kiplinger expected an antidepression push by the administration, he soon realized that it would be largely psychological, or what some historians have decided was more presidential declaration and exhortation than action. However, as spring broke, Kiplinger, like the president, read the economic signs optimistically and avoided any suggestion of increased federal intervention. Many responsible observers agreed with Kiplinger and Hoover that the bottom of the depression had been reached. A few days later, Arthur W. Page, vice-president of A T & T, expressed to Stimson encouragement about the economy. The president was probably most persuaded by his own Bureau of Foreign and Domestic Commerce, which saw business "at the bottom" and that "recovery should be well under way in the last half of this year."[27]

Even in this moment of optimism, however, the president was now hearing more clearly a call to arms—from the Left and the Right. Insurgents, only somewhat muted, did not believe the economic signs and urged a special session of the Congress, the last thing that Hoover wanted. Conservatives such as Arthur Page wanted the president to release industry from its commitment to hold up wages, and Yale Professor Irving Fisher wanted Hoover to persuade the Federal Reserve System to lower interest rates and buy bonds. The Yale economist was convinced that the governor of the New York Federal Reserve, Benjamin Strong, had avoided depressions in 1921, 1922, 1924, and 1927 by buying securities.

Although Hoover resisted the various calls to action by the Left and the Right, he tired of Treasury Secretary Mellon's laissez-faire "child-like narrations of the economic situation" in cabinet meetings.[28] The president anxiously left such meetings to devour departmental reports on the progress of their antidepression efforts to date. Although he held extensive conferences with his department heads to encourage them to strain to keep their activities within balanced budgets, he argued in a late-May cabinet meeting that the times were like wartimes, and "in wartime no one dreamed of balancing budgets." Besides, the times seemed to be propitious for borrowing on good terms."[29]

While the time might have been ripe for the government to borrow on good terms, increasing numbers of Americans viewed the times as being bad. They were so viewed especially by the nearly 28 percent of the factory labor force who by June of 1931 were unemployed (or by the some 15 percent of the total labor force that was unemployed). And among the employed, vastly more Americans were becoming conscious of the weakness of the economy, largely because of the perspective of time that was afforded by the year and a half that had elapsed since the crash. Heretofore most Americans had placed the economic slump of

1930 in the category of the several other economic downturns during the decade. But by the late spring of 1931 enough economic data had surfaced to confirm the fact of depression that millions of Americans were acutely feeling. The increase of the national public debt alone was a frightening statistic. Whereas in the fiscal year ending in June 1930 it had decreased by nearly $750 million, by the end of the following fiscal year, in June 1931, it had increased by almost the same amount, approximately $720 million. The reasons for the massive turnaround in the retirement of the debt were not lost on many Americans. The internal revenue of the United States had decreased by over $600 million in 1931, and during the same fiscal year, federal expenditures had increased by over $300 million, with much of the increase being due to additional expenditures on public works, agricultural programs, and the bonus bill that had been passed in February 1931.

Other signs of depression became apparent after an economic upturn during the first quarter of the year. Although Standard and Poor stock prices had risen dramatically by nearly a billion dollars in early 1931, by spring they began a descent which reached nearly $4 billion by the end of the year. Personal income, which had risen dramatically during the first quarter, soon began a precipitous slide, which did not end until the president left office in 1933. Industrial production and freight-car loading, which rose in the first quarter, began a steady decline that was almost unbroken until the summer of the following year. Department-store sales, which dropped during the Christmas season, picked up several percentage points during the first quarter, but by spring began a decrease that continued until midsummer of the following year.

The nation reacted variously to the downturn in the economy during the second quarter of 1931. Many Americans still continued to express optimism, including some economists whose credibility seemed to be enhanced by the growing lack of credibility in regard to business leaders. The president, although faced with discouraging data, again, largely for psychological reasons, expressed optimism. He spoke with the visiting mayor of Liverpool, England, who then reported to a New York audience that the president saw the "slump" as "mental." The *New York Times* editorialized that the use of psychology as a resolution of the much-worsening economic condition was "a perilous thing"; this criticism seemed to be sustained by a growing chorus of objections to the apparent federal inaction. Social workers and labor leaders were foremost in their expressions of concern—the former fearing for the condition of children, especially among minority Americans; the latter fearing for adult males. William Green called upon the president and suggested that he call a national parley of industrial, labor, and governmental economists to consider a gamut of economic solutions, such as a five-day week, the maintenance of wages, a modification of antitrust legislation, a cancellation of war debts, taxation according to ability to pay, industrial planning, and security for workers. Leo Wolman, of the Amalgamated Clothing Workers of America, wanted the federal government to float a $3-billion bond loan to employ 750,000 unemployed workers; and he especially wanted federal control of the economy.

Increasing numbers of politicos, especially presidential contenders, protested what appeared to be White House irresolution. Albert C. Ritchie, the conservative Democratic governor of Maryland, although he agreed with Hoover that the international scene was the source of the problem, decried the administration's policies on tariffs, debts, and reparations, and he asked for a reduction in all three. Roosevelt, representing the party's more liberal wing, was as critical of Hoover as was Ritchie and was also about as short on suggestions. He placed more emphasis on the domestic scene, rather simplistically mentioning, among other things, the need to reduce the excess cost of local government. In his address to fellow governors, who were listening attentively for ideas on how to end the depression, he helped little by talking about his state's survey of land to replace marginal agriculture with reforestation and the development of factories to hire the unemployed.

Most Americans complained less about the economy than did those social workers, labor leaders, and politicos who spoke up; and Hoover appealed to them to remain confident. At Indianapolis, on June 15, the president spoke with a vigor and assurance that perhaps he never again attained. He spoke glowingly of an America whose future prosperity depended, he believed, on individual reliance and voluntary relief. Without minimizing the economic trials that were being visited on many Americans, he concluded that the world-wide depression would not be resolved by nostrums at home but by the character of people who were determined to avoid the "vicious tyranny" of bureaucratic solutions. In fact, he stressed that the federal government would hereafter avoid federal appropriations that were actually inhibiting the individualism of Americans. "Shall we abandon the philosophy and creed of our people for 150 years by turning to a creed foreign to our people?" he asked stolidly. "Shall we establish a dole from the Federal Treasury? Shall we undertake Federal ownership and operation of public utilities instead of the rigorous regulation of them to prevent imposition? Shall we regiment our people by an extension of the arm of bureaucracy into a multitude of affairs?"[30]

A year or two hence many Americans would have shouted yes to the president's questions—more than likely they would have added unkind epithets. Not so in June of 1931. The protest of social workers, labor leaders, and some politicos did not yet reflect the American mood. President Glenn Frank of the University of Wisconsin seemed, however, to speak for an increasing number of Americans when he answered the president by suggesting that we needed to rethink important words such as "individualism," which was important "only in terms of what it does to and for the individual. . . . There is nothing sacred in the name," he said, almost blasphemously adding: "The fact is that the old and somewhat anarchaic individualism which was a superb virtue in simpler pioneer days has become a vice in this complicated, technical, interdependent age."[31]

As if to respond to Kiplinger's assurance that there would be administrative action after the adjournment of Congress and in answer to Democratic charges of an administrative lack of effort, on June 20 Herbert Hoover announced his proposal for a one-year moratorium on all intergovernmental debts. The plan, which was consistent with the president's attention to Europe as the source of America's economic problem, was described by Henry L. Stimson as the boldest step taken by the United States in Europe since 1918.

The moratorium did not represent altruism. In May the Credit Anstalt, the important central bank in Austria, had failed, thereby shaking world confidence in all of Austria's banks and in the ability of the Austrian government to stay on the gold standard. Although many foreign creditors descended upon Austria to withdraw short-term funds, foreign central banks offered their aid, but they only partially stabilized the economic situation. To save itself, the Austrian government imposed a strict control over all transactions in gold and foreign exchange—a nationalistic action that was then followed by Hungary and Germany, whose currencies were also affected by the failure of Credit Anstalt and other Central European banks. It was in this context of international runs on European banks that Hoover searched for an international solution and reached for the moratorium as a "shot in the arm" to leave hundreds of millions of dollars intact to help in stabilizing European currencies. Of course, Germany's annual reparations of nearly $400 million went to England and France, two-thirds of which was then turned over to the United States to meet their World War I debts. The president was acutely aware that when Germany had defaulted on the reparation payment in 1923, the French had taken the Ruhr Valley in retaliation.

Stimson was thrilled by Hoover's assumption of leadership regarding the moratorium, and the weeks of its preparation were the most exciting of Stimson's long public life. He gloried in a president who could act as if he were in a war, although he was depressed by the apprehension that the president had manifested until he made the final decision. Secretary of State Stimson abetted somewhat the president's low spirits, for he argued "intensely" with his chief about the obvious connection between the German reparations payments and the payment of Allied debts to the United States. For good political reasons the president insisted on maintaining the fiction that they were separate. The American people would not stand for expunging the Allied debts after one year if Germany was not able to resume the reparations payments.

The announcement of the moratorium was electric, and for the moment there were again confident prognoses about both European and American economies. As dramatic as the announcement itself was the administration's success in achieving congressional support at home and French support abroad. The latter support was largely Stimson's bailiwick, which helped make it the most stirring period of his professional career. Just as Hoover understood that Americans would never forgive the war debts (they agreed with Coolidge, who had said: "They hired the money, let them pay it"), Stimson understood that the French, who had suffered at the hands of German imperialists for decades, were even more emotional about getting their just reparations. Stimson helped bring the French to the support of the moratorium, however, and, even more, got them to throw their weight against liquidation of short-term credits to Germany.

Getting congressional support was Hoover's job, a responsibility that he addressed with unusual vigor. The president lobbied congressmen with little of his previous compunction. He sought the personal support of over forty important members of both parties in the Congress and telegraphed to the rest, asking for their support. He acquired sufficient assurances that Congress would vote the moratorium when it convened in December. The support, however, was by no means unanimous. "For the first time since he has been president," wrote George Norris to John Simpson of the Farmer's Union, "he has communicated with me and has sent me a long telegram." The gist of Norris's three-page letter to Simpson was that he would not support any moratorium. Ironically, he agreed with Coolidge that England and France would use it as an excuse to get their war debts canceled, which would be as unthinkable as our government's repudiating "its debts in the shape of the Liberty Bonds which our own people own and which our own people must pay." Norris represented the minority of Americans. In midsummer the nation hoped that the moratorium would turn the economy around.[32]

It is another quirk of history that as Hoover had exulted at Congress's adjournment in the spring of 1931, he reluctantly turned to it to give him his finest presidential hour. After the March adjournment of Congress, it was not the president's singular administrative talent that offered the possibility of relief for the depression. It was, rather, the moratorium which the president could effect only with assurances from congressional leaders that a majority would approve of it when they next convened in December as the new Seventy-second Congress.

Hoover's sigh of relief at the adjournment of Congress hardly meant relaxation for the president. Never one to "lie back," even in the best of times, Hoover plunged on even more grimly as economic conditions deteriorated into the third quarter of 1931. Now the Kiplinger thesis of administrative success vis-à-vis congressional failure at addressing the depression would be tested. That the thesis had some merit would be evidenced in coming months by achievements that would enhance any administration: the one-year moratorium on all intergovernmental debts and the establishment of the Reconstruction Finance Corporation. The latter, which was intended to infuse $2 billion of credit into the economy, became the hallmark of the forthcoming Seventy-second Congress. It is discussed at length in the following chapter. The former, the president's boldest foreign-policy action, is more thoroughly covered in the ensuing chapter on foreign policy. Both, of necessity, were subject to approval by Congress, which the president happily watched take its leave of Washington in the spring of 1931. And the moratorium marked a shift of depression resolution to the foreign field and away from the national domestic scene, where Kiplinger had expected Hoover's administrative talents to work best. Albeit, as 1931 drew to a close, the confidence of many quarters still reposed in the president.

8

★ ★ ★ ★ ★

DEPRESSION AND THE
SEVENTY-SECOND CONGRESS

Hoover, indeed, was always happier when Congress was not in session, and particularly so in the spring of 1931, as economic conditions worsened and as congressional corridor and cloak-room rumblings about the depression were surfacing in both the chambers and the *Congressional Record*. While nonagricultural production was up one industrial index point from a previous month, it was down 38 points from the high of 125 in the months prior to the crash. Such a decrease in production, of course, affected factory employment, reducing it 25 points from a high of 103 points prior to the crash. And the GNP continued a steady decline from nearly $105 billion in the late summer of 1929, to approximately $75 billion in the late spring of 1931.[1]

The president's relief at Congress's adjournment was not just bound to congressional complaints about the administration's ineffective antidepression program. Other reasons were tied to what might be called the president's dogmas. For one, because he took seriously the federal idea of separation of powers, he felt that the Executive Branch could operate far better when it was assured more independence of and noninterference from the Congress during times when it was not in session. Another reason was that he strongly feared congressional relief measures which would carry federalism far beyond his belief in decentralization of government. The president also feared that congressional programs might disproportionately strengthen government, business, or labor. And Congress seemed to be ready to repudiate Hoover's great emphasis on state, local, and philanthropic responsibility for relief aid. Also, Hoover thought that the Congress was too constituency-oriented to have his larger disinterested view. (He disapproved what he perceived to be their constant partisanship.) Perhaps the summer of 1931 was the time that David Hinshaw was referring to when he said that his Quaker friend did not learn soon enough the broader responsibilities of the presidency. Hoover, said Hinshaw in a moment of reflection, was too much an administrative president. He should address more seriously the politics of congressional tension. As Jordan Schwarz has noted, Hoover considered Congress's role in the depression to be that of a spectator, not a provider of solutions.

Senators and congressmen were generally mute during the summer of 1931. Some weeks after their March adjournment, the president, by various means of communication, got from them enough promises of support to assure the passage of a year's moratorium on foreign debts when the Seventy-second Congress would convene in December. George Norris and other westerners had grumbled about such a procedure of verbal commitment and called for an immediate special session of Congress to address the moratorium and other measures affecting economic conditions. During the summer, Hoover held onto the votes to sustain the moratorium; and the White House staff counted fifty-seven senators who agreed that there should be no special session. Rather than manifesting loyalty to the president, however, such members of Congress were probably reflecting a lack of their own solutions to the depression. Indeed, Hoover's staunch House supporter, Charles L. Underhill of Massachusetts, could only count on eight colleagues to "stand by at anytime and all time for attack or defense [of the president]."[2]

The most important extracongressional criticism of the president's relief efforts came from Pennsylvania's progressive Republican governor, Gifford Pinchot, in August 1931, in the form of a compelling demand to convene a special session immediately. With nearly one-fourth of Pennsylvania's laborers unemployed, Pinchot feared for their economic condition in the forthcoming winter. He wrote in an open letter to the president: "Wages are decreasing. Distress in many counties is acute. Many children are suffering from partial starvation because of unemployment. The hospitals are overburdened and the demand for charity shows no decrease this summer over the high record of last winter." He wanted federal relief to be greatly increased.[3]

Although the chairman of the House Appropriations Committee, Will R. Wood, was not among Hoover's eight congressional defenders, he continued to support the president in opposing a special session, which would muddy legislative waters with federal "dole" proposals.

Pennsylvania's Senator David Reed, the leader of Pinchot's Republican opposition in the Keystone State, also deprecated the idea of a special session. Agreeing that the Hoover administration had already done "about all" that it could, Reed concluded that "each one of us owes a clear duty to do his best to mitigate and end . . . the depression."[4]

Not a few observers caught the significance of the Pinchot-Hoover exchange. They were the nation's foremost Republican elected officials, and shortly, the zealous Pinchot would attempt unsuccessfully to take the presidential nomination from Hoover. Certainly few people recognized the common Progressive political heritage of Hoover and Pinchot. Most people thought the two were polar opponents. Actually, both had similarily straddled progressivism; the president and the governor had been equally committed to both New Nationalism and New Freedom, the two ideological images of progressivism.

New York's Governor Franklin D. Roosevelt was not yet ready for a confrontation with the president. Indeed, he did what the president wished that more state governors would do, for he began assuming responsibility for state and local aid to the unemployed. Roosevelt increased the New York income-tax rate by nearly one-half and asked the state legislature to appropriate $20 million for unemployment relief. The New York governor, like Pinchot, harbored a design on the White House, although more plausibly and more cautiously. In requesting his state relief program, Roosevelt noted that the nation's eight million unemployed could not wait for Hoover to act, although he believed that the president might yet adopt a thought-out approach and thus eradicate the causes of the depression. Roosevelt's direct relief action vis-à-vis Hoover's more indirect action in 1931 would be noted by politicians and academicians for months and years to come. At the time, however, the two men essentially agreed on having the states assume such responsibility.

In spite of rumblings from certain factions in Congress and from various statehouses, Hoover's prestige with the general public was still creditable in midsummer 1931. Colonel Woods, having recommended more federal actions to effect relief, quietly left the chairmanship of the President's Emergency Committee on Employment, which, on 17 August 1931, was subsumed under a new organization, the President's Organization on Unemployment Relief, or POUR for short. The new organization was headed by Walter S. Gifford, president of the American Telephone and Telegraph Company. It was basically a continuation of Woods's organization and, for all intents and purposes, was run by Fred C. Croxton, one of Woods's assistants. There were cosmetic changes in the new relief organization, with the appointment of five national committees to help in the mobilization of relief resources, to aid in the administration of relief matters, to advise on employment plans and suggestions, to recommend federal public-works projects, and to coordinate national organizations and agencies. True to the president's desire, POUR avoided recommending direct federal relief programs. The editors of the *Kiplinger Washington Letter* warned, however, that if the Gifford organization did not generate "very large local charity funds" in September and October, "Mr. Hoover would receive more bitter denunciation from Congress than any president since Cleveland." The distinction between the president and his vociferous opposition in Congress, noted the *Kiplinger Washington Letter,* would be "between the theory of private business responsibility with minimum government, and the theory of social business responsibility with maximum of government." It is obvious, concluded the *Letter,* that the "latter forces would gain momentum."[5]

Kiplinger was right about the momentum. As the Gross National Product continued to fall during the second two quarters of 1931, some of the Gifford committee's efforts began to appear foolish against the grim backdrop of the overall unemployment, which reached approximately 13 percent. Its subcommittees, in part, recommended charitable contributions solicited through mass-media events; "the resumption of normal buying on a nation-wide scale by all elements of the population having available income"; and the substitution of more constructive plans for the public bread line, soup kitchens, and "other emergency methods." It also advocated the "maintenance of healthy, character-building [groups] and other similar organizations to keep community morale on a high level"; the emphasis "upon the continuing need for plain old-fashioned neighborliness in helping the unemployed to solve their trying problems"; and focusing "attention upon the need for encouraging and assisting students to continue their education during the emergency when it . . . [was] so difficult to obtain employment."[6] It is little wonder that historian Albert U. Romasco, in *The Poverty of Abundance,* had a field day with the POUR effort, especially when he could quote Gifford as having told the president, as late as November 1931, that "there is every indication that each state will take care of its own this winter" and could quote Gifford as a month later having told Congress that he really did not know how many unemployed Americans there were.[7]

POUR must be viewed in the context of Hoover's considerable antidepression efforts before and after the second half of 1931. Although the president believed in the mutual self-help tenets that the organization propounded, POUR was only one of many of his administration's antidepression efforts, which included federal public works, stabilization conferences, supports for prices of agricultural commodities, a decrease in taxes, the expanding of currency through decreased discount rates and open-market purchases, and the moratorium. POUR, to a large degree, was really a holding action, to quiet the voices of a growing camp of veteran and newly elected congressmen who were demanding that Congress take strong action when it would convene on 7 December 1931. By then the president would have moved on new administrative fronts and would have prepared a substantial program for congressional action. The Congress appeared to cooperate. Jordan Schwarz had described what was about to take place in the new Congress as a "kissing bee."

The heart of Hoover's administrative front in the fall of 1931, and of his legislative program in December, involved the availability of credit for banks, industries, and consumers. It was representative of Hoover's presidential activism and was precedent setting in many respects.

Since the crash, Hoover, time and again, had called upon bankers, generally, and the Federal Reserve System, specifically, to stimulate the economy with the availability of credit. While the president always deplored the excessive use of credit in inflationary and speculative periods, in 1930 he noted that "a wise direction of credit [in deflationary periods] provides a large contribution to recovery from depressions."[8] By 1931 the contribution was not forthcoming. In fact, many banks lacked enough liquidity to survive, as evidenced by a doubling of failures in 1930 and a quadrupling in 1931. When the governor of the Federal Reserve Board, Eugene Meyer, questioned the Federal Reserve System's statutory authority to implement Congressman Adolph J. Sabath's plea for a liberalization of eligibility requirements for borrowing, the congressman replied that if ever there were a time for the system to act in accord with its purpose for being, it was then. Sabath concluded: "I insist it is within the power of the Federal Reserve Board to relieve the financial and commercial distress."[9]

History now records that the credit mechanism of the Federal Reserve System indeed did not provide the economy with its needed liquidity and credit. Milton Friedman and Anna Jacobson Schwatz insist that the system failed to use its authority over discount rates and open-market operations and thus caused what they called the "Great Contraction" of the money supply. They argue persuasively that the system followed a "passive, defensive, hesitant policy from 1929 to 1933."[10] The analysis of that contraction is beyond the purview of this study except to note again that the death in 1929 of Benjamin Strong, the governor of the New York Federal Reserve Bank who guided the whole system throughout much of the decade of the 1920s, had thrown the system's operation into a confused state just prior to Hoover's entrance into the presidency. Struggles within the system—between the twelve Federal Reserve banks and the Federal Reserve Board, among various schools in the board itself, and among the governors of the twelve banks—put the whole intricate network beyond anybody's influence, let alone control. The president did have a credit "expansionist" friend in the system when he appointed Eugene Meyer as governor of the Federal Reserve Board in 1930. But Meyer was unable, throughout 1931, to persuade the Open Market Policy Conference to approve of large-enough purchases on the open market to save banks let alone to assure them of enough liquidity to engage in making loans that would stimulate the economy.

The folly of the bankers and the Federal Reserve System, as well as the consequent bank failures and credit losses to the nation, was not lost on the president. It became an obsession with him. He viewed it, along with foreign economic instability, as the principal cause of the economic deterioration. On 8 September 1931, Hoover called Eugene Meyer to the White House and suggested that the depression could be solved by having the leading bankers form a private credit corporation to aid troubled banks. On September 15 he suggested that the bankers create a $500-million credit pool. The governor of the Federal Reserve Board doubted that bankers would commit such sums for such a purpose.

Meyer did agree that relief for bankers, businessmen, and consumers was desperately needed; that bankers had been more concerned about their own liquidity than about funding for borrowers; and that the depression would continue until substantial commercial lending was revived. Meyer was willing to contact leading New York bankers and some Federal Reserve governors across the nation to consider the president's suggestion. The bankers, however, were reluctant. In late September they nevertheless were willing to talk with the president about his proposal, surreptitiously, in Treasury Secretary Andrew Mellon's Washington home. There Hoover was articulate in spelling out the problem and his solution. He stressed the voluntary nature of the operation and its lack of governmental constraints. Unexpectedly, the president threatened governmental intervention to save banks and to increase the availability of credit if the large banks did not act. Even more unforeseen was the banking leaders' insistence that their organization of a pool in the form of the National Credit Corporation be contingent upon federal intervention if their organization were to fail.

Indeed, only with such a guarantee would bankers proceed to establishing the National Credit Corporation. Needless to say, bankers were averse to establishing a voluntary organization to rescue distressed banks. Nevertheless, the governor of the New York Reserve, George Harrison, proceeded to organize a committee of New York bankers to pledge $500 million in subscription and to issue $1 billion in debenture notes.[11]

The nation and most congressmen applauded the president's action, although John Nance Garner, who was about to become the Democratic Speaker of the House of Representatives, would have preferred a special session of the Congress to legislate the matter. The nation's press seemed to be supportive of the large voluntary effort. Hoover's friend Will Erwin wrote to the president from New York City: "I have made it a point to circulate and talk with all manner of men. From the yiddish newsdealer to the pastor of the church on the corner and on to Wall Street, the reaction has been one of hope, relief, and appreciation for your cleverness in conceiving this plan and putting it through."[12] Hoover became highly enthusiastic about his plan.

Praise of the president's credit plan was nonetheless mixed with malice. The publication of *The Mirrors of 1932*, a devastating anonymous criticism of the president, must have hurt. The president was said to be unpopular and unloved, inefficient, and incapable of governing, a man who wouldn't be assured of a footnote in history. However, William Allen White wrote to Walter Newton that the attacks in *Mirrors* and other places were unjustified. Although the Kansas editor said that he could not account for them, he, in fact, did so by noting the president's reticence to "go public" and by observing that "the president doesn't fight back. . . . He sublimates his indignation . . . instead of spitting on his hands . . . and beating the tar out of his enemies. The people are low in the mind and want to be cheered by a fight."[13]

By November, Hoover could see that the voluntary banking-pool effort was a failure. The bankers lent paltry sums to save banks and to ease credit. So, as promised, the president proceeded with drafting legislation for the Reconstruction Finance Corporation (RFC), modeled on the War Finance Corporation, which had financed the nation during World War I. The RFC would avoid the structural weaknesses of the National Credit Corporation (NCC) and especially the latter's inability or unwillingness either to aid the weakest banks or to provide credit to monetary institutions other than commercial banks. Also, the RFC, unlike the NCC, would provide new credit for the nation, not just redistribute available credit. In sum, the RFC would prove to be more of a governmental intrusion into the banking industry than the president had bargained for.

On 7 December 1931 the president included his request for the RFC in his State of the Union message to Congress. Congress delayed acting on such a bill until January 22. The bill principally provided $500 million of capital appropriation and $1.5 billion in RFC bonds and debenture notes, which would support federal loans to banks, railroads, and certain agricultural organizations (such as livestock and agricultural credit corporations and Federal Land Banks). It passed the Congress handily as the first act of the "kissing bee," but not without acquiring its vociferous critics. Progressives in Congress were made suspicious by the bankers' enthusiasm for the bill. Specifically, they variously criticized it as a banker "bail-out" at taxpayers' expense; a bill without provision to aid depressed cities; and a bill that was not justified because of the bankers' inability to make the predecessor organization, the National Credit Corporation, work. But as was frequently true with Hoover's congressional critics in early 1932, they presented no acceptable alternative to the president's plan.

The president appointed Federal Reserve Governor Eugene Meyer as chairman of the RFC and former Vice-President Charles Gates Dawes as its president. There were seven additional members. The corporation immediately organized into eight divisions and thirty-three local offices and proceeded with a massive infusion of credit, which seemed only to alleviate rather than to stimulate the economy, as the president had hoped it would do. Although the story of the RFC appears throughout much of the remainder of Hoover's presidency and the New Deal that followed, the organization proved to be inadequate for resolving the depression. It did, however, contribute to saving some banks and to postponing the depths of the depression.

Basically, in weighting so heavily the RFC as a principal antidepression mechanism, the president and the bankers probably erred in emphasizing what in later decades would be termed the "supply side" of credit, as opposed to the "demand side." The year 1932 was too late to right the economy with an infusion of credit. Much confidence in the economy had been lost, a problem that Hoover was aware of but still thought could be corrected by the infusion of credit. If the Federal Reserve System had provided it sooner and more liberally, the banks might not have failed in as great numbers, and producers and consumers might have spent money in ways that would have stimulated the economy in time to turn it upward, especially given the other antidepression efforts. James Olson, the definitive historian of the RFC, notes poignantly that what the president initiated as another "corporatist" idea of having government and capital cooperatively construct a large credit-infusion operation became, in fact, a federal subsidization of the private money market. "He sacrificed," writes Olson of Hoover, "his personal philosophy to objectives that he could never achieve."[14]

The RFC was probably the most important of Hoover's legislative programs which he presented to the new Seventy-second Congress. Much of the whole program was viewed as very creditable: a balanced budget, liberalization of Federal Reserve eligibility requirements, substitution of government bonds for gold as partial coverage of currency, authorization of the Federal Reserve System to expand credit, additional capital for Federal Land Banks, the establishment of the Home Loan Discount Bank system, reorganization of railroads, and the ratification of the moratorium. Other recommendations were less important and received less consideration. Republicans saw the program as "constructive"; Democrats viewed it as too "general." Insurgent Republicans said that it was vexing. A *New York Times* editorial described it as "correct but cold."[15] The *Times*'s reaction was probably the most accurate.

By early 1932 the president seemed to have lost all but his devoted followers. "Today," wrote Edward Clark to former President Coolidge, "there seems to be no class nor section where Hoover is strong or where a decision is respected because [he] made it. . . . Wilson provoked . . . violent hostility but nobody was contemptuous of him." "Who advises him?" mused Clark. "There is the implication that he has no fundamental principles which guide his cause, no definite goal, no essential purpose."[16]

Strangely enough, while Clark, an administrative insider, reflected a common view about advisement in the White House, he should have known better. Hoover consistently adhered to certain fundamental principles which he viewed as being essential in order to guide the nation to economic stability and prosperity without impairing freedom and equality of opportunity, which he thought were so necessary to the system. For a man who had succeeded so brilliantly in manipulating public support of great causes, it was hard for Clark and others to believe that the president could fail now when in the ultimate leadership position and when he was most greatly in need of securing support for his personal performance and program.

In retrospect, we can see that what Hoover did was plausible. The moratorium was to stabilize the increasingly important international economic conditions. The RFC would provide credit to induce domestic production and consumption. The Federal Reserve System would liberalize the availability of its credit to supplement that of the RFC. The construction industry was to be revived by a system of Home Loan Banks. Railroads would be reorganized. Taxes would be increased, and the budget would be as nearly balanced as possible. Insurgent Republicans and Democrats had no such detailed program. Reflective people, such as Walter Lippmann and even Rexford G. Tugwell, thought well of it. But the president outlined his program unemotionally and coldly, and "Americans still . . . [longed] for a public man who could rise to the great crisis in a great way."[17] Crises in American presidential history seem to require inspirational leadership for their resolution, and tragically, Hoover's stolid ways, along with an inflexible ideology, would become increasingly inadequate to the challenge.

Although the nation as a whole had been remarkably restrained about the economic slump, no one doubted by 1 January 1932 that it had reached crisis proportions. It was without question a depression. While industrial production in 1931 had fallen 14 points, as compared to 26 during the previous year, the total drop since the high of 119 points in 1929 had been a decrease of 51 points. Still, the president was looked to by most Americans as the only leader who could resolve the crisis, and Congress still would do his bidding. For all its rumblings prior and subsequent to its convening, the Seventy-second Congress, in its first "one hundred days," gave the president much of what he asked for: the moratorium, the liberalization of Federal Reserve eligibility requirements, the strengthening of the Federal Home Loan Bank system, and the Glass-Steagall Act, which substituted federal securities for gold as partial backing of Federal Reserve currency. Of course, some insurgents wanted far more by way of the "demand side" legislation, but they were still in the minority. While the large spending recommendations of a few insurgents were now appearing less radical, their articulation still lacked force. Indeed, many Democrats wanted to spend less than the president did. Some "slashed away" at appropriations so as to be able to say one day that they had maintained the government's solvency.

In many ways, Hoover appeared to be very assertive. Although he wanted a balanced budget, he did not radically reduce the budget. In fact, he increased spending for federal public works. He was a fiscalist, but he was more a monetarist and counted on the RFC and the Federal Reserve's liberalization of the availability of currency to turn the economic tide. By the early spring of 1932, Hoover's credit approach still had considerable support in Congress.

Hoover's congressional support, however, now reflected less and less national support, and the president was less and less able to rally the nation behind his program. To his sorrow, he admitted that he was no Teddy Roosevelt, preaching from a "bully pulpit"; to his credit, he did not try to be. Conservatives across the nation had always suspected his liberal commitment and still did. Insurgents could not see him as being one of them. The president's image seemed to be moribund.

Even the appointment of Benjamin Cardozo to replace Oliver Wendell Holmes on the Supreme Court had little effect on Hoover's image among liberals. Understanding the fact that the Cardozo appointment gave the state of New York overrepresentation on the high court, the president might have gone to one of several other eminently qualified candidates: John W. Davis, George Wharton Pepper, Newton D. Baker, or William E. Borah. He took the highest of roads in selecting the eminent Cardozo. This was not foreign to Hoover's apolitical nature.

In spite of his image problem, the president, with considerable justification, looked upon his record in the new Congress with confidence—a confidence that would sustain him for a while yet. Arthur Krock, Washington correspondent of the *New York Times*, reported on April 20 that "the president looked well and spoke vigorously, with many 'damns.'" As usual, Hoover "wishes Congress would adjourn soon so he [could] get down to uninterrupted business. . . . He smiled a good deal and chuckled . . . at the 'phony' performance of the Democrats."[18]

Press Secretary Theodore Joslin continually tried to plant in the press the human side of Hoover that Arthur Krock and others close to the president saw. Joslin's attempt continued to fail badly, but this did not affect the discerning and frequently commendable analyses that columnists such as Krock and Walter Lippmann accorded to the president's earnest efforts at recovery. They were frequently needled by associates as the economy worsened and as Congress debated relief measures and the presidential election loomed on the horizon.

Lippmann, of course, was the intellectual dean of American columnists. While catholic in his relationship with important people, such as Hoover, Alfred Smith, and Franklin D. Roosevelt, Lippmann had always had a particular admiration for the president. He had liked Hoover's firm administrative control of matters, although now Felix Frankfurter was working hard to dispel any such view of the president's actions. From his Harvard office the brilliant professor of law voraciously read Lippmann's columns and corresponded with the great critic in an effort to detract from the president. Frankfurter did not always succeed, although he was colorful and telling in his arguments. He wrote: "This Administration is already [so] loaded down with such a heavy burden of demonstrable blundering, that I have no appetite for more fault-finding.'' Then Frankfurter catalogued his opposition to the RFC provisions: the issuance of bonds for the relief of financial institutions; a bill that was founded in psychology rather than in finance; the ''bolstering up false values . . . by shoveling out government money.'' When Lippmann responded that he still liked the idea of the RFC and its chairman, Eugene Meyer, Frankfurter replied obscurely that ''the government will hold the bag. . . . You know as well as I do that our financial institutions . . . are loaded with cats and dogs.'' On top of it all, Frankfurter was incredulous that the $2 billion in bonds would be immune from taxation. Frankfurter kept up the pressure. In the coming months, Lippmann's support of Hoover would falter, probably more because of time and events than because of Frankfurter's badgering.[19] Lippmann no longer called his president ''a considerable fellow,'' as he had eighteen months before. Now the nation and Congress would face the tax issue and the end of the ''kissing bee.''

Herbert Stein, chairman of Richard Nixon's Council of Economic Advisors, looked back upon Hoover as a fiscalist in the White House. In addition to Hoover's 1930 public-works and tax-reduction endeavors to stimulate the economy, his presidency was not averse to public borrowing and deficit spending in an attempt to end the depression. Hoover drew the analogy between fighting a war and fighting a depression and the need for borrowing in order to do both. He continued to be of that mind as economic conditions worsened in late 1931. Then he changed his thinking. To avoid further increasing the federal deficit, he recommended tax increases to the Seventy-second Congress when it convened in December. Stein has surmised that the tax increase was part of the program to save the dollar, which was being threatened by an external gold flow that was caused by England's going off the gold standard on 21 September 1931—a condition that caused investors here and abroad to assume that the United States would follow suit. Perhaps the president's advisers, Secretary of State Henry L. Stimson and Treasury aides Ogden Mills and Arthur A. Ballantine, persuaded him to recommend the tax increase. They argued that although the budget could not be balanced under any circumstances in 1933, new taxes should be levied ''as an educational instrument so that [the president] could get the minds of the people behind solid finances.''[20] Along the same line, Walter Lippmann wrote: ''The first duty of the government, then, is to show that it has the courage to draw upon the resources of the people. If it has not that courage, its credit is at once impaired, for it is then demonstrating that it is not willing to place all the resources of the nation behind its obligations."[21]

Hoover read Lippmann's columns. Indeed, practically all whom Hoover listened to or read agreed that an increase in taxes was needed in order to make up for the nearly 40 percent loss of federal revenues after the stock-market crash. There were exceptions, such as William T. Foster and Waddill Catchings, two prominent economists who had long advocated massive spending on the part of the public sector. A more recent exception was Professor E. R. A. Seligman of Columbia University, who, in Undersecretary of the Treasury Ogden Mills's presence at a New York City forum, argued for more borrowing and less tax increase than the administration proposed in December 1931. Mills partially agreed with Seligman, noting that the budget could not be balanced for twenty-four months, during which time the government would borrow $313 million by selling bonds. A more pointed criticism of the administration was that it had not balanced the budget sooner. Felix Frankfurter wrote to Walter Lippmann that "the financial advisors of the administration were urged . . . a year and a half ago to plan to balance the budget by heavier taxes."[22]

Frankfurter wanted a tax increase on his terms, which meant higher taxes at the higher-income brackets and certainly not a regressive sales tax. So, in December 1931, the big question was this: Who should be taxed more? It was a tricky economic problem, for Mills had correctly observed that taxes "should not be so great as to retard business recovery, upon which restoration of the normal flow of revenue depends." The Treasury undersecretary's outline of the administration's position seemed to be acceptable when it was presented to the prestigious Economic Club of New York: an increase in the graduated income tax from $1\frac{1}{2}$, 3, and 5 percent, respectively, to 2, 4, and 6 percent; a reduction of personal exemptions from $3,500 to $2,500; an increase of existing surtaxes of 20 percent on incomes over $100,000 to a graduated surtax from 37 to 40 percent; an increase in corporation taxes by one-half of one percent; an increase of taxes on estates and stock transfers; and certain excise taxes, such as one on tobacco. Startling to historians might be the remark made to the Economic Club by the revered and eminent economist Richard T. Ely, who praised the proposed tax program "because it does spread out the burden, reaching down to lower income groups."[23] Lippmann also felt that lower-income Americans should be taxed, and even Frankfurter agreed "to some extent," although the latter felt, in terms of his own income, that he should pay more. "I feel as though I'm living on a graft," wrote Frankfurter.[24]

While Americans such as Lippmann, Frankfurter, and Richard Ely were not reluctant to see lower-income Americans assume more tax responsibility, many of them were affronted by a turn of events in the Ways and Means Committee of the Democratic House of Representatives. On 7 March 1932 the committee voted 24 to 1 to secure one-half of the revenue measure from a two-and-one-half-percent manufacturers' sales tax and the remaining half from income, corporate, and excise taxes. While the president was developing his more conventional tax-increase program during the fall of 1931, congressional conservatives opted for the sales tax. The new tax form had caught on in many southern states during the 1920s and now seemed to them to be the most painless way of securing needed revenue without taxing people in upper-income levels, whose investments were needed to stimulate the economy. And Ogden Mills was not unhappy with the Democrats' sales-tax proposal. Mills, of course, frequently showed conservative stripes, as evidenced by his "fast friendship" with Speaker Garner and his intense interest in a balanced budget. But Mills's influence with Garner and the acting chairman of the Ways and Means Committee, Charles Crisp, was minimal as compared to the force of Democratic patriarchs like Bernard Baruch, who lobbied in many important quarters for the sales tax.

What appears to have been a conservative southern cause in the Ways and Means Committee spawned a southern opponent. The one dissenter in the final Ways and Means 24 to 1 vote was an unobtrusive congressman from North Carolina, Robert L. Doughton, whose rather courageous opposition inspired an alliance of liberal Democrats and insurgent Republicans to beat the measure on the floor of the house.

Ogden Mills, now secretary of the Treasury, did support the Ways and Means revenue package of $1.245 million, which included the two-and-one-half-percent sales tax, and he urged that the cabinet also support it. The president agreed to support it, provided "that there would be no tax on staple food or cheaper clothing." House Democratic leaders thought they could contain the insurgent Republicans and liberal Democrats, but what started as a skirmish against the sales tax eventually became a war. Representative Fiorello H. La Guardia, Mills's ideological Republican opponent from New York, led the eastern insurgents in their fight against the sales tax. He wrote to Ogden Mills, wondering how he could square his December tax program without the sales tax, which he presented to the New York Economic Club, with his March 12 statement in support of the sales tax. It was easy for Mills, who wrote: "In the first [speech] I stated the means [by] which I preferred to meet the present emergency. In the second, I stated that the means proposed [at that time] by a practically unanimous vote of the Ways and Means Committee was acceptable. There was no inconsistency. The main objective is a balanced budget.''[25] Mills did not like La Guardia, especially when the latter tried to compensate for eliminating the sales tax by increasing the surtax to 65 percent.

Hoover's fortunes turned. Whereas two months previously the president had been having his way with the Congress, now he was identified with sales-tax supporters who blossomed overnight in the public view as conservative ogres. Once Hoover had committed himself, he typically stayed with it to defeat. But the Revenue Act that he ultimately signed increased the surtax to 55 percent, raised corporation taxes three-fourths of 1 percent, increased estate taxes to 45 percent, and placed an excise tax on certain items. It contained no manufacturers' sales tax. New revenues were expected to exceed $1 billion.

The tax rebellion had profound effects on the political leadership of both parties. John Nance Garner, in spite of all of his support from important conservative Democrats such as Bernard Baruch and William Randolph Hearst, never recovered from the defeat in the House. His chances for presidential nomination were irreparably damaged. Hoover had probably been badly advised by Ogden Mills, on whom he was then relying most heavily. And while Lippmann did not support the sales tax, it did not become a matter of conscience for him until Frankfurter described the fight against the tax as ''one of the basic social issues'' of the day.[26] The dean of columnists might have begun his very slow trek to the liberal Democrats on the day when he heard Frankfurter's opinion about the tax. Hoover as president probably would have survived the sales-tax defeat had it not been compounded by more serious challenges, particularly the matter of relief and the Great Bonus March.

When Hoover increased taxes by signing the Revenue Act on June 7, he strove for what the majority of Americans then supported—a balanced budget. He knew that it would not be balanced, a fact that bothered him less than it would have bothered Andrew Mellon, had he still been secretary of the Treasury. Ogden Mills had told the Economic Club of New York that by the end of 1933 there would be a $1.5 billion deficit. But both Hoover and Mills strove for a balanced budget. In addition to tax increases to obtain a balanced budget eventually, they would effect economies in government, although, here again, the president was not as demanding as were some of his advisers and critics. Bernard Baruch, who was both an adviser and a critic, carried on a disagreeable correspondence with Hoover, insisting that the president cut $500 million from the budget's so-called fixed charges of $1.4 billion. Baruch wrote that the nation had spent fewer than $1 billion on such charges before 1929. "I am sure we need not apprehend jail deliveries and half-strength armament on that minimum for 1933."[27] However, Hoover had to run a government and had to ward off "meat-ax" suggestions such as Baruch's. Nevada's Senator Tasker L. Oddie wanted a 10 percent cut in the number of federal employees, which Mills said would mean dismissing thirteen hundred deputy collectors of revenue, who would be needed to collect the new taxes just passed by Congress. Ten percent seemed to be a magic figure. Speaker Garner said that $400 million could be saved by a 10 percent cut across the board, but he forgot that the debt and veterans' services were mandated by law. Interior Secretary Wilbur "cut" costs thoughtfully and valiantly in his department, only to have his problems "multiplied by the arbitrary and inconsiderate nature of [congressional] reductions," particularly those according to the "McKellar 10% rule," which were named for Tennessee's tough Kenneth McKellar of the Senate Appropriations Committee.[28] When the president did send up a budget reduction of $369 million, the House of Representatives accepted only $98 million of it. Hoover thought that some savings in the executive branch could be carried out by some administrative organization, but Garner said that that was a legislative responsibility. On economy matters, testiness became the order of the day. When some senators wanted the Atlantic Fleet, which was carrying out exercises off the West Coast, to divide its time between the North and the South Pacific Ocean and to visit Hawaii, the president rejected the idea if it would cost "an additional dime."[29]

While the federal government in the spring of 1932 was squabbling over economy in government, general unemployment approached 23 percent, and attendant harsh conditions were affecting more and more Americans. Studs Terkel's *Hard Times* vividly describes 1932 as having been the real beginning of the depression—especially in the blighted areas of the urban cities and the most depressed agricultural sections of the nation. To people in such areas, the president's "remedial" program, which was submitted to Congress on 8 December 1931, had not been very remedial. To them the title seemed to be a misnomer.

The president had expected the Reconstruction Finance Corporation to utilize its available $2 billion to infuse banks, railroads, and building-and-loan organizations with plentiful credit. The credit, in turn, was supposed to induce a massive commercial lending and borrowing by capital investors to start up a productivity that would employ people who would buy the goods and services that were necessary in order to stimulate the economy. But this turn of events did not materialize. The new corporation, which Hoover turned to because of the cautiousness of the Federal Reserve System, became comparably circumspect about lending its money. Whereas bankers always preferred a liquid position to a risky lending position, the RFC, which was run by bankers, could not break the habit. In loaning out its money, it went rigidly by the law, insisting on heavy collateral for all "fully secured" loans and on the repayment of loans within six months. What financial institutions and railroads needed were unusually long-term loans and new capital in the economy (not money that was secured by the purchase of RFC bonds). Of course, there was some justification in the RFC's fear that if its money were lent out too easily, the corporation would be competing with private loans and would therefore impede the recovery of the banking industry. The RFC did serve the purpose of saving many businesses from failure in February and March of 1932, during which time 160 banks, 60 railroads, and 18 building-and-loan organizations received a total of $238 million. By sustaining outstanding loans, many businesses and jobs were saved. Thus, the economy was kept from worsening for a while—no small achievement for the RFC. However, enabling banks to liquefy their position did not stimulate the commercial lending, as Hoover had wanted.[30]

So, the economy continued its descent. The unemployed and their spokesmen became vociferous in their criticism of the RFC. They saw money going to "plutocrats." Their increasing criticism, particularly in the press and in Congress, was fanned not only by general economic conditions but also by particular factors, such as a $5.85-million loan to the Missouri-Pacific Railroad and an ideological split on the board of the RFC—a conservative Republican wing, which favored loans such as that to the Missouri-Pacific Railroad, and a liberal Democratic wing, which believed that smaller financial institutions were being discriminated against. The elitist Federal Reserve System was paradoxical in its criticism. On the one hand it accused the RFC of being too "tight fisted," but, on the other hand, of loaning money so freely as to cut into their banking responsibility. By late spring, Hoover was very downcast over the RFC's inability to increase commercial lending and by the inability of the Federal Reserve System to do the same. No little problem for the president—a public relations one—was the RFC's loan of $90 million to its president, Charles Dawes, who was also president of Chicago's important Central Republic Bank and Trust Company.

James Olson notes that with the failure of the RFC, Hoover, in the late spring of 1932, turned somewhat to the left, and soon thereafter, on July 21, he signed the nation's first massive-relief legislation, the Emergency Relief and Construction Act of 1932. The evolution of events that led to the signing of the act is revealing of the president's character and the running of his office.

Even before the president had signed the RFC Act in February, some members of Congress, of various ideological persuasions, had been seeking more direct public-work relief for the unemployed. A pair of liberal senators—Democrat Edward P. Costigan and Republican Robert M. La Follette, Jr.—had introduced a bill in December which provided for an appropriation of $375 million for direct aid to the states. It was defeated in February. Shortly thereafter, three Democrats—Hugo L. Black, Thomas J. Walsh, and Robert J. Bulkley, the latter a conservative—introduced a bill providing the same amount of relief assistance, but in the form of loans rather than grants. It was defeated, to be followed by a bill of New York's liberal Democratic senator, Robert Wagner, which made the loan assistance more palatable by assuring conservative senators that the loans, if necessary, would be paid back from federal highway appropriations, commencing in 1937. That failed, and out of desperation, Wagner, in March, threw into the Senate hopper a $1.1-billion appropriation bill to be supported by federal bonds—a procedure that was not acceptable to almost the whole senate. Edward Costigan, in May, came back with a bill for $500 million in bonds to be supported by grants-in-aid to the states, which was as unacceptable as the previous bond-supported bill.

The objections to these bills were obvious to most economic and political leaders. Federally appropriated congressional measures would unbalance the budget even further, and measures that were federally bonded would increase the federal debt. Either of these actions would shake confidence in the federal government, which had already been hurt by a currency that was being threatened by an outflow of gold which was needed to support it. Walter Lippmann noted that what was at stake was "a struggle to preserve the credit of the United States by demonstrating that the government is in command. . . . The government must exercise its sovereignty."[31]

Relief resources of states, cities, and charities were being rapidly depleted in late spring, as capital refused to borrow in order to invest in productivity and as Congress voted down relief measures. New York's former Governor Alfred E. Smith blamed the president for overlooking "the need of finding immediate productive employment for millions of people." Lippmann chided Smith, insisting, first, that Hoover was quite "as sincere" and as "persistent" in trying to restore employment as "any man living" and, second, that the problem "has to do with recovery and not with relief." In his various newspaper columns, Lippmann noted that hundreds of millions of dollars had been spent on relief since the crash, but to no avail. If $2 billion were to have been appropriated immediately, it would have provided employment for less than 10 percent of the estimated unemployed. It would not have been worth the extreme threat to the credit of an already burdened economy. Yet Lippmann recognized that the nation could not "rest in an attitude of negation." He commended to his readers the ideas of Bernard Baruch, Senate Democratic leader Joseph Robinson, and the president— namely, that federally bonded relief programs be limited to self-liquidating projects. Baruch suggested to Robinson, for example, that money be loaned for the construction of a self-supporting toll tunnel under the East River between Manhattan and Long Island. The president already had suggested that federally bonded support be provided for sound businesses that would be assured of sufficient profits to pay back such loans.[32]

A critical network of important political thinkers and activists was evolving around some form of direct relief. The Emporia, Kansas, editor William Allen White, who was close both to the president and to western insurgents, urged Lippmann on his course of deliberation, stressing at the same time the fundamental need for "a redistribution of wealth."[33] Frankfurter, like Lippmann, agreed that it was time to move " 'the loaded ass' [a]cross the torrent," but he was skeptical of "our leaders" and their "panaceas."[34] Senate Democratic leader Robinson wrote to Bernard Baruch that he would compromise to get action, even though "the president bitterly opposes the incorporation of any funds for public works."[35]

The president now was constantly being engrossed in the quest for some kind of public-works relief. When his loyal American Society of Civil Engineers suggested to him "a large issue of federal government bonds to finance a new program of huge expansion of 'public works' construction," he answered with a litany of all his antidepression efforts, past and present. He repeated further his opposition to the kind of massive public works that they proposed: they would only be of "remote usefulness"; they would be great "burdens upon the taxpayer"; they would unbalance the budget; and they would demoralize government credit. Still, after six single-spaced pages, Hoover concluded: "A larger and far more effective relief to unemployment at this stage can be secured by increased aid to 'income-producing works.' I wish to emphasize this distinction between what for purposes of this discussion we may term 'income-producing works' (also referred to as 'self-liquidating works') on the one hand and non-productive 'public works' on the other."[36]

It was not easy to move Frankfurter's so-called loaded ass across the torrent. From mid May through mid July the White House and the Congress went back and forth in producing the first of the nation's massive relief measures, the principal thread being a $1.5-billion federally bonded program of state-aid relief, which would be based on self-liquidating public works. There were tensions and snags along the way—as when Speaker Garner threw into the House hopper a $2.2-billion relief program, one-half for non-self-liquidating public works, the other half in the form of RFC loans to states, cities, businesses, and individuals. Hoover was appalled by what he considered to be Garner's reckless measure, and even though Congress and the White House seemed to agree on a bill of many compromises, the president vetoed it because the aid to states was based on population and not on need, but also and more important because it contained a Garner provision that unlimited RFC loans not be secured with collateral. The bill that the president signed on July 21 provided for the $1.5 billion for public construction of income-producing projects; $300 million in loans to states for direct relief (reimbursable from 1935 federal highway appropriations); and $200 million to assist in liquidating closed banks. Speaker Garner further angered the president with a provision that all RFC loans be made public, an action that Hoover feared would undermine depositor confidence in any bank that received a loan. The bill was path breaking and might have boded well for the relief of the unemployed had the depression not been descending so rapidly and had the nation not been thrown into a great national election, in which the depression was the critical issue.

Before assessing the election of 1932 and its aftermath, it is essential to examine the foreign policy of the Hoover presidency, which affected the nation as surely as domestic policy, although far less obviously at the time.

9

★ ★ ★ ★ ★

FOREIGN POLICY

For a half-century after his presidency, Hoover's foreign policy was generally explained as a combination of the influence of Quaker pacifism, the rising tide of depression, and the overriding strength of his secretary of state, Henry L. Stimson. From such assumptions it seemed to follow that Hoover's Quakerism inclined the president toward isolationism; that the depression so absorbed him that he gave foreign policy only limited attention, and that Stimson usually made foreign policy. Such conclusions are simplistic generalities that miss the mark widely.

George Fox, the founder of Quakerism, did say that Friends would never "fight any war against any man with outward weapons, neither for the Kingdom of Christ, nor for the kingdoms of this world."[1] Such was a heavy charge laid on Quakers, including those in the milieu of Hoover's "education." Hoover's valiant efforts for peace before and during his presidency were undoubtedly influenced by the Quaker tenet. (Stimson frequently thought they were.) But some Quakers have supported war, as did Hoover during World War I. Hoover was no pacifist. Perhaps his shift from sectarian to secular Quakerism worked to remove any strong pacifist inhibitions. Quaker influence on Hoover's foreign policy does become important when one sees in his thought and life a combination of both the Friends' penchant for peace and their consistent search for orderliness "everywhere."[2] Although the "ordered freedom" of Quakers impressed Hoover far more than did pacifism, for him the latter tenet seems to have affected the former.

Hoover believed, for example, that the real force for peace and order was moral, not military. Indeed, he would lend his good offices during his presidency to effect more disarmament than had his predecessors. He expected to succeed. "It seems to me," he wrote to his new secretary of state, "that there is the most profound outlook for peace today that we have had at any time in the last half century."[3]

Without question, the depression did affect Hoover's foreign policy. It was, after all, one of the world's most disturbing events since the industrial revolution of the late eighteenth century. Until the Great Depression the Western world assumed that its nations would move from strength to strength. But, as Robert H. Ferrell points out, during the twentieth century the West lost its "classical reckoning." Adam Smith, the patron saint of the free and vigorous trade that so strengthened the Western nations during the Pax Britannica of the nineteenth century, would have been shocked by the nationalistic turn of economic and political events.

Hoover, in late 1930, came to see the selfish interests of Western nations as the primary cause of the world-wide depression and, as we shall see, attempted to find international solutions, such as a moratorium on foreign debts and the planning of a great economic conference of Western nations to effect international economic stability. At times, even Hoover sought nationalistic solutions. More often than not, however, he hewed to an internationalism that was consistent with his Wilsonian experience. Nor did the depression so absorb him with domestic crises that he left the making of foreign policy to Secretary of State Stimson. Hoover was a strong president. Throughout his term he made foreign policy.

Herbert Hoover was well equipped to direct American foreign policy. It has been said that probably no American president since John Quincy Adams had had as much experience on the foreign scene before becoming president. His mining experiences had made him knowledgeable about world affairs. He entered public life by providing food for war-ravaged people in much of Europe. It will be recalled that John Maynard Keynes commented that Hoover was the one statesman who came out of the Versailles proceedings with his reputation enhanced. As secretary of commerce during the 1920s he had become highly involved in international economic matters and other areas of foreign policy, including the Washington Arms Conference and the fight for United States participation in the World Court. After his election in 1928 he traveled extensively in South America, designing his administration's foreign policy for that area of the world. Such experiences did not always make Herbert Hoover an internationalist. Indeed, his belief in protective tariffs, his distrust of Europe, and his support of immigration restriction showed a nationalist, even an isolationist, coloration.[4] But, on balance, he practiced what Joan Hoff-Wilson has described as an "independent internationalism,"[5] a position that he, not his secretary of state, imposed upon his administration.

Still, Hoover's secretary of state, Henry L. Stimson, was far more forceful than were most others who have held that high office. He did influence foreign policy strongly. What was fascinating was to see such strong men as Hoover and Stimson work in tandem. Their personalities were in such juxtaposition as to warrant a digression here in order to examine the relationship, not only because they often conferred and frequently vied in making foreign policy but also because the personality of the aristocrat Stimson is a foil for understanding the character of Hoover, the Quaker.

Henry L. Stimson's family lines ran back to the Massachusetts Bay Colony of the early seventeenth century and evolved to an aristocratic status two centuries later that afforded "Harry" all of its privileges and responsibilities. The former included education, travel, and associations that assured Stimson of having tremendous competence and self-confidence regarding what he thought and what he did. The responsibilities of class, a spirit of noblesse oblige, caused Stimson, as a brilliant young attorney in a prestigious law firm, to avoid "the green goods business" (i.e., big corporations and large fees) and instead to engage in public duties. In the performance of public duties he worked his way up to a seat on the powerful New York County Republican Committee and then, respectively, to the offices of United States attorney for the Southern District of New York, secretary of war, governor general of the Philippine Islands, and secretary of state. In periods between holding these various offices he returned to the private practice of law, always, however, with an eye to his next public service. Sometimes he failed, as when he lost the New York governorship race in 1910. Without exception, however, he seemed to learn. He came to the Hoover administration very wise politically and more self-assured than ever, two attributes that the president seemed to lack most.

Vignettes extracted from Stimson's lengthy diaries of the Hoover presidency years offer an insightful contrast of personalities between the secretary of state and the president. For example, the secretary very early in the administration enjoyed joshing with the "press boys," and after heavy cross-examination, he usually brought them "in line again." Later in the administration, when the "press boys" did not, for various reasons, get the story straight, the secretary frequently took the senior reporters aside and got them to understand the situation. Where

Stimson got away with playing favorites, Hoover did not. The secretary continued to meet with all reporters down in the State Department, but the president met less and less often with the press.

Stimson was spirited and enjoyed the ironies of life. He had a strong sense of humor. Hoover was frequently dispirited, usually oblivious to ironies, and seldom showed his humor. The president's way, rather than the secretary's, dominated the administration, though. In his diary the secretary constantly deplored the humorlessness in the administration. In October 1930, he wrote: "It has been dreadfully dull and stale, nothing but work, no play . . . and the ever present feeling of gloom. . . . I really never knew such unenlivened occasions as our cabinet meetings. . . . I don't remember that there has even been a joke cracked in a single meeting of the last year and a half."[6]

Stimson often enjoyed sports. Very frequently, in midafternoon, he would return to his palatial home, Woodley, in northwest Washington, for a choice of sports: tennis, horseback riding, bowling, golf, deck tennis, "bowling on the green," or if not a sport, an automobile ride through the countryside. He often commented on his scores in his various athletic activities. Stimson seemed to be so often absent from the State Department that the president often thought that Stimson was ill. On the other hand, Stimson wished that the president would enjoy recreation as much as he did. The president threw a heavy leather medicine ball every morning, but for physical conditioning, not for pleasure. Hoover did enjoy fishing immensely. However, the sternness and insecurities of his childhood, quite in contrast to Stimson's, appeared to affect his ability to relax, even when fishing. Frequently, when he was at Rapidan, rather than fish, he would slosh through mud and water carrying rocks to "build" a dam. Even when he played, which was seldom, he seemed to be compelled to work.

The secretary of state accepted the challenge of his task day by day. World events, he felt, could not be planned and had to be met as they unfolded. He rather believed the same about domestic affairs. He thought that Hoover planned the impossible: for example, the president planned what Congress should do. However, the actions of such senators as William E. Borah were beyond planning. When Borah opposed the president on an issue, Hoover saw a conspiracy and thought that the Idaho senator was "bitter" toward him. Stimson, who was as different from the "wild jackass" Borah as he was from the Quaker president, cultivated the senator, who happened to be the chairman of the Foreign Relations Committee. Borah and Stimson grew to like each other; Borah and Hoover grew to dislike each other. Yet in 1931, when Borah and other senators kept urging the president to call a special session of Congress, Stimson suggested that Hoover tell them to "go to hell." The president was shocked.[7]

Unlike Hoover, Stimson was not inclined to harbor ill feelings. To the same person, Stimson could express wrath one day and sincere congeniality the next day. Stimson, from his class position, could be confidently patronizing. He would speak of Andrew Mellon as "childlike" and Hoover as the "poor old president." Hoover, who had been born to poverty, lacked the class position and self-assurance to be condescending, despite his later wealth. The secretary of state knew when not to "strong arm" or "push" too hard, and he frequently advised the president not to so treat, for example, the French on the moratorium, the Japanese on Manchuria, and even Governor Franklin Roosevelt on the St. Lawrence Seaway.

Stimson had a sense of constructive optimism; Hoover had a knack for destructive pessimism. Stimson often wished that the president would see the bright side—the potential for productive action. Yet the bright side that the secretary of state usually saw did not blind him to the reality of the moment. He thought that the president was too frequently unrealistic, as when Hoover laid out the ten American points to be established at the 1932 disarmament conference, which seemed to Stimson to be a Quakerly "Alice in Wonderland" position.

Stimson was often charming, while Hoover was frequently the opposite—terse. Stimson could be short, but his short-temperedness seemed to be more acceptable than Hoover's. The secretary recovered quickly, whereas the president brooded. What is revealing is that Stimson could be blunt with the president. When Hoover excitedly phoned the secretary to put out an anti-English and anti-French statement when they had procrastinated on the debts that they owed to the United States, Stimson said that he would talk to Secretary of the Treasury Ogden Mills about it, and then quickly hung up. When, on another occasion, Hoover expressed displeasure at a Stimson *aide-mémoire* on a statement by Benito Mussolini that might have had an adverse effect on relations with Germany, the secretary noted in his diary that "I finally took the paper away and told him that at this rate I would have to declare a moratorium on foreign affairs."[8]

Actually, Hoover and Stimson complemented each other to the benefit of the nation's foreign policy. The implicit tension in the relationship was usually salutary. One observer concluded: "It is doubtful whether any statesman could have built better with the materials which were available than did Secretary of State Henry L. Stimson." And the author of that conclusion does not include Hoover among difficult "materials" with which Stimson worked. The president's knowledge, experience, and commitment earned the secretary's respect and affection—even though Stimson would one day serve Hoover's Democratic successor. This leads to one final difference in personalities. Stimson was eclectic; Hoover was not. Stimson did serve well as Franklin Roosevelt's secretary of war. Hoover seems later not to have forgiven his former secretary of state for joining the administration of his successor. In 1948, when Hoover read the account of Stimson from which the above conclusions are drawn, the former president described it as another "build-up for Stimson." Hoover came to regret that he had not made Charles Francis Adams his secretary of state.[9]

On 5 October 1929, Hoover and the British prime minister, Ramsay MacDonald, sat on a log in a secluded area down the hill from the president's summer camp, Rapidan. They were messengers of peace. There they discussed what the *New York Times* on the previous day had predicted would be "a momentous undertaking," to "clothe" the Kellogg-Briand (war-renouncing) Pact of 1928 in such a way as not just to outlaw war between great nations but actually to eliminate it.[10] A decade later, World War II would erupt.

The meeting of the two statesmen was not as naïve as it appears from the perspective of history. Stimson, who hovered over the discourse, agreed with the president that rationality and order should reign. Certainly if he, Stimson, could bring order to primitive areas of Nicaragua and the Philippine Islands, as he thought he had effectively done during the 1920s, he could do the same between great civilized nations. The secretary of state was confident that what Charles Evans Hughes had gained in the limitation of capital naval ships at the Washington Arms Conference in 1922, he (Stimson) could achieve for auxiliary ships in a forthcoming conference of the great sea powers. It mattered not that the Coolidge administration had failed to achieve such a limitation in 1927. The Quaker president, who had particularly enjoyed addressing foreign problems before being burdened by the depression, interested himself in disarmament causes: they are moral causes. The British, who are not prone to move with dispatch, especially in foreign affairs, became particularly serious about naval limitation when the United States Congress, in 1928, passed the Cruiser bill, which provided for the completion of fifteen heavily armed ships and an aircraft carrier. The British were hurting more financially than was the United States. Therefore, the new Labour prime minister had asked for an invitation to the White House and had come quickly to the United States to plan another attempt at naval disarmament.

It was a brilliant autumn day—the view and the colors from the Blue Ridge Mountain top were kaleidoscopic. In the rough garb of the camp, the prime minister and the president walked briskly to the clearing, with Hoover occasionally pointing to natural curiosities along the mountain-stream path. The prime minister was amused by one unnatural phenomenon, a small Stimson "fish-sunning" dam, built by the hands of the secretary on a former recreational outing to the camp. In the clearing the leaders discussed the possibilities of placing a limitation on naval auxiliary ships, freedom of the seas in time of war, the presence of the British navy in the Western Hemisphere, and even the smuggling of liquor from the British possessions into the United States, which was a problem during prohibition.

In reality, however, little of substance came from this highly publicized meeting. Few of the items on the agenda were consummated. More significant than that was the absence of any thorny items of importance, such as America's nonparticipation in the World Court, the protective United States tariff, and the war debts owed to the United States. A surfacing nationalism, as much on the part of the United States as Great Britain, precluded discussion of these matters. In this instance, however, style might have been more important than substance. The British prime minister was warmly received everywhere—down Broadway in New York, in the halls of Congress, at the White House, and, of course, in the Virginia mountains. The good will between the two English-speaking nations, as manifested by Hoover and MacDonald, was a presage of alliance in the war that was to come in the late 1930s.

Hoover and MacDonald, at the Rapidan meeting, did plan to do everything possible to bring together the "Big Five" naval nations—the United States, Great Britain, Japan, France, and Italy—and to show good faith by appointing as delegates the best of their public and diplomatic servants. The president was determined not to repeat the grievous error of 1927, when Coolidge had sent second-rate delegates to the Geneva Naval Limitations Conference. Stimson therefore headed the United States delegation to the subsequent London Naval Conference. He was accompanied by Senate Democratic leader Joseph T. Robinson; Pennsylvania Senator David Reed, an influential Republican; Dwight W. Morrow, a highly regarded Republican and lately successful ambassador to Mexico; Navy Secretary Charles F. Adams, a descendant of former presidents; the United States ambassador to Belgium, Hugh Gibson, a confidant of the president's; and the inimitable Charles G. Dawes, ambassador to the Court of St. James's. The presence of the United States delegation was matched by a combination of British political and royal elite. No less a personage than King George V himself opened the proceedings in the awesome historical setting of the House of Lords. After His Majesty's greetings, which were heard by radio in faraway places, including the basement of the White House, where members of the medicine-ball cabinet listened in gym clothes, Secretary Stimson moved that MacDonald be elected as permanent chairman of the conference. It was, again, however, a matter of style over substance.

As contrasted to the prime minister's meeting with the president in the United States, where style had effect, both style and substance in London seemed to be lacking. As is probably true in all international conclaves where the actuality of danger, such as war, is not imminent, the London conference would have few meaningful results. Peace seemed so inevitable as to make disarmament unnecessary. The conference nearly collapsed at the start, surely an early indication to Stimson and Hoover that international relations during their administration might be very difficult. Ramsay MacDonald had predicted as much when he told Ambassador Dawes that experts and lawyers make the reefs on which states founder. But even MacDonald could not have predicted the technical morass that engulfed the conference. It proved to be impossible to extend to all naval vessels the existing tonnage ratios, which had been established for capital ships at the Washington Arms Conference. Simple tonnage was not enough for the experts. What, they asked, of comparative age, speed, armor, and general fighting value of all shapes and sizes of ships? And who knows, without battle experience, what ships would be effective under varying conditions? To begin, the conferees asked themselves how many 9,850-ton British cruisers with 7.5-inch guns it would take to equal the United States' larger 10,000-ton cruisers with 8-inch guns. And whether lighter 6-inch-gun cruisers might not outmaneuver the heavier cruisers! The fact of the matter was that "old sea dogs," who were most influential in the conference, were not interested in naval parity. With their national and professional pride, they looked to future naval victory against all comers, unencumbered by naval limitations.

Secretary Stimson was far too strong a personality to let the "old sea dogs" undo what he and Hoover had dreamed and planned. In typical fashion, he cut through the experts' mystification by writing to France's Premier André Tardieu: "The whole purpose of the appointment of committees is to gain time so that the real issues may be settled by informal discussion outside."[11] The dialogue among political leaders smacked of the experts' confusion. France would not consider the limitation of armaments without having some assurance of security against its traditional enemy, Germany, and the threatening enemy, Mussolini's Italy. The United States, Great Britain, and France engaged in long discussions over European security as assured by the League of Nations Covenant, the Four Power Treaty of the Washington Arms Conference, the Kellogg-Briand Pact, and the Five-Power Locarno Treaty, but never to the satisfaction of the French. All nations that were represented in London were, of course, constrained by political situations at home. Actually, Stimson favored a security arrangement with France but knew that the Senate would never agree to such a treaty arrangement. He then told France's Foreign Minister Aristide Briand, who frequently walked out of meetings in a huff, that he would support a "consultative pact" if it were not tied to the Naval Limitations Treaty. But not unlike the hawkish-dovish differences between Stimson and Hoover on the upcoming Manchurian crisis, Hoover vetoed the idea of a "consultative pact" that might morally commit the United States to defend France, if the latter were attacked. The British were about as cool toward any French special-security arrangements at the London Naval Conference as were the Americans. When that fact became readily apparent, the French left the conference, and Stimson reconciled himself to a three-power naval agreement among Great Britain, the United States, and Japan. At this point the secretary was tiring of the ordeal and wished he were back at Woodley, his Washington estate.

Secretary Stimson's next major problem at the London Naval Conference, which was only slightly better handled, was Japan's insistence that the ratio for auxiliary ships give her a higher standing than that accorded to her in the Washington Arms Conference's 5:5:3 ratio of capital ships. After considerable haggling, in which the American delegate, Senator David Reed, played an important part, England and the United States agreed to a cruiser ratio of 10:10:6 in principle, which was in fact closer to a 10:10:7 ratio. In addition, the United States agreed not to build up to the London-allotted strength until after 1936, at the same time permitting Japan to construct a total of twelve heavy cruisers (which would give Japan a 72 percent ratio in all small cruisers and destroyers) and parity with the United States and Great Britain in submarines. Unfortunately, the military atmosphere at home in Japan rendered its people sufficiently humiliated by the agreements that, in the long run, the conference might not have been worth the British and American efforts.

Italy's role in the London Naval Conference was a less significant problem to Stimson and Hoover. Italy's enmity toward France had been such that Italy had left the conference. Hoover now tired of haggling and was eager to get provisions that would be confirmed by the United States Senate. These were: extension of the capital-ship holiday to 1936; an "escalator clause," which would permit the United States to exceed the ratio if other powers did so; limitation of the 10:10:7 tonnage levels until 1936; a series of agreements on various ship replacements and conversions. Not surprisingly, the Senate procrastinated on its agreement but finally yielded on 21 July 1930, 58 to 9. The conference seemed in many respects to have been a failure. Still, for the first time, modern naval forces had consented to restrictions in all classifications of ships.

The centerpiece of any chapter on Hoover's foreign policy, for several reasons, is the Stimson Doctrine. For one, New Left revisionists, decades later, would applaud Hoover for restraining his secretary of state and for staying out of a Far Eastern war. Second, the event characterized distinctly the streams of noninterventionist and interventionist foreign policy, the former being reflected by the strong-minded president, the latter by an equally strong-minded, though deferential, secretary of state. Third, the story of the doctrine provides another account of the personality differences between Hoover and Stimson. Last, it reveals the important relationship of Hoover foreign policy to the immediate past and future—the past of the Washington and other treaties and the future of Japan's attack on Pearl Harbor.

The setting for the Stimson doctrine of nonrecognition (of the Japanese puppet Manchukuo government) was Manchuria, an agriculturally and resource-rich part of northern China, where both Russia and Japan had treaty rights and considerable economic interests. The beginning of the crisis came early in the Hoover presidency, when in July 1929 China proceeded to dislodge the Russians by taking over the Soviet-dominated Central Eastern Railway, which traversed Manchuria from the USSR on the west to the Russian port city of Vladivostok on the Sea of Japan. It was an adventure of the Chinese leader Chiang Kai-shek, who sought a show of power that, even if unsuccessful, might well eliminate a political adversary, the "Young Marshal" Chang Hsueh-liang, the Chinese warlord of Manchuria. While this distant activity was not bothersome to much of the rest of the world, it was to the new American secretary of state, fresh from his Far Eastern tour as governor general of the Philippines. He felt that something should be done to prevent a possible war between two adherents to the Kellogg-Briand Peace Pact, which was to be formally proclaimed in the East Room of the White House on 24 July 1929.

Of the three treaties that Stimson considered using in the Far Eastern crisis—the Nine Power (Washington) Pact of 1922, the Kellogg-Briand Pact of 1928, and the League of Nations Covenant—Russia was not a signatory to the first, and the United States was not to the last. So if Stimson were to act, he would have to use the new Kellogg nonaggression pact. In fact, it was the best choice, being the most thoroughgoing commitment to peace that had ever been made by great powers. The secretary moved with dispatch in mid July by getting important signatory nations to call for a peace in Manchuria that would be consonant with the pact. On the day after the United States formally proclaimed the pact, the eager secretary proposed that an international commission of conciliation be appointed to arbitrate the matter. Stimson soon learned that his diplomacy was somewhat simplistic ("shirt-sleeved"), when the Japanese ambassador in Washington, Katsuzi Debuchi, wondered what the United States would do if conciliation were rejected. Would it use pressure to enforce the commission's findings?

Secretary Stimson dropped the commission idea, but he did so without really having heard the Japanese ambassador's implied advice against Western meddling in the Far East. When, in the fall of 1929, Russia made border raids on Manchuria, Stimson took a page from one of his eminent predecessors, John M. Hay, and sent messages to the Kellogg-Briand Pact signatories, admonishing China and Russia to adhere to "the most sacred processes" of the Kellogg nonaggression pact. Stimson announced that "the replies were favorable in principle to my proposal." The fact of the matter was that war in Manchuria was not imminent. China and Russia had agreed to a settlement. Stimson, particularly, should have been more responsive to Japan's extreme sensitivity to American "meddling." But the secretary of state and his president, who concurred in the American action, were learning quickly that diplomacy requires caution. It is possible, also, that the matter taught the president something about his secretary of state.

Hoover should have learned that his secretary of state shunned the slowness and subtleties of diplomacy, although Stimson quickly adjusted to the latter, if not the former. And Stimson might have learned from the Sino-Russian conflict that moral suasion in diplomacy has its limitations in implementation and effectiveness. When the second Manchurian crisis between Japan and China developed in 1931, the president, though he was much burdened by the depression, watched over the affair much more closely, for reasons stemming from his experience in the first crisis.

That Hoover directed foreign affairs is seen by the nation's policy toward Japan's takeover of all of Manchuria and by the Stimson Doctrine of Nonrecognition, a policy that clearly should be labeled the Hoover-Stimson Doctrine, principally because of Hoover's restraint on

Stimson and also because Hoover had conceived the idea in the first place.

It was a complicated and important policy-making affair. To begin with, Japan's interests and treaty rights in Manchuria were every bit as important to that island nation as Russia's interests were; in fact, Japan's concerns were the more serious because she viewed Manchuria as a buffer against the Russians. When on the night of 18 September 1931 a small section of Japan's South Manchuria Railway line, north of Mukden, was destroyed, a Japanese patrol shot and killed several Chinese soldiers who were fleeing from the scene. No investigation, then or since, has been able to assign blame for the "missing track." The story of the incident became so confused that some years later, Stimson believed that it had never really happened.

At first, both Hoover and Stimson had little interest in the Mukden incident. In fact, Stimson was disposed to think the best of Japan, for our security in the area seemed to be tied to Japan's stabilizing influence there. When, however, Japanese troops fanned out beyond the railroad area into the Chinese countryside and did not return to the railroad zone, Stimson became anxious, as did the League of Nations, which, differently from what it had done in the first Manchurian affair, now looked to Washington for leadership. China also appealed to the United States, as a cosponsor of the Kellogg Pact, for some sign of support. Stimson, having once been burned by "shirtsleeve" diplomacy, did not act. The president was in agreement. The League of Nations passed a resolution unanimously calling on the contending parties in Manchuria to restore normal relations, but to no avail. Japanese planes were soon bombing the city of Chinchou in southern Manchuria. Now the secretary became agitated at the news and, in Hoover's presence, strongly urged some United States action, which provoked the president to demand caution in the matter. The two agreed on a policy to await League of Nations action, and they did support the league when, in November 1931, it passed a second resolution calling upon Japan to leave the Chinese territory.

Although dangerously simplistic, it is interesting to note somewhat parallel dialogues that took place within the Japanese and United States foreign offices. A long-term dialogue between peace and war factions in Japan resulted in the military's assuming control in 1931, in support of the military control of Manchuria. The dialogue between Hoover and Stimson on Manchuria also marks a difference regarding American reaction to the Manchurian affair. It did so along noninterventionist and activist lines, although the Hoover-Stimson split was mild as compared to the peace-war differences within the Japanese government and, of course, was carried out here in a democratic tradition. The differences between Hoover and Stimson particularly caught the attention of historians during the 1960s as they watched war elements in Washington win out and entrap the nation in another war in the Far East.[12]

Hoover, who was fearful that the nation might become involved in an Asian conflict by taking an untoward action, expressed the view in a cabinet meeting that the League of Nations must not deposit "the baby" (bombing of Chinchou) on "the Americans."[13] Stimson agreed, but mused in his diary about the importance of our own treaty commitments.

In early November the League of Nations in Geneva, and Stimson in Washington, discussed various options to be taken in the Manchurian affair. Stimson wrote in his diary: "An embargo [is] an attempt to put on economic pressure [and the president] ruled it out on the ground that it . . . would be provocative and lead to war. His idea was that we might withdraw an ambassador [from Japan], and, if we did so, he would give out a statement at the same time putting war out of the question, an announcement that we would not under any event go to war and that that was contrary to our present policy and to all treaties and contrary to the view of the world. I concur with him as to the danger of a blockade leading to war. It's almost [as] . . . belligerent [a] step [as] in the case of Jefferson, although the situation there was entirely different in 1807, it did eventually take this country to war."[14]

Two days later, the secretary further reported to his diary: "He [the president] is beginning to swing against the idea of withdrawing the ambassador and thinks his main weapon is to give an announcement that if the treaty is made under military pressure we will not recognize it. . . . This matter I also discussed afterwards with [the staff]. [Far Eastern Affairs chief, Stanley] Hornbeck [said] the remedy didn't amount to anything because we had tried it in 1915. But there the situation was wholly different. . . . Under present situations, particularly if the disavowal is made by all the countries, it ought to have a very potent effect."[15]

The above selections from Stimson's diary for November 7 and 9 are important to understanding two key elements in the relationship between the president and the secretary of state during the course of the Sino-Japanese crisis—namely, that Hoover would not support economic sanctions and that he originally conceived the doctrine of nonrecognition.

Stimson thought over the nonrecognition approach—some experts in the State Department thought it too drastic—but he delayed taking further action, thinking that the Japanese might halt their aggressions or that the League of Nations might take a stronger position. On 2 January 1932 the Japanese occupied the city of Chinchou. Then Stimson acted. After a sleepless night, at 6:00 A.M. on January 3 he went to his library "and wrote out in long hand a short note to the Chinese Government and to the Japanese Government."[16] It was the Stimson Doctrine, which, following discussion of it with his aides and the president, was sent on 7 January 1932. In effect, it said that the United States would not recognize any treaty of agreement that was not in accord with any existing treaties, such as the Kellogg and Nine Power pacts. Short and profound, its origins were in a 1915 State Department action to restrain Japan's demands on China. Actually, it was suggested by Hoover and by Walter Lippmann, in a letter proposing that since "all resort to force is barred to us why not persuade the signatories of the Nine-Power Pact to declare that they should not recognize as legal any agreements which may result from Japanese action since September 18th." Lippmann hoped that nonrecognition would work to Japan's economic disadvantage and that "it would be fair to hope the military party would eventually be overthrown."[17]

It is difficult to determine just when the doctrine came to be called the Stimson Doctrine. Probably it was so named as events moved through January 1932, especially late in the month, when Japan attacked the "old city" of Shanghai, an event that was really not planned by the military in Tokyo. The military action resulted in the death of hundreds of Chinese and angered foreigners in Shanghai, as well as their home governments, including the United States and, especially, Stimson, who became increasingly disenchanted with the Japanese.

By late December 1932 the secretary of state was ready to send naval forces to protect Americans in Shanghai, and at first, the president actually seemed to concur. Secretary of Navy Adams had reservations about such an overt act, and Secretary of War Patrick Jay Hurley, who was usually not reluctant to use military force, sharply questioned Stimson when the secretary of state mentioned to the cabinet "the importance of having Japan fear this country." Hoover, in the cabinet, took a middle position, praising Stimson for the nonrecognition notes but warning of the "folly of getting into a war with Japan on this subject." He wanted no policy of threat. Stimson's diary account that night reflected "the great difference and difficulty" he was having with the president: "He has not got the slightest element of even the fairest kind of bluff."[18]

When the Japanese bombed the civilian quarter of Shanghai and the secretary then talked to the president about the need for "leadership" to avoid Wilson's timid example in 1915, Hoover recoiled and the two clashed. Throughout February, Stimson talked, but mostly mused, about the "Open Door," the Nine-Power Pact, the Kellogg Pact, and other responsibilities that the nation had in the affair. While the divergence between Hoover and Stimson as to what role the United States should play in the matter widened, it must be remembered that Stimson's musings in his diary were quite different from what he in fact did. He loyally carried out the president's more cautious policy of noninterference. Still, Stimson was frustrated, not only with the president and the cabinet, which more accurately reflected American opinion, but also with the League of Nations and the British foreign minister, Sir John Simon, who would not publicly support the nonrecognition doctrine.

Assistant Secretary of State James G. Rogers suggested that Stimson write "a letter to somebody," reiterating his strong feelings on the subject. Stimson did so, to the chairman of the Senate Foreign Relations Committee, William E. Borah, in which he emphasized that Japanese aggression was contrary to all the Washington treaties of 1922—the 9-Power, 5-Power, and 4-Power pacts—and that if Japan persisted in its aggression, the United States would view itself as being released from any treaty limitation on its navy and Pacific bases. Hoover supported the missive, although he wanted to assure the world that the United States would not support any sanctions against Japan. Stimson talked the president out of a "no-sanctions" statement.

After the Borah letter of 14 February 1932, the League of Nations, at the urging of Sir John A. Simon, adopted a resolution of nonrecognition. Stimson was emboldened again and talked (and mused) again about economic sanctions and a naval presence in Shanghai. However, only the threat of nonrecognition remained as United States anti-Japanese policy in Manchuria. It seems, however, that the doctrine meant different things to the president and to the secretary of state—the maximum action to the former, possibly the beginning of action to the latter, including economic and military sanctions.

In late spring of 1932 Stimson attended the disarmament conference in Europe, and while Stimson was out of the country, Undersecretary of State William R. Castle made two speeches in which he assured the American people that the government did not expect to use any economic or military pressure in carrying out its Manchurian policy. Reporters sensed a difference between Hoover and Stimson on Far Eastern policy—the former seemed to be pacifistic; the latter, military-minded. Stimson reported in his diary that Hoover took responsibility for the statements given out during Stimson's absence, telling the secretary of state that he permitted their release because he feared that the Japanese might take military action against the United States. While Hoover's explanation lacked candor, Stimson seemed to be genuinely relieved that the president "apparently had no thought of differing with me seriously."[19]

However, Hoover differed from Stimson far more than Stimson thought at the time and perhaps less than historians later thought. At the time, Hoover, who was in the midst of the 1932 presidential campaign, wanted Stimson to make a speech proclaiming nonrecognition as the Hoover Doctrine. The president felt that as it stood, it was his, for the "secretary wanted always to go in for withdrawal of diplomats or an economic embargo, either or both of which would almost inevitably lead to war." Stimson refused Hoover's suggestion, saying to him that in his (Stimson's) letter to Senator Borah he had already credited the president with the instigation of the doctrine.[20]

In due course, the Japanese left Shanghai but consolidated their position in Manchuria. In February 1933 the League of Nations issued the Lytton Report, which thoroughly and accurately documented the Japanese aggression. The report preceded the nearly unanimous vote of the League Assembly "against Japan for virtually every action taken by her in Manchuria." In February the Japanese representative to the League of Nations pleaded the rightness of his nation's position in Manchuria and led his delegation out of the league.

In his memoirs, which were published in 1948, Stimson called the nonrecognition doctrine "the greatest constructive achievement" of his public life. Although inadequate as only a moral condemnation, it had "secured a united front against approval of conquest by military power."[21] The president, in his *Memoirs*, published five years after Stimson's, noted that "besides effective defense of the Western Hemisphere, America can take either of two roads in international relations: The one is to develop moral standards. . . . The other is to use economic and inevitably military force against aggressors." Hoover still stood on the former; Stimson seemed to stand on both. The distinction between the two seemed to build up with the passage of time.[22]

As the centerpiece of foreign policy, one can argue that the Stimson Doctrine represented the Hoover presidency at its best. The dialogue between a president—who leaned toward peace and reflected public opinion—and a secretary of state—who leaned toward force and possibly war—reflected the reality of future events. Nevertheless, the dialogue had no stabilizing effect on the Manchurian crisis, which George F. Kennan has described as "a vast and turgid process, involving immensely powerful currents of human affairs over which we Americans had little control or influence."[23]

Hoover's foreign policy elsewhere, in Latin America and in Europe, had a "hands-on" quality which distinguished it from his Far Eastern policy. The president had spent ten weeks touring Latin America in the interregnum before his inauguration, and the secretary of state had made two lengthy missions to Europe during the presidency. Both Hoover and Stimson had close contact with the leaders and representatives of Latin America and Europe, but with varying results. United States foreign policy in the Western Hemisphere was highly successful; the policy in Europe was about as unsuccessful as was that in the Far East. Still, White House and State Department foreign-policy efforts in all places were of a high order during the Hoover years.

A brief examination of Latin American diplomacy reminds historians that it was a "good neighbor" policy. In the public perception, that policy is attributed to Franklin Roosevelt. In fact, Roosevelt, in his Inaugural Address in 1933, enunciated a "good neighbor" policy toward all the nations of the world. He obviously drew from what Hoover had called the established policy toward Latin America.

Hoover's ulterior motive for going to Central and South America—to stay out of Coolidge's way—had faded as he planned the most extended foreign tour by any president or president-elect up to that time. The grand affair—passage by battleship, naval escorts, large entourages, palace receptions—had become a learning experience for the president as he studied and as he wrote some twenty-five speeches to be delivered in ten nations. He adopted a "good neighbor" course. In his very first address, delivered at Amapala, Honduras, on 26 November 1928, he said:

> I come to pay a call of friendship. In a sense I represent on this occasion the people of the United States extending friendly greeting to our fellow democracies on the American continent. I would wish to symbolize the friendly visit of one good neighbor to another. In our daily life, *good neighbors* call upon each other as the evidence of solicitude for the common welfare and to learn of the circumstances and point of view of each, so that there may come both understanding and respect which are cementing forces of all enduring society. This should be equally true amongst nations. We have a desire to maintain not only cordial relations of government with each other but the relations of *good neighbors*. [24]

Latin American audiences had reason to be pleased, although they also had reason to be suspicious. For more than two decades the Theodore Roosevelt corollary to the Monroe Doctrine had justified United States intervention in the internal affairs of many, if not most, of the nations south of the United States border. Frequently invited, and frequently uninvited, the United States too often had manifested an imperial presence in Latin America. Of course, the nation felt that its interest required stability in the Western Hemisphere, to be assured by United States military and economic presence. However, with the passage of time from its proclamation by Theodore Roosevelt in 1904—"brutal wrongdoing, or an impotence . . . may finally require intervention . . . [and] the United States cannot ignore this duty"—the Roosevelt Corollary had become onerous. Because Senate debate over the Kellogg-Briand Pact of 1928 might include discussion of the corollary, Under-secretary of State J. Reuben Clark, Jr., made a lengthy study of the Monroe Doctrine and the Roosevelt Corollary and concluded that the latter really was not consonant with the former, that the doctrine was originally intended as a shield from Europe, not as a lance held by the United States. Hoover pondered Clark's study, which was called the Clark Memorandum, and other recent efforts to assuage Latin America—such as the appointment of Dwight W. Morrow as ambassador to Mexico (with which Morrow came to have a "love affair") and the presence of both Charles Evans Hughes and President Coolidge at the Sixth Latin American Conference in Havana in 1928.

Latin nations might have thought Hoover's "good neighbor" pronouncements only rhetorical when no signs of such a policy were evinced during the first year of his presidency. But evidence was forthcoming in September 1930, when the State Department replaced Woodrow Wilson's moralistic policy of recognition with a threefold basis for recognition of Latin American governments: de facto control, an intent to fulfill international obligations, and plans to hold elections "in due course." Shortly thereafter, the Hoover administration's new policy was tested in connection with removing United States military forces from Nicaragua and Haiti. Most accounts emphasize the withdrawal of United States marines from the former and a planned withdrawal from the latter. While this is essentially true, Stimson's diary in October 1930 interestingly records that the president had wanted to withdraw very early in his administration. An old hand in the State Department, Dana C. Munro, warned Stimson that if we got out of Haiti, we would not get back in. The president apparently was taking seriously the advice of the president of Tuskegee Institute, Robert R. Moton, who said that Haiti's President Eugene Roy would not be a mere puppet "in the hands . . . of Americans." Hoover told Stimson that, regardless of the consequences of our leaving Haiti, "we should get out anyway."[25] The secretary dictated to his diary: "I am rather afraid that he [the president] is on the wrong track." Stimson prevailed, perhaps wisely. The withdrawal was "planned" but was not effected until 1934. Hoover had wanted out in 1930.[26]

Basically, Hoover and Stimson thought alike on the withdrawal of United States military forces from Latin America. The president at times seemed the more eager to expedite the policy. Stimson, if just as firm, was more cautious. Fundamentally, they worked in concert. When, in the spring of 1931, the New Orleans Banana Company and other interests wanted military protection of American citizens who were conducting business in the unstable interior of Nicaragua, Hoover emphatically supported the secretary in not providing such. At that, it took another year and a half to get all of the marines out. Hoover and Stimson seemed to rely on each other in developing the new policy of nonintervention. When, in the spring of 1932, a visitor asked Stimson if he would protect American interests in Chile and Colombia, Stimson replied: "Not on your life."[27] Both Hoover and Stimson naturally were influenced by the Manchurian affair, which was raging at the time. While the withdrawal policy in Latin America would have come in spite of the Far Eastern problem, the United States was very anxious not to be seen using her military forces in foreign lands, as Japan was doing in Manchuria.

The Clark Memorandum in June of 1930 had stated the administration's abrogation of the Roosevelt Corollary to the Monroe Doctrine. Unfortunately, as is often the case with his initiatives, Hoover has not been credited with the promulgation because it was not delivered to Latin American governments. Former Secretary of State Frank B. Kellogg and Stimson urged that the memorandum be officially dispatched, but the president had questions about some of its details. He thought a celebration of delivery might "provoke a great deal of debate."[28] Also, domestic matters were occupying his time. Hoover's policy of recognition and both his withdrawal and his planned withdrawal of military forces gave Latin American governments proof of his "good neighbor" policy. But it was the succeeding president, Franklin D. Roosevelt, with his flamboyance, who captured imaginations by telling the world what he was doing by way of freeing Latin America from the "Colossus of the North."

Illustrative of effective foreign policy during the Hoover presidency was Stimson's quiet attempt at resolving Latin American disputes between Paraguay and Bolivia over the Chaco, and between Peru and Colombia over Leticia. In a sense these represented the best in United States diplomatic intervention. In the first case, Stimson and his competent assistant secretary for Latin American Affairs, Francis White, worked through the Pan American Union to declare a Stimson Doctrine of nonrecognition of Bolivia's seizure of the Paraguayan outpost Fort Carlos Antonio Lopez. It was ironic that while the United States was giving up its nonrecognition policy in Latin America, it supported nonrecognition in this case. Mexico's suggestion that the nineteen members of the Pan American Union send a joint telegram to Paraguay and Bolivia, as a warning on nonrecognition, pleased the secretary of state. The joint telegram was sent on 3 August 1933, but the war between the two nations continued until 1935. Stimson worked even harder to resolve the Colombia-Peru borderland dispute. In this case he even brought representatives of European powers and Japan to Woodley to consider sending a joint admonitory note to the two nations, which included the Kellogg-Briand prohibition against aggression. All agreed to do so except Japan, which was then engaged in its own aggression. The Leticia affair between the two nations was finally settled by the League of Nations in 1934. Henry L. Stimson, however, had taken the first important moves to resolve the crisis.

When all had been said and done about Hoover's Latin American policy, Franklin Roosevelt picked it up, barely dropping a stitch. The New Deal did introduce one major reform, a reciprocal-trade program, which lowered the high Smoot-Hawley tariff schedules. In so doing, it further enhanced Latin-American good will, which had begun with Hoover's "good neighbor" policy.

While the "good neighbor" policy was the most successful part of the foreign policy of the Hoover presidency, the high point was the one-year "moratorium" on German reparations and on foreign debts that were owed to the United States. It yielded up a national sigh of relief and was almost everywhere viewed as being imaginative. Whereas it seemed to bode well as an American action in Europe, the World Disarmament Conference, which was conducted simultaneously with the moratorium, manifested failure from the start.

The massive war debts that Western nations owed the United States were not a particular problem or an issue until the depression set in, thus interrupting the international exchange of money. Prior to the depression, American banks had loaned Germany vast sums of money at high interest rates; Germany used the loans largely to meet Versailles reparation payments to Allied nations, especially to England and France, which in turn used the reparations to pay off much of their indebtedness to the United States. It all worked for awhile, especially because the Dawes and Young plans successfully reduced the reparations. In fact, by the end of the decade, just prior to the depression,

Germany was recovering remarkably from its highly inflationary post-war economic slump. However, Germany had borrowed to the hilt, many times more than it needed for its reparation payments. In view of the depression squeeze, Germany complained about the cost of her reparations. France and England, however, did not listen, because they needed the money to pay their own war debts to the United States.

Washington consistently refused to see the connection between the reparations and debts. Secretary Stimson saw it, but he was not elected to office. It was well and good for him to talk of "these damn debts," but he was not as accountable as Hoover was to the public who remembered Coolidge's aphorism: "They hired the money, didn't they?"[29] Nevertheless, by early 1931 Germany was not able to pay both its debts to the United States and its reparations to England and France. Its threat of default on reparations caused bank runs in America. Loans to Germany dried up at the American source. By the spring of 1931 Germany and Austria allied in a customs union to save themselves by cutting foreign imports; France retaliated by withholding funds for German and Austrian banks. The central bank of Austria, Creditanstaldt, failed. The United States ambassador to Germany, Frederic M. Sackett, who was home on leave, explained to the president how serious Germany's economic plight had become. It now was experiencing a massive flight of gold.

The idea of a one-year moratorium on intergovernmental debts was Hoover's, but in retrospect, we see that he had no choice. Still, Stimson and, later, French Ambassador Paul Claudel were surprised by the boldness of the move. Stimson naturally supported it. Aside from the grave economic conditions, Europeans were bitter about the idea of the debt. Not long before, Stimson and Elihu Root had agreed on the scenario that Europeans saw—that the United States had made money on the last war. By refusing to join the League of Nations or the World Court, the United States, they calculated, would abet the next war in which it would make still more money. Ogden Mills was ready to extend the moratorium to two years. But what might have seemed like no choice to those close to the White House was viewed as a bad choice to some unhappy congressmen and some French leaders. Hoover worked to convince congressional leaders of the need for their support; the State Department tried to persuade France to adopt the moratorium.

Stimson described the efforts to secure support for the moratorium on many fronts as "quite like a war." At times he worried about the president's dark side. "The president was tired," wrote Stimson, and "he went through all the blackest surmises. . . . But I think he is moving at last."[30] But to Stimson's delight, Hoover got in touch with thirty members of Congress and won them over to support the moratorium when they convened the next December. Congressional leaders reflected the supportive mood of the nation on the issue. Of course, not all of them did. Senator George Norris, long one of Hoover's opponents, strung out his pejorative comments to the president of the Farmers' Union, John A. Simpson: "the so-called Hoover moratorium proposition!"; "first time he has communicated with me"; "members of congress . . . with unprejudiced minds and unpledged action [should] debate questions of this kind"; "I am suspicious that . . . Great Britain . . . has communicated this idea and had Hoover father it"; "the first step toward an attempt to cancel all [debts]"; "England and France would make no sacrifice whatsoever."[31] The French leaders appeared to be as adamantly opposed as was Norris. As the Nebraska senator seemed to condone English and French suffering, so France seemed to feel the same way about Germany. But the French bowed to pressure from Washington and concurred on July 6; they even agreed to a one-year "stand-still" agreement on private short-term credits.

The moratorium was credited with having warded off an economic and political crisis in Germany. In the end, it only prolonged the worsening of the crisis. In January 1932, at Lausanne, Switzerland, the Western nations agreed to forgive the German reparations, assuming that the United States would forgive the war debts, something that no American president in an election year could agree to do. Economic and political confusion continued to reign over Europe. In September 1932 England went off the gold standard. Some observers thought that this was the end of Western civilization. The American president plodded on through a presidential campaign and more planning, this time for the great London Economic Conference to be convened in 1933; again he proposed to bring order and stability to the Western world and, of course, to the United States. Hoover had principally in mind the restoration of the gold standard and, perhaps, a quid pro quo: United States consultation on war debts in exchange for British tariff concessions.

The World Disarmament Conference, which convened in Geneva in early 1932, is accurately described by Robert H. Ferrell as having been "an unmitigated nuisance." Leaders of the Great Powers went through the motions. It had been anticipated very long; the people wanted it and thought that the mass of delegates could make it work. The depression, however, was closing in on the president, who believed that he had little time to waste. He was downright annoyed that French Premier Pierre

Laval paid a state visit to the United States prior to the conference. "What has he come for, anyway?" Hoover asked in his blunt way. Stimson noted that the president acted as if Laval had come "to pick his pocket."

Laval had probably come for what he considered to be two good reasons: one, to get political mileage back home by looking like a hard worker in Washington; two, to lay the groundwork for the one thing that the French wanted at the disarmament conference—security against the historical German threat. Laval got no satisfaction. In fact, Hoover said that the conference would deal with land armies—a European, not an American, problem. Some excitement ensued during the visit, when Senator Borah told the press that the Versailles Treaty should be revised to return the Polish Corridor to Germany and to redraw the Hungarian frontiers. Laval exclaimed: "Why, the man lives in Mars!"

Actually, when Stimson got Borah and Laval together at Woodley, they charmed one another; but as little substance came from their meeting as from any other conference that Laval experienced in Washington. The communique issued upon his departure was innocuous: "We find that we view the nature of these financial and economic problems in the same light and this understanding on our part should serve to pave the way for helpful action by our respective governments."[32]

The United States delegation to the Disarmament Conference, which met in Geneva in February 1932, was ordinary as compared with the one that had represented the nation at the London Naval Conference in 1930. Stimson was the head, but it was well understood that the ambassador to Belgium, Hugh Gibson, would do the work. Actually, the secretary of state spent much time securing support for his nonrecognition doctrine in the Far East. His memoirs, however, do reveal interesting discussions with the leaders of Europe on a range of subjects.

At the conference itself, the French talked about an international police force, and Ambassador Gibson offered many suggestions, ranging from reducing many classifications of capital and auxiliary ships by one-third to abolishing submarines, airplanes, and tanks. These suggestions were actually the president's. Stimson thought that they reflected the president's "Quaker nature" and had a dreamlike quality about them.[33] Although sincere, the president seemed to be playing on rhetoric rather than exercising a leadership role. Stimson put it plainly when he told the French that the United States should not lead the conference because we already had restricted or reduced our armaments and, besides, were out of air range of Europe. The conference got nowhere for many reasons, but foremost, especially for the French, was the problem of Continental security. France wanted a "consultative" pact with the United States and England as the price for reducing armaments. Both nations feared that a commitment to consultation with France would imply support if France were to be attacked, which would mean war.

By June, Hoover, who was tired of watching the "dawdling," proposed an all-around 30 percent reduction in armaments, which seemed reasonable to Germany, Italy, and Russia but not to France, which still feared another German invasion. The conference continued to "lag" and "slipped into limbo." In the ensuing year, Great Britain suggested a draft convention which would result in an international conference if any nation broke the Pact of Paris. The United States offered consultation if nations would first reduce armaments. Nothing happened, except that in October 1933 Chancellor Hitler withdrew Germany both from the disarmament conference and from the League of Nations. Secretary Stimson still thought that he had served an important purpose with the conference by bringing the leaders of the powerful nations together. Furthermore, the conference had given the United States an opportunity to proselytize for the Far Eastern policy of nonrecognition.

Though the Disarmament Conference of 1932 was "an unmitigated nuisance," Hoover expected that the forthcoming London Economic Conference of 1933 would more than compensate for the very limited success of the Geneva meeting. The president's enthusiasm for the possibilities of success for the Economic Conference seemed to be in inverse proportion to his feeling about the disarmament conclave. Particularly would he feel so as his term came to an end early in 1933, a subject that is fully discussed in chapter 11, "The Rites of Passage."

It is clear that Quaker pacifism, the Great Depression, and the forcefulness of Henry L. Stimson affected Hoover's foreign policy far less than has been presumed heretofore. Noncoercion did become the hallmark of much of the Hoover administration's actions overseas, as is demonstrated by the avoidance of economic and military sanctions against Japan in Manchuria, the withdrawal of United States marines from Nicaragua, and armament reduction at the London Naval Conference. But such was not pacifism. Noncoercion was vigorously pursued without abandoning the nation's military capability. United States forces were stationed where they were needed, as in Shanghai, the Philippine Islands, and certain parts of Latin America and Europe. The president believed firmly, however, that the nation's military capability abroad should not entail intervention. Nor should it portend intervention. Its only function was to maintain peace and order, profound Quaker characteristics.

To say that the depression was the determining force in Hoover's foreign policy is to misunderstand the consistency of that policy almost everywhere, both before and after the depression. Foreign policy was usually unrelated to economic conditions at home and abroad. It is true, as the Stimson diaries demonstrate, that the president's time came more and more to be taken up by a continually failing economy. In the process he undoubtedly did defer more frequently to Stimson; and at times the president manifested a testy economic nationalism. Almost always, however, he strove for a policy of noncoercion and seemed always to adhere to the goal on American terms that were consonant with his independent internationalism.

Franklin Roosevelt spoke advisedly when he said at the time that "old Hoover's foreign policy has been pretty good" on two scores: first, it really was Hoover's policy and not Stimson's and, second, it was about as successful as it could be.[34] Although the nonrecognition policy in Manchuria did not free China from Japanese occupation, there is little evidence to say that Stimson's more aggressive stance would have done more good than harm. The Good Neighbor Policy was devised by Hoover before Stimson appeared on the scene early in the term. Stimson credited Hoover with the moratorium and thought it was one of Hoover's finest hours, as it was one of the most exciting times of the secretary's long career. Such foreign-policy endeavors overshadowed the weaknesses of the administration: those nationalistic and ethnocentric efforts such as the high tariff, nonforgiveness of debts, and at the end of his term, his seeming use of the forthcoming economic conference to commit his successor to his domestic policy.

Alexander De Conde has recently made what might be the two most telling points about Hoover's conduct of United States foreign policy. They are that Hoover's spirit of noncoercion was so pervasive that it made void any trappings of "the imperial executive" and that the president was absolutely accountable to the people and to the Congress.[35] Also, surely of service to the nation was the demonstration that a president can have at his side a forceful secretary of state who actually vies for policies. Stimson obviously had many strengths, not the least of which was knowing his constitutional place in the making and directing of foreign policy.

10

★ ★ ★ ★ ★

DEFEAT

"I find a number of intelligent students of politics, here and there, who think Hoover is now at his nadir and will get stronger; some even profess to believe he can be re-elected."[1] So wrote, on 4 September 1931, the Pulitzer-prize-winning journalist Herbert B. Swope to William Borah. This is one of the few expressions of hope for Hoover's reelection that I found in researching the subject. At that, Swope's comment was mostly sarcastic, for he refuted his comment in the next sentence by stating the "simple" fact that Franklin Roosevelt would win his party's nomination and the election, unless the Democrats became overly confident, a remote danger. Borah admitted that Roosevelt was the Democrats' strongest vote getter. The exchange reflected political reality. Still, in the fall of 1931, Hoover was at a "nadir" of sorts. The descent of the GNP during the third quarter had not yet been recorded. The debt moratorium held out promise for an international stability that would bode well for America. And Democratic antidepression proposals were in disarray.

The depression, however, was hurting the president badly, even though by election time in 1932 the GNP was actually leveling off and industrial production, factory employment, and freight-car loadings were up in the four months prior to the election, respectively, by 8, 3, and 6 percent. The comparison of the data with that of the period prior to the crash of 1929 was too staggering. In that comparison, the GNP had dropped over 30 percent, and industrial production, factory employment, and freight-car loadings were all down about 40 percent. As

193

Hoover's political fortunes fell, Roosevelt's rose. The president, nevertheless, became increasingly determined to win reelection after his perfunctory nomination in 1932. Roosevelt's role would be somewhat reversed. The governor would have to fight for his party's presidential nomination, but less so for the election.

As the incumbent president, Hoover would demand that his party renominate him. All elected Republican presidents, except for Rutherford B. Hayes, had successfully done so. In addition, Hoover's ability as a bureaucratic politician assured him of the continued control of the Republican organization, if not of the electorate. There would be more intraparty rumblings in 1932 than had been the case for most Republican presidents who in times past had sought renomination. As Republicans approached their convention, many talked wistfully of nominating Calvin Coolidge, Dwight Morrow, or Charles G. Dawes. Coolidge had had enough of the high office and was not in good health; Dwight Morrow died on 5 October 1931; and Charles Dawes knew that he could not get the nomination away from Hoover even if he wanted it. Mrs. Ruth Hanna McCormick, who in 1930 had suffered defeat as Illinois's Republican nominee for the United States Senate, pleaded in her Rockford, Illinois, newspaper that Republicans not repeat their 1912 fiasco of blindly nominating a loser. Former Bull Mooser Harold Ickes also remembered 1912. As he had then supported Theodore Roosevelt for the Republican nomination, he now looked for another insurgent candidate to support in 1932. He put out a feeler to Senator Hiram Johnson to run against Hoover. The idea was probably fascinating to Johnson, for, as Theodore Roosevelt's 1912 running mate, he was a legitimate heir to the Progressive crusade. In fact, he had already suggested that Hoover retire. But the California senator, for a variety of reasons—the most likely of which was the memory of Theodore Roosevelt's failure to secure the Republican nomination in 1912—would not run.

Perhaps Pennsylvania's governor, Gifford Pinchot, would try for the Republican nomination. Pinchot, another former Bull Mooser, thought well of the idea. He asked Ickes to make some soundings in the party on his behalf. Ickes spent $3,500 to canvass prominent Republican leaders about the possibility. He got far more "brick bats than bouquets" for his effort. A former Taft supporter, New York's Charles D. Hilles, who really did not like Hoover, immediately swore allegiance to the president. Chief Justice Charles Evans Hughes was furious that Ickes would approach him on such a "political subject." William Allen White reflected the ambivalence of the party about replacing Hoover with another candidate when he told the president's friend David

Hinshaw that "the calf's eyes were sought and that [Pinchot's] entrance into the fight would only make a row and not either revive a cause or effect the principles." Somewhat hypocritically, White mused to Ickes: "I wish I could think that Gifford had a chance."[2]

Herbert Hoover largely dominated the Republican Convention in Chicago in mid June—from the choosing of the temporary and permanent chairmanships, respectively those of Senator Lester J. Dickinson and Congressman Bertrand Snell, to the platform, to the slate of Hoover and Curtis. The president's principal surrogates were Ogden Mills, Henry L. Stimson, Agriculture Secretary Arthur Hyde, Postmaster General Walter F. Brown, and his secretaries, Walter Newton and Larry Richey. To many Americans, as *Time Magazine* pointed out, a sad commentary on the Republican program was that while "the platform was full of . . . plans for the reconstruction of the nation, the convention debated only the subject of prohibition."[3]

Hoover fanned the fires of the prohibition debate among Republicans by standing firm on the enforcement of the amendment, even when most Republicans and the vast majority of Americans favored its drastic revision, if not its repeal. Although the irresolute Wickersham report at midterm was a tip-off of the nation's opposition to the amendment, it actually seemed to stiffen the president's support of it. For reasons of his ideological development by stages, which has previously been discussed, the president clung tenaciously to the amendment. Only on the very eve of the Republican National Convention were Ogden Mills and Henry L. Stimson finally able to move Hoover to see the political necessity of compromising on the issue. After much soul-searching, the president expressed his willingness to accept a plank that would repeal prohibition but give the federal government the power to keep dry those states that wished to remain that way and to prohibit the open saloon from being established in those states that wished to be wet. Had Mills and Stimson been able to convince the president sooner to accept such repeal, they might have avoided the spectacle of having Republicans, in their national convention, debate a dead issue instead of the live one of economic depression. So, dry Republicans such as former Kansas Governor Henry J. Allen, then the Republicans' publicity director, continued to push for a dry plank. Stimson, who at the White House had favored a modified repeal plan, would have done so on the floor of the convention had this been necessary. The president wavered on the issue during the weeks before the convention, but he finally stayed with the Stimson-Mills compromise plank, which handily carried the day. Allen and the drys lost at the convention. Hiram Bingham moved an outright minority wet plank, which lost by a ratio of 6 to 4 on the convention floor.

The president unenthusiastically insisted upon the vice-presidential renomination of Charles Curtis, a rather run-of-the-mill politician, who was described by Ted Clark to Coolidge as one who was "carried away by the lure of Washington society."[4] The president would have preferred Theodore Roosevelt, Jr., but the New Yorker was probably too liberal for the convention. Some Republicans wanted Dawes to be vice-president, but he did not want that job again. Twenty Republican state delegations opposed Curtis, but there seemed to be no viable alternative. Thus, with the president's support, he won the nomination.

Some grim humor was injected into the convention when an Oregon delegate by the name of Lawritz Bernard Sandblast tried to nominate for president a former United States senator, Dr. Joseph I. France of Maryland. However, Hoover's organization prevailed when Sandblast's microphone went dead and when France himself was denied access to the dais from which he hoped to decline the nomination and to nominate Coolidge. France was not a delegate. Following the convention, Hoover's floor leaders returned to the White House to be congratulated for a job that had been so expeditiously accomplished. Curtis posed for pictures with the president. The new campaign was about to begin. The president would run it, although with a new chairman, Everett Sanders, who was disparagingly described by *Time Magazine* as "chunky, slow-minded."[5]

While Republicans had become increasingly discouraged during the months prior to the conventions, Democrats waxed jubilant. The joy of the Democrats was not only tied to Republican misfortune; it had an ideological as well as a partisan cast. As the Republican national leadership looked more conservative, the Democrats looked more liberal and thus appealed to increasing numbers of the insurgents. The North Carolina editor Josephus Daniels, Franklin Roosevelt's former chief at the Navy Department, had caught the significance of the 1930 election when he applauded insurgent victories in both parties: Thomas Walsh, the Senate Democrat who had fought the oil scandals; George Norris, the Senate Republican who had fought the Muscle Shoals "take-over"; Gifford Pinchot, Pennsylvania's maverick Republican governor who had fought the power trusts; and Franklin Roosevelt, the New York governor who had fought power companies in New York. Roosevelt was less the insurgent and battler than others and certainly was more pragmatic and politically successful. The aristocratic governor seemed to be even more democratic than the Quaker president, although at heart he probably was not. It was revealing of Hoover's image problem that his good friend William Allen White wrote to Josephus Daniels: "I think . . . [Hoover] is a great president in many ways . . . [but] I don't admire his boundless respect for the plug hat section of American life."[6]

Roosevelt had proved his democratic, pragmatic, and political skill throughout two decades of elective and administrative efforts at the state and national levels, as New York state senator, as assistant secretary of the navy, and as governor of New York. His only defeat had come when he had lost the vice-presidency in 1920, but was valuable nevertheless because of the national experience and exposure. In 1921 Roosevelt had suffered from poliomyelitis, which crippled him permanently but which many observers think gave him a humane sensitivity that enhanced his relationship with other downtrodden Americans—an attribute that befitted the times of increasing economic depression. As governor, elected in 1928, Roosevelt was a rather cautious progressive, especially during his first term and even during his second term down to late 1931, when the depression entered a precipitous slide. His transformation to being a fighter against the depression had been slow. At the Governors Conference in the summer of 1930 Roosevelt had criticized the Hoover administration, specifically for pouring money into public works and, generally, for departing from laissez faire. His serious attack on the depression came only in late 1931 with the establishment of the Temporary Emergency Relief Administration, which provided relief for 10 percent of the state's families. Only then did he seem to assume the character of large leadership, although he had always been an attractive political personality. It is another paradox that prior to his reelection as governor in 1930, Roosevelt had always been the junior member of the Hoover-Roosevelt relationship, going back to the Wilson presidency. Even during the 1920s Roosevelt had happily served Secretary of Commerce Hoover as the head of a trade association, the American Construction Council.

After his reelection as governor of New York in 1930 Roosevelt slowly emerged as an innovative leader of the nation's largest and most diversified state, striving for antidepression mechanisms: banking reform, distribution of employment, unemployment insurance, interstate employment compacts, and state emergency relief. While the New York governor was no political radical, he soon gave the conservative Democrats, such as Bernard Baruch, reason to pause over his qualifications to be president. The closer Roosevelt came to the nomination, the more Baruch grumbled.

Of course, Baruch, for all of his conservatism, was not far from the Democratic center in 1932. Roosevelt's appeal covered the spectrum from George Norris, on the left, to Bernard Baruch on the right. George

Norris knew that Roosevelt would be "right" on public power. Baruch saw Roosevelt moving ideologically to the left and warned him against unbalanced budgets and centralization of government. But Baruch closed no door to Roosevelt, and Roosevelt always kept it ajar. He wrote ambiguously to Baruch: "There is a very definite line of demarcation, of course, between national and state problems, for the state must confine itself to matters which from their nature do not require federal action."[7] Roosevelt did not fool Baruch. The financier liked conservatives such as Garner and Democratic Senate leader Joseph Robinson. Baruch wrote to Robinson: "It seems terrible to me that two men are going to be nominated by the two great political parties and they are not really wanted. . . . It does seem to me that men like you . . . and others who have borne the brunt of Democratic battles for the last twelve years ought to have something to say about this nomination."[8]

Unlike Hoover, Roosevelt could not demand the nomination in the Democratic Convention, which convened in late June in the same setting as the Republic Convention—Chicago. It was too highly coveted. Speaker John Nance Garner, former Secretary of War Newton Baker, Senators James H. Lewis and James A. Reed, Governors Albert Ritchie and William Henry ("Alfalfa Bill") Murray, General Electric's president Owen D. Young, investigative counselor Samuel Seabury, and Al Smith—all wanted the nomination. But in short, Roosevelt had what it took to win the prize, even with the Democratic Convention's two-thirds rule for nomination.

In retrospect, one might wonder why the Democrats even hesitated to nominate Franklin D. Roosevelt. He had campaign, legislative, and executive experience at the state and national levels; a famous name; physical attractiveness and charm—*charisma*, to use the worn term; supreme confidence—an "active-positive" type, according to James David Barber; uncanny political sensitivity; and a pair of advisers—Louis Howe and James A. Farley—who were unsurpassed in presidential elections. For a decade the gnomelike Louis Howe had been planning much of the strategy that led to the nomination. And in later years the affable James Farley had implemented the strategy with his own Irish embellishments. The massive correspondence and contacts of Howe and Farley came to fruition when the latter canvassed eighteen states in 1931, reporting solid support for the New York governor. Still, the presidential nomination came hard, a story that has been told many times in many places: how Walter Lippmann said that Roosevelt was just "a pleasant young man" who wanted to be president; how Al Smith and his managers, John Jacob Raskob and Jouett Shouse, were not permitted to deadlock the convention by their various shenanigans;

how the Roosevelt team tried to rescind the convention's two-thirds rule; how the New York governor appealed to the important influence of William Randolph Hearst by almost shamefully renouncing internationalism; how Speaker Garner, at the behest of Hearst and California's McAdoo, released his delegates to the New Yorker; how these events led to Franklin Roosevelt's nomination on the fourth ballot; and how the candidate dramatically flew to Chicago to accept the nomination of the Roosevelt-Garner slate.

Few scenes so dramatized what America wanted as that of the Democratic Convention's last hours—a change in procedure. The fact that the candidate flew to Chicago, against strong headwinds, to appear personally before the convention and to accept his party's nomination, was breath-taking. The acceptance speech was necessarily general, synthesizing what the candidate had campaigned for and what the platform now advocated: economy in government, crop reduction, relief and mortgage financing, public works, regulation of the sale of securities, and last, the repeal of prohibition. It was symbolic that, unlike the Republicans, emphasis was put on the economic issues and not on prohibition. It was no radical declaration; in many ways it was similar to the Republican economic enunciations. But aside from similarities in substance, the style was profoundly different. The candidate stood closer to his party than did Hoover and talked far more simply and more inspirationally:

> On the farms, in the large metropolitan areas, in the smaller cities and in the villages, millions of our citizens cherish the hope that their old standards of living and of thought have not gone forever. These millions cannot and shall not hope in vain.
>
> I pledge you, I pledge myself, to a new deal for the American people. Let us all here assembled constitute ourselves prophets of a new order of competence and of courage. This is more than a political campaign; it is a call to arms. Give me your help, not to win votes alone, but to aim in this crusade to restore America to its own people.[9]

The adage that when one thing goes wrong, everything goes wrong, applied unquestionably to Hoover's reelection campaign. The march of the Bonus Army on Washington in late July to demand that veterans immediately receive full payment of the World War I bonus should have been largely extraneous to the presidential campaign. Instead, it became a nightmare, at the dawn of the campaign, from which Republicans never seemed to awaken. That the horror lingered on to the end of the campaign was evident on November 5, in St. Paul, Minnesota, when a very tired Candidate Hoover blurted out extemporaneously: "Thank God, you have a government in Washington that knows how to deal with a mob."[10] The remark brought applause from the partisans who were present, but it reminded much of the nation of the media event of three months earlier which had flashed grotesque scenes of armed-to-the-teeth military units seemingly "blasting" away at helpless "hungry" American veterans when the Hoover administration drove the Bonus Army out of Washington.

Such a tragic end of the bonus affair seemed both to typify and to symbolize Hoover's whole campaign against his presidential opponent—indeed, against the depression itself. All that the president had done for veterans and all that he had done to alleviate the depression had come to nought. Little wonder that Hoover called the people a harsh employer, though, in retrospect, the harshness is understandable.

The picture of Hoover-administration mistreatment of veterans in July 1932 did not square with the record and public approval of the president's policies in behalf of veterans during the previous three and one-half years. The establishment of the Veterans' Administration to enhance aid to veterans was one of Hoover's major bureaucratic reforms; and federal expenditures for such veterans' benefits as housing, hospitalization, and disability payments reached a massive annual total of $675.8 million. When the president very occasionally did say no to veterans, as in his unsuccessful veto of the 1931 bill to permit veterans to borrow up to 50 percent on their World War I bonus (a paid-up life insurance policy collectable in 1945), he was applauded by such liberal journals as the *Nation* and the *New Republic*. Also, when the president appeared personally before the American Legion to oppose a second bonus bill (to make collectable the remaining 50 percent), the *Nation* saw "courage and leadership" in Hoover. Important personages, such as Franklin Roosevelt, Fiorello La Guardia, and Walter Lippmann, agreed with Hoover and the *Nation* in opposing the second bonus. Yet, when some eleven thousand veterans marched on Washington to lobby the Congress for the bill, Hoover not only defended their civil liberty to do so but quietly provided materials and quarters to comfort many of them.[11]

Why the tragic ending from such worthy beginnings? It suffices here to say that the "Bonus Expeditionary Force," including women and children, fanned out from provided camps to unoccupied buildings and areas in the business district of the city of Washington and very near to Capitol Hill, where the "Force" employed various strategies to pressure Congress. The marchers were usually constrained, thanks largely to the enlightened District of Columbia superintendent of police, Pelham D. Glassford, at least until the administration chose to evict the marchers from the buildings near Capitol Hill. The administration thought that it would be necessary to raze the buildings so that longstanding public-works plans to construct new ones in their place could be carried out. Not only were the new buildings needed, but so was the employment that their construction would provide.

A majority of the bonus marchers had left the capital by the time of the eviction incident. Congress had not met their second bonus demand, and the president had signed a $100,000 authorization to pay for their transportation home. A portion of the remaining ones continued their petition for the second bonus by occupying the buildings that were scheduled for demolition. District police were unable to carry out the eviction and apparently called upon federal authorities to aid in the effort. The record shows considerable confusion over whether the district commissioners or the police authority requested the federal assistance. Secretary of War Patrick Hurley saw that a potential for riot existed; therefore he requested that the president declare martial law. Hoover refused to do so and gave Hurley precise instructions for moving the occupants from the buildings to their own camps nearby. According to Donald J. Lisio's definitive account of the incident, Hurley took it upon himself to instruct the chief of staff, Gen. Douglas MacArthur, to move the marchers, not to nearby camps, but out of the business district and across the river to Camp Marks, on Anacostia Flats. MacArthur, in turn, assumed even more authority, personally directing his forces to drive the remnants of the Bonus Expeditionary Force (BEF) even beyond Camp Marks and their hovels on Anacostia Flats—by tanks, guns, and tear gas. These were the scenes of military action that had flashed across the nation and were on the minds of many Americans as Hoover, at the end of the campaign, thanked God for a "government . . . that knows how to deal with a mob." MacArthur not only disobeyed the president's orders when Hoover tried to stop the army from driving the BEF across the Anacostia bridge; the chief of staff proclaimed that he did "not want either himself or his staff bothered by people coming down and pretending to bring orders." It did not matter that high-ranking officers personally delivered the president's orders. Of course, if the arrogant chief of staff could ignore with impunity the orders of the president, it is not difficult to understand that he would ignore the army's own plans of an eventual orderly transport home of any rioting veterans, or the question of the legality of the eviction, which was raised by his own adjutant general, or the advice of his aide, Maj.

Dwight D. Eisenhower, that it was "highly inappropriate" for the chief of staff to assume personal command of such an operation.[12] But MacArthur conspicuously presented himself, hands on hips, with distinctive britches, cap—insignia and all—for the media to record for posterity.

The deed was done. The Quaker president was appalled by it all—the treatment of American veterans and MacArthur's studied disobedience of the commander in chief. The president was not so nonpolitical as to fail to realize the political implications.

Another president two decades later would fire the same MacArthur for publicly complaining about and even ignoring presidential policy. In 1932 Hoover merely requested that both MacArthur and Hurley acknowledge their responsibility for the military action or so inform a congressman who could defend the president against an expected outcry from critics of the administration. That, too, the general and the secretary of war refused to do. MacArthur said that it would be "bragging"; Hurley said that it would be "trying ourselves" before a "fickle public," and besides, the secretary concluded inconsistently, the public was "with" the president and he should "glory" in that fact.[13] Then Hoover showed his Quaker and nonpolitical side by assuming the responsibility himself and by withdrawing his requests that MacArthur and Hurley confess to their disobedience.

Hoover's assumption of responsibility was "a crucial blunder," particularly since Hurley was more right in his prediction of the public's fickleness than of its glorying in the issue. On the day after the "riot," Hoover, Hurley, and the public seemed to accept MacArthur's charge that "revolution . . . animated" the rioters. The president liked the good press, a very scarce commodity in those months. Because Hoover was prone to self-delusion, once it set in, it took hold. Even though investigations made immediately after the riot by the FBI, the Secret Service, the Washington police, the Veterans' Administration, the War Department, and a federal grand jury found no evidence of "insurrection," the president and his attorney general believed differently, both at the time and subsequently. In his *Memoirs*, published twenty years later, Hoover declared that "as abundantly proved later on, the march was in considerable part organized and promoted by the Communists and included a large number of hoodlums and ex-convicts determined to raise a public disturbance."[14]

The rout of veterans in late July became a political liability in the presidential campaign that followed, as the lack of evidence of insurrection became apparent. Liability turned to political disaster when Washington's Police Superintendent Glassford insisted that the Communists had mustered no more than 210 men in the 11,000-man Bonus Army and that the attorney general's desperate attempt to associate the Bonus Army not only with Communists but also with "criminals" had been a blatant attempt to mislead the American public. The *New Republic,* which had at first defended the administration's action, later described the Justice Department's report of criminal and Communist charges as being a "campaign document, pure and simple."[15] The public came to view the administration's defense in much the same light. Twelve years later, former Attorney General Mitchell blamed MacArthur and Hurley for the bad public reaction, "the stories and motion pictures of armored cars bristling with machine guns and all that tom-foolery." Mitchell concluded that MacArthur had "always been the flashy, 'showy' kind, and Hurley also liked to 'strut.' "[16]

The high price that Hoover finally paid for the bonus fiasco did not by itself determine the outcome of the presidential campaign, but it was an integral part of the mosaic that was crafted during the months between July and November 1932, which seemed to portray the fall of a leader more in terms of Greek tragedy than of American politics.

As with Martin Van Buren, his White House predecessor of nearly a century before who had suffered defeat in the wake of the depression of 1837, Herbert Hoover also was ordained to lose the presidency in 1932. Although his political situation was compounded by the bonus fiasco, it was more gravely affected by his strong technocratic, objective, and impersonal approach to economic depression, which the people perceived to be an approach that had failed. It was also adversely affected, according to Hoover, by Franklin Roosevelt's pliable approach to problems—"chameleon on plaid"—which was viewed by the people as being pragmatic and experimental, with a great potential for success.

Craig Lloyd has well documented Hoover's successful public-relations efforts to sell great programs when he had administered various World War I food programs and the Commerce Department. Lloyd concluded his book by noting that the presidency called for different skills.[17] Indeed, the American presidency is a very personal affair between the office and the people. The story of the Hoover presidency thus far has demonstrated a lack of people-to-people interaction, which is necessary in order to draw political feeling (and knowledge) from a range of people and, in turn, to sustain the people in their trials. It is significant that Hoover disliked crowds; he thought them mindless. That lack of communion contributed to the administration's failure and severely handicapped the president in seeking reelection, not only in trying to sell his program, but in selling himself. What he had done, by campaign fiat in 1928, required far more personal appeal in 1932, especially for the millions of Americans who were most deeply affected by the depression. Justice Stone said plainly to Hoover in 1932 that he should not forget that the people elect the presidents.

It is difficult to imagine that Hoover, who had so expertly practiced public relations over a decade prior to his presidency, could not adjust to the kind of public relations that were required by the presidential office. And it is a paradox that his opposition party was the first in United States history to employ public relations so devastatingly to discredit a president, from the time of his inauguration to his defeat. Charles Michelson shrewdly discerned that both parties in the 1928 campaign had successfully overbuilt their candidates as supermen, a view, in fact, that Hoover recognized and lamented. After the 1928 election, Democratic Party Chairman John Jacob Raskob, embittered by the religious bigotry that Al Smith had suffered, sought retribution. He was aided by Michelson, who discovered that the public-relations effort that had built Hoover up could also bring him down. Every slip of the new administration, no matter what its distance from the president, would, if at all possible, be attributed to him: the Smoot-Hawley Tariff, which the president had very reluctantly signed, became the "Hoover Tariff"; the stock-market panic, which had no relationship to the president, became the "Hoover Panic"; the depression became the "Hoover Depression"; and the hovels in which people had to live became "Hoovervilles." In addition, Michelson's committee frequently planted among congressmen information that if libelous, would be immune from prosecution. Quite naturally, such stories frequently made news headlines. The press had many a field day. George Creel, a World War I propagandist, understood particularly well what was happening. Reporters had tales galore; and to reporters, "nothing in the world was worth so much as a story."[18]

In addition to inspiring Shouse's and Michelson's aversion to him, which provoked their propagandistic tactics, the president played into the hands of his critics, not only the Democratic publicity committee, but also the White House reporters. He increasingly avoided the press, distributing mimeographed handouts in a way that reflected his reticence with the public. Little did the president understand what a politician of yesteryear had grasped when he said of a supplicant, Theodore Roosevelt: "Waiter, pull up the curtains and let the people see the President eat."[19] Presidents are fascinating to their people; especially was this so in "an era of personalities" such as the 1920s and 1930s. The period frequently descended into an "era of the gutter journalism," sometimes beyond even what Democratic publicity director Charles Michelson wished. It was a rather new formula for American politics. Michelson entered the presidential politics of the 1932 campaign with far more acumen than had publicity directors in any prior campaigns. On 30 December 1932 William Allen White wrote to his close friend Henry Allen: "These [are] malevolent times. Did it ever occur to you that we went through the . . . campaign and the preliminary campaign of that year before last June without one kindly story circulated about Hoover or about any of his friends? And all sorts of gossip, malicious, dirty, grotesque gossip was dramatized into little wise-crack episodes about Hoover and all who surrounded him, and repeated across the nation, crackling like flames of hell as they went. Lord, what a time. The malice in men's hearts rises in their adversity."[20]

What White saw happening from a distance, Ted Clark, Coolidge's former secretary, knew from personal experience. Brought in to help press relations during the campaign, Clark was shocked by "the bitter personal hatred which [Hoover] . . . has inspired in so many of the newspapermen." Again, the atmosphere seemed to attract the trivial as well as the substantive event. Clark wrote to Coolidge: "The final blow was the investigation by the Secret Service of an insignificant story out of the Rapidan Camp. The investigation was made, not because the story had done any harm, but because the president was determined to get rid of anyone who was dropping hints to the newspapermen. Man after man was brought over to Moran's office in the Treasury Department and put through the third degree. Since then news has been distorted in an effort to injure Mr. Hoover to a degree that I never imagined possible."[21]

A few days after the election, Clark wrote to Coolidge, as he did after the Rapidan camp incident, that the state of unfortunate press relations was attributable to both "the newspapers' propaganda against [Hoover] headed by Charles Mikelson [sic] of the Democratic Committee and the terrorism which the White House tried to exercise through [Larry] Richey."[22]

The link between White House press relations and the reporters' treatment of the issues that Hoover propounded during the campaign is not known. In any case, the depressed times, like those of Van Buren, probably spelled defeat; but if they had not, the president's press relations might well have done so.

Historical analysis of the 1932 campaign in recent years frequently adds up to far more similarities than differences on issues between the major presidential candidates. Such a point of view is given credence by the fact that Roosevelt has come to be viewed as having moved to the left after his inauguration, rather than before the election. And Hoover's charge that his opponent's 1932 positions were frequently adjusted to a conservative "chameleon-on-plaid" attitude seems to ring true. The difference between the candidates, it can be argued, was far more in manner than in substance. On the specific issues of agriculture, labor, foreign policy, public works, economy in government, prohibition, and the tariff, the candidates frequently were more in agreement than in disagreement. For example, it can be contended that Roosevelt's Topeka speech on agriculture was so vague as to disaffirm support for the "radical" domestic allotment plan; that on labor, the Democrats, like the Republicans, hardly mentioned collective bargaining; that Roosevelt said that the foreign policy of "old Hoover" was "pretty good"; that Hoover had broken all records with his administration's public-works expenditures; that while Roosevelt had promised relief in his Pittsburgh speech, he had vowed to economize in government; that on prohibition both candidates supported repeal and opposed the return of the saloon; and that on the tariff, while Roosevelt deplored Smoot-Hawley protection, he backtracked at the end of the campaign, provoking Hoover's "chameleon" comment.

This "similarity view" of the 1932 campaign, however, does not really square with the facts. The candidates did differ on specific issues. Hoover took pride in pointing out the ideological disparity, as confirmed by his many campaign allusions to individualism, which he so meticulously catalogued in his memoirs. Roosevelt was not the big-government advocate that Hoover said he was, but the New Yorker's pragmatism moved him to emphasize the need for more government, as he obviously ennunciated in his speech at the Commonwealth Club in San Francisco.

Substantive differences between Herbert Hoover and Franklin D. Roosevelt on specific issues can be easily tallied. Roosevelt's agriculture speech, at Topeka in September 1932, entailed the input of some twenty-five experts (or near-experts) on the subject, including M. L. Wilson, the authority who came closest to being the father of the domestic-allotment plan. Wilson and Roosevelt held such similar opinions on the subject that neither knew who was influencing whom. While the "six-points"—tarifflike benefits, self-financing, nonforeign dumping, decentralization, cooperation, and voluntarism—might have looked like "glittering generalities" to Republican Senator Lester Dickinson, to Hoover they constituted a disguise for the "price-fixing" domestic-allotment scheme. Roosevelt, who probably took agriculture more seriously than any other issue, delivered at Topeka a farm speech that appealed to nearly all of agriculture's diverse schools.

On labor, Roosevelt was rather silent. Still, Roosevelt, in Boston, criticized his opponent for vetoing the Wagner public-employment-office bill. Hoover was sufficiently nettled by the charge to explain in his memoirs that he had vetoed the bill because it was an attempt by Tammany Hall and other city machines to obtain control of the federal employment service. On foreign policy, differences, while minimal, still existed. For one thing, Roosevelt's ''isolationism,'' as Hoover surely knew, had been mandated by William Randolph Hearst. Second, while sometimes for and sometimes against tariff reduction, Roosevelt, at heart, was for it, even if his political consideration caused him to take a position favoring protection. On the issue of public-works efforts, Hoover supported the self-liquidating concept. Roosevelt went beyond that concept and pushed as essential such federally sponsored community efforts as public playgrounds and public housing.

Roosevelt's October 19 ''Economy'' speech in Pittsburgh, where he swore to reduce current federal expenditures by 25 percent, haunted him in subsequent years. Roosevelt, of course, believed in a balanced budget. The fact that he demanded 25 percent reductions in federal operations does point up his conservatism at this late stage of the campaign. A partial explanation was that he was persuaded by his conservative advisers, in this case particularly the main writer of the speech, Hugh S. Johnson, a protégé of Bernard Baruch. The speech seemed to be filled with conservative shibboleths and fears of federal extravagance, unbalanced budgets, and other ''economic heresies.'' Little wonder that in subsequent years Judge Samuel I. Rosenman advised the president to deny that he had ever made the speech. Did the speech reflect a Hooverlike economy-mindedness in 1932, or does it justify the charge of political deceitfulness that has frequently been hurled at Roosevelt by his opponents? Although Roosevelt's political success has frequently been explained by his political flexibility, a pang of conservative conscience seems to have struck home in the ''Economy'' speech.

On the prohibition issue the candidates unquestionably had fundamental differences. Roosevelt was wet; Hoover was dry.

Roosevelt's fluctuations for and against the tariff issue proved to be the most embarrassing of his candidacy. Particularly striking was the contrast between his early adamant opposition to what he described in late September as ''the notorious indefensible Grundy tariff . . . a ghastly plot'' and his late October comments: ''It is absurd to talk of lowering tariff duties on farm products'' and ''I favor continued protection for American agriculture as well as American industry."[23] This latter position was a political appeal on the eve of the election and was quite contrary to the candidate's internationalist, low-tariff stance before the campaign, the vehemence with which he attacked the Smoot-Hawley Tariff early in the campaign, and the low-tariff history throughout his long presidency.

Issues were prolific during the campaign. Hoover begot them and combed Roosevelt's speeches for purposes of rebuttal, either in his omnibus speeches or in his memoirs, which were published twenty years later. To scrutinize other issues here, such as gold, currency, taxation, monetary policy, conservation, bank-deposits insurance, and stock-market control, would belabor the fact that Roosevelt frequently equivocated, although he leaned heavily toward change, and that although Hoover rarely hedged, his positions were far more moderate than liberal historians have reported.

Two distinctions in regard to issues remain to be made: on public-utility power and the general philosophy of government. Without gainsaying Hoover's enlightened position on the federal construction and regulation of electric power, Roosevelt went further and called, where necessary, for federal ownership and distribution. This became the basis for the Tennessee Valley Authority, which has been described by Eric Goldman as epitomizing the New Deal centralization-decentralization. The Commonwealth Club speech, delivered in San Francisco in late September, was a portent of the New Deal to come, which reflected, in bold relief, the nuance of most of Roosevelt's campaign rhetoric—namely, that we "are providing a drab living for our own people" and that "our task now is . . . the business . . . of administering resources . . . [and] distributing wealth and products more equitably."[24] Frequently it has been said that Roosevelt had not seen the speech prior to delivering it. He was no fool. The speech was the culmination of a long dialogue with his brain trust.

In regard to campaign strategy and tactics, the Democrats, somewhat fortuitously, got off to a head start, a disadvantage that Republicans could ill afford. For one thing, Republicans were caught napping when they expended needed efforts and talents to resolve their prohibition stance, thus sacrificing their dire need to alert the nation to their antidepression efforts. Second, and much related to that mistake, the Democrats, conversely, used the depression as their first issue, as indeed Michelson had been doing for years. So indelibly have Democrats associated Hoover with the depression that more than a half-century after the campaign, they are still using it as an issue against Republicans. Third, the immediate launching of the Democratic campaign by Franklin Roosevelt's air flight to Chicago to accept the presidential nomination was dramatic, especially when compared to the time-honored custom of having a committee from the convention, weeks later, call upon the candidate to inform him of their party's nomination. And last, Democratic campaign strategy jelled quickly as compared to the Republicans' slow start and decreasing effectiveness.

The press, as always, was strategically important to both parties, but more successfully so to the Democrats in this election because Michelson had attuned so many reporters to his prejudicial views and because Roosevelt was able to win back most of the southern papers that had opposed the wet Catholic Smith. Republican editors, who dominated the editorial columns of most papers in the nation, found that their readers were frequently staying with the front-page stories about the depression president or the progressive New York governor. The Republican campaign tried to mitigate the Michelson vilification with ongoing endorsements from such shrinking numbers of Hoover supporters as former President Coolidge, the popular novelist Mary Roberts Rinehart, and the editor William Allen White. Those who were approached for support frequently balked. Coolidge could not provide daily help, as requested. White did not like the pressure, even from his fellow Kansan Henry Allen, "When I . . . write something . . . under orders, the little devil balks." Allen came to appreciate the small favors, such as having Coolidge and White occasionally yield and even having Louis Howe refuse to buy a story that during the war Hoover was seen eating beefsteak on a meatless day.[25]

Radio, too, was of strategic importance, especially by 1932. Here, Roosevelt had the edge. John D. Hicks had noticed that in 1928 campaigner Hoover's words had come out of the airways better than they had gone in, as compared to those of Smith, who caused a staccatolike sound by not standing still before the microphones. However, in 1932 Roosevelt's melodious voice sounded better than his opponent's tonal evenness, especially when Hoover persevered, seemingly for hours. Agriculture Secretary Hyde once forcefully delivered to an associate a paragraph from a Hoover speech and remarked that "the President failed to capitalize on his opportunities throughout the entire speech."[26] Roosevelt not only modulated, he entertained with his own Alice-in-Wonderland anecdotes. One example is when, in Columbus, Ohio, he spoke about the dreary subjects of the tariff and the "moratorium":

A puzzled, somewhat skeptical Alice asked the Republican leadership some simple questions.

"Will not the printing and selling of more stocks and bonds, the building of new plants and the increase of efficiency produce more goods than we buy?"

"No," shouted Humpty Dumpty. "The more we produce the more we can buy."

"What if we produce a surplus?"

"Oh, we can sell it to foreign consumers."

"How can the foreigners pay for it?"

"Why, we will lend them the money."

"I see," said little Alice, "they will buy our surplus with our money. Of course, these foreigners will pay us back by selling us their goods?"

"Oh, not at all," said Humpty Dumpty. "We set up a high wall called the tariff."

"And," said Alice at last, "how will the foreigners pay off these loans?"

"That is easy," said Humpty Dumpty, "did you ever hear of moratorium?"[27]

Anecdotes, allusions, slogans, and symbols, used as political shorthand messages to millions of Americans, are frequently as important and revealing as prepared speeches, although Roosevelt's Topeka speech, with its input from many advisers, was short, had a common touch, and was profoundly notable. Hoover's speech in Madison Square Garden on October 31, one of his last major campaign speeches, was cumbersome, five times as long as Roosevelt's campaign finale in the same place two days later, and probably more harmful than helpful. That allusions and symbols were important in 1932 is evidenced by their ring of familiarity after a half-century. They are a part of the strategy, often as fortuitous as not. The term "New Deal" was accidental, but Democratic singing of "Happy Days Are Here Again" was not. The Democrats had the better of it. Roosevelt's gay, upraised, confident face, with his famous grin or upward-pointed cigarette holder, was viewed by some observers as being supercilious, while it displayed to many Americans an air of sincerity and optimism, especially as contrasted to the Quaker stoicism and grimness on the face of Herbert Hoover, set above his frequently stiff high collar.

Political shorthand communication told Americans more than what a thousand words from either candidate could have conveyed. Hoover usually found such communicating too trivial. While Franklin Roosevelt taught his granddaughter to sing "Happy Days," Hoover grimly warned that if Roosevelt's tariff proposals were adopted, the "grass would grow in the streets of America." Hoover was almost unique among American presidents in finding the game of symbolism repugnant. When he stayed in the "Rose Garden" in the early part of the campaign, he stayed there to work, not just to look as though he were working. When he left to campaign, as he did increasingly in the weeks before the election, he did not leave on cue, but left only because at last he felt he could be spared. And when he left, he went plodding onward, avoiding the dilettantism of symbols. He could not and would not be directed. His friend John C. O'Laughlin suggested to Hoover that Mrs. Theodore Roosevelt, Jr., accompany him to California. "This would completely offset the Franklin Roosevelt propaganda that he is regarded as T.R.'s living representative." O'Laughlin continued: "It would be helpful also for Lindbergh to pilot a Victory Flight; and it would add to the public interests if Amelia Earhardt [sic] would accompany him. They could be met at different landing fields by escorts of planes and by Republican committees. There is an excellent chance for publicity, and the few words Lindbergh would utter undoubtedly would be helpful, and if Mrs. Roosevelt could be brought back by Lindbergh to vote for you, the dramatic effect would be heightened."[28] Hoover probably cringed at the idea, although he had in fact previously entertained Mrs. Roosevelt, Colonel Lindbergh, and Amelia Earhart at the White House, with no personal "public relations" in mind. One proposed slogan that was found in the Hoover papers probably was not suggested to the president: "Boy! wasn't that some Depression."

Hoover did spend much time at dispatching his few remaining agents out into the country. Unfortunately, there were too few of them, usually only cabinet members. Treasury Secretary Ogden Mills was the workhorse of the campaign. Intelligent, articulate, confident, and aristocratic in bearing, he served his president best among eastern establishment audiences. Postmaster General Walter Brown was, of course, the president's most effective liaison with party workers. Secretary of War Patrick Hurley worked the veterans' organizations, as William N. Doak did the labor organizations that wanted to hear the Republican point of view. Hoover wanted Stimson, particularly, to attack Governor Roosevelt, his fellow New Yorker. Stimson, as secretary of state, would not do this. He did defend the administration's foreign policy, and he applauded Hoover's many antidepression efforts. But his few speeches were far from what Hoover wanted. Stimson said, "I tried not to get into any general criticism of . . . [Roosevelt] or any calling of names." Hoover never forgave him for his reluctance to criticize Roosevelt. "He [Stimson] was the first Cabinet leader in history to take that view," wrote Hoover in his *Memoirs*.[29]

As for his campaign spokesmen, Roosevelt's experience was the opposite of Hoover's. All shades of Democrats, including even Al

Smith, spoke on Roosevelt's behalf. Most notable, although not surprising, were insurgent Republicans: George Norris, Robert La Follette, Hiram Johnson, Bronson W. Cutting, Donald Richberg, and Harold Ickes. Western Republican support for Roosevelt saddened William Allen White, who, from early in the Hoover presidency, had hoped to be the president's link with these western progressives. Having long lost that coveted role, White stayed loyal to the president—but with little enthusiasm.

By election time, Hoover's supporters seemed to have narrowed down to habit-voting Republicans, a cluster of industrialists, those farmers who still favored the independence of the soil, organization Republicans, and a coterie of Hoover's admirers. At that, Roosevelt received a substantial share of these elements and many of the rest: the unemployed, the poor, the small businessmen, exporters, investors, professionals, veterans, and an ever-increasing fraternity of Roosevelt's advisers as well as all "good" Democrats.

The nation's economy actually picked up during the third quarter of 1932, but signs of economic distress were everywhere prevalent: farm foreclosures, business and bank failures, raging unemployment, and malnutrition. The press no longer needed Michelson to describe conditions in America. Now, reporters were picturing the difficulties on their own.

On the eve of the election, Hoover still believed that he had a chance, which was typical of his self-delusion. Others around the president thought that victory was possible—perhaps their degree of optimism being in direct proportion to their closeness to the "Chief." Henry Allen was not very hopeful. He would have been had they been able to get the president on the campaign trail in September instead of October. Mills thought that Hoover would win. Hurley and Stimson faced reality. "The people of sobriety," Stimson wrote in his diary, "and intelligence and responsibility are on Mr. Hoover's side and yet we have a feeling that the immense undercurrent is against us."[30]

The president lost, by about 22,800,000 to 15,750,000 in the popular vote and by 472 to 59 in the electoral vote. He carried only six eastern states: Connecticut, Delaware, Maine, New Hampshire, Pennsylvania, and Vermont.

Feeling about the election results depended upon the individual's personal identification with the president. "I am stunned," wrote Edgar Rickard; "it is a great calamity."[31] William Allen White was sorry but not distraught. He told Gifford Pinchot that he did not think "that Roosevelt was worth a bolt. I don't trust his fiber."[32] Stimson thought more of himself than he did of Hoover: "I have taken an active part in the campaign and have made some vigorous speeches against Roosevelt which cannot make him friendly toward me. . . . I am in the lap of the gods.''[33] The president, in the way of Friends, was sparse in his comments and feeling about defeat: ''As we expected, we were defeated in the election.''[34]

11

★ ★ ★ ★ ★

RITES OF PASSAGE

Rites of passage between presidencies have taken various forms, although few were as difficult and acrimonious as that from Hoover to Roosevelt. All presidential transitions are, at best, stressful. Examples of magnanimity in giving up the great office and the White House are scarce. Theodore Roosevelt grinned and then bore it with the help of a long African safari. Wilson would have preferred to die in office, and almost did, rather than leave. Coolidge had many bitter things to say about his successor. President Taft differed from his White House brethren: he gladly left the office, sharing with Hoover the uncommon experience of being forced by the electorate to leave involuntarily.

Henry L. Stimson, from the perspective of a cabinet post, had watched the passage from Taft to Wilson. Now again, also from a cabinet post, he witnessed another transition. Stimson hoped that Hoover would take the defeat and transition as Taft had done, cheerfully and philosophically. He remembered that Taft rather enjoyed it: "He went everywhere and saw everybody and made [cheerful] speeches" and "really had a good time." Not so with Hoover! Stimson continues in his diary: "He had wrapped himself in the belief that the state of the country really depended on his re-election. . . . All through the three-and-a-half years, I could see that the question of his re-election was constantly on his mind." Little wonder, thought Stimson, that the president was very depressed upon losing the election. While Taft was forever through with partisan politics after his defeat, Hoover was "full of fight" and still smelled "the aroma of battle." Stimson tried to ease

Hoover's burden by telling him that "the currents of American life were so immensely strong that no individual could control them." But the secretary knew that Hoover was his own man, and not a cheerful Taft. Stimson also suggested Grover Cleveland as a model. That strong New Yorker, who had left the presidency in defeat after one term, was still a partisan but "paid no attention to politics" upon his departure. "And then . . . the current became so strong that nothing could stop his [re]nomination and re-election." Hoover seemed to listen to Stimson but again became moody—a condition that was exacerbated by the president-elect's temperament and ideology.[1]

The transition accelerated quickly after the election, when on November 10 the British ambassador dropped a "bombshell" during Stimson's "Diplomatic Hour," a time set aside for ambassadorial calls. Ambassador Sir Ronald Charles Lindsay requested that the United States hold up on the December 15 deadline for Britain's next debt payment, pending a consideration to reduce the interest and principal on the debt. Stimson and Mills wanted Hoover to work harmoniously with the president-elect on the request, but they could not restrain the president from putting his own campaign views of noncancellation of foreign debts into a telegram to Roosevelt on the subject of the British request. Stimson felt the message "took away the simple and magnanimous tone which [he and Mills] tried to put in the telegram." Roosevelt probably believed as Stimson did, that the president was finding it hard "to lift himself above the [political] plane on which he has been for so many months."[2] In a telegraphed invitation to Roosevelt, Hoover also strongly urged that the discussion of the foreign debts be accompanied by an interchange of views on disarmament and the forthcoming international economic conference. The president was apparently trying to score two points: first, that the British note was wrong in reading into the Hoover-Laval communique of the previous month a suggestion of debt adjustment—for, indeed, Hoover at that time had informed both Laval and the American people whom he met on the campaign trail that the debts must be paid; and second, that by getting Roosevelt to accept a tying of debts to disarmament and the economic conference, the president-elect would be agreeing that the American depression was part of a world-wide phenomenon and not a domestic one to be laid on the outgoing president.

The fact was that Roosevelt had very indefinite ideas about debts and their relationship to foreign affairs and the American economy. If he had a view, he leaned in Hoover's direction on these matters as he did on budget balancing and sound currency. Here temperamental differences surfaced. Hoover was grimly sure of his international-credit approach to the world's depression. Roosevelt was unperturbedly ambivalent about the relationship but was confident that by inaugural time his administration would have some solutions to economic problems. Hoover's power of analysis surpassed Roosevelt's, which is not to say that the president-elect was not addressing an array of depression problems, with the aid of numerous advisers from diverse schools. But Roosevelt had a distinct temperamental advantage over Hoover. As Oliver Wendell Holmes poignantly implied at the time, Roosevelt's "second-class intellect" was of lesser importance than his "first-class temperament."

Roosevelt's response to the president's telegram reflected the "chameleon-like" quality that Hoover had accused him of having. Because the president-elect's counsel was very much divided on the debt question and its ramifications, Roosevelt's wire to Hoover was courteously general, indicating his desire to have "your views" but noting that "the responsibility . . . rests upon those now invested with executive and legislative authority."[3] Obviously, Roosevelt needed time to choose—indeed, if he had to choose—between the international and the domestic wings of his advisers, Col. Edward House and Owen D. Young representing the former; Raymond Moley and Rexford Tugwell, the latter. And other advice impinged upon the general nature of his reply to Hoover. Felix Frankfurter suggested that Roosevelt keep his meeting with Hoover "informal and personal."[4] Senator Key Pittman's advice was that Roosevelt watch out for Hoover's "pre-prepared [press] statements," thus implying the possibility of entrapment.[5]

Hoover, who was dissatisfied and scornful of Roosevelt's very general reply, telephoned to him on November 17 to make specific arrangements for the two of them to meet when the president-elect was planning to travel through Washington within a fortnight. The president indicated that he would like to include in the conference Ogden Mills, "because I would like to give you an outline of what is going on abroad."[6] Roosevelt agreed, saying that Raymond Moley would accompany him. Stimson, who concurred that the debt problem was more a Treasury Department issue than a State Department matter, was not to attend the meeting but was to be readily available for consultation, if needed. Hoover, who was always more comfortable with Mills anyway, may have become disenchanted with Stimson. Perhaps he sensed Stimson's suspicion of Hoover and Mills, which the secretary of state recorded in his diary—"the president [wants] to protect his record in the past, and Mills to protect his future." Stimson agreed that there were reasons for distrusting Roosevelt, but he suggested to Hoover that "the way to make a person trustworthy is to trust him."[7]

The meeting took place in the Red Room at 3:45 P.M. on November 22, the four men sitting in a circle against the backdrop of a wood-burning fire and portraits of Presidents Adams, Jefferson, Madison, and Grant. Immediately the president expostulated at length on the need to avoid cancellation of foreign debts but at the same time to recognize the need for debt adjustment, an adjustment that would best be addressed by reconstituting a debt commission of presidential appointees, named with Roosevelt's approval. Moley demurred, preferring diplomatic, rather than the special commission, route for negotiating with debtor nations. Roosevelt let Moley do much of the talking. Hoover undoubtedly wondered about the prominence of this professor in the dialogue and directed much of his "education" toward him. He subsequently described him as "ignorant." Roosevelt, by nodding, seemed to be agreeing to the principle of negotiation with debtor nations, if not by the special-commission route. Again, while Hoover knew quite specifically what he wanted by way of proceeding, Roosevelt knew only generally. The president-elect's instinct was to feel his way and not be bound by a machinery that might tie foreign issues such as debts, disarmament, and the forthcoming economic conference in such a way as to restrict his own resolution of great economic problems. The new administration might well decide to emphasize internal rather than external solutions to the nation's depression. Such Hoover-Roosevelt differences in approaching the depression were quite naturally left unmentioned in the meeting; and when the two men agreed to make separate press statements, Hoover expected Roosevelt's support for the reconstituted debt commission. He did not get it. In nodding assent to negotiation, Roosevelt probably had been favoring Moley's diplomatic route. Furthermore, in his press statement, Roosevelt reiterated that debt negotiation was primarily the responsibility of the Hoover administration. The meeting, as Frank Freidel describes it, had been "pleasant enough, but relations between the men turned sour."[8] Even Stimson was pained by Roosevelt's "let down" of the president. For once, Stimson, like the president, was discouraged. "The quicker we get these damn debts out of the way . . . the better off we'll be," he wrote in his diary. The difference was that Hoover was far less willing than Stimson to drop the debts at any cost.[9]

While the outgoing and incoming administrations developed differences on procedures for dealing with debt negotiations and other European matters, Hoover answered the British note, insisting on that nation's paying, but suggesting the possibility of future negotiation. It took considerable effort on Stimson's part to tone down Hoover's draft of the note. The secretary of state often complained in his diary that the president had swung "off the high plane."[10] At one point the president told Stimson that the two of them were "ten million miles apart on the debt issue."[11]

The British paid their debt installment on December 10; and Hoover and Stimson debated the issue again, the former still wanting Roosevelt to join in appointing a debt commission. Stimson felt that Hoover was still pursuing old campaign goals, whether in his relations with Roosevelt or with the British. Stimson noted in his diary: "Our leader is showing his worst side. . . . He seems to be unable to divest himself of personal and partisan politics." Hoover was amazed by Stimson's attitude and "joked" with him and Mills about "our friend who is for protecting every other nation except his own."[12] It was like Hoover, of course, to worry about what he had said and to apologize to his secretary of state—a refreshing posture for a president, a stance that Stimson much appreciated.

Hoover, on December 17, again asked Roosevelt to cooperate in appointing a debt commission. Roosevelt waited a few days before replying, probably to see what Hoover would say on the subject to a special session of the lame-duck Congress. As Roosevelt had expected, Hoover intertwined debts, disarmament, and the agenda of the economic conference, whereupon the president-elect replied to Hoover's latest invitation by insisting that the three items should be kept separate. Stimson now thought that Roosevelt was being uncooperative, but he again influenced President Hoover to tone down another message to the president-elect. "I am unwilling," wrote Hoover, "to admit that cooperation cannot be established between the outgoing and incoming administrations which will give earlier solutions and recovery from these difficulties." Roosevelt answered on the next day, saying that the "difficulties" between them were not "the means or the intelligence [needed] for cooperation but, rather, in defining clearly those things concerning which cooperation between us is possible." On the next day Hoover threw up his hands and released in total to the press all the Hoover-Roosevelt communications, "in order that there may be no misunderstanding." Roosevelt replied through the press with a counter communique: "I have made to the president the definite suggestion that he select his representatives to make preliminary studies. I have asked to be kept advised as to the progress of these preliminaries. I have offered to consult with the president freely between now and March 4th." Needless to say, free and easy consultation did not seem to be in the offing.[13]

On the day that Hoover and Roosevelt exchanged charges of noncooperation, fur flew in their respective camps. Hoover pondered a memorandum from Larry Richey, which told of Lewis L. Straus's information that Roosevelt seemingly was planning to ignore Hoover's ideas on foreign debt and to settle things himself with British Prime Minister MacDonald in a "big dramatic" White House meeting in April.[14] In the other camp, Baruch wrote to James M. Cox, applauding Roosevelt's unwillingness to cooperate and concluding that the word to Hoover meant that he was "to have his own way."[15] Yet both camps had calmer heads than might have been expected.

Herbert Feis, an economic adviser to the secretary of state, while attending a Harvard function, telephoned to his old friend, law professor Felix Frankfurter, who had been invited to be with Roosevelt that very evening in the Governor's Mansion in Albany. Feis and Frankfurter quite naturally discussed the Hoover-Roosevelt liaison problem, and just as naturally concluded that their mutual mentor, Henry L. Stimson, might effect a liaison between the president and the president-elect. (Frankfurter had admired the secretary for over twenty-five years. When Stimson was the United States attorney for the southern district of New York, young Frankfurter had served on his staff.) Frankfurter, in his discussion with Roosevelt that evening, undoubtedly related the question of the liaison to Stimson's possible role, evoking Roosevelt's response: "Why doesn't Harry Stimson come up here and talk with me and settle this damn thing that nobody else seems able to do?" Shortly thereafter, Frankfurter called Stimson and reported Roosevelt's regret at the breakdown of cooperation and added that if the secretary were to call the president-elect, the latter would invite him to come to Hyde Park on the day after Christmas. Stimson liked the idea, but Hoover and Mills did not, although the secretary of the Treasury admitted his "good opinion of Frankfurter." Hoover insisted that communication between the incoming and outgoing administrations could be reopened only if Roosevelt were to send down to Washington two or three men of proper eminence to talk to Stimson and Mills.[16]

When Frankfurter again called Stimson about the idea of a visit, the secretary of state said that he "was much gratified that Roosevelt wanted to meet him" but that he "could not see at present that it would do any good." Stimson then pressed Hoover's suggestion that the president-elect should send to Washington several prominent men to talk to Hoover and to Mills. For several days, Frankfurter, directly or through Feis, kept in touch with Stimson, saying on one occasion: "Trust my accuracy in this matter; Roosevelt is anxious to see you." Four days later, on December 28, Frankfurter, thinking that Stimson was reluctant about having a meeting, sketched Roosevelt's character, causing Stimson to admit that the picture of the president-elect was "more attractive [than] . . . that we have been getting from . . . [our] side." After a few days, on January 2 of the new year, Stimson told Hoover that "it was a ticklish responsibility to refuse to give foreign policy information to . . . [the president-elect] even supposing he was as bad as [the president] thought." "It was more dangerous," Stimson said, "to give him . . . [the] grievance of not seeing him." The secretary of state concluded by saying that Hoover's foreign policy was what he wanted to pursue in any conversation with Roosevelt. Hoover finally acquiesced, murmuring doubts "of the possibility of success."[17]

Roosevelt was as eager as ever for the meeting. (Even before he had heard about Hoover's approval, the president-elect asked a mutual friend of the two administrations, Norman Davis, for any sign of approval.) Now, Stimson immediately got in touch with Frankfurter, who in turn made known the turn of events to Roosevelt, who amusedly handled it as Hoover wanted, by writing to the president and formally asking to see the secretary of state. Hoover made the most of it, releasing to the press the news of the forthcoming meeting and thinking about the press mileage that would be achieved from the meeting. He told Charles Evans Hughes and Stimson that if the two administrations could agree on the joint appointment of a debt commission, "by doing so and giving a good deal of publicity [to] it, there will be an impression given to the country that something is being done and that this may serve to stave off the bad effects of another panic."[18]

So, on January 9 the liaison between the administrations was renewed at Hyde Park, and there began a relationship between the secretary and the president-elect that had consequences far beyond the interregnum, to a far-off day when Stimson would serve in yet another cabinet, as Roosevelt's World War II secretary of war. The thought of this at that time, however, was as unlikely as the idea that Stimson "connived" to steer Roosevelt's solutions to the depression in Hooverlike internationalist approaches, a belief that was then and thereafter adhered to by Raymond Moley.[19]

Roosevelt and Stimson were caught up in the moment, enjoying a wide-ranging conversation in the old home, with its "confusion from the accumulation of [Christmas] packages" and a miscellany of "general furnishings . . . [which the secretary] felt sure would not meet with [his wife] Mabel's approval." They talked of United States policy regarding Cuba, the Far East, disarmament, the economic conference, foreign debts, Haiti, the Philippine Islands, and Russia, as well as the "character of our Foreign Service," in that order. Stimson expressed pleasure that Roosevelt was in agreement with Stimson's Manchurian policy. He cautioned the president-elect to consider the possibility of complications in the upcoming economic conference. And he listened closely to Roosevelt's two reasons for opposing the idea of having a debt commission: (1) the president-elect could not jointly appoint members because he had not yet selected his cabinet members and policy makers, and (2) he thought that he could get a better debt settlement through Congress than through a commission. Roosevelt "spoke of the unpopularity of Mr. Hoover's commission." Stimson loyally reported the president's desire "to obtain the necessary psychological effect in the country to stop this [economic] deterioration." That evening Stimson concluded in his diary that "none of the president's forebodings [about Roosevelt] were realized."[20]

The important immediate consequence of the Hyde Park session was the arrangement of another Hoover-Roosevelt meeting, to take place when the president-elect would next pass through Washington. When Stimson reported this to Hoover two days later, he expressed the hope that the president would not flatly object to Roosevelt's ideas of avoiding a debt commission and separating the debts from the economic conference. The president "said he would think it over, overnight." After reflecting upon it, Hoover still wanted Roosevelt to name three or more experts, whom the president would appoint to sit down with the best British representatives "to work out a plan to reverse the economic forces now working in the world." Stimson understood what Roosevelt wanted—an informal contact with an Englishman, such as the lord president of the council, Stanley Baldwin. "If the Governor," Hoover told Stimson, "wants an Englishman to come over, and if he will do all of the negotiating, we can facilitate it." Such hyperbole aside, the president agreed to meet again with the president-elect.[21]

Stimson left the White House, crossed the street to the State, War, and Navy Building, and telephoned Roosevelt to make final arrangements for a meeting with the president and to spell out some difficulties that were inherent in some of the issues to be discussed. In his lengthy and cordial conversation with the president-elect, the secretary seemed to accommodate successfully his own views to those of Hoover and Roosevelt. Stimson recorded the points in his telephone conversation with Roosevelt. For one, he suggested that even if the foreign debts and the economic conference were to be separated, the United States needed some assurance of British cooperation in stabilizing currency, unless the two nations were prepared to enter an inflation race. Roosevelt emphatically opposed—at least so Stimson thought—such an "inflation race." Second, the British would want to send over "several men" to negotiate the debts and the agenda for the economic conference. Roosevelt reiterated to Stimson his opposition to too many British negotiators, to what would seem like the formation of commissions of experts. Third, Stimson told the president-elect that continual study would have to ensue immediately, so that there would be men who would be ready to talk. Roosevelt agreed. Fourth, Stimson quite correctly predicted that the debt issue would "crop up" early in any preliminary discussion with the British. Last, Stimson warned Roosevelt against too much conferring in Washington, where press and Congress would get involved as soon as a stage of negotiating was reached. The secretary was anxious to arrange negotiations on a European site. Stimson closed his conversation by urging that the British not arrive until March 1, so that they could discuss matters with Roosevelt's secretaries of state and of the Treasury, thus avoiding "as far as possible the idea of a commission." While deferring to Roosevelt on the latter point, Stimson, in deference to Hoover, pressed for an early announcement of a meeting with the British so that the nation would have "the psychological advantage" for the recovery of the country.[22]

The ground for the forthcoming meeting seemed to be firmly set. Harvey H. Bundy and Herbert Feis, who had listened to their chief's talk with Roosevelt on auxiliary phones, were pleased; and when Stimson reported his conversation to Mills and Hoover, they also seemed to be contented. The president, however, had his usual caveat. He urged Stimson to prepare a debt-paying demand note for France, which Roosevelt could approve when he was in Washington, thus doubling the pressure on that recalcitrant nation. Stimson commented frustratedly in his diary: "It is an old and favorite suggestion of his."[23]

On the morning of January 19 Stimson talked forthrightly to Ambassador Lindsay during the diplomatic hour, bringing the British envoy up to date on the renewed Hoover-Roosevelt cooperation and asking particularly if the British were prepared to send over representatives if Roosevelt approved of holding discussions. The ambassador said they were so prepared. Stimson then had lunch with the president, who at the moment was satisfied with the progress in the new "cooperation" and looked forward to his second meeting with the president-elect on the morrow. Then, in midafternoon the secretary answered Roosevelt's request that he call at the Mayflower Hotel. He was warmly greeted by the president-elect: "We are getting so that we do pretty good teamwork, don't we?" Stimson smiled and agreed. The secretary loyally brought up the president's idea of the new French note. Stimson was not bothered when Roosevelt demurred on the subject of the note, but he became concerned that now the president-elect was "hesitant and confused," particularly on the point of the importance of not giving up our debts until we had received some assurances as to Great Britain's attitude on other things, particularly her stabilization of currency. However, Stimson thought that he had brought the president-elect and Raymond Moley back on the administration's foreign-debt and economic-conference track. Norman Davis, whom Roosevelt brought into the conference, had been supportive of Stimson's position all along.[24]

On the next day, Hoover and Roosevelt had their second meeting with Mills and Moley, this time with Stimson and Norman Davis also. Again they sat in a circle in the Red Room. Following some pleasantries and then some comments by the president on debt negotiation, Stimson was surprised that Moley vehemently opposed any connection between the debts and the general economic situation. And Roosevelt seemed "wobbly" on the relationship between debts and economic conditions that they had agreed to the day before. Stimson reported in his diary that he had told Roosevelt that since he had to conduct negotiations with the British, he had to know if the president-elect would accept British "assurances" regarding favorable trade adjustment (such as lower tariffs) for "concessions which we might make on the debts." He noted that Roosevelt and Moley saw the two subjects of economic conditions and foreign debts as related, but in the form of "twins," which should be "treated as physically two different discussions of which the results of one might be made conditional on the other." Stimson's diary account reveals an annoyance with an appearance of coyness on the part of Roosevelt and Moley. "Their conditions," he concluded, "seemed to be based upon some relics of the campaign in the shape of positions which Roosevelt may have taken." Stimson was certainly right. Roosevelt undoubtedly wanted to protect his freedom of movement in his new administration and not to be bound domestically by any foreign economic agreements prior to that time.[25]

Moley seemed to stand alone in his vehemence about separating debts and economic conditions, although Roosevelt did support his idea that discussions on the debts and economic conditions be kept separate. After the meeting, Roosevelt went off to Warm Springs, Georgia, leaving it to Moley and Stimson to work out a statement to be sent to the British on debts and other economic matters. Because Moley and Tugwell insisted, the aide-mémoire on which the British note was based said that "any discussion of debts . . . must be concurrent with and conditional upon a discussion of world economic problems."[26] Although the statement seemed in fact to connect debts and economic conditions, Stimson knew what Moley and Tugwell meant by it and therefore signed it unhappily.

In the short and long runs, the anxiety in the two administrations regarding the forthcoming London Economic Conference was more debilitating and time-consuming than necessary. Shortly thereafter, in Warm Springs, Roosevelt had the whole matter in his hands after a soothing talk there with British Ambassador Lindsay, which afforded Roosevelt the time to handle the debt issue and the economic conference in his own way during the months following the inauguration. The weeks-long dialogue during the interregnum was revealing of political contests, particularly of the outgoing and incoming presidents—the former, for quite understandable reasons, being far more set in the *modus operandi* of his office, with his long-evolved solutions to problems, and with a frequently intractable personality; the latter, conversely, being far looser and open in his style of political operation, with different solutions to problems and with his amenable personality. (Roosevelt's flexibility during his new administration was perhaps no better demonstrated than when he sent his secretary of state and entourage to the London Economic Conference in early June in order to effect some international solutions to the Great Depression; and within days he dispatched Raymond Moley to London to, simply put, scuttle the conference. The new president wanted freedom to resolve the domestic crisis without interference from foreign commitments.)

Raymond Moley complained that far too much of the interregnum was being consumed by the issue of foreign debts and its relationship to other foreign affairs. Roosevelt and others of the brain trust agreed, except for Norman Davis and Col. Edward House. Almost all looked more to national solutions for the depression. Hoover and his reduced coterie of advisers looked more and more to world solutions, almost as a reflex to the failure of their own domestic efforts. And as Inauguration Day approached, the president worried increasingly about the Democrats' national solutions. He seemed gripped by what Moley called a "damn duty" to keep his saving hold on the reigns of government. If during the campaign he had feared for the nation's going "off gold" under the Democrats, causing grass to "grow in the streets," and cracking "the timbers of the constitution," now he seemed to be apoplectic.[27]

Hoover's near state of apoplexy was physical as well as philosophical. Momentary disorientation, which he manifested late in the campaign, was replaced after defeat by what was reported as weeping within the solitude of the White House; on one occasion, after discussing the campaign, he was said to have been "convulsed with sobbing."[28] According to Ogden Mills, the president was, by the end of the long interregnum, a "very tired man."[29]

Fortunately, the president was not always morose during the interregnum. Thirty-five years later, Moley recalled glimpses of a mellowed rather than a "duty-gripped" president. He remembered the grace and generosity that Hoover had expressed in his Gridiron Club speech of 12 December 1932, saying about his defeat, "As nearly as I can learn, we did not have enough votes on our side." Hoover then insisted that his countrymen owed him no debt upon turning him out of office, for they had given him "the highest honor that comes to man," and that "only a few rare souls in a century . . . count much in the great flow of the Republic"—not, he added, that he was necessarily among them. Moley must have been particularly moved by what Hoover said next:

> The life stream of this Nation is the generations of millions of human particles acting under impulses of advancing ideas and national ideals gathered from a thousand springs. These springs and rills have gathered into great streams which have nurtured and fertilized this great land over these centuries. Its dikes against dangerous floods are cemented with the blood of our fathers. Our children will strengthen these dikes, will create new channels, and the land will grow greater and richer with their lives.

Moley was right. There was grace to Hoover's words, but even in them the president could not escape the duty of warning: "God help the man or group who breaks down these dikes." And less blatantly but as assuredly, Hoover concluded that Democrats and Republicans together could "maintain the very foundations of our stability"—if only they would rise above partisanship and "consider major action in cooperation with other nations."[30]

Hoover's mix of equanimity and duty in the Gridiron speech had surfaced frequently during the interregnum. Not long after he gave this speech, the Hoovers gave the William Allen Whites three pleasurable days and nights at the White House. They "were delightful," wrote White to David Hinshaw. The president "took a terrible wallop in November, but he wasn't groggy and I think the bruises are healing fast. Mrs. Hoover was a dear."[31] White wrote to Colonel House about the visit in the same vein, but interestingly he revealed the president's preoccupation with the need for the new president to pursue the outgoing administration's international solutions for the depression. White wrote that the president had "no pride, no plan, no project which he would not subvert to any plan or project which the incoming president might have . . . to put out the world conflagration."[32]

Hoover enjoyed some equanimity—vis-à-vis the sternness of duty—as he always had, by having close at hand old friends with whom he was comfortable, such as the Whites. He shunned the public, as he was frequently inclined to do. (On January 16 he held his first meaningful press conference in about six months.) Also, as in the past, no little equanimity was restored by fishing; he caught a 7'8" sailfish off Palm Beach, which was just slightly under the record catch there. And as clerks packed his private papers for shipment to Palo Alto, "he riffled old letters between his fingers, chuckled as he read bits here and there." However, duty invariably called, as, for example, the February 12 Lincoln Day speech, which he viewed as his valedictory, and yet another opportunity was given him to say what was paramount in his mind: "The solution [to the depression] can only be found now and found quickly through the reestablishment of gold standards amongst the important nations. . . . The American people will soon be at the fork of three roads. The first is the highway of cooperation amongst nations. . . . The second road is to rely upon our high degree of national self-containment . . . and thus to secure for us a larger measure of economic isolation. . . . The third road is that we should inflate our currency, abandon the gold standard, and with our depreciated currency attempt to enter a world economic war."[33] The president's equanimity during the interregnum seemed constantly to be threatened by the duty to head the incoming administration to the first fork in the road.

Hoover represented the concave side of the interregnum lens—with its view of somberness, rather closed dialogue, and international solutions to the depression; Roosevelt depicted the convex side—the picture of gaiety, diverse dialogue, and emphasis on great domestic issues. After Roosevelt had left the Red Room conference on foreign affairs on January 20 to make his way to Warm Springs, Georgia, he visited the Tennessee Valley, where he enunciated the vast domestic program that would become the hallmark of the New Deal.

The Tennessee River area where Roosevelt had stopped—Muscle Shoals—was the site of the Wilson Dam, built during the war to produce electrical power and nitrates for munitions. Although the war had ended before the dam had been finished, southern farmers and congressional progressives of both parties had wanted the government to complete the dam for purposes of distributing cheap electrical power and fertilizers to the depressed people of the area. The leader of the movement was Senator George Norris of Nebraska, who had even greater designs for the dam than his Tennessee Valley followers—a design that also was to encompass irrigation, navigation, recreation, reforestation, and a general economic uplift. Norris had the power to block the lease of the dam to private promoters, such as Henry Ford, and to see through Congress a bill to implement his vision. Both Presidents Coolidge and Hoover had vetoed the measure, the latter insisting that the development of the dam was a state and private matter.

Roosevelt thought otherwise, although many observers at first reasoned that his stopover was a symbolic gesture. They should have known that as governor of New York, he had shown interest in a strong public-power policy. He moved toward eventual support of a federal policy as he surveyed public-power possibilities in the Tennessee Valley. Several times during the day, Roosevelt reiterated that his administration's policy would develop extensive hydroelectric power in the valley. He said to George Norris at his side, "This should be a happy day for you, George." Norris, through tears, replied: "It is, Mr. President [sic]. I see my dreams come true." At the conclusion of his trip, from the portico of the Alabama Capitol in Montgomery, Roosevelt went further than he had all day and prophetically called for using federally constructed and operated power dams to reinvigorate the whole multistate area of the Tennessee River. Here, he said: "We have an opportunity of setting an example of planning, planning not just for ourselves but planning for the generations to come, tying in industry and agriculture and forestry and flood prevention, tying them all into a unified whole over a distance of a thousand miles so that we can afford better opportunities and better places for millions of yet unborn to live in in the days to come." He concluded that he saw it, if successful, as "the forerunner of similar projects in other parts of the country, such as in the watersheds of the Ohio, Missouri, and Arkansas Rivers and in the Columbia River in the Northwest."[34] The president-elect was not yet a grand planner and a large spender. He was telling Baruch at the same time that he would "make a good stab at" reducing federal expenditures by 25 percent.[35] One thing was certain, however: Roosevelt was moving left toward domestic solutions to the depression and away from the international approach, which his new friend Henry Stimson had impressed him with.

Norris, a progressive Republican, and Baruch, a conservative Democrat, probably represented the ideological spread that Roosevelt was exposing himself to during the interregnum—a diffusion that was duplicated in the intimate advisers who were close at hand and in the cabinet, which was soon to be announced. The spread, lending a dynamic confusion to the incoming administration, was in marked contrast to the narrow ideological range of the incumbent administration, a contrast as marked as the internationalist-domestic distinction between the two administrations.

The other contrast, somberness versus gaiety, became apparent shortly after the Tennessee Valley trip and a few days at Warm Springs. Roosevelt decided that it was a time for amusement at sea for eleven days on Vincent Astor's yacht, *Nourmahal*. In fact, the merriment began at Warm Springs, where, on his fifty-first birthday, he gave cake to frolicking children who gathered there. Hoover, too, cared much for children—and proved it often enough—but never as buoyantly as Roosevelt. Nor did Hoover go to sea in as blithe a fashion. In a holiday atmosphere the president-elect jested with the press as he and friends of his own social class shoved off. Frank Freidel describes the events that then followed:

> Under Roosevelt's leadership, the group gave itself over to much elaborate, almost ritualistic tomfoolery—ceremonies honoring Father Neptune, and joking so adolescent that a later generation of Harvard's Hasty Pudding Club would have disowned it with scorn. Through horseplay, sunning, and some fishing, Roosevelt relaxed. "I am getting a marvelous rest—lots of air and sun," he wrote his mother. "Vincent is a dear and a perfect host. . . . When we land on the 15th I shall be full of health and vigor—the last holiday for many months."[36]

"No rest for the wicked" might be the phrase with which Roosevelt could have perceived Hoover's next attempt at "cooperation." No sooner had the president-elect returned from his Florida respite, which was marred in its latter days by an attempt on his life in Miami, than he received a lengthy handwritten letter from the president. It was delivered personally by a Secret Service agent late on the night of February 18, while Roosevelt was attending the Inner Circle dinner, New York City's counterpart of the Washington Gridiron shows. In fact, Hoover had been trying to get in touch with the president-elect for ten days. The president's concern now was the internal state of the nation, particularly as it was being manifested by the deteriorating nature of the banking situation. His disquietude was so acute that he addressed the president-elect as "Roosevelt." Roosevelt perused the letter, undoubtedly giving special notice to the most salient points. Hoover described the "critical situation" in the country, particularly the "state of the public mind" and the nation's "degenerating confidence." He attributed such conditions to "two profound examples"—one, "the aggregate of actions" in the Democratic House of Representatives, after this administration had demonstrated to the country that "inflation of the currency and bonus were defeated, that the government credit would be maintained, [and] that the gold standard would be held"; and two, the adverse impact of the presidential election on the national confidence which the administration had restored during the second half of 1932. Hoover catalogued the recent actions of the House of Representatives that had compounded the "hesitation" in the economy, such as budget-busting proposals, publication of the RFC loans, and the failure to enact banking legislation, and all "the clatter about dictatorship" in the nation. The president concluded:

> I therefore return to my suggeston . . . [that] it would steady the country greatly if there could be prompt assurance that there will be no tampering or inflation of the currency; that the budget will be unquestionably balanced . . . ; that the Government credit will be maintained. . . . I am taking the liberty of addressing you because both in my anxiety over the situation and my confidence from four years of experience that such tides as are now running can be moderated and the process of regeneration which are always running can be released.[37]

Having studied it, Roosevelt passed it under the table to Moley, who, after glancing at it, expressed astonishment and shared it with his companions. Upon returning to his home, Roosevelt discussed it briefly with Moley, Basil O'Connor, Samuel Rosenman, and Louis Howe. One can imagine the snare they perceived, an assumption that has been justified by the knowledge, held by future historians, that the president, three days later, wrote to Pennsylvania Senator David A. Reed that "if these declarations be made by the president-elect, he will have ratified the whole major program of the Republican Administration; that is, it means the abandonment of 90% of the so-called new deal."[38] Yet, given the condition of banks, Hoover's concern was justified. His suggestions, which he found satisfying because of their potential for sidetracking the New Deal, had the support of reasonable people. Even Henry Stimson earlier in the day had spoken to Roosevelt about the banking trouble's being so grim that continual sessions between the two administrations were needed in order to stem the tide of closings. Roosevelt had agreed with Stimson about the need for cooperation but probably had changed his mind after receiving the president's letter, which the secretary of state had encouraged Hoover to write, although not in the way that he did.

Without question, banking conditions were deteriorating rapidly. Ever-decreasing commodity prices, low levels of trade, stagnating industry, and general business failures caused banks to see their assets go down in value, their investments become unproductive, and their loans uncollectable. And the assets that had been pledged by borrowers were unacceptable to banks because they, too, were worth little in the prevailing markets. Strong city banks, especially the New York banks, could borrow on their assets and survive, but "country banks" soon ran out of money. The Reconstruction Finance Corporation had somewhat stemmed the tide of failures in 1932, but in January 1933 the closing of country banks and intermediate city banks had accelerated. Bank runs, hoarding, and the flight from the dollar (as speculators and investors put their money into foreign currency) became common occurrences. In February, conditions in Michigan reached a "crisis" stage when two of Detroit's largest banks threatened to go under. Hoover, with Secretary Mills and Undersecretary Ballantine, would have saved the banks there had they succeeded in getting Michigan Senator James Couzens to contribute $1 million to a pool of deposits that had been agreed to by Henry Ford and the officials of General Motors and Chrysler companies. Couzens refused, evoking the president's comment: "If 800,000 small bank depositors in my home town could be saved by lending 3 percent of my fortune, even if I lost, I would certainly do it." Only the governor of Michigan was able to save the depositors by declaring, on February 14, a "banking holiday." The Michigan "holiday" shocked the nation, causing even greater panic elsewhere. By March 2 the governors of nine other states had followed Michigan's lead, and even New York was beginning to feel the effects of the massive closings and "holidays."[39]

On the eve of the great banking storm, Hoover and Roosevelt were at another impasse. Obviously, the president-elect pondered how he should react to the president's request. Roosevelt appreciated the need for stability of the currency, yet he wanted some inflation. He wanted his administration to reduce federal deficits; yet he saw the need for federal relief. Dare he commit himself irrevocably to the gold standard and the balanced budget, both of which would prohibit even mild inflationary and relief measures? Hoover was probably right. Such a cause would call for abandonment of 90 percent of the New Deal. The president-elect's answer was not to answer. To Moley he appeared to be blithely unperturbed. To Hoover, he appeared to be a "madman." Stimson, who watched the president, Mills, and Undersecretary Ballantine valiantly struggle against the collapse, wondered "who in God's name, will take their places" in the new administration.[40] By Sunday February 26 Roosevelt still had not answered Hoover's request. He went to St. James Church in Hyde Park and was consoled that he had not acted to save bankers. He heard clearly the words from the pulpit: "The money changers have fled from their high seats in the temple of our civilization."[41]

Roosevelt's uncertainty kept pace with Hoover's certainty. The president-elect's search for immediate and varied solutions to the depression was matched by the president's long-range, far-narrower solutions. To Hoover "the major fault in the system as it [now] stands is in the financial system." So he wrote to his old friend Arch W. Shaw on the day before he sent his plea to Roosevelt. His letter to Shaw consisted of "broad conclusions I have formed from experience of the last four years as to the functioning of our economic system." The president tightly and very logically argued: "Our whole economic system naturally divides itself into production, distribution, and finance. By finance I mean every phase of investment, banking, and credit." But as he had done so often, Hoover emphasized the particular importance of "the credit system." He saw it as the necessary "lubricant" of the system; that it should expand with "the needs of production"; that it should not be used for speculative purposes. He noted that even though these needs of the system were frequently not met, "we could have weathered them" if it had not been for "the rain of blows from abroad." Although stressing the foreign influence for upsetting the economy of his administration, the president rather inconsistently returned to the domestic scene for solutions. He concluded: "Clearly we must secure sound organization of our financial system as a prerequisite of the functioning of the whole economic system. The first steps in that system are sound currency, economy in government, balanced budgets, whether national or local."[42]

While through the remaining days of February, Roosevelt still did not respond to Hoover's plea of the eighteenth, the administration had the president-elect's reply. On February 23, Secretary Mills had returned from New York, where he had met with Treasury Secretary-designate William H. Woodin, who had informed Mills that there would be no pronouncement. Still, on February 28 the president wrote again to Roosevelt, stating that "the financial situation has become even more grave," and "I am confident that the declaration even now on the line I suggested . . . would contribute greatly to restore confidence and save losses and hardships to millions of people."[43]

Roosevelt lamely responded on March 1, stating that he had written on February 20, but that his secretary, thinking that the letter was only a draft, had not sent it. He noted that Woodin and Mills were conferring on the problem and that he agreed with the president that "a very early special session [of the Congress] will be necessary." In his letter of February 20, which he enclosed, the president-elect confirmed what Woodin had told Mills, that his idea was that the banking situation was "so very deep-seated that the fire's bound to spread in spite of anything that is done by way of mere statements."[44] Such a statement very likely reminded the president of an earlier report to the White House that economist Rexford Tugwell had presented to James H. Rand over lunch: that the banking system "would collapse within a few days, which would place the responsibility in the lap of President Hoover," and that Roosevelt should worry about nothing except "rehabilitating the country after March 4."[45]

In addition to getting Roosevelt to "steady" the economy with pronouncements, Hoover was looking for a course of specific action. In January he had supported the Glass banking-reform bill. The president saw it through the Republican Senate, only to watch it get buried in the Democratic House of Representatives. Legislation to ease the process of bankruptcy met a similar fate. In February, Hoover even considered supporting the use of the Trading with the Enemy Act to suspend special payments in order to halt hoarding and the flight of capital abroad—an action that Mills had supported for some time. Hoover asked the Federal Reserve Board if it would endorse such action. It would not. Several days later, on February 28, the president asked the board if it would support some form of a federal guarantee of bank deposits or the issuance of special scrip by clearing houses. Or, asked the president, would the board "allow the situation to drift along under the sporadic state and community solutions?" The board, annoyed by the "drift" charge, debated the proposals and told the president on March 2 that it had no recommendation to make.

On that same day Hoover thought again about the bank-deposit-guarantee approach; it might be attached to the Glass banking-reform bill, which was languishing in the House Banking Committee. Senators Glass and Robinson were amenable but thought that Roosevelt opposed the deposit-guarantee idea. Late on the same day the Federal Reserve Board reconsidered its negative response of the morning and asked the president if he would use the Trading with the Enemy Act to declare a national bank holiday. Hoover's attorney general questioned the legality of such action on the basis of that particular act. The president then said that although he would not declare a bank holiday, he would use the act to restrict bank withdrawals and trading in gold, if the Federal Reserve Board and the president-elect would approve. The board wanted the holiday, and Roosevelt did not think that restricting bank withdrawals would work. The president-elect reported that he would declare the holiday, if necessary, after he had been sworn in and that if Hoover wanted to close the banks before then, he could do so on his own authority. The president then got word to Roosevelt that he would issue a proclamation to control hoarding—but not to close the banks—if the incoming administration would not repudiate his action. Roosevelt would make no such commitment.

On Friday morning March 3 Hoover made one last try at joint action with the president-elect to abate the banking crisis. Refusing the protocol of having the president-elect to dinner, Hoover did invite the Roosevelts to tea and there broached the subject of the crisis again. Also present were Federal Reserve Governor Eugene Meyer and Secretary Mills. Roosevelt had been escorted by his son James and had called Moley to come over from the Mayflower Hotel. Then a dialogue ensued between Meyer, who argued for a proclamation to close the banks, and Hoover, who wanted a proclamation only to regulate withdrawals. Roosevelt would not support either, saying that he would have to discuss the matter with his advisers. What next transpired was later reported by the president-elect:

> I decided to cut it short. It is the custom for an outgoing President to return the call of an incoming one. I knew that Hoover didn't want to go through the strain involved in this custom, so I tried to give him a way out. I mentioned the custom to him, and then said, "I realize, Mr. President, that you are extremely busy so I will understand completely if you do not return the call." For the first time that day, he looked me squarely in the eye and said: "Mr. Roosevelt, when you are in Washington as long as I have been, you will learn that the President of the United States calls on nobody." That was that. I hustled my family out of the room. I was sure Jimmy wanted to punch him in the eye.[46]

The bank crisis continued to weigh heavily on the president. Just before dinner he recounted to Stimson his distress at Roosevelt's unwillingness to cooperate and at the incoming president's refusal to persuade New York's Governor Herbert H. Lehman to declare a bank holiday in that state. Stimson reported in his diary that "Roosevelt . . . evidently [wants] to get the benefit of having matters as bad as they can be." When, on the next day, Stimson learned from Mills that apparently Hoover himself had refused to act on a national bank holiday when Roosevelt finally agreed to it, late on the third, the secretary of state saw "a bit too much politics on both sides."[47]

The third of March was not entirely a loss to the president—at least in personal terms. The cabinet's gift of an elaborate desk set was far from perfunctory. Stimson made the presentation, noting that "this country has lost its best friend." Hoover was appreciatively humorous, remarking that while the barometer on the desk set didn't indicate "very dry," he was glad that it didn't indicate "very wet." Well-wishers came and went during the day. It is interesting that most were little known, perhaps revealing the state of the president's public relations at that late hour of the administration. He met reporters for the last time, looked at them quizzically, and almost inaudibly said: "I have not any news today. . . . And, so I will say goodby." Their farewells, too, were more than perfunctory, especially of those nearby whose hands he shook. On balance, however, the reticent president was finding the last rites of passage increasingly burdensome, most particularly because of the unresolved banking crisis. It made him very late for his last repose in the White House.[48]

The president arose at 7:30 on the morning of March 4. As he surely gazed out from the White House windows and porticos at the great monuments of Washington; especially conspicuous was that of the first president. Early buds had appeared on the trees, although they were too faint to brighten the gray dawn. It was a cold morning. There would be no medicine ball on that last morning.

Instead, the president dutifully thanked White House employees as they filed by. Although he did so somewhat rigidly and somewhat awkwardly, his sincerity was quite apparent. A Secret Service agent, trying unobtrusively to remove some artifacts from the farewell scene, found himself in an intimate and unreserved conversation with the president, the agent learning to know the subject of his protection for the first time. Also during the morning the president took many phone calls, quite the reverse from all of those times when he had initiated calls to many people in many places.

At approximately eleven o'clock President Hoover emerged from the north portico of the White House and joined Roosevelt for the ride to the Capitol. The ride has been described frequently: the general feeling of depression, the somberness of the riders and the crowd, Hoover's single doffing of his hat to faint cheers, Roosevelt's frequent tipping of his hat when he was not engaged in conversation with the president, and Hoover's monosyllabic responses. The president extended his commentary only to ask if the president-elect might find a federal position for Walter Newton. Roosevelt agreed to fulfill that request. Upon arrival at the Capitol, the president and the president-elect parted company—the former to go to the president's room to sign his last bills;

the latter, to the Military Affairs Committee Room. Then both went to the Senate to attend the swearing in of the vice-president. At noon, Hoover walked to the great rotunda of the Capitol and then to the inaugural stand. Roosevelt followed and entered the stand to the strains of "Hail to the Chief."

Chief Justice Hughes administered the oath of office, and Roosevelt began his Inaugural Address with historic utterances which assured him a prominent place in inaugural history but which, just as assuredly, distressed the outgoing president. Hoover must have pondered Roosevelt's emphasis on such concepts as "charity," "fear," "broad executive powers," "discipline"—all of which the outgoing president had addressed. No president had called more for "charity," struggled more with the psychology of "fear," and avoided more the tyranny of "executive power" and "discipline" than had Hoover. Even Eleanor Roosevelt had qualms about such terms as "power" and "discipline." Upon the conclusion of the address, Hoover hastily shook the new president's hand and made his way to Union Station for his trip to New York and the Waldorf-Astoria Hotel.[49]

Dourness turned to delight at Union Station. There friends applauded their chief, no half-hearted applause as had affronted Herbert Hoover in other places during the day. Most were devoted public servants of the former president, some of long standing, but not all. Devoted citizens were there, one shouting, "Good luck, Herbie"—an unlikely farewell. Hoover must have enjoyed the occasion as he appreciated the crowd. Generally, he only tolerated crowds, but it had been a long time since he had enjoyed one. As if to relish it more, he worked his way to the rear platform of his train to again acknowledge their presence. Then he turned to the train's recesses to be with his intimate family and friends, the latter comprising the Wilburs, the Rickards, Lewis Straus, Walter Hope, and a very few others. Mrs. Hoover and a party left the train at Philadelphia and transferred to another one for the transcontinental trip to Palo Alto, to make ready their new home.[50]

12

★ ★ ★ ★ ★

EPILOGUE

Few presidents, perhaps none, have been subjected to such a wide range of interpretation as has Herbert Hoover, from hero to villain, from genius to naïf. The determination of the most creditable assessment of the Hoover presidency presents a daunting challenge. Certainly, at least two questions must be considered, in all fairness. One is whether Hoover attained the goals outlined in his Inaugural Address: justice, ordered liberty, equality of opportunity, encouragement of individual initiative, freedom of opinion, integrity in government, growth of religious spirit, strengthening of the home, and advancement of peace. The other is whether he attacked the causes of the depression: international, cyclical, sectoral (such as agriculture), fiscal, and monetary. Both questions can be as readily answered either yes or no. In regard to the first, Herbert Hoover was what Walter Lippmann said a president should be, "a custodian of a nation's ideals." And with regard to the second, Hoover did attack the causes of the depression with vigor and imagination. Nevertheless, on election day 1932, he was turned out of office in a landslide. He clearly had not met the expectations of most of his fellow Americans.

Rather than weigh here the diverse interpretations of Hoover as president, emphasis shall be given to the observations of his associates during the dawn of the New Deal. Although the passage of a half-century since Hoover left the White House has not stopped scholars from entertaining ideological views of his presidency, more knowledge has been gained of what the intimates of the thirty-first president thought of their chief and their times. This record is revealing for appraising Hoover's presidency.

On the evening of 4 March 1933 Hoover dined quietly with Larry Richey in his high tower apartment at the Waldorf-Astoria. He retired early, slept twelve hours, and on the next day motored in Ogden Mills's car to New Canaan, Connecticut, where he had lunch with Mr. and Mrs. Edgar Rickard. The former president returned to New York late in the afternoon, again retired early, and again slept for twelve hours. The pattern of well-earned rest was broken only by consonant activity, such as enjoying automobile drives, taking long walks, and looking after some charitable organizations that he headed.

In fact, however, Hoover stood ready to answer the new president's call to service to help resolve the great bank crisis. The call was not forthcoming. The new administration had declared a national bank holiday on March 6 and had set to work to write legislation to assist in the reopening of the nation's banks. History records that Ogden Mills and Arthur Ballantine not only stayed on to give invaluable and wearisome help to the new Treasury Department staff but actually to provide the framework for the Banking Act of 9 March 1933.

Hoover gave public support to the new administration's bank efforts. Privately, however, he was of a different mind. On March 9 Larry Richey complained by telephone to the exhausted Mills about the Mills–New Deal liaison and the consequent bank program. Mills listened and exasperatedly replied: "This job had to be done and unless I and Ballantine . . . stayed here it would not have been done. We have a country you know."[1] On the next day Hoover expressed grave doubts about the legislation to Mills. The idea of having the federal government close banks and then decide which should be opened surely was repugnant to Hoover's concept of federalism. What banks were to be saved? The former president must have feared for thousands of country banks. And how would the New York matrix of the nation's banking system cope with their dependent banks, whose doors would remain closed? Hoover's answer was still the credit approach, based on confidence in stable government here and abroad. "I think . . . [the Banking Act] is going to raise the most appalling difficulties here," he said to Mills. Then the former Treasury secretary patiently explained how the banks, under the plan that he and Ballantine had so much influenced, would be reopened under the New Deal.[2] In fact, another Republican, Hoover's comptroller of the currency, F. Floyd Awalt, stayed on as acting comptroller and advised Mills and the New Deal's Treasury Department as to which banks should be opened, conditionally opened, or not opened, Although Hoover and Mills differed on the banking matter, the two would shortly meet in Chicago, travel together to California, and commiserate with each other about the evils of the First One Hundred Days.

Walter Lippmann, in spite of Felix Frankfurter's badgering, had found it difficult to speak ill of Hoover during much of his friend's presidency. Even when Frankfurter seemed to be compelling in his criticism, the great commentator still had thought Hoover "a considerable fellow." But as during the interregnum Hoover had feared the executive power that would be forthcoming in the new administration, Lippmann had moved to the left of both Hoover and Roosevelt, saying to the latter: "The situation is critical, Franklin. You may have no alternative but to assume dictatorial powers." That Lippmann meant what he said became clear to his many readers when he wrote, prior to the inauguration, that the special session of Congress must not be allowed "to obstruct, to delay, to mutilate, and to confuse"—that "the danger . . . is not that Congress will give Franklin D. Roosevelt too much power, but that it will deny him the powers he needs." Frankfurter, in luring Lippmann away from Hoover's reluctance to use executive power, must have wondered what seeds he had sowed. He pleaded with Lippmann to educate the public to the relevance of "wise decisions" by a deliberative Congress and not to "abdication of everybody's reason." Lippmann answered by saying that Frankfurter seemed to be "a little bit hesitant about breaking the eggs to make the omelet." Lippmann approved quick action on the New Deal measures, which assured strong executive authority, including what had been essentially Mills's banking bill.[3]

William Allen White, who had so often failed in getting Hoover to heed western Republicans on farm policy, nevertheless stayed loyal to Hoover to the end. It was not easy. For some time, White had sided with western restlessness about Hoover's cooperative approach to resolving the nation's farm problems. During the trials of the interregnum, the Whites and the Hoovers had enjoyed one another's company in the White House. However, very shortly into the New Deal era, White thought that the new administration's farm bill—the domestic-allotment plan that Hoover abhorred—was "better than fairly good. I have been trying to support the president in every possible way in his emergency measures," he wrote to Col. Edward House. For Hoover, of course, the New Deal federal controls of agricultural production were anathema. The Kansas editor urged Congress to approve the whole Roosevelt farm program—in fact, the whole New Deal, "the whole alphabet thereunto pertaining." He even "spanked" some Kansas Democrats for at times not supporting Roosevelt. Lippmann and White seemed to complement each other. Where the former emphasized strong presidential leadership, the latter stressed congressional support of the new president.[4]

The public view of Hoover's equanimity in the environs of the Waldorf-Astoria was matched by a similar view when, very shortly, he crossed the continent to join his family at Palo Alto. There, in his home on a hill overlooking his beloved Stanford University, the former president was "surrounded by his dogs and visited by his friends and an occasional . . . dignitary . . . [and discovered] a new zest in the mere fact of being alive." He walked, read, traveled, and fished; slept and ate when he pleased; and held open house, seemingly at any time, for old friends and neighbors. If not the "life of Riley," as the press reported, it was believably idyllic. He had, it was reported, no plans to be active in politics or to write a book.[5]

The serenity of Hoover in New York and Palo Alto matched that of his friends who made their peace with the New Deal—as did Ogden Mills with bank legislation, White with agricultural legislation, Lippmann with executive power, and as Harlan F. Stone and Henry L. Stimson would do with the restriction of liberty and foreign policy, respectively. Nonetheless, in fact, Hoover seethed at the first One Hundred Days of the New Deal. Rather than accept the views of his friends of stature, he seemed to thrive on partisan views of friends of far-lesser eminence, such as Larry Richey, J. C. O'Laughlin, Walter Brown, Henry Robinson, and Edgar Rickard. As noted, Richey and Hoover both reproved Mills over the bank legislation. O'Laughlin, who detailed to the former president his bitter opposition to all of the One Hundred Days' legislation, evoked a response in kind, as Hoover wrote: "February, March, and April of 1933 will someday be known as the winter of the Roosevelt hysteria. The panic over the possibilities of the New Deal . . . , the unnecesaary closing of the banks . . . , the passage of fiscal matters which increased . . . governmental expenditures, the authorization of white rabbits by Congress in the spirit of the total abandonment of responsibility for the first time in 150 years are just part of what we shall see." Hoover, who was not frequently given to writing long letters, did so now. Four days later he wrote again to O'Laughlin: "Our fight is going to be to stop this move to gigantic socialism of America. . . . We have a big job ahead and the first step is to let the country know the real facts behind . . . the greatest issues which . . . have confronted our people in half a century."[6] And when Walter Brown, a month later, wanted to know what message Hoover might have for "our friends in Washington," the former president replied with seven single-spaced typewritten pages, stating his opposition to the New Deal measures to date, with special references to the bank act, the Economy Act, the Civilian Conservation Corps, and the inflationary measures. In regard to the last—and to leaving the gold standard—the former president concluded: ''There never has been so dangerous a proposal laid before the American Congress. . . . The Administration in reversing our policies has brought the country to the brink of the precipice, and it is a desperate act.''[7]

In September, accompanied by Edgar Rickard, Hoover traveled to Chicago and there met with various groups, perhaps most importantly with a dozen faculty members from the University of Chicago. There the former president exchanged views over whether public opinion was demanding the administrative authority that was evolving in Washington. Not surprisingly, New Deal manipulation of currency and National Recovery Administration (NRA) planning, as being most representative of the new administration, dominated much of the discussion. Rickard reported in his diary that while the academics agreed with Hoover on the unsoundness of the NRA's planning and New Deal inflation, they saw both as being inevitable. All accorded Hoover ''great respect.'' The irony of the occasion was perhaps lost on Rickard—that surely many of the same faculty members had contributed heavily to the recent *Report of the President's Committee on Recent Social Trends*, which was far more consistent with the New Deal's than with the Hoover administration's philosophy. The conclusions contained in that report seemed to typify New Deal performance: the recognition of the low standard of living and the consequent growth of government; the need for a reduced-hour working day, a solvent unemployment fund, the extension of old-age pensions, the surrender of some property rights, the speed-up of social invention, and the humanizing of labor. Such is not to deny the relationship of the report to Hoover's concerns and to his abortive efforts at resolution of them.[8]

Revealing of the narrow scope of Hoover's friends of lesser stature was Rickard's subsequent diary entry of November 23. He reports that on that day he had met at the University Club in New York City with Robert A. Millikan, Robert Lamont, and Henry Robinson. All had commiserated about the key men in the New Deal. Henry Robinson deplored the fact that all of them were Jews who had been nominated by Felix Frankfurter. The conversation addressed analogies between the domination of European countries and America by an unacceptable class of Jews, notwithstanding that there were desirable types, less aggressive Jews such as James P. Warburg, Bernard Baruch, and Lewis Straus. The lesson of Rickard's diary entry is that Hoover's more partisan friends conceived the world about them in far-narrower terms than did the former president's loftier associates: Mills, Lippmann, White, Stone, and Stimson. Hoover now listened to the former more than the latter. Or more likely, he listened to what he wanted to hear. He appreciated their anti–New Deal diatribe, if not their anti-Semitism. Certainly, Hoover was not anti-Semitic.[9]

The irony of Rickard's diary entry is that Frankfurter influenced not only Franklin Roosevelt but also Hoover's truly important friends. Mills had spoken highly of Frankfurter when the latter was working so diligently to bring Roosevelt and Stimson together during the interregnum. Perhaps no American encouraged Lippmann so much to see the weaknesses of the Hoover presidency as did Frankfurter. Frankfurter and White had a history of congeniality, going back to the Sacco-Vanzetti case. Harlan Stone and Felix Frankfurter were truly brethren before the bar, even in advance of their shared service on the Supreme Court. And Frankfurter had admired Stimson and had served him diligently when the latter had been the United States attorney for the Southern District of New York.

Henry L. Stimson, the first of Hoover's insiders to make an accommodation with Franklin Roosevelt during the interregnum, continued his spirit of accommodation, although seldom by betraying his ideology or his loyalty to Hoover. Early in the New Deal, on 13 March 1933, Stimson wrote to Hoover, defending the bank bill as "on the whole a good job." Hoover replied cryptically, "I am not reconciled."[10] The two leaders saw each other occasionally, though less so as war clouds grew later in the decade, and as they again had differences over foreign policy—Hoover still being the noninterventionist; Stimson becoming more inclined toward intervention. Only Stimson, of Hoover's friends, went so far as to join the first rank of the Roosevelt administration, as secretary of war, although Lippmann, White, and Stone gave important service to the New Deal.

Harlan Fiske Stone had always esteemed Herbert Hoover. Notwithstanding the justice's appointment by President Roosevelt to the chief justiceship, Stone in 1940 again wanted Hoover to be president. But in 1934 he gravely questioned his friend's views on the fate of liberty at the hands of New Dealers. Stone responded thoughtfully to a lengthy Hoover paper on individual liberty, which shortly would take book form under the title of *The Challenge to Liberty*, a sequel to *American Individualism*. Stone agreed with the charge that the New Deal was threatening individual liberty: "I think even more could be said about present tendencies to depart from traditional forms of democratic government under the Constitution. The steady absorption of power by the President, the failure of Congress to perform its legislative duties, the absence of debate in Congress, and of open public discussion of the public's problems, the creation of drastic administrative procedures, without legislative definition and without provision for their review by courts, are, I believe, an even greater menace than the programs for whose advancement these sacrifices have been made.''

Stone went on with his criticism of Roosevelt. Surely, Hoover, up to this point in the letter, was pleased, for Stone was no O'Laughlin or Walter Brown or Henry Robinson. But then Stone told his "Chief" what he had said to him so many times before: that the people govern, that they want reform, that they "expect that objection will be made . . . on the ground that . . . [reforms] infringe [upon] the principle of freedom of the individual.'' Such has been the case for seventy-five years, said Stone. Hoover's paper, Stone sadly concluded, would be viewed as just another objection to American reform. It would not matter that the former president had devoted much of his life to encouraging that American reform.

Then Stone explained to his friend where the two of them differed— namely, that "the necessities of an increasingly complex civilization, in which every individual and group within the state becomes increasingly interdependent" required "restrictions on individual liberty.'' The Jeffersonian state would not suffice. "The issue [of industrial depression] cannot be settled by an appeal to the eighteenth-century philosophy of individualism in the abstract, for that philosophy cannot be completely adapted to the twentieth century.'' Any appearance of hyperbole was not intended by Stone. He knew Hoover's reform spirit. But he also knew that "now the people are disposed to endure the evils of the administration program in the hope that they may bring a better day, freed from the dangers which they are now suffering. . . . [The people] would be overjoyed if some one could point the way to accomplish it without the sacrifices of liberty which they are being called to make.'' Hoover just as sadly rejected his friend's challenge. He published his book, which heaped scorn on the New Deal for denying the "God-given right" of liberty; and he received much of the public condemnation that Stone had predicted.[11]

It is revealing that during his presidency, Hoover had consulted with and earned the affection and respect of leaders of eminence such as Mills, the brilliant fiscalist; Lippmann, the seminal commentator of the day; White, the spokesman for Mid-America; Stimson, a living statesman; and Stone, "the pillar of the law.'' But it is also revealing that when these Americans accommodated themselves to the times and the New Deal, they were fulfilling obligations that they frequently had advocated in the dialogue with Hoover and just as frequently had failed to achieve during his presidency. Singly, they were no more on the side of the angels than was Hoover. Together, however, their search for accommodation seems to have been a more creditable model for governing during the Great Depression than does Hoover's monolithic plan for the United States, brilliant and principled though it was.

Why did an American president who entered office with such high qualifications leave with such a reversed image? Was it the times, such as those when Martin Van Buren, nearly a century before, had suffered defeat at the hands of a great depression that also had gripped the nation? That, of course, is an important part of the answer. But the nation seemed to forgive Van Buren for his "depression" presidency when, in fact, it probably had less cause to blame Hoover for the economic downturn of the 1930s, given his antidepression concerns and actions before and during the Great Depression. Indeed, astute historians for decades have viewed the Hoover presidency as the logical transition from progressivism to the New Deal—that it was both the last of the old and the first of the new presidencies.

Then, the important question about Herbert Hoover that remains is not why the people refused to reelect him, but why the reversal of the nation's image of him was so overwhelming and long-lasting. Democrats, every four years for more than half a century, seemed to be running against Herbert Hoover. And each quadrennial chastisement seemed to make the superb reputation that Hoover had enjoyed upon entering his presidency increasingly irretrievable. (The fifty-year drumbeat against Hoover was not unlike the fifty-year Republican campaign against Democrats for having supposedly perpetrated the Civil War.) To be sure, Hoover's image has been somewhat rehabilitated because of his many important postpresidency performances during his long life, which have been observed by an increasing number of historians in recent years.

Most baffling, however, is the fact that many Americans have been adamant in refusing to recognize the attributes and services of Herbert Hoover. Two observations may explain the mystery. For one, the public's attitude appears in proportion to Hoover's firm refusal to make the kinds of accommodation with the statist spirit of the New Deal that the general public and Hoover's own associates of "high stature" made. A second observation necessarily qualifies the first. Hoover's determined opposition to the New Deal becomes less mysterious when one considers the meaning of "ordered freedom" to America's only practicing Quaker president. This Quaker formula, by and of itself, does not explain Hoover's adamantine posture, for others in America also believed in "ordered liberty." But the escalation of it over nearly six decades of Hoover's life seems to be the best explanation of the posture.

Herbert Hoover's absolute commitment to his interpretation of and belief in ordered freedom mounted uncannily, seemingly in geometric progression, as he moved from one stage of his life to another: as the principal tenet of his Quakerism, both sectarian and secular; as a principal tool of "rationalization" in his business and engineering professionalism; as a synthesis of New Nationalist and New Freedom thought during his service in the Progressive Era; as the theme of *American Individualism*, his guide during his decade of political service prior to his presidency; as the essence of his presidency, when he said upon entering it: "My concept of America is a land where men and women may walk in ordered freedom"; and as the basis for his criticism of the New Deal in *Challenge to Liberty*. Herbert Hoover did "risk" his ideal of ordered freedom "to the tender mercies of a world," only to discover that "the world [was] not yet ripe for [it]."

It has often been said that the jury on the Hoover presidency is still out—that scholars who seek to assess American presidents react differently depending upon their sources of information, their times, and their values. In fact, however, the jury on the Hoover presidency is in, with a verdict that is compelling enough to make it unlikely that it will ever be overturned. The jury consists of three important constituencies: Hoover's close associates of high stature at the close of his presidency; the majority of Americans throughout the half-century following his presidency; and historians at the half-century mark after his presidency. The constituencies agree that the Hoover presidency was a failed one. They do so notwithstanding three arguments in defense of the administration: that its goals and antidepression efforts were in many respects without precedent; that it was surely as much failed by American capital as by presidential leadership; and that probably no American elected in 1928 could have survived the nation's greatest depression. Ironically, Herbert Hoover's very success in pursuing his goals and antidepression efforts were probably paramount in creating the misfortunes of his presidency. His unalterable commitment to ordered freedom as a canopy for solutions to the depression proved to be more telling to this jury than did either the iniquities of capital or the seeming facileness of his political opponents. Of course, Hoover's friends of eminence saw the many magnificent qualities of the whole life of Hoover, if not of his singular presidency; and increasing numbers of historians, including this author, see them now. It is regrettable that as the twentieth century nears its end, many of the nation's citizens continue to see in the man Herbert Hoover what he himself frequently saw in his own presidency—"the dark side first." Given the emphasis that is placed on the presidency in American public affairs, it is improbable that this assessment will ever change.

NOTES

CHAPTER 1
THE EDUCATION OF HERBERT HOOVER

1. No. 878, *Addresses upon the American Road,* 11 Aug. 1928, p. 36; "Religious Tolerance," Hoover Papers (hereafter cited as HP), Herbert Hoover Presidential Library, West Branch, Iowa (hereafter cited as HL).

2. William Hard, "Friend Hoover," *Christian Herald,* 15 Sept. 1928, HP.

3. Preston Wolfe, oral history, HP.

4. For the Quaker life style see William Wistar Comfort, *Just among Friends: The Quaker Way of Life* (New York: Macmillan Co., 1941) and *Quakers in the Modern World* (New York: Macmillan Co., 1949), chap. 7; Herbert Hoover, Address at the Republican National Convention, Chicago, Illinois, 25 July 1960, HP.

5. J. William Frost, "The Dry Bones of Quaker Theology," *Church History,* Dec. 1970, pp. 503–23; J. William Frost stressed the importance of "corporate individualism" in a conversation with me at Swarthmore, Pa., on 27 Aug. 1982.

6. James R. Bowers, "Herbert Hoover: Ambivalent Quaker" (master's thesis, Sangamon State University, Springfield, Ill., 1981), chap. 5; William Friar Dexter, *Herbert Hoover and American Individualism: A Modern Interpretation of a National Ideal* (New York: Macmillan Co., 1932), passim; Hoover used "ordered freedom" and "ordered liberty" interchangeably; for example, the former in his Madison Square Garden speech on 22 Oct. 1928 and the latter in his Inaugural Address.

7. David Burner, *Herbert Hoover: The Public Life* (New York: Alfred A. Knopf, 1979), p. 19.

8. George Nash, *The Life of Herbert Hoover,* vol. 1: *The Engineer, 1874–1914* (New York: W. W. Norton & Co., Inc., 1983), chaps. 3 and 27.

9. Herbert Hoover, *Principles of Mining* (New York: McGraw-Hill Book Co., 1901).

10. Burner, *Herbert Hoover,* p. 74.

11. Keynes is quoted in Burner, *Herbert Hoover,* p. 138.

12. Elizabeth Gray Vining, *Friend of Life: The Biography of Rufus M. Jones* (Philadelphia: J. B. Lippincott Co., 1958), chaps. 1 and 2.

13. Hoover to Rufus Jones, 1 Nov. 1919 and 21 Sept. 1921, the Quaker Collection, Haverford College Library, Haverford, Pa.

14. N. V. Peale, oral history, 16 Sept. 1971, HP.

15. Alpheus T. Mason, *Louis D. Brandeis: A Free Man's Life* (New York: Viking Press, 1946), p. 520.

16. Quoted in Frederick B. Tolles, *Quakers and the Atlantic Culture* (New York: Macmillan Co., 1960), p. 52.

17. Burner, *Herbert Hoover,* p. 151.

18. Ibid., p. 152.

19. Herbert Hoover, *American Individualism* (West Branch, Iowa: Herbert Hoover Presidential Library Association, 1971; originally published by Doubleday, Page & Co. in 1922).

20. Ibid., "American Individualism."

21. Ibid., "Philosophical Grounds."

22. Ibid., "Spiritual Phases."

23. Ibid.

CHAPTER 2
VICTORY

1. Donald R. McCoy, "To the White House: Herbert Hoover, August, 1927–March, 1929," in *The Hoover Presidency: A Reappraisal,* ed. Martin L. Fausold and George T. Mazuzan (Albany: State University of New York Press, 1974), pp. 31–32.

2. Roy V. Peel and Thomas C. Donnelly, *The 1928 Campaign: An Analysis* (New York: Richard R. Smith, Inc., 1931), p. 24.

3. Ibid., pp. 28–29; *New York Times,* 15 June 1928.

4. Peel and Donnelly, *1928 Campaign,* p. 30.

5. *New York Times,* 16 June 1928.

6. Carter Glass to Harry F. Byrd, 8 Aug. 1928, Papers of Carter Glass (#2913), Manuscripts Department, University of Virginia Library, Charlottesville, Va. (hereafter cited as Glass Papers, University of Virginia).

7. David Burner, *The Politics of Provincialism: The Democratic Party in Transition, 1918–1932* (New York: Alfred A. Knopf, 1967), chap. 7 passim.

8. Kent M. Schofield, *The Figure of Herbert Hoover in the 1928 Campaign* (Ann Arbor, Mich.: University Microfilms, Inc., 1966), passim.

9. John D. Hicks, *Republican Ascendency, 1921–1933* (New York: Harper & Row, 1960), p. 211.

10. *New York Times*, 12 Aug. 1928.

11. Franklin D. Roosevelt to Julius H. Barnes, 25 Sept. 1928, and Barnes to Roosevelt, 26 Sept. 1928, HP.

12. Vaughn Davis Bornet, *Labor Politics in a Democratic Republic: Moderation, Division, and Disruption in the Presidential Election of 1928* (Washington, D.C.: Spartan Books, Inc., 1964), p. 236.

13. George Akerson to Hoover, 6 Feb. 1929, HP.

14. Louis J. Taber to Hoover, 26 Sept. 1928, HP.

15. See an undated lengthy statement signed by Jane Addams, HP.

16. Harold Ickes to Hiram W. Johnson, 2 Oct. 1928, Ickes Papers, Library of Congress (hereafter cited as LC).

17. Hiram Johnson to Harold Ickes, 25 Feb. 1928, Ickes Papers, LC.

18. See "William Allen White Says," HP.

19. See press release in Hoover's handwriting, 24 Sept. 1928, HP; also see Mabel W. Willebrandt to Hubert Work, 27 Sept. 1928, HP.

20. Harold Ickes to Hiram Johnson, 28 Sept. 1928, and Johnson to Ickes, 29 Sept. 1928, Ickes Papers, LC.

21. H. E. Mize to Carter Glass, 23 July 1928, Glass Papers, University of Virginia.

22. Benjamin J. Kunkel to Robert H. Wagner, 11 Nov. 1928, Wagner Papers, Georgetown University, Washington, D.C.

23. Hoover to Elihu Root, 16 Nov. 1928, HP; see LeRoy Ashby, *The Spearless Leader: Senator Borah and the Progressive Movement in the 1920s* (Chicago: University of Illinois Press, 1972), pp. 275–84.

24. George Moses to Hoover, 9 Nov. 1928, HP.

25. Memorandum from Mark Sullivan, undated, HP.

26. Hoover to Elihu Root, 16 Nov. 1928, HP.

27. Herbert Hoover, *The Memoirs of Herbert Hoover*, vol. 2: *The Cabinet and the Presidency, 1920–1933* (New York: Macmillan Co., 1951, 1952), pp. 210–15; Charles Evans Hughes to Hoover, 13 Feb. 1929, Hughes Papers, LC; Alexander De Conde, *Herbert Hoover's Latin-American Policy* (New York: Octagon, 1970), p. 49.

28. Henry L. Stimson to Dwight F. Davis, 19 Jan. 1929, HP.

29. Hugh Gibson to Hoover, 21 July 1928, HP.

30. *New York Times*, 13, 26, 27 Jan. and 1 Mar. 1929; William Donovan to Hoover, handwritten, undated, and Hoover handwritten memorandum to himself re Donovan appointment, HP.

31. Hoover, *Memoirs*, 2:218; William R. Castle to Hoover, undated, HP.

32. John Q. Tilson to Hoover, 12 Nov. 1928, and Christian Herter to Lawrence Richey, 31 Jan. 1929, HP.

CHAPTER 3
A NEW BEGINNING

1. *New York Times*, 5 Mar. 1929; *Public Papers of the Presidents of the United States, Herbert Hoover, Containing the Public Messages, Speeches and Statements of the President, Mar. 4 to Dec. 3, 1929* (Washington, D.C.: Government Printing Office, 1974), pp. 1–11.

2. Howard William Runkel, "Hoover's Speeches during His Presidency" (Ph.D. diss., Stanford University, 1950), pp. 37, 57; Theodore Joslin, *Hoover off the Record* (Garden City, N.Y.: Doubleday, Doran & Co., 1934), p. 13; Barry D. Karl, "Herbert Hoover and the Progressive Myth of the Presidency" (paper presented to Hoover Centennial Seminar, HL, 1974).

3. *New York Times*, 4, 18, and 31 Mar., 21 and 26 Apr., 5 and 12 May, and 7 July 1929.

4. John Lee Westrate, "The Administrative Theory and Practice of Herbert Hoover" (Ph.D. diss., University of Chicago, 1968), chap. 8 passim; Robert Sharon Allen and Drew Pearson, *Washington Merry-Go-Round* (New York: Blue Ribbon Books, Inc., 1931), chap. 14 passim.

5. Henry Lewis Stimson, diaries, x, 3, 8/28/30 (microfilm edition, reel 2), Henry L. Stimson Papers, Manuscripts and Archives, Yale University Library, New Haven, Conn. (hereafter cited as Stimson, diaries). Some of these observations by Stimson are on reels 3, 4, 5.

6. Irwin Hood ("Ike") Hoover, *Forty-two Years in the White House* (Boston and New York: Houghton Mifflin Co., 1934), p. 184.

7. Westrate, "Administrative Theories," chap. 8.

8. William Allen White to Hoover, 10 Apr. 1919, White Papers, LC; Harold Ickes to White, 7 May 1929, Ickes Papers, LC; White to Henry J. Allen, 1929, and Allen to White, 30 Sept. 1929, White Papers, LC.

9. M. L. Requa, memorandum to Lawrence Richey, 27 May 1929, HP.

10. Karl, "Herbert Hoover," chap. 8 passim.

11. John Knox Boaz, "The Presidential Press Conference" (Ph.D. diss., Wayne State University, 1969), pp. 73–82; press conferences, Mar., Apr., May 1929, HP; Stimson, diaries, ix–xiii, reels 2–5 passim.

12. Martin L. Fausold, "President Hoover's Farm Policies, 1929–1933," *Agricultural History* 51, no. 2 (Apr. 1977): 362–77; Herbert Hoover, *The New Day* (Stanford University, Calif: Stanford University Press, 1929), pp. 53–54, 194–95; *New York Times*, 17 Apr. 1929.

13. Fausold, "President Hoover's Farm Policies," p. 366; *New York Times*, 21, 25, and 26 Mar., 14 and 15 Apr. 1929.

14. Hoover to Charles L. McNary, 20 Apr. 1929, HP.

15. *New York Times*, 9 and 13 May 1929.

16. Fausold, "President Hoover's Farm Policies," pp. 367–68.

17. *New York Times*, 16 June 1929.

18. Fausold, "President Hoover's Farm Policies," passim.

19. Hoover, *Memoirs*, 2:293–94; Joseph R. Grundy to Hoover, 19 Aug. 1929, HP; *New York Times*, 27 Sept., 1, 3, and 13 Oct. 1929; Editorial Summary Week Ending November 7, 1929, HP.

20. Edward H. Hobbs, "Executive Reorganization in the National Government" (master's thesis, University of Mississippi, 1953), chaps. 1, 2, 3; Peri E. Arnold, "Executive Reorganization & the Origins of the Managerial Presidency," *Polity* 13 (Summer 1981): 568–99, p. 592 for Hoover quotation.

21. Herbert Hoover, *Hoover after Dinner* (New York: Charles Scribner's Sons, 1933), p. 10 (3 Apr. 1929 address before the Gridiron Club).

22. Karl, "Herbert Hoover."

23. David Burner, "Before the Crash: Hoover's First Eight Months in the Presidency," in *The Hoover Presidency: A Reappraisal*, ed. Martin L. Fausold and George T. Mazuzan (Albany: State University of New York Press, 1974), pp. 57, 62–63.

24. Barry D. Karl, "Presidential Planning and Social Service Research: Mr. Hoover's Experts," in *Perspectives in American History*, vol. 3 (1969); *New York Times*, 22 Dec. 1929.

25. Andrew Sinclair, *Era of Excess: A Social History of the Prohibition Movement* (New York: Harper & Row, 1962), pp. 357–58; *New York Times*, 9 Mar. and 24 Oct. 1929; Mabel Willebrandt to Walter Newton, 30 Mar. 1930, George Wickersham to Franklin D. Roosevelt, 5 July 1929, and "Wickersham Letters; Newspaper Editorials," HP.

26. William G. McAdoo to George F. Milton, 21 Apr. 1929, McAdoo Papers, LC.

CHAPTER 4
THE CRASH

1. *New York Times*, 1 Sept. 1929.

2. Ibid., 1 Apr. 1933.

3. *Historical Statistics of the United States: Colonial Times to 1970*, Bicentennial edition (Washington, D.C.: U.S. Government Printing Office, 1975), p. 680.

4. Ibid., p. 224.

5. Jim Potter, *The American Economy between the World Wars* (New York: John Wiley & Sons, 1974), chaps. 2 and 3 passim.

6. Broadus Mitchell, *Depression Decade: From New Era through New Deal, 1929–1941* (New York: Rinehart & Co., Inc., 1947), p. 26; *Recent Economic Changes in the United States*, ed. Edward Eyre Hunt, 2 vols. (New York: McGraw-Hill Publishing Co., 1929).

7. Mitchell, *Depression Decade*, pp. 25–26.

8. *Recent Economic Changes*, 1:94.

9. Ibid., 1:218.

10. Ibid., 2:909.

11. *Statistical Abstract of the United States, 1940* (Washington, D.C.: United States Government Printing Office, 1941), p. 502.

12. Potter, *American Economy,* chap. 3 passim.

13. Ibid.

14. George Henry Soule, *Prosperity Decade: From War to Depression, 1917–1929* (New York: Rinehart & Co., 1947), p. 142.

15. Frank R. Forrest to Franklin D. Roosevelt, 30 Aug. 1938, Roosevelt Papers, Franklin D. Roosevelt Presidential Library, Hyde Park, N.Y. (hereafter cited as Roosevelt Papers).

16. Herbert Hoover, *The Memoirs of Herbert Hoover,* vol. 3: *The Great Depression 1929–1941* (New York: Macmillan Co., 1952), pp. 9–10.

17. John Kenneth Galbraith, *The Great Crash, 1929* (Boston: Houghton Mifflin Co., 1955), p. 21.

18. Christian Herter to George Akerson, 5 Apr. 1929, HP.

19. George Akerson to Christian Herter, 2 Apr. 1929, HP.

20. George Akerson to Christian Herter, 8 Apr. 1929, HP.

21. Hoover, *Memoirs,* 3:17; Galbraith, *Great Crash,* p. 47.

22. Bernard Baruch to Herbert B. Swope, 13 Feb. 1929, Baruch to Frank Kent, 8 Apr. 1929, and Baruch to Carter Glass, 15 Feb. 1929, Baruch Papers, Princeton University, Princeton, N.J. (published with the permission of the Princeton University Library).

23. William G. McAdoo to John F. Sinclair, 12 Apr. 1929, McAdoo Papers, LC; Hoover, *Memoirs,* 3:18.

24. Carter Glass to C. S. Hamlin, 6 Apr. 1931, Glass Papers, University of Virginia.

25. Bernard Baruch to Charles Mitchell, 27 Mar. 1929, Baruch Papers, Princeton University; Jordan A. Schwarz, *The Speculator: Bernard M. Baruch in Washington, 1917–1965* (Chapel Hill: University of North Carolina Press, 1981), chap. 6.

26. C. S. Hamlin to Carter Glass, 26 Mar. 1931, Glass Papers, University of Virginia; Garrard Winston to Ogden Mills, 27 Aug. 1929, Mills Papers, LC.

27. Eugene Meyer to Hoover, 1 Feb. 1929, Meyer Papers, LC; Henry H. Bond to Garrard Winston (for O. Mills), 17 Mar. 1929, Ogden Mills Papers, LC.

28. William Starr Myers and Walter H. Newton, *The Hoover Administration: A Documented Narrative* (New York: Charles Scribner's Sons, 1936), p. 23; James J. Davis to Hoover, 7 May 1929, HP.

29. *New York Times,* 18–31 Oct. 1929.

30. Ibid., 2 Oct., 1 Nov., and 1 Dec. 1929, 1 and 2 Jan., 1 and 2 May 1930, 1 and 2 Jan. 1931, 1 and 2 Jan. 1933. The price of industrial stocks is used. See Robert Sobel, *Herbert Hoover at the Onset of the Great Depression, 1929–1930* (Philadelphia: J. B. Lippincott Co., 1975), chap. 4.

31. Tom Shachtman, *The Day America Crashed: A Narrative Account of the Great Stock Market Crash of October 24, 1929* (New York: G. P. Putnam's, 1979), pp. 22, 130–32.

32. Edwin Jassaross (*sic*), president, Globe & Rutgers Fire Insurance Co., to Hoover, 23 Oct. 1929, HP.

33. *New York Times,* 31 Oct. 1929.

34. Myers and Newton, *Hoover Administration,* p. 23.

35. *New York Times,* 30 Oct. 1929.

36. J. J. Davis to Hoover, 12 Nov. 1929, and Robert P. Lamont to Hoover, 14 Nov. 1929, HP.

37. Hoover to all cabinet members, 18 Nov. 1929, HP; Hoover, *Memoirs,* 3:42; *New York Times,* 19 Nov. 1929; Lester V. Chandler, *American Monetary Policy, 1928–1941* (New York: Harper & Row, 1971), chap. 5 passim; *New York Times,* 4 Dec. 1929.

38. Myers and Newton, *Hoover Administration,* pp. 23–31.

39. Ibid.

40. Hoover to Robert P. Lamont, 5 Dec. 1929, HP.

41. James J. Davis to Hoover, 23 Nov. 1929, HP.

42. Hoover, *Memoirs,* vol. 3, chap. 1.

43. Charles P. Kindleberger, *The World in Depression, 1929–1939* (Berkeley: University of California Press, 1975, c. 1973), pp. 33, 292–94.

44. Lester V. Chandler, *America's Greatest Depression, 1929–1942* (New York: Harper & Row, 1970), pp. 92–93.

45. Paul A. Baran, *The Political Economy of Growth* (New York: Marzana and Munsell, 1957), pp. 1–2, quoted in David Martin, "The Onset of the Great Depression: An Institutional Diagnosis" (paper, Geneseo, N.Y., 1978).

46. Gunnar Myrdal, *Beyond the Welfare State: Economic Planning and Its International Implications* (New Haven, Conn.: Yale University Press, 1960), pp. 30–40.

47. Arnold Toynbee, *The Industrial Revolution* (Boston: Beacon Press, 1956), p. 60.

48. Alan Sweezy, "The Keyneseans and Government Policy, 1933–1934," *American Economic Review* 62 (May 1972): 121; J. A. Swanson and S. H. Williamson, "Estimates of National Product and Income for the United States," *Explorations in Economic History* 10, no. 1 (Fall 1972): 55–70.

49. Potter, *American Economy,* pp. 102–3 passim.

50. Ibid., pp. 103–4; Milton Friedman and Anna Jacobson Schwartz, *The Great Contraction, 1929–1933* (Princeton, N.J.: Princeton University Press, 1965), passim.

51. Potter, *American Economy,* pp. 104–7.

52. Ibid., pp. 109–10; Peter Temin, *Did Monetary Forces Cause the Great Depression?* (New York: W. W. Norton & Co., Inc., 1976), pp. 169–79.

CHAPTER 5

1930

1. Stimson, diaries, x, 49, reel 2, 10/4/30.

2. Stimson, diaries, x, 78–80, reel 2, 10/17–18/30.

3. *New York Times*, 2 Mar. 1930.

4. Ibid., 12 Aug. 1930.

5. Mark Sullivan, "Hoover's First Year," *New York Herald-Tribune* (undated), HP.

6. Stimson, diaries, ix–x, 118, reel 2, 11/1/30.

7. *New York Times*, 15 May 1930; Mason, *Louis D. Brandeis*, p. 520.

8. Felix Frankfurter to Walter Lippmann, 5 Feb. 1930, Frankfurter Papers, LC.

9. Alpheus Thomas Mason, *Harlan Fiske Stone: Pillar of the Law* (New York: Viking Press, 1956), chap. 17 passim.

10. Ibid., p. 267.

11. Ibid.; Alpheus Thomas Mason, *William Howard Taft: Chief Justice* (New York: Simon & Schuster, 1964), p. 297; Merlo John Pusey, *Charles Evan Hughes* (New York: Macmillan Co., 1951), chap. 63.

12. Mason, *Harlan Fiske Stone*, chap. 17.

13. *Confirmation of Honorable John J. Parker, To Be an Associate Justice of the Supreme Court of the United States* (hearing before a subcommittee of the Senate Committee on the Judiciary, 71st Cong., 2d sess.), 5 Apr. 1930, passim; Richard L. Watson, Jr., "The Defeat of Judge Parker: A Study in Pressure Groups and Politics," *Mississippi Valley Historical Review* 50, no. 2 (Sept. 1963): 213–34; "Memorandum on the Opinion of Circuit Judge John J. Parker," in *International Organization, United Mine Workers of America* v. *Red Jacket Consolidated Coal and Coke Co.*, 18 F (Ind) 839 (prepared by the Department of Justice), HP.

14. Ibid.; *Confirmation of Honorable John J. Parker*, statement by William Green, pp. 23–27 HP.

15. Memorandum re John J. Parker, by Harlan Stone (undated, not titled), HP; see David J. Danelski, *A Supreme Court Justice Is Appointed* (New York: Random House, 1964), pp. 190–99.

16. *New York Times*, 12 May 1930; Parker memorandum, "Answer to Charge That Judge Parker Advocated . . . ," HP.

17. *New York Times*, 1 and 2 May 1930.

18. My telephone conversation with Herbert Wechsler, professor of law at Columbia University, on 9 July 1977 revealed that Attorney General Mitchell had advised Parker not to appear before the committee because there was no precedent for it. Wechsler also reported that Parker was "burdened" by the defeat for the rest of his life.

19. Felix Frankfurter to Harlan F. Stone, 22 May 1930, Stone Papers, LC; Henry J. Allen to William Allen White, 12 May 1930, and White to Allen, 23 May 1930, White Papers, LC; *New York Times*, 10 May 1930.

20. See Duane F. Guy, "The Influence of Agriculture on the Tariff Act of 1930" (Ph.D. diss., University of Kansas, 1964), chap. 6 passim; William Allen White to Henry J. Allen, 9 May 1930, White Papers, LC.

21. For Hoover's farm policies see Joan Hoff-Wilson, "Hoover's Agricultural Policies, 1921–1928," *Agricultural History* 51 (Apr. 1977): 335–62;

Fausold, "President Hoover's Farm Policies," pp. 362–79; Guy, "Influence of Agriculture," chap. 3 passim.

22. Guy, "Influence of Agriculture," chap. 6 passim; "Comparison of the Flexible Provisions of the Tariff: Section 336, Tariff Act of 1930, Section 315, Tariff Act of 1922," HP; *New York Times*, 15 May 1931.

23. Frank W. Taussig, *The Tariff History of the United States* (New York: G. P. Putnam's Sons, 1931), chap. 11 passim.

24. William A. White to Henry J. Allen, 9 May 1930, White Papers, LC.

25. Thomas W. Lamont to Hoover, 3 Jan. 1930, HP.

26. "Steps Taken by the Federal Government towards Expediting Public Works Construction," 23 Jan. 1930, and an untitled statement of 7 Mar. 1930, HP; see also Harris Gaylord Warren, *Herbert Hoover and the Great Depression* (New York: Oxford University Press, 1959), chap. 7 passim, and Albert U. Romasco, *The Poverty of Abundance: Hoover, the Nation, the Depression* (New York: Oxford University Press, 1965), chap. 4 passim.

27. E. D. Durand to Thomas W. Lamont, 6 Mar. 1930, HP.

28. Felix Frankfurter to Walter Lippmann, 28 Feb. 1930, Frankfurter Papers, LC.

29. William Green to Hoover, 12 Mar. 1930, and Hoover to Green, 13 Mar. 1930, HP.

30. Hoover to Robert P. Lamont, 29 Apr. 1930, HP.

31. Hoover to Roy A. Young, 24 Mar. 1930, Young to Hoover, 28 Mar. 1930, and E. A. Goldenweiser to Hoover, 11 Apr. 1930, HP.

32. Hoover to Wesley Jones and Will R. Wood, 18 Apr. 1930, HP.

33. Eugene Meyer to Hoover, 2 July 1930, HP.

34. Arthur Wood to Hoover, 21 Nov. 1930, HP; *Federal Reserve Bulletin*, Feb. 1931.

35. Franklin D. Roosevelt to Louis Howe, 21 May 1929, Roosevelt Papers.

36. Thomas S. Barkley, "The Publication Division of the Democratic Party, 1924–30," *American Political Science Review* 25 (Feb. 1931): 69–73.

37. Stimson, diaries, x, 53, reel 2, 10/6/30.

38. *New York Times*, 6 and 7 Nov. 1930; Stimson, diaries, reel 2, 11/5/30.

39. Edward Clark to Calvin Coolidge, 6 Nov. 1930, Clark Papers, LC.

40. William Allen White to David Hinshaw, 10 Nov. 1930, White Papers, LC.

CHAPTER 6
THE CORPORATIST BALANCE

1. Arthur M. Schlesinger, Jr., "Hoover Makes a Comeback," *New York Review of Books*, 8 Mar. 1979, p. 11.

2. Ellis W. Hawley, "Herbert Hoover and American Corporatism, 1929–1933," in *The Hoover Presidency: A Reappraisal*, ed. Martin L. Fausold and

George T. Mazuzan (Albany: State University of New York Press, 1974), pp. 101–23.

3. William Appleman Williams, "What This Country Needs . . . ," *New York Review of Books*, 5 Nov. 1970, p. 9.

4. Vaughn Bornet to author, 11 May 1981.

5. Hoover, *American Individualism*, passim; William Appleman Williams to author, 23 Feb. 1977, 15 June 1981.

6. Milton S. Eisenhower, ed., *Yearbook of Agriculture, 1930* (Washington, D.C.: United States Government Printing Office, 1930), pp. 19–20.

7. Ibid.; *Statistical Abstract of the United States, 1940*, p. 673.

8. Julius H. Barnes to Hoover, 4 Mar. 1930, HP.

9. Alexander Legge to Hoover, 6 Mar. 1930, HP.

10. Henry J. Allen to William Allen White, 15 July 1930, White Papers, LC.

11. Roger Lambert, "Food from the Public Crib" (paper delivered to NEH Seminar, HL, summer 1979).

12. Carter Glass to A. S. Burleson, 6 Aug. 1931, Glass Papers, University of Virginia.

13. Grover Cleveland to House of Representatives, 16 Feb. 1887, HP.

14. Lambert, "Food from the Public Crib," passim; John G. Brown, confidential agent, USDA, to Hoover, 16 July 1931, HP.

15. Lambert, "Food from the Public Crib," p. 27.

16. Fausold, "President Hoover's Farm Policies," p. 372.

17. Louis Galambos, "The Emerging Organizational Synthesis in Modern American History," *Business History Review* 44 (Autumn 1970): 279–90; Ellis W. Hawley, "Neo-Institutional History and the Understanding of Herbert Hoover" (paper presented at George Fox College, spring 1982).

18. M. Browning Carrott, "The Supreme Court and American Trade Associations, 1921–1925," *Business History Review* 44 (Autumn 1970): 320–38.

19. Ibid., pp. 234–38; also National Industrial Conference Board, *Trade Associations: Their Economic Significance and Legal Status* (New York: National Industrial Conference Board, Inc., 1925), pp. 88–93.

20. Carrott, "Supreme Court"; William G. Robbins, "Voluntary Cooperation and the Search for Stability: The Lumber Industry in the 1920s" (paper delivered to NEH seminar, HL, summer 1979), passim.

21. William Tanner, "Secretary of Commerce Hoover's War on Waste, 1921–1928" (paper delivered to NEH seminar, HL, summer 1979), passim; Edward Eyre Hunt, "Economic Changes in 1929," reprinted from *Mechanical Engineering*, Feb. 1930, Hunt Papers, HP.

22. Carrott, "Supreme Court," p. 327.

23. Felix Frankfurter to Walter Lippmann, 6 Jan. 1930, Frankfurter Papers, LC.

24. Robert F. Himmelberg, contributor to *Herbert Hoover and the Crisis of American Capitalism*, ed. J. Joseph Huthmacher and Warren I. Sussman (Cambridge, Mass.: Schenkman Publishing Co., 1973), pp. 35–87.

25. *Public Papers of the Presidents of the United States, Herbert Hoover, 1930* (Washington, D.C.: United States Government Printing Office, 1976), pp. 420–27.

26. Ibid., *1931* (Washington, D.C.: United States Government Printing Office, 1976), pp. 272–77.

27. Hoover, *Memoirs*, 3:334.

28. Julius H. Barnes to Hoover, 7 May 1932, HP.

29. Peri Ethan Arnold, "Herbert Hoover and the Department of Commerce: A Study of Ideology and Policy" (Ph.D. diss., University of Chicago, 1972), pp. 133–37.

30. Herbert Hoover hearings before U.S. Senate Education and Labor Committee, 14 May 1920, Public Statements File, vol. 3, HP; James E. Cebula, "Herbert Hoover, the Corporative State and the Right to Strike" (paper delivered at NEH seminar, HL, summer 1979), passim.

31. Herbert Hoover, Foreword, *Business Cycles and Unemployment* (New York: McGraw-Hill Book Co., Inc., 1923), vol. 6.

32. Robert K. Murray, *The Harding Era: Warren G. Harding and His Administration* (Minneapolis: University of Minnesota Press, 1969), p. 256; note, Robert Murray to Ellis Hawley, summer 1974.

33. Jules Abels, *The Degeneration of Our Presidential Election: A History and Analysis of an American Institution in Trouble* (New York: Macmillan Co., 1968), p. 165.

34. Vaughn Davis Bornet, *Labor Politics in a Democratic Republic*, p. 167.

35. Cebula, "Herbert Hoover," pp. 22–23.

36. William D. Mitchell to Hoover, 23 Mar. 1932, Mitchell to Hoover, confidential, 23 Mar. 1932, and Walter Newton to Bertrand Snell, 8 Mar. 1932, HP.

37. Edward Eyre Hunt, "Planning: A Technique of Balance," box 6, Hunt Papers, HL.

CHAPTER 7
1931: THINGS GET WORSE

1. *New York Times*, 14 Jan. 1930.

2. Ibid., 12 Jan. 1928.

3. Ibid., 21 Jan. 1931.

4. Norman H. Clark, *Deliver Us from Evil: An Interpretation of American Prohibition* (New York: W. W. Norton & Co., Inc., 1976), p. 192.

5. Author's conversation with J. William Frost, Swarthmore, Pa., 27 Aug. 1982.

6. *New York Times*, 22 Oct. 1928.

7. Edward T. Clark to Calvin Coolidge, 15 Dec. 1930, Clark Papers, LC.

8. David Lawrence to Lawrence Richey, 8 Nov. 1930, HP.

9. Bernard Baruch to Franklin D. Roosevelt, 13 Nov. 1930, Roosevelt Papers, private correspondence.

10. William Allen White to Franklin D. Roosevelt, 17 Dec. 1930, White Papers, LC.

11. Edward M. House to Franklin D. Roosevelt, 30 Dec. 1930, House Papers, Franklin D. Roosevelt Presidential Library, Hyde Park, N.Y.

12. *New York Times,* 2 Jan. 1931.

13. William Allen White to David Hinshaw, 13 Feb. 1931, White Papers, LC.

14. *Public Papers, Hoover, 1930,* pp. 509–23; *New York Times,* 3 Dec. 1930.

15. Franklin D. Roosevelt to N. E. McIntosh, 7 Jan. 1931, Roosevelt Papers.

16. *New York Times,* 15 Nov. 1930.

17. Ibid., 9 Dec. 1930.

18. Ibid., 4, 19, 23 Jan., 13 Feb. 1931.

19. Hoover, *Memoirs,* 3:310.

20. William Allen White to Judson King, 13 Mar. 1931, White Papers, LC.

21. Paul A. Kellogg to Lawrence Richey, 30 Mar. 1931, HP; J. Joseph Huthmacher, *Senator Robert F. Wagner and the Rise of Urban Liberalism* (New York: Atheneum, 1968), p. 84.

22. *Kiplinger Washington Letter,* 14 and 21 Mar. 1931.

23. Stimson, diaries, xv, 205, reel 3, 3/30/31.

24. Irwin Hood Hoover, *Forty-two Years in the White House,* pp. 192–97; *New York Times,* 4 Apr. 1931.

25. Stimson, diaries, xvi, 168, reel 3, 6/18/31.

26. Ibid., xviii, 46, reel 3, 9/19/31.

27. J. E. Dewhurst to Julius Klein, 19 Mar. 1931, HP.

28. Stimson, diaries, xvi, 83, reel 3, 5/19/31.

29. Ibid., xvi, 104, 105, reel 3, 5/26/31.

30. *New York Times,* 16 June 1931; *Public Papers, Hoover, 1930,* pp. 295–307.

31. *New York Times,* 22 June 1931.

32. George Norris to John A. Simpson, 30 June 1931, Norris Papers, LC.

CHAPTER 8
DEPRESSION AND THE SEVENTY-SECOND CONGRESS

1. *Federal Reserve Bulletin* (Washington, D.C.: Federal Reserve Board, Dec. 1932), p. 760; *Historical Supplement to Federal Reserve Chart Book on Financial and Business Statistics* (Washington, D.C.: Board of Governors of Federal Reserve System, 1959), p. 79.

2. White House Number Count on Special Session, Congress, 1932/33, and Charles L. Underhill to Hoover, 7 Dec. 1931, HP.

3. *New York Times,* 20 Aug. 1931.

4. Ibid., 21 Aug. 1931.

5. *Kiplinger Washington Letter,* 5 Sept. 1931.

6. Description of P.O.U.R., 16 Dec. 1931, HP.

7. Romasco, *Poverty of Abundance*, pp. 165–66.

8. *Public Papers, Hoover, 1930*, p. 398.

9. Adolph J. Sabath to Eugene Meyer, undated, HP. To make sure that the Federal Reserve System had power to relieve "distress," Sabath proposed legislation to broaden its discount authority (*New York Times*, 27 Nov. 1930).

10. Milton Friedman and Anna Jacobson Schwartz, *A Monetary History of the United States, 1867–1960* (Princeton, N.J.: Princeton University Press, 1963), p. 411.

11. James Stuart Olson, *Herbert Hoover and the Reconstruction Finance Corporation, 1931–1933* (Ames: Iowa State University Press, 1977), chap. 3 passim.

12. Will Irwin to Herbert Hoover, 5 Oct. 1931, HP.

13. *Mirrors of 1932* (New York: Brewer, Warren & Putnam, Inc., 1931), passim; *New York Times*, 26 July 1931; William Allen White to Walter Newton, 13 Oct. and 10 Nov. 1931, White Papers, LC.

14. Olson, *Herbert Hoover*, p. 119.

15. *New York Times*, 9 Dec. 1931.

16. Edward Clark to Calvin Coolidge, 11 Nov. 1931, Clark Papers, LC.

17. *New York Times*, 9 Dec. 1931.

18. "Private Office Memorandum," 20 Apr. 1932, Arthur Krock Papers, Princeton University, Princeton, N.J.

19. Felix Frankfurter to Walter Lippmann, 13 and 19 Jan. 1932, and Lippmann to Frankfurter, 23 May 1930, Frankfurter Papers, LC.

20. Jordan A. Schwarz, *The Interregnum of Despair: Hoover, Congress, and the Depression* (Urbana: University of Illinois Press, 1970), passim.

21. Walter Lippmann, "Today and Tomorrow," *New York Herald Tribune*, 3 May 1932.

22. Felix Frankfurter to Walter Lippmann, 12 Apr. 1932, Frankfurter Papers, LC.

23. *New York Times*, 15 Dec. 1931.

24. Felix Frankfurter to Walter Lippmann, 1 Apr. 1932, Frankfurter Papers, LC.

25. Ogden Mills to Fiorello H. La Guardia, 17 Mar. 1932, Mills Papers, LC.

26. Felix Frankfurter to Walter Lippmann, 1 Apr. 1932, Frankfurter Papers, LC.

27. Bernard Baruch to Hoover, 11 Apr., 10, 18, and 21 May 1932, Baruch Papers, Princeton University, Princeton, N.J.

28. Roy L. Wilbur to Hoover, 22 Apr. 1932, HP.

29. Hoover to Senators, 12 Mar. 1932, HP.

30. Olson, *Herbert Hoover*, chaps. 5 and 6.

31. Lippmann, "Today and Tomorrow."

32. Walter Lippmann, *Interpretations, 1931–1932*, ed. Allan Nevins (New York: Macmillan Co., 1932), pp. 78–91.

33. William Allen White to Walter Lippmann, 26 Apr. 1932, White Papers, LC.

34. Felix Frankfurter to Walter Lippmann, 27 Apr. 1932, Frankfurter Papers, LC.

35. Joseph Robinson to Bernard Baruch, 27 May 1932, Baruch Papers, Princeton University.

36. Hoover to Herbert S. Crocker, 21 May 1932, HP.

CHAPTER 9
FOREIGN POLICY

1. Tolles, *Quakers and the Atlantic Culture*, p. 42.

2. Ibid., p. 64.

3. Robert H. Ferrell, *American Diplomacy in the Great Depression: Hoover-Stimson Foreign Policy, 1929–1933* (New Haven, Conn.: Yale University Press, 1957), p. 19.

4. Alexander De Conde, "Herbert Hoover and Foreign Policy: A Retrospective Assessment," in *Herbert Hoover Reassessed: Essays Commemorating the Fiftieth Anniversary of the Inauguration of Our Thirty-first President,* sponsored by Mark O. Hatfield (Washington, D.C.: United States Government Printing Office, 1981), p. 319.

5. Joan Hoff-Wilson, "Herbert Hoover's Foreign Policy," in *The Hoover Presidency: A Reappraisal,* ed. Martin L. Fausold and George T. Mazuzan (Albany: State University of New York Press, 1974), p. 165.

6. Stimson, diaries, x, 112–14, 11/1/30.

7. Ibid., x, 228, reel 2, 12/15/30.

8. Ibid., xxiii, 172–88, reel 4, 9/14–18/32.

9. Hoover to Ray Lyman Wilbur, 8 Mar. 1948, HP; Graham Stuart, *The Department of State: A History of Its Organization, Procedure and Personnel* (New York: Macmillan Co., 1949), chap. 24; Frank J. Merli and Theodore A. Wilson, eds., *Makers of American Diplomacy from Benjamin Franklin to Henry Kissinger* (New York: Charles Scribner's Sons, 1974), pp. 407–36.

10. *New York Times*, 4 Oct. 1929.

11. Ferrell, *American Diplomacy*, p. 94.

12. William Appleman Williams, *Americans in a Changing World: A History of the United States in the Twentieth Century* (New York: Harper & Row, Publishers, 1978), pp. 234–35.

13. Henry L. Stimson and McGeorge Bundy, *On Active Service: In Peace and War* (New York: Harper & Brothers, 1947), pp. 222–24.

14. Stimson, diaries, xix, 18–19, reel 4, 11/7/31.

15. Ibid., xix, 23–24, reel 4, 11/9/31.

16. Ibid., xx, 4, reel 4, 1/3/32.

17. Walter Lippmann to H. L. Stimson, 22 Dec. 1931, Stimson Papers, Yale University Library, New Haven, Conn.

18. Stimson, diaries, xx, 103, reel 4, 1/26/32.

19. Ibid., xxii, 14, reel 4, 5/19/32.

20. Ibid., xxi, 60, reel 4, 3/12/32.

21. Stimson and Bundy, *On Active Service*, p. 262. It must be noted that by the time both Stimson and Hoover wrote their memoirs, "the two were bitter enemies because of Stimson's service to FDR whom Hoover detested" (Selig Adler to author, 25 May 1981).

22. Hoover, *Memoirs*, 2:377.

23. Elting E. Morison, *Turmoil and Tradition: A Study of the Life and Times of Henry L. Stimson* (Boston: Houghton Mifflin Co., 1960), p. 369.

24. Alexander De Conde, *Herbert Hoover's Latin-American Policy*, p. 18.

25. Robert R. Moton to Hoover, memorandum, 28 July 1930, HP.

26. Stimson, diaries, x, 113, reel 2, 11/1/30.

27. Stimson and Bundy, *On Active Service*, p. 182.

28. De Conde, *Herbert Hoover's Latin-American Policy*, pp. 49–50.

29. Stimson and Bundy, *On Active Service*, p. 211; Donald R. McCoy, *Calvin Coolidge: The Quiet President* (New York: Macmillan Co., 1967), p. 190.

30. Stimson and Bundy, *On Active Service*, pp. 204–5.

31. George Norris to John A. Simpson, 30 June 1931, Norris Papers, LC.

32. Ferrell, *American Diplomacy*, pp. 198–204.

33. Stimson, diaries, xxii, 35, reel 4, 5/24/32.

34. De Conde, "Herbert Hoover and Foreign Policy," p. 329.

35. Ibid., p. 328.

CHAPTER 10

DEFEAT

1. Herbert B. Swope to William E. Borah, 4 Sept. 1931, and Borah to Swope, 20 Sept. 1931, Borah Papers, LC.

2. Harold Ickes to Charles P. Hilles, 14 Mar. 1932, and Hilles to Theodore G. Joslin, 16 Mar. 1932, HP; William Allen White to David Hinshaw, 24 Mar. 1932, White to Harold Ickes, 17 Mar. 1932, and Ickes to White, 18 Mar. 1932, White Papers, LC.

3. *Time Magazine*, 27 June 1932.

4. Edward T. Clark to Calvin Coolidge, 11 Apr. 1932, Clark Papers, LC.

5. *Time Magazine*, 27 June 1932.

6. William Allen White to Josephus Daniels, undated, White Papers, LC.

7. Franklin D. Roosevelt to Bernard M. Baruch, 19 Dec. 1932, Roosevelt Papers.

8. Bernard M. Baruch to Joseph T. Robinson, 13 June 1932, Baruch Papers, Princeton University.

9. Arthur M. Schlesinger, Jr., and Fred L. Israel, *History of American Presidential Elections, 1789–1968* (New York: McGraw-Hill Book Co., 1971), 3:2784–2805.

10. *New York Times*, 6 Nov. 1932.

11. Donald J. Lisio, "A Blunder Becomes Catastrophe: Hoover, the Legion, and the Bonus Army," *Wisconsin Magazine of History* 51 (Autumn 1967): 37–50.

12. Ibid.

13. Ibid.

14. Hoover, *Memoirs*, 3:225.

15. Lisio, "Blunder," pp. 37–50.

16. William Mitchell to Ray Lyman Wilbur, 8 Sept. 1944, HP.

17. Craig Lloyd, *Aggressive Introvert: A Study of Herbert Hoover and Public Relations Management, 1912–1932* (Columbus: Ohio State University Press, 1973), p. 175.

18. Will(iam Henry) Irwin, *Propaganda and the News: Or, What Makes You Think So?* (New York: McGraw-Hill, 1936), p. 295. Charles Michelson tells it differently, emphasizing that his pieces on Hoover were simply drawn from the president's own speeches and those of his critics (*The Ghost Talks* [New York: G. P. Putnam's Sons, 1944], pp. 28–29).

19. Clinton Rossiter, *The American Presidency* (New York: New American Library, 1956), p. 97.

20. William Allen White to Henry J. Allen, 30 Dec. 1932, White Papers, LC.

21. Edward T. Clark to Calvin Coolidge, 16 Sept. and 11 Nov. 1932, Clark Papers, LC.

22. Ibid.

23. Frank Freidel, *Franklin D. Roosevelt*, vol. 3: *The Triumph* (Boston: Little, Brown & Co., 1956), pp. 356–57.

24. Ibid., p. 354.

25. Lawrence Richey, memorandum, Sept. 1932, HP; William Allen White to Henry J. Allen, 20 Sept. 1932, and Allen to Theodore Joslin, 15 Aug. 1932, HP.

26. Richard Lowitt, ed., *Journal of a Tamed Bureaucrat: Nils A. Olsen and the BAE, 1925–1935* (Ames: Iowa State University Press, 1980), p. 143.

27. Schlesinger and Israel, *History of American Presidential Elections*, 3:2736.

28. J. C. O'Laughlin to Hoover, 8 Oct. 1932, O'Laughlin Papers, LC.

29. Stimson, diaries, xxiii, 224–26, reel 4, 10/1–2/32; Hoover, *Memoirs*, 3:233.

30. Stimson, diaries, xxiv, 69, reel 5, 11/8/32.

31. Edgar Rickard, diary, 8 Nov. 1932, HL.

32. William Allen White to Gifford Pinchot, 18 Nov. 1932, White Papers, LC.

33. Stimson, diaries, xxiv, 71, reel 5, 11/9/32.

34. Hoover, *Memoirs*, 3:343.

CHAPTER 11
RITES OF PASSAGE

1. Stimson, diaries, xxiv, 89–97, reel 5, 11/14–16/32.

2. Ibid., xxiv, 76, reel 5, 12/10/32.

3. *The Public Papers and Addresses of Franklin D. Roosevelt,* vol. 1 (New York: Russell & Russell, 1938), pp. 876–77.

4. Felix Frankfurter to Franklin D. Roosevelt, 15 Nov. 1932, Frankfurter Papers, LC.

5. Key Pittman to Franklin D. Roosevelt, 17 Nov. 1932, Roosevelt Papers.

6. Frank B. Freidel, *Franklin D. Roosevelt,* vol. 4: *Launching the New Deal* (Boston: Little, Brown & Co., 1973), pp. 26–27.

7. Stimson, diaries, xxiv, 111–12, reel 5, 11/14/32, and xxiv, 123–31, reel 5, 11/22/32. Other explanations of Stimson's absence from the conference include the fact that Hoover trusted Mills's harder line against Roosevelt.

8. Freidel, *Franklin D. Roosevelt,* vol. 4, chap. 3. There are many other accounts of the meeting, such as that in Raymond Moley, *The First New Deal* (New York: Harcourt, Brace & World, Inc., 1966), chap. 1.

9. Stimson, diaries, xxiv, 120–30, reel 5, 11/23/32.

10. Ibid., xxiv, 167, reel 5, 12/3/32.

11. Ibid., xxiv, 176, reel 5, 12/4/32.

12. Ibid., xxv, 16, reel 5, 12/17/32.

13. Ibid., xxv, 24–26, reel 5, 12/20/32; Freidel, *Franklin D. Roosevelt,* vol. 4, chap. 3.

14. Lawrence Richey, memorandum, 21 Dec. 1932, HP.

15. Bernard Baruch to James Cox, 22 Dec. 1932, Baruch Papers, Princeton University.

16. Herbert Feis, *1933: Characters in Crisis* (Boston: Little, Brown & Co., 1966), chap. 5; Stimson, diaries, xxv, 25–53, reel 5, 12/20–24/32.

17. Ibid., xxv, 55–77, reel 5, 12/27/32–1/4/33.

18. Ibid., xxv, 86–87, reel 5, 1/7/33.

19. Oral history interview with Raymond Moley by Raymond Henle, 13 Nov. 1967, p. 5, HP.

20. Stimson, diaries, xxv, 92–105, reel 5, 1/9/33.

21. Ibid., xxv, 110, 123, reel 5, 1/11/33.

22. Ibid., xxv, 120–28, reel 5, 1/15/33.

23. Ibid., xxv, 141, reel 5, 1/18/33.

24. Ibid., xxv, 142–47, reel 5, 1/19/33.

25. Ibid., xxv, 148–55, reel 5, 1/20/33.

26. Feis, *1933,* chap. 6; "Conference on Jan. 29, 1933 between President Hoover and Governor Roosevelt," HP.

27. *Time Magazine,* 14 Nov. 1932.

28. R. M. Washburn to Colonel Edward House, 18 June 1933, Roosevelt Papers.

29. Stimson, diaries, xxv, 177, reel 5, 1/23/33.

30. Oral history, Moley and Henle, p. 27; *Public Papers of the Presidents: Herbert Hoover, 1932–1933* (Washington, D.C.: United States Government Printing Office, 1977), pp. 891–95.

31. William Allen White to David Hinshaw, 30 Dec. 1932, White Papers, LC.

32. William Allen White to Colonel Edward House, 11 Jan. 1933, White Papers, LC.

33. *Time Magazine*, 9, 16, 23, 30 Jan. and 6, 13, 27 Feb. 1933; *Public Papers, 1932–33*, pp. 985–97.

34. Freidel, *Franklin D. Roosevelt*, 4:161–65.

35. Ibid., p. 167.

36. Ibid., pp. 168–69.

37. Hoover to Franklin D. Roosevelt, 18 Feb. 1933, HP.

38. Hoover to David Reed, 22 Feb. 1933, HP.

39. For a good general analysis of the banking crisis see Susan Estabrook Kennedy, *The Banking Crisis of 1933* (Lexington: University Press of Kentucky, 1973), chaps. 2–5; Hoover, *Memoirs*, 3:206–7.

40. Stimson, diaries, xxvi, 84–85, 113–16, reel 5, 2/28/33.

41. Freidel, *Franklin D. Roosevelt*, 4:186.

42. Hoover to Arch Shaw, 17 Feb. 1933, HP.

43. Freidel, *Franklin D. Roosevelt*, 4:188.

44. Franklin D. Roosevelt to Hoover, 20 Feb. 1933, HP.

45. James Rand telephone message to White House, 25 Feb. 1933, HP.

46. Freidel, *Franklin D. Roosevelt*, 4:192–93.

47. Stimson, diaries, xxvi, 126–36, reel 5, 3/3–4/33.

48. Ibid.; *New York Times*, 4 and 5 Mar. 1933.

49. Freidel, *Franklin D. Roosevelt*, 4:202–7.

50. *New York Times*, 5 Mar. 1933; *Chicago Tribune*, 5 Mar. 1933.

CHAPTER 12
EPILOGUE

1. Ogden Mills to Lawrence Richey, telephone call, 9 Mar. 1933, HP.

2. Ogden Mills to Hoover, telephone call, 10 Mar. 1933, HP.

3. Felix Frankfurter to Walter Lippmann, 11 Mar. 1933, and Lippmann to Frankfurter, 14 Mar. 1933, Frankfurter Papers, LC; Ronald Steel, *Walter Lippmann and the American Century* (Boston: Little, Brown & Co., 1980), pp. 300–302.

4. William Allen White to Colonel Edward House, 10 and 18 Mar. 1933, White Papers, LC; Walter Johnson, *William Allen White's America* (New York: Henry Holt & Co., 1947), pp. 436–39.

5. *New York Times*, 23 July 1933.

6. J. C. O'Laughlin to Hoover, 21 Mar. 1933, and Hoover to O'Laughlin, 25 Mar. 1933, O'Laughlin Papers, LC.

7. Hoover to Walter Brown, 25 and 26 Apr. 1933, HP.

8. Edgar Rickard, diary, 27 Sept. 1933, HP.

9. Ibid., 23 Nov. 1933.

10. Henry L. Stimson to Hoover, 13 Mar. 1933, and Hoover to Stimson, 14 Mar. 1933, HP.

11. Harlan F. Stone, memorandum, 1 May 1934, Stone Papers, LC; see Herbert Hoover, *The Challenge to Liberty* (New York: Charles Scribner's Sons, 1934); Mason, *Harlan Fiske Stone*, pp. 369–82.

BIBLIOGRAPHICAL ESSAY

There are two parts to this essay: a General section of secondary and primary sources that are germane to the entire book and a section mostly of secondary sources that are applicable to individual chapters. The works in the General section usually are not listed again in the chapter bibliographies, even though they frequently relate to some chapters far more than to others.

GENERAL

Books

Almost immediately after the end of his presidency, Hoover and many of his associates launched an effort to establish their record of the Hoover administration. Their books are, of course, invaluable for factual information and for an understanding of their perceptions of the Hoover presidency. In 1934 Hoover published *The Challenge to Liberty* (New York: Charles Scribner's Sons), which, in ideological content, is a sequel to, and remarkably consistent with, his book *American Individualism* (Garden City, N.Y.: Doubleday, Page & Co.), published in 1922. The two books envelop the political philosophy of the Hoover presidency. Hoover's memoirs are essential sources to an understanding of the presidency, although they are subjective and are occasionally inaccurate: *The Memoirs of Herbert Hoover*, vol. 1: *Years of Adventure, 1874–1920*, vol. 2: *The Cabinet and the Presidency, 1920–1933*, and vol. 3: *The Great Depression, 1929–1941* (New York: Macmillan Co., 1951, 1952).

More accurate, although sympathetic to the former president, are the accounts by some of his associates: Ray Lyman Wilbur and Arthur Mastick Hyde, *The Hoover Policies* (New York: Charles Scribner's Sons, 1937); William

Starr Myers and Walter H. Newton, *The Hoover Administration: A Documented Narrative* (New York: Charles Scribner's Sons, 1936); Theodore G. Joslin, *Hoover off the Record* (Garden City, N.Y.: Doubleday, Doran & Co., 1934). Very favorable biographies by close friends are Will Irwin, *Herbert Hoover: A Reminiscent Biography* (New York: Grosset & Dunlap, 1928); William Hard, *Who's Hoover* (New York: Dodd, Mead & Co., 1928); Edwin Emerson, *Hoover and His Times: Looking Back through the Years* (Garden City, N.Y.: Garden City Publishing Co., 1932); and an insightful account by a fellow Quaker, David Hinshaw, *Herbert Hoover: American Quaker* (New York: Farrar, Straus & Co., 1950). A eulogistic biography, helpful nevertheless because it is based on interviews with Hoover associates, is Carol Green Wilson, *Herbert Hoover: A Challenge for Today* (New York: Evans Publishing Co., 1968). A very helpful compilation is William Starr Myers, ed., *State Papers and Other Public Writings of Herbert Hoover* (Garden City, N.Y.: Doubleday, Doran & Co., Inc., 1934), although it has been made less essential by the recent publication *Public Papers of the Presidents: Herbert Hoover, Containing the Public Messages, Speeches and Statements of the President* (Washington, D.C.: United States Government Printing Office), published in six volumes between 1974 and 1976. An important memoir is that of Hoover's lifelong associate and his secretary of the interior, Ray Lyman Wilbur, *Memoirs, 1875-1949*, edited by Edgar Eugene Robinson and Paul Carroll Edwards (Stanford, Calif.: Stanford University Press, 1960). A very useful sympathetic study by an academic friend of Herbert Hoover's, published many years after the presidency, is Edgar Eugene Robinson and Vaughn Davis Bornet, an associate of Robinson's, *Herbert Hoover: President of the United States* (Stanford, Calif.: Hoover Institution Press, 1975).

Caustic contemporary views of the Hoover presidency, which are often as important to an understanding of the administration as the above, are Robert Sharon Allen and Drew Pearson, *Washington Merry-Go-Round* (New York: Blue Ribbon Books, Inc., 1931) and *More Merry-Go-Round* (New York: Liveright, Inc., Publishers, 1932); and [Ray Thomas Tucker], *Mirrors of 1932* (New York: Brewer, Warren & Putnam, 1931). A very thoughtful and important contemporary analysis is Walter Lippmann, *Interpretations, 1931-1932*, ed. Allan Nevins (New York: Macmillan Co., 1932).

Secondary accounts of Hoover's life and presidency have become, according to Forrest McDonald, rather a cottage industry. Several scurrilous accounts were written immediately after the presidency. The serious works were initiated by two apologies, the former more favorable than the latter: Eugene Lyons, *Our Unknown Ex-President: A Portrait of Herbert Hoover* (Garden City, N.Y.: Doubleday, 1948; Hoover was so sensitive about Lyons's title that it was changed for the 1964 edition); and Harris Gaylord Warren, *Herbert Hoover and the Great Depression* (New York: Oxford University Press, 1959). The first scholarly revision (and the first to be based on the Hoover Papers at the Hoover Presidential Library in West Branch, Iowa) was *The Hoover Presidency: A Reappraisal*, edited by Martin L. Fausold and George T. Mazuzan (Albany: State University of New York Press, 1974). A fine collection of papers is that published under the direction of Senator Mark Hatfield, *Herbert Hoover Reassessed* (Washington, D.C.: United States Government Printing Office, 1981). Two Hoover scholars have written well-received revisionist biographies of the former president: Joan Hoff-Wilson, *Herbert Hoover: Forgotten Progressive* (Boston: Little, Brown & Co., 1975); and David Burner, *Herbert Hoover: The Public Life* (New York: Alfred A. Knopf, 1979). The first volume of a multivolume biography, authorized and subsidized by the Hoover Presidential Library Association, Inc., is George H. Nash, *The Life of Herbert Hoover,* vol. 1: *The Engineer, 1874–1914* (New York: W. W. Norton & Co., Inc., 1983). The series will consist of definitive source books in the life of Herbert Hoover. A very keen study of Hoover's public behavioral traits is Craig Lloyd, *Aggressive Introvert: A Study of Herbert Hoover and Public Relations Management, 1912–1932* (Columbus: Ohio State University Press, 1973).

A number of general secondary works of the period are essential to an analysis of the Hoover presidency. First is a cautiously corrective chapter, "Herbert Hoover and the Crisis of American Individualism," in Richard Hofstadter, *The American Political Tradition and the Men Who Made It* (New York: Alfred A. Knopf, 1948). A somewhat dated work on the twenties is John D. Hicks, *Republican Ascendency, 1921–1933* (New York: Harper & Brothers, Publishers, 1960). The best recent general account of the interwar period is Donald R. McCoy, *Coming of Age: The United States during the 1920's and 1930's* (Baltimore, Md.: Penguin Books, 1973). The following two multivolume biographies of Franklin D. Roosevelt offer extensive coverage of the era: Frank Freidel, *Franklin D. Roosevelt,* vol. 3: *The Triumph,* and vol. 4: *Launching the New Deal* (Boston: Little, Brown & Co., 1956, 1973); and Arthur M. Schlesinger, Jr., *The Age of Roosevelt,* vol. 2: *The Crisis of the Old Order, 1919–1933,* and vol. 3: *The Coming of the New Deal* (Boston: Houghton Mifflin & Co., 1957, 1958). A provocative interpretation of Democratic party politics of the decade is David Burner, *The Politics of Provincialism: The Democratic Party in Transition, 1918–1932* (New York: Alfred A. Knopf, 1967).

Certain tangential secondary works are necessary to an understanding of the Hoover era: Albert U. Romasco, *The Poverty of Abundance: Hoover, the Nation, the Depression* (New York: Oxford University Press, 1965); Irving Berstein, *The Lean Years: A History of the American Worker, 1920–1933* (Boston: Houghton Mifflin Co., 1960); Robert H. Zieger, *Republicans and Labor, 1919–1929* (Lexington: University of Kentucky Press, 1969); Joan Hoff-Wilson, *The Twenties: The Critical Issues* (Boston: Little, Brown & Co., 1972); Jordan A. Schwarz, *The Speculator: Bernard M. Baruch in Washington, 1917–1965* (Chapel Hill: University of North Carolina Press, 1981); Carroll H. Wooddy, *The Growth of the Federal Government, 1915–1932* (New York: McGraw-Hill Book Co., Inc., 1934). Two books that are helpful to a perception of Hoover—the first a psychological study, the second an ideological one—are James David Barber, *The Presidential Character: Predicting Performance in the White House* (Englewood Cliffs, N.J.: Prentice-Hall, Inc., 1972); William Appleman Williams, *The Contours of American History* (Cleveland, Ohio: World Publishing Co., 1961). Dated, although still classic, works on the period are Frederick Lewis Allen, *Only Yesterday: An Informal History of the Nineteen-twenties* (New York: Harper & Brothers, 1931); and Karl Schriftgiesser, *This Was Normalcy: An Account of Party Politics during Twelve Republican Years, 1920–1932* (Boston: Little, Brown, 1948).

MANUSCRIPTS

Most important to this book and to an interpretation of the Hoover presidency are several manuscript collections. Foremost, of course, are the Hoover manuscripts at the Herbert Hoover Presidential Library in West Branch, Iowa, which must be closely combed, particularly because of Hoover's economy in regard to letter writing, especially during his presidency. Other useful collections in the Hoover Library are those of George Edward Akerson, Edgar French Strother, Ray Lyman Wilbur, Julius Barnes, and Edward Eyre Hunt. Certain oral histories in the Hoover Library were helpful: those by Raymond Moley, Robert S. Allen, David Lawrence, and Edgar Eugene Robinson. The diary of Hoover's close associate and personal financial adviser, Edgar Rickard, is revealing of inner-circle attitudes.

Essential to an appraisal of the Hoover presidency are the following collections in the Library of Congress: those of Felix Frankfurter, William Allen White, Edward T. Clark, Eugene Meyer, William E. Borah, John Callan O'Laughlin, Harold L. Ickes, Henry J. Allen, and Harlan Fiske Stone. Important collections, although less essential, are those of Victor Murdock, Raymond Clapper, Charles McNary, James J. Davis, Jesse Jones, Ogden Mills, Gifford Pinchot, George Norris, and Key Pittman.

Collections in other libraries were very useful. Of paramount importance are the diaries and letters of Henry L. Stimson at the Yale University Library. Also at the Yale Library are the papers of Walter Lippmann and Charles D. Hilles. Certain collections at the Princeton University Library proved to be surprisingly helpful: those of Bernard Baruch, Arthur Krock, and Fred I. Kent. On Federal Reserve actions, I found useful the papers of Carter Glass at the University of Virginia and the papers of George Harrison and Wesley Mitchell at Columbia University. Collections at the Franklin D. Roosevelt Presidential Library at Hyde Park, New York, were disappointing, although of some assistance were those of Roosevelt's New York governorship and of the 1932 elections, and the papers of Charles Michelson and Louis M. Howe.

NEWSPAPERS, JOURNALS, ARTICLES, AND GOVERNMENT DOCUMENTS

All researchers of twentieth-century American history use heavily the *New York Times* and its invaluable index. I tried to balance the *Times*'s Democratic bias with the Republican bias of the *Chicago Tribune*. Contemporary popular journalistic articles are too prolific to be listed here. Aside from the *Congressional Record*, which applied to nearly every chapter in the book, those government documents that are applicable to specific chapters are noted under individual chapters. Although the nation lacked the economic literacy that it had achieved by the time of the full employment of 1946, the following publications were of inestimable value for understanding economic conditions: *The Kiplinger Washington Letter* (semimonthly; Washington, D.C.: Kiplinger Washington Agency); *The Federal Reserve Bulletin* (monthly; Washington, D.C.: Federal Reserve System Board of Governors Publishing Service); Edward Eyre Hunt, ed., *Recent Economic Changes in the United States,* 2 vols. (New York: McGraw-Hill Publishing Co., 1929).

I have been much influenced by several seminal articles whose titles explain their general application to the Hoover presidency as a whole: William Allen White, "Herbert Hoover—Last of the Old Presidents or the First of the New?" *Saturday Evening Post,* 4 Mar. 1933, pp. 6–7, 53–56; Barry D. Karl, "Herbert Hoover and the Progressive Myth of the Presidency" (paper presented to Hoover Centennial Seminar, West Branch, Iowa, 1974); Walter Lippmann, "The Permanent New Deal," *Yale Review* 24 (June 1935): 649–67; Barry D. Karl, "Presidential Planning and Social Science Research: Mr. Hoover's Experts," *Perspectives in American History,* vol. 3 (Cambridge, Mass.: Charles Warren Center for Studies in American History, Harvard University, 1969), pp. 347–409; Herbert Stein, "Pre-Revolutionary Fiscal Policy: The Regime of Herbert Hoover," *Journal of Law and Economics* 11 (Oct. 1966): 189–223; Victor L. Albjerg, "Hoover: The Presidency in Transition," *Current History,* Oct. 1960, pp. 213–19. Two important titles are not self-explanatory: Carl N. Degler discusses the commonality of the Hoover and Franklin D. Roosevelt administrations as active antidepression presidencies in "The Ordeal of Herbert Hoover," *Yale Review* 52 (Summer 1963): 563–83; a bizarre yet creditable account of Hoover as a statist liberal is Murray N. Rothbard, "Herbert Clark Hoover: A Reconsideration," *New Individualist Review* 4 (Winter 1966): 3–12.

Although doctoral dissertations frequently come last in bibliographies, some should come first. Such is particularly true of John Lee Westrate, "The Administrative Theory and Practice of Herbert Hoover" (University of Chicago, 1968); Clair E. Nelsen, "The Image of Herbert Hoover as Reflected in the American Presidency" (Stanford University, 1956). An essential background doctoral dissertation for understanding Hoover's public life prior to his presidency is Peri E. Arnold, "Herbert Hoover and the Department of Commerce: A Study of Ideology and Policy" (University of Chicago, 1972). Doctoral dissertations about important political associates are Lawrence L. Murray, "Andrew W. Mellon, Secretary of the Treasury, 1921–1932: A Study in Policy" (Michigan State University, 1970); Orde Sorensen Pinckney, "William E. Borah and the Republican Party, 1932–1940" (University of California, Berkeley, 1958).

CHAPTER BIBLIOGRAPHIES

Chapter 1: The Education of Herbert Hoover
This chapter has been in germination for more than the decade that I have spent in doing the research for and writing of this book. Although the development of Hoover's ideology began with his Quaker origins, my understanding of it first emanated from corporatist thought as described by William Appleman Williams, "What This Country Needs . . . ," *New York Review of Books*, 5 Nov. 1970, pp. 7–11; and various works by Ellis W. Hawley: "Herbert Hoover, the Commerce Secretariat, and the Vision of an 'Associative State,' 1921–1928," *Journal of American History* 61 (June 1974): 116–40; "Herbert Hoover and American Corporatism, 1929–1933," in *The Hoover Presidency: A Reappraisal,* edited by Martin L. Fausold and George T. Mazuzan (Albany: State University of New York Press, 1974), pp. 101–19; and an unpublished paper by Hawley presented at George Fox College in the spring of 1981, "Neo-Institutional History and the Understanding of Herbert Hoover."

Hoover's corporatist thought in many respects was a reinforcement of his Quaker beginnings, which are described in Quaker materials in the Herbert Hoover Presidential Library and such published works as David Hinshaw, *Herbert Hoover: American Quaker* (New York: Farrar, Straus & Co., 1950); Gerald D. Nash, in *Herbert Hoover and the Crisis of American Capitalism,* edited by J. Joseph Huthmacher and Warren I. Sussman (Cambridge, Mass.: Schenkman Publishing Co., 1973); and such unpublished works as James R. Bowers, "Herbert Hoover: Ambivalent Quaker" (master's thesis, Sangamon State University, Springfield, Ill., 1981); and David Burner, "A Quaker in the White House: Toward an Understanding of Herbert Hoover" (at Herbert Hoover Centennial Seminar, Herbert Hoover Presidential Library, 1974).

Particularly helpful regarding Quaker background generally were Elizabeth Gray Vining, *Friend of Life: The Biography of Rufus M. Jones* (Philadelphia: J. B. Lippincott Co., 1958); William Wistar Comfort, *Just among Friends: The Quaker Way of Life* (New York: Macmillan Co., 1941); Frederick B. Tolles, *Quakers and the Atlantic Culture* (New York: Macmillan Co., 1960).

Essential to an understanding of Hoover's thought was his work *American Individualism* (Garden City, N.Y.: Doubleday, Page & Co., 1922); Gary Dean Best, *The Politics of American Individualism: Herbert Hoover in Transition, 1918–1921* (Westport, Conn.: Greenwood Press, 1975); Walter Friar Dexter, *Herbert Hoover and American Individualism: A Modern Interpretation of a National Ideal* (New York: Macmillan Co., 1932).

Chapter 2: Victory
Very basic tools for understanding the election of 1928 are these factual, yet interpretative, works: Roy V. Peel and Thomas C. Donnelly, *The 1928 Campaign: An Analysis* (New York: Richard R. Smith, Inc., 1931); Donald R. McCoy, "To the White House: Herbert Hoover, August, 1927–March, 1929," in *The Hoover Presidency: A Reappraisal,* edited by Martin L. Fausold and George T. Mazuzan

(Albany: State University of New York Press, 1974), pp. 29–49; Lawrence H. Fuchs, "Election of 1928," in *History of American Elections*, edited by Arthur M. Schlesinger, Jr., and Fred L. Israel, vol. 3 (New York: McGraw-Hill Co., 1971), pp. 2585–2704.

Important works on the election which emphasize particular themes are Gilbert C. Fite, "The Agricultural Issues in the Presidential Campaign of 1928," *Mississippi Valley Historical Review* 37 (Mar. 1931): 653–72; Vaughn Davis Bornet, *Labor Politics in a Democratic Republic: Moderation, Division, and Disruption in the Presidential Election of 1928* (Washington, D.C.: Spartan Books, Inc., 1964); Edmund Arthur Moore, *A Catholic Runs for President: The Campaign of 1928* (Gloucester, Mass.: P. Smith, 1968); Richard Hofstadter, "Could a Protestant Have Beaten Hoover in 1928?" *Reporter,* 17 Mar. 1960, pp. 31–33; Samuel J. Eldersveld, "The Influence of Metropolitan Party Pluralities in Presidential Elections since 1920: A Study of Twelve Key Cities," *American Political Science Review* 43 (Dec. 1949): 1189–1206; Earland I. Carlson, "Franklin D. Roosevelt's Post-Mortem of the 1928 Election," *Midwest Journal of Political Science* 8 (Aug. 1964): 298–308; Jerome M. Clubb and Howard W. Allen, "The Cities and the Election of 1928: Partisan Realignment?" *American Historical Review* 74 (Apr. 1969): 1205–20; Kent Michael Schofield, "The Figure of Herbert Hoover in the 1928 Campaign" (Ph.D. diss., University of California, Riverside, 1966).

Chapter 3: A New Beginning

A very worthwhile piece that is devoted solely to the early presidential years is David B. Burner, "Before the Crash: Hoover's First Eight Months in the Presidency," in *The Hoover Presidency: A Reappraisal,* edited by Martin L. Fausold and George T. Mazuzan (Albany: State University of New York Press, 1974), pp. 50–65.

For the operation of the presidency the following are essential works: Peri E. Arnold, "Executive Reorganization & the Origins of the Managerial Presidency," *Polity* 13 (Summer 1981): 568–99. A useful background source is Edward Henry Hobbs, *Executive Reorganization in the National Government* (University: University of Mississippi, 1953); and Thomas E. Cronin and Sanford D. Greenberg, eds., *The Presidential Advisory System* (New York: Harper & Row, 1969).

Works that delineate specific aspects of the precrash period are Howard William Runkel, "Hoover's Speeches during His Presidency" (Ph.D. diss., Stanford University, 1950); Martin L. Fausold, "President Hoover's Farm Policies, 1929–1933," *Agricultural History* 51, no. 2 (Apr. 1977); 362–77; E. A. Stokdyk and Charles H. West, *The Farm Board* (New York: Macmillan Co., 1930); and John Knox Boaz, "The Presidential Press Conference" (Ph.D. diss., Wayne State University, 1969). A favorable view of the Hoover presidency from inside the White House is Theodore G. Joslin, *Hoover off the Record* (Garden City, N.Y.: Doubleday, Doran & Co., 1934); an unfavorable view is Irwin Hood ("Ike") Hoover, *Forty-two Years in the White House* (Boston and New York: Houghton Mifflin Co., 1934).

Important doctoral dissertations regarding agricultural policy are Gary H. Koerselman, "Herbert Hoover and the Farm Crisis of the Twenties: A Study of the Commerce Department's Efforts to Solve the Agricultural Depression, 1921–1928" (Northern Illinois University, 1971); and Bernard M. Klass, "John D. Black: Farm Economist and Policy Adviser, 1920–1942" (University of California, Los Angeles, 1969).

Chapter 4: The Crash
Very useful background secondary sources on the economics of the 1920s are Jim Potter, *The American Economy between the World Wars* (New York: John Wiley & Sons, 1974); and Ellis W. Hawley, *The Great War and the Search for Modern Order: A History of the American People and Their Institutions, 1917–1933* (New York: St. Martin's Press, 1979). Dated, though useful if used cautiously, are companion volumes in the series the Economic History of the United States: George Henry Soule, *Prosperity Decade: From War to Depression, 1917–1929* (New York: Rinehart & Co., Inc., 1947); and Broadus Mitchell, *Depression Decade: From New Era through New Deal, 1929–1941* (New York: Rinehart & Co., Inc., 1947). The classic though liberally oriented work on the crash is John Kenneth Galbraith, *The Great Crash, 1929* (Boston: Houghton Mifflin Co., 1955).

For the crash and its immediate aftermath see Robert Sobel, *Herbert Hoover at the Onset of the Great Depression, 1929–1930* (Philadelphia: J. B. Lippincott Co., 1975). Very instructive to me was an unpublished paper by a colleague, David Martin, SUNY, Geneseo, "The Onset of the Great Depression: An Institutional Analysis." The most helpful book on the crash and the depression is Lester V. Chandler, *America's Greatest Depression, 1929–1942* (New York: Harper & Row, Publishers, 1970). Important thematic books on the depression are Charles P. Kindleberger, *The World in Depression, 1929–1939* (Berkeley: University of California Press, 1975, c. 1973); Lester V. Chandler, *American Monetary Policy, 1928–1941* (New York: Harper & Row, Publishers, 1971); Peter Temin, *Did Monetary Forces Cause the Great Depression?* (New York: W. W. Norton & Co., Inc., 1976); Milton Friedman and Anna Jacobson Schwartz, *The Great Contraction, 1929–1933* (Princeton, N.J.: Princeton University Press, 1965).

Two excellent edited works on the general subject of the Hoover presidency and the economy are J. Joseph Huthmacher and Warren I. Sussman, *Herbert Hoover and the Crisis of American Capitalism* (Cambridge, Mass.: Schenkman Publishing Co., 1973); and Robert F. Himmelberg, ed., *The Great Depression and American Capitalism* (Boston: D. C. Heath & Co., 1968). The latter work, a volume in the Problems in American Civilization series, puts emphasis on the New Deal. A useful edited work is David A. Shannon, *The Great Depression* (Englewood Cliffs, N.J.: Prentice-Hall, Inc., 1960).

Chapter 5: 1930
Although the works, manuscript collections, and newspapers listed in the introductory paragraph to this annotated essay provide a detailed account of Hoover's first year in the presidency, the most thorough single account, and the

most sympathetic, was Mark Sullivan, "Hoover's First Year," *New York Herald Tribune* (undated, summer 1931). For the social scene, particularly the Dolly Gann controversy, see Alice Roosevelt Longworth, *Crowded Hours: Reminiscences of Alice Roosevelt Longworth* (New York: Charles Scribner's Sons, 1933); and James Brough, *Princess Alice: A Biography of Alice Roosevelt Longworth* Boston: Little, Brown & Co., 1975).

On the matter of judicial appointments the biographies by Alpheus Thomas Mason are indispensable: *Harlan Fiske Stone: Pillar of the Law* (New York: Viking Press, 1956) and *William Howard Taft: Chief Justice* (New York: Simon & Schuster, 1964). Also important is Merlo John Pusey, *Charles Evans Hughes* (New York: Macmillan Co., 1951). The essential secondary source on the John Parker appointment to the Supreme Court is Richard L. Watson, Jr., "The Defeat of Judge Parker: A Study in Pressure Groups and Politics," *Mississippi Valley Historical Review* 50, no. 2 (Sept. 1963): 213-34. The Judiciary File in the Hoover Papers gives extensive coverage to the Parker appointment.

For the coverage of agriculture during the prepresidency and presidency period see the above bibliographic section on chapter 3 and Joan Hoff-Wilson, "Hoover's Agricultural Policies, 1921-1928," *Agricultural History* 51, no. 2 (Apr. 1977): 335-62; and Martin L. Fausold, "President Hoover's Farm Policies, 1929-1933," *Agricultural History* 51, no. 2 (Apr. 1977): 362-77. For the relationship of agriculture to the tariff see Duane F. Guy, "The Influence of Agriculture on the Tariff Act of 1930" (Ph.D. diss., University of Kansas, 1964). An important contemporary view of the tariff issue is Frank W. Taussig, *The Tariff History of the United States* (New York: G. P. Putnam's Sons, 1931).

Chapter 6: The Corporatist Balance

On the definition of corporatism the seminal works are Ellis W. Hawley, "Herbert Hoover and American Corporatism, 1929-1933," in *The Hoover Presidency: A Reappraisal,* edited by Martin L. Fausold and George T. Mazuzan (Albany: State University of New York Press, 1974), pp. 101-19; William Appleman Williams, *Contours of American History* (Cleveland, Ohio: World Publishing Co., 1961); James Weinstein, *The Corporate Ideal in the Liberal State, 1900-1918* (Boston: Beacon Press, 1968). For corporatist balance in government and agriculture and for agriculture during the period see Fausold, "President Hoover's Farm Policies"; Murray Reed Benedict, *Farm Policies of the United States, 1790-1950: A Study of Their Origins and Development* (New York: Twentieth Century Fund, 1953); Gertrude Almy Slichter, "Franklin D. Roosevelt and the Farm Problem, 1929-1932," *Mississippi Valley Historical Review* 43 (Sept. 1956): 238-58. Two unpublished NEH papers, prepared under my directorship at the Herbert Hoover Presidential Library in 1974, were Roger Lambert, "Food from the Public Crib"; and Bernard M. Klass, "The Federal Farm Board and the Antecedents of the Agricultural Adjustment of 1933."

Very helpful regarding the relationship of government and aggregate capital were Louis Galambos, "The Emerging Organizational Synthesis in Modern American History," *Business History Review* 44 (Autumn 1970): 279-90;

Robert F. Himmelberg, *The Origins of the National Recovery Administration: Business, Government, and the Trade Association Issue, 1921–1933* (New York: Fordham University Press, 1976), and in *Herbert Hoover and the Crisis of American Capitalism* (1973); M. Browning Carrott, "The Supreme Court and American Trade Associations, 1921–1925," *Business History Review* 44 (Autumn 1970): 320–38; Peri Arnold, "Herbert Hoover and the Department of Commerce." Again, two papers done at the NEH seminar in 1979 were William G. Robbins, "Voluntary Cooperation and the Search for Stability: The Lumber Industry in the 1920s"; and William Tanner, "Secretary of Commerce Hoover's War on Waste, 1921–1928."

The relationship of government and labor is partially covered in Louis Galambos, "AFL's Concept of Big Business: A Quantitative Study of Attitudes toward the Large Corporation, 1894–1931," *Journal of American History* 57 (Mar. 1971): 847–63; Ronald Radosh, "The Corporate Ideology of American Labor Leaders from Gompers to Hillman," in *Beyond Liberalism: The New Left Views American History*, comp. Irwin Unger (Waltham, Mass.: Xerox College Pub., 1971); and an unpublished paper prepared at the NEH seminar in 1979, James E. Cebula, "Herbert Hoover, the Corporative State and the Right to Strike."

Chapter 7: "1931: Things Get Worse"

Creditable and scholarly interpretations of the prohibition movement are Norman H. Clark, *Deliver Us from Evil: An Interpretation of American Prohibition* (New York: W. W. Norton & Co., Inc., 1976); Sean Dennis Cashman, *Prohibition: The Lie of the Land* (New York: Free Press, 1981).

An array of journalistic books exist on the subject, the better ones being Andrew Sinclair, *Era of Excess: A Social History of the Prohibition Movement* (New York: Harper & Row, Publishers, 1964); and Herbert Asbury, *The Great Illusion: An Informal History of Prohibition* (Garden City, N.Y.: Doubleday & Co., 1950). An essential source is George W. Wickersham, *U.S. National Commission on Law Observance and Enforcement Report* (Washington, D.C.: United States Government Printing Office, 1931).

The conflict between the president and Congress on labor matters is well described in J. Joseph Huthmacher, *Senator Robert F. Wagner and the Rise of Urban Liberalism* (New York: Atheneum, 1968); Robert Allen Karlsrud, "The Hoover Labor Department: A Study in Bureaucratic Divisiveness" (Ph.D. diss., University of California, Los Angeles, 1972); John Bruce Dudley, "James J. Davis, Secretary of Labor under Three Presidents, 1921–1930" (Ph.D. diss., Ball State University, 1972).

For an excellent contemporary analysis of the first half of the term see Arthur Krock, "President Hoover's Two Years," *Current History*, July 1931, pp. 488–99. See also Joseph M. Jones, Jr., *Tariff Retaliation: Repercussions of the Hawley-Smoot Bill* (Philadelphia: University of Pennsylvania Press; London: Oxford University Press, 1934).

Chapter 8: Depression and the Seventy-second Congress

Invaluable secondary accounts on the Seventy-second Congress are Jordan A. Schwarz, *The Interregnum of Despair: Hoover, Congress, and the Depression* (Urbana: University of Illinois Press, 1970); James Stuart Olson, *Herbert Hoover and the Reconstruction Finance Corporation, 1931–1933* (Ames: Iowa State University Press, 1977); Gerald D. Nash, "Herbert Hoover and the Origins of the Reconstruction Finance Corporation," *Mississippi Valley Historical Review* 46 (Dec. 1959): 455–68. The chapter, however, marks such a vast descent of the Hoover presidency into depression as to require practically all sources listed in the introductory part of this Bibliographical Essay.

Chapter 9: Foreign Policy

Still the definitive book on Hoover's foreign policy is Robert H. Ferrell, *American Diplomacy in the Great Depression: Hoover-Stimson Foreign Policy, 1929–1933* (New Haven, Conn.: Yale University Press, 1957). A fine updating of Ferrell is Alexander De Conde, "Herbert Hoover and Foreign Policy: A Retrospective Assessment," in *Herbert Hoover Reassessed* (Washington, D.C.: United States Government Printing Office, 1981), pp. 313–35. Essential to understanding the foreign policy of the period are William Starr Myers, *The Foreign Policies of Herbert Hoover, 1929–1933* (New York: Charles Scribner's Sons, 1940); and of course, the memoirs of Hoover and of Secretary of State Henry L. Stimson. Many scholarly works have been written on Stimson's conduct of foreign policy, though these are somewhat dated, such as Richard Nelson Current, *Secretary Stimson: A Study in Statecraft* (New Brunswick, N.J.: Rutgers University Press, 1954); Armin Rappaport, *Henry L. Stimson and Japan, 1931–33* (Chicago: University of Chicago Press, 1963); Elting E. Morison, *Turmoil and Tradition: A Study of the Life and Times of Henry L. Stimson* (Boston: Houghton Mifflin Co., 1960). An excellent recent work is Alexander De Conde, *Herbert Hoover's Latin-American Policy* (New York: Octagon, 1970). A fine background work is Joseph Brandes, *Herbert Hoover and Economic Diplomacy: Department of Commerce Policy, 1921–1928* (Pittsburgh, Pa.: University of Pittsburgh Press, 1962).

Excellent accounts of the conduct of United States foreign policy during the interwar period are Selig Adler, *The Uncertain Giant, 1921–1941: American Foreign Policy between the Wars* (London: Collier-Macmillan Ltd., 1965); William Appleman Williams, *The Tragedy of American Diplomacy* (Cleveland, Ohio: World Publishing Co., 1959).

Chapter 10: Defeat

The best sources on the election of 1932 are the near-contemporary study by Roy V. Peel and T. C. Donnelly, *The 1932 Campaign: An Analysis* (New York: Farrar & Rinehart, 1935), and a more recent analysis, Frank Freidel, "Election of 1932," in *History of American Presidential Elections, 1789–1968*, edited by Arthur M. Schlesinger, Jr., and Fred L. Israel (New York: McGraw-Hill Book Co., 1971), vol. 3, pp. 2707–2806. For the record of the Hoover administration on the eve of the election see Allan Nevins, "President Hoover's Record," *Current History,* July 1932, pp. 385–94.

On the bonus march, which so damaged Hoover's campaign, there are two equally creditable works: Roger Daniels, *The Bonus March: An Episode of the Great Depression* (Westport, Conn.: Greenwood Pub. Co., 1971); and Donald J. Lisio, *The President and Protest: Hoover, Conspiracy, and the Bonus Riot* (Columbia: University of Missouri Press, 1974). A fine synthesis of the latter is Donald J. Lisio, "A Blunder Becomes Catastrophe: Hoover, the Legion, and the Bonus Army," *Wisconsin Magazine of History* 51 (Autumn 1967): 37–50.

Two views of the effort of Charles Michelson, publicity director for the Democratic National Committee, to discredit the Hoover presidency are Will(iam Henry) Irwin, *Propaganda and the News: Or, What Makes You Think So?* (New York: McGraw-Hill, 1936); and Charles Michelson, *The Ghost Talks* (New York: G. P. Putnam's Sons, 1944). As suggested in the bibliography for chapter 2 ("The Election of 1928"), the following works should be examined in order to understand this election: Samuel J. Eldersveld, "The Influence of Metropolitan Party Pluralities in Presidential Elections since 1920: A Study of Twelve Key Cities," *American Political Science Review* 43 (Dec. 1949): 1189–1206; Craig Lloyd, *Aggressive Introvert*; David Burner, *The Politics of Provincialism: the Democratic Party in Transition, 1918–1932* (New York: Alfred A. Knopf, 1967).

Chapter 11: Rites of Passage

To understand the important period of transition from the Hoover presidency to that of Roosevelt, most of the sources in the introductory paragraph must be consulted. In addition, particular attention should be given to Frank B. Freidel, *Franklin D. Roosevelt,* vol. 4: *Launching the New Deal* (Boston: Little, Brown & Co., 1973); Raymond Moley, *The First New Deal* (New York: Harcourt, Brace & World, Inc., 1966); Herbert Feis, *1933: Characters in Crisis* (Boston: Little, Brown, & Co., 1966); and a fine oral history piece, Raymond Henle, "Oral History Interview with Raymond Moley," 13 Nov. 1967, HP.

The best secondary account on the banking crisis is Susan Estabrook Kennedy, *The Banking Crisis of 1933* (Lexington: University Press of Kentucky, 1973). A helpful work is Laurin L. Henry, *Presidential Transitions* (Washington, D.C.: Brookings Institution, 1960).

Chapter 12: Epilogue

Although the Epilogue is based almost solely on primary sources, most important are the papers of Herbert Hoover, Felix Frankfurter, J. C. O'Laughlin, and William Allen White and the diaries of Edgar Rickard and Henry L. Stimson. The following secondary sources, particularly, provided an important context: Walter Johnson, *William Allen White's America* (New York: Henry Holt & Co., 1947); and Ronald Steel, *Walter Lippmann and the American Century* (Boston: Little, Brown, & Co., 1980).

Index

Adams, Charles Francis, 126, 173, 180; as secretary of navy, 35–36; cabinet role of, 45; Hoover wants for secretary of state, 172
Adams, John Quincy, 104
Addams, Jane, 28, 56
Agricola, Georgius, 8
Agriculture, 51, 81, 206; Agriculture Marketing Act, 49, 52, 106–7, 111–12; McNary-Haugen bills, 50; in 1920s, 65–66, 108; Agriculture Adjustment Act, 239–40. *See also* chap. 6, ''The Corporatist Balance''
Akerson, George, 69, 139; as press secretary, 22, 32, 41, 47–48
Albright, Horace M., 57
Allen, Henry J., 42, 46, 48, 93–94, 97, 109, 195, 205, 209, 212
Allen, Robert, 41
American Association of Civil Engineers, favors public-works relief, 165
American Citizens Relief Committee, 8–9
American Column and Lumber Company v. United States, 113–14
American Construction Council, headed by FDR, 118, 197
American Friends Service Committee, works for Hoover in World War I, 11
American Hardwood Manufacture Association, 113–14

American Individualism (Hoover), 17–19, 72, 105–6. *See also* its sequel, *Challenge to Liberty*
Anacostia Flats, dinner for Bonus Army from, 201
Antitrust cases during Hoover's presidency, 116
Ashurst, Henry F., 92
Aswell, James B., 111
Austria, forms customs union, 187
Awalt, F. Floyd, 238
Ayers, William A., 25

Babson, Roger W., 73, 77
Baker, George F., 68
Baker, Newton D., 62, 157, 198
Baldwin, Stanley, 222
Ballantine, Arthur A., 158, 231; aids New Deal, 238
Banks: 1933 crisis in, 233–34; Banking Act of 1933, 238–39. *See also* Reconstruction Finance Corporation
Barkley, Alben W., 101
Barnes, Julius H., 14, 27, 76–77; opposes wheat purchases, 109; for Swope plan, 118
Baruch, Bernard M., 70, 207; and FDR, 130, 198, 220; demands balanced budget of Hoover, 161–62
Bates, Sanford, 76
Bewick, Moreing & Co., 6–7

Bingham, Hiram, 196
Black, Hugo L., 164
Black, John D., 112
Bolivia, and boundary dispute, 185–86
Bolt & Nut Association, 116
Bonus, for veterans, 134, 161; march on Washington in 1932, 199–202
Borah, William E., 89, 102, 157, 189, 193; on agricultural legislation, 37, 51; on tariff, 93; on prohibition, 127; on bonus bill, 134; on public works, 165; on Manchurian incident, 181
Brandeis, Louis D.: his attitude toward Hoover, 12, 87; on trade associationalism, 114–15
Branner, John C., 6
Brewster, Ralph O., favors prosperity reserve fund, 33, 72
Briand, Aristide, 175. See also Kellogg-Briand Pact
Brookhart, Smith W., 37, 50, 101
Brown, Walter F., 22, 36, 196, 211; cabinet role of, 45
Bulkley, Robert J., 164
Bundy, Harvey H., 223
Business Cycles and Unemployment (1923 study), 64
Butler, William M., 26
Byrnes, James F., 129
Byrns, Joseph W., 101

Cabinet, Hoover's, 34–36
California Petroleum Refiners, 116
Cannon, James, Jr., 127
Capper, Arthur, 50–51
Caraway, Thaddeus H., 132
Cardozo, Benjamin N., 88, 93, 156–57
Castle, William R., Jr., 34, 37, 182
Catchings, Waddill, 159
Catholicism, as campaign issue in 1928, 29
Central Republic Bank & Trust Co., 163
Chaco (in Bolivia, Paraguay, Argentina), 185–86
Challenge to Liberty (Hoover), 245
Chamber of Commerce, favors Swope plan, 118
Chang Hsueh-liang, 176
Chiang Kai-shek, 176
Chinchou, Manchuria, 178, 180
Christgau domestic allotment bill, 112
Chrysler Corp., 231
Churchill, Winston, 9
Clarence Hatry Enterprises, 77

Clark, Edward T., 103, 129, 155, 196, 205
Clark, J. Reuben, Jr., 184–85
Claudel, Paul, 187
Cleveland, Grover, 111, 216
Collier, James W., 101
Colorado dam project, 136
Columbia River, 228
Commerce Department, 16
Commission for Relief in Belgium, 9–10
Commissions, committees, and conferences arranged by Hoover, 59
Committee on Business Cycles, 124
Committee on Recent Economic Changes, 124. See also chap. 4, "The Crash"
Commonwealth Club of San Francisco, Hoover's speech at, 206, 208
Conference on Unemployment, of 1921, 137
Congress, United States, 37, 50–51, 102; and Hoover, 48, 51, 156
Connally, Thomas T., 101
Coolidge, Calvin, 22, 39, 129, 144, 155, 184, 194, 205, 215; on Hoover's advice, 21
Corporatism, 27, 106, 113, 116, 124, 154; defined, 105–6. See also chap. 6, "The Corporatist Balance"
Costigan, Edward P., 164
Cotton, Joseph P., 88
Cotton, stabilization of, 110
Couzens, James, 231
Cox, James, 14, 220
Crash, 63; causes of, 77–78; Hoover explains causes of, 97. See also chap. 4, "The Crash"
Credit Anstalt, 143, 187. See also chap. 7, "1931: Things Get Worse"
Crisp, Charles R., 101, 160
Crissinger, Daniel R., 68–69
Croxton, Fred C., 149–50. See also President's Organization on Unemployment Relief
Cuba, 221–22
Curtis, Charles, 21, 24, 84, 195
Curtis, Cyrus, 13
Cutting, Bronson W., 212
Cycles, trade, 80

Daniels, Josephus, 196
Daugherty, Harry M., 15, 114, 120
Davis, James J., 36, 45, 71, 120–21, 135
Davis, John W., 130, 157

Davis, Joseph S., 112
Davis, Norman, 221, 224, 225
Davison, F. Trubee, 37
Dawes, Charles G., 21, 163, 186–87, 194, 196; as president of Reconstruction Finance Corporation, 154
Debts, foreign, 221–22
Democratic Party: its candidates for president in 1928, 24–25; its candidates in 1932, 198, 199; its fifty-year drumbeat against Hoover, 244
Depression: explanations for, 77–82; seen as world-wide, 168; its effects on foreign policy, 191; Hoover-Roosevelt differences on, 218. See also chap. 4, "The Crash"
DePriest, Mrs. Oscar, 59
Dickinson, Lester J., 195, 206–7
Dill, Clarence C., 92
Dixon, Joseph M., 91
Doak, William N., 35, 211
Domestic-allotment agricultural proposal of 1932, 206–7
Donovan, William J.: controversy over his appointment, 34–35; on antitrust prosecution, 116
Doughton, Robert L., 160. See also Revenue Act of 1932
Drought of 1930, 110–11
Du Pont, Pierre Samuel, 76
Durand, Edward Dana, 97–98
Durant, Will(iam James), 85

Earhart, Amelia, 211
Economy, the national: in the 1920s, 63–67; in 1931, 141, 147; in 1932, 156, 193, 207; in 1933, 231. See also chap. 4, "The Crash"
Edison, Thomas A., 73
Eighteenth Amendment, 61; and the Wickersham report, 125–27
Eisenhower, Dwight D., 201–2
Elections: of 1928, 21–30, results of, 30–31; of 1932, 194–212, results of, 212
Ely, Richard T., 159
Emergency Relief and Construction Act, 163–66
Erwin, Will, 153
Export debentures, 50, 94
Ezekiel, Mordecai, 112

Fall, Albert B., 120–21
Farley, James A., 198

Federal Farm Board: functions of, 49–52, 107; antidepression efforts of, 108–9. See also Agriculture, Agriculture Marketing Act
Federal Land Banks, 155
Federal Reserve System, 98; and stock market, 68–74; its authority questioned, 151; is critical of RFC, 163
Federal Trade Commission, 68, 116
Feis, Herbert, 220, 223
Fess, Simeon D., 23, 51, 85
Fisher, Irving, 140
Fisher, John, 26
Food Administration, United States, 9
Ford, Henry, 73, 76, 231
Fordney-McCumber Tariff, 94, 96
Foreign Policy: Hoover's direction of, 58, 167–69; its impact on depression, 191. See also chap. 9, "Foreign Policy"
Foster, William T., 159
Fox, George, 4, 167
France: on moratorium, 144, 188; on disarmament, 173, 190; on debt, 223
France, Joseph I., 196
Frankfurter, Felix, 98, 116, 157, 165, 217, 220, 239; on appointment of chief justice, 86–92; on tax increase, 159–61; his influence on Hoover's associates of high stature, 242
Friedman, Milton, 80, 151. See also Depression: explanation for

Galbraith, John Kenneth, 69. See also Crash: causes of
Gann, Mrs. Dolly, 84
Garner, John Nance, 101, 132, 153, 161, 166, 198; and Hoover, 49
General Motors Corp., 231
Geneva Naval Limitations Conference, 173
George, Walter F., 25
Germany, 144, 186–87, 190
Gibson, Hugh, 13, 34, 173, 189
Gifford, Walter S., heads POUR, 149–50
Glass, Carter, 25, 71, 110, 129, 156, 233
Glassford, Pelham D., 200, 202–3
Glenn, Frank, 143
Goff, Guy D., 24
Gompers, Samuel, 13, 119
Good, James W., 26, 36, 45, 138
Good Neighbor policy, 58, 183, 186, 191. See also chap. 9, "Foreign Policy"

Great Britain, 188; and London Naval Conference, 173; on reparations, 187; on war debts, 219, 223–24

Great Depression: its comparative effects on Hoover and Van Buren, 244

Green, William, 90, 98, 100, 135, 141–42; supports Hoover in 1928, 28, 121

Gridiron Club, 129, 226

Gross national product (GNP), 1923–29, 64

Grundy, Joseph R., 37, 53

Haiti, 58, 184

Hall, William, 48

Hamlin, Charles S., 71

Hand, Learned, 34

Hansen, Alvin H., 81

Harding, Warren G., 14

Hard Times, 162

Harriman, Henry I., 118

Harrison, George L., 70, 153

Harrison, Pat (Byron Patton), 101

Hawley, Ellis W., 105. *See also* chap. 6, "The Corporatist Balance"

Hay, John M., 177

Hayes, Rutherford B., 194

Hays, Will H., 120–21

Hearst, William Randolph, 199, 207

Herter, Christian A., 34

Hilles, Charles D., 26, 194

Hillman, Sidney, 28

Hillquit, Morris, 133

Hinshaw, David, 131, 148

Hitchman Coal and Coke case, 90

Holmes, Oliver Wendell, 114

Home Loan Discount Bank, 155

Hoover, Andrew (forebearer), 2

Hoover, David (forebearer), 2

Hoover, Herbert Clark
—his background: family heritage of, 1–3; his early life and education, 3–5; his experience in mining, 6–7; his marriage, 6
—presidential career of: and Panama-Pacific exposition, 8; and American Citizens Relief Committee, 8; as author—*Principles of Mining* (1901), 8, *American Individualism* (1922), 17–19, *Challenge to Liberty* (1934), 245, *The Memoirs of Herbert Hoover* (1951, 1952), 267; as commissioner for Relief of Belgium, 9; and U.S. Food Administration, 9; at Versailles, including Inter-Allied Food Council,

10, 168; is considered for presidency in 1920, 13–14; as secretary of commerce, 15–16
—and election of 1928: Coolidge's role in, 21–22; Hoover's nomination, 26–27, 195; campaigns, 28–30; and Catholicism issue, 29–30, 127; is victorious, 31
—as president: forms cabinet, 34–35, 44; and controversy over Donovan, 34–35; his inauguration, 39–40; administrative reforms of, 39; and White House staff, 41; routine of, 42, 44, 84; nonpartisanship of, 45–46; his relations with public and press, 47, 203–5; and agriculture, 49–52, 107, 110–12; and President's Committee on Recent Social Trends, 59–60; his first year, 62, 85; and banks, Federal Reserve System, 68, 70, 98; and the crash, 72–74, 97; his antidepression efforts, 72, 75–76, 81, 98; and public power, 73, 136; on economy, 78, 140, 141, 155, 164, 165, 166, 232; and court appointments—J. Parker, 89–93, O. Roberts, 93, C. E. Hughes, 87–88, B. Cardozo, 157; and tariffs, 93–94; and PECE, 99–100; and election of 1930, 103; and capital, 112–16; and Swope plan, 117; and labor, 120–22, 138; and POUR, 120; and prohibition, 125–28, 195; his speeches, 142, 226–27; and NCC, 152–53; forms RFC, 154; and bank crisis of 1935, 233–34
—and Congress: his relations with, 49; gets his program through, 100; looses support in, 129–30; his 1931 program in, 132; Bonus bill vetoed by, 134; Hoover on Congress, 147; weak Republican support in, 147–48; David Reed defends Hoover in, 149; and State of Union Message, 154; and Revenue Act of 1932, 161, 167
—and foreign relations: South American trip of, in 1929, 32–33; Central American trip of, in 1931, 138; and moratorium, 143, 182, 187; meets with J. Ramsay MacDonald, 172; and Japan, 179–80; and Clark Memorandum, 185; Laval's visit with, 188–89, 216; and World Disarmament Conference, 190; after the 1932 election, 216–17; and Stimson-FDR meeting, 221–22

—and election of 1932: Republican opposition to his nomination, 148–49; seeks credit for Stimson Doctrine, 182; and Bonus Army, 202; Michelson's activity in, 204; Hoover's public relations in, 204–5; issues of, 206; use of radio in, 209; campaign spokesmen in, 211–12; defeat in, 212

—after the election of 1932: meets with FDR, 48, 224; on war-debt issue, 219; receives gift from cabinet, 235; Washington's farewell, 236; his routine after leaving White House, 238–40; his attitude about first 100 days, 240; meets with faculty of University of Chicago, 241

—descriptions of: by Stimson, 42, 187–88; by "Ike" Hoover, 43; by Edward Clark, 155

—his ideology, 124; and ordered freedom, 4–5, 40, 245; evaluation of, 17–19; and corporatism, 27, 106; and progressive myths, 46–47; and associationalism, 113; and individualism, 117

—his life style, 169; his treatment of children, 83–84; and fishing, 137–38

—and Quakers, 4–12. *See also* Prohibition *and* chap. 12, "Epilogue"

—his relations with (and comparison to): Henry L. Stimson, 45, 101–3, 164, 182, 221; Harlan F. Stone, 87–88, 242–43; Franklin D. Roosevelt, 149, 218, 224, 227, 229, 231–32

—author's conclusions about, 237–46

Hoover, Herbert Clark, Jr. (son), 138
Hoover, Huldah (mother), 2, 4
Hoover, Irwin ("Ike") Hood (chief usher at White House), describes Hoover, 43
Hoover, Jesse Clark (father), 2
Hoover, John (uncle), 2
Hoover, Lou Henry (wife), 4, 6
Hoover, Mary (sister), 2
Hoover, Rebecca (great grandmother), 2
Hoover, Theodore (brother), 2
Hope, Walter E., 42, 236
Hopkins, Richard J., 46
Hornbeck, Stanley, 179
House, Col. Edward M., 13, 130, 217, 226
Howard University, 59
Howe, Louis M., 100, 198, 230
Hughes, Charles Evans, 14, 21, 33, 59, 172, 184, 194; appointed chief justice, 88
Hughes, Charles Evans, Jr., 37, 88
Hull, Cordell, 25
Hunt, Edward Eyre, 16, 42, 60, 115; on corporatist balance, 124
Hurley, Patrick Jay, 138, 180, 211; and Bonus march, 201–3; expects Hoover's defeat in 1932, 212
Hyde, Arthur M., 36, 209; on Agriculture Marketing Act, 106–7; on wheat-acreage restriction, 109–10

Ickes, Harold L., 28, 30, 194–95, 212
Inaugurations, presidential: in 1929, 39–40; in 1933, 235–36
Indianapolis, Hoover's speech at, 142
Ingalls, David S., 37
Italy, 173, 175, 190

Jahncke, Ernest Lee, 37
Janin, Louis, 6
Japan, 173, 182. *See also* chap. 9, "Foreign Policy"
Jardine, William M., 51
Johnson, Hiram W., 14, 135; opposes Hoover in 1928, 28; in 1932, 194
Johnson, Hugh S., 207
Joint Committee on Reorganization, of 1920–24, 54
Jones, Jesse H., 25
Jones, Rufus M., 3, 10–11
Jones, Wesley L., 72, 98
Jordan, David Starr, 5–6
Joslin, Theodore G., 42, 139, 157

Katsuzi Debuchi, 177
Keep Commission, 54
Kellogg, Frank B., 185
Kellogg-Briand Pact, 172, 176–77, 180–81, 184, 186. *See also* chap. 9, "Foreign Policy"
Kennan, George F., on Manchurian crisis, 182
Kent, Frank R., 48, 70
Kenyon, William S., 62
Kenyon bill of 1920, 72
Keynes, John Maynard, 81, 168; describes Hoover at Versailles, 10
King, Judson, 136
Kings Mountain, Hoover's speech at, 117

Kiplinger Washington Letter, 137, 145, 150
Klein, Julius, 16, 37, 74
Klots, Allen, 83
Krock, Arthur, praises Hoover, 157

Labor: in 1920s, 67; Hoover and, 118; and Wilkerson injunction, 120–21; and 1928 election, 121, 207. *See also* Wagner, Robert F., *and* chap. 6, "The Corporatist Balance"
La Follette, Robert M., 28, 86, 101, 164, 212
La Guardia, Fiorello H., 160, 200
Lamont, Robert P., 36, 45, 77, 97, 126, 241–42
Lamont, Thomas W., 74
Lausanne, Switzerland, 188
Laval, Pierre, 188–89
Lawrence, David, 48
League of Nations, 176–77, 181, 182
Legge, Alexander, 52, 108–10
Lehman, Herbert H., 234
Lenroot, Irvine, 68–69
Leticia (Colombia), 185–86
Lever Act, 9
Lewis, James H., 198
Lewis, John L., 28
Lincoln Day speech by Hoover, 227
Lindbergh, Charles A., 211
Lindsay, Sir Ronald Charles, 216, 225
Lippmann, Walter, 25, 180, 198, 200, 237; on Hoover's first year, 86; supports Hoover early in 1932, 156–57; favors balanced budget, 158–59; favors sound money, 164; favors self-liquidating public works, 164–65; supports FDR, 234
London Economic Conference, 188, 190, 224–25
London Naval Conference, 96–97, 102, 190; provisions of, 173–76
Longworth, Alice Roosevelt, and society feud, 84
Longworth, Nicholas, 51, 84
Lowden, Frank O., 21
Lucas, Robert H., 171
Lytton Report, 186

McAdoo, William Gibbs, 62, 70, 199
MacArthur, Gen. Douglas, 201–3
McClintic, George W., 90
McCormick, Anne O'Hare, 85
McCormick, Ruth Hanna, 97–98, 194

MacDonald, James Ramsay, 73
McDuffie, John, 191
McGrath, Myra, 41
McKellar, Kenneth, 91, 162
McNab, John L., 23
McNary, Charles L., 36, 51
McNary-Haugenism, 50, 94
Madison Square Garden, Hoover's and Roosevelt's speeches at, in 1932, 210
Manchuria incident, 177–81, 190, 221–22. *See also* chap. 9, "Foreign Policy"
Maple Flooring Association v. *The United States,* 114
Martin, Edward, 26
Massachusetts Public Utilities Department, 77
Mellon, Andrew W., 14–15, 44, 76, 97, 152, 161, 171; his "child-like" narrations, 140
Merriam, Charles E., 60–61
Mexico, 185–86
Meyer, Eugene, 71, 99, 152, 154, 158, 234; questions authority of Federal Reserve System, 151
Michelson, Charles, 85–87, 204–5
Michigan, bank holiday in, 231
Millikan, Robert A., 241–42
Mills, Ogden L., 26, 36, 37, 42, 44, 66, 166, 171, 187, 211, 216, 217, 225; on bank crisis, 133, 231–32; on tax increase, 158–59; on prohibition, 195; a Hoover associate of high stature, 238
Minthorn, Henry John, 2
Mirrors of 1932, The, 153
Missouri-Pacific Railroad, 163
Missouri River, 228
Mitchell, Broadus, 65
Mitchell, Charles, 70, 101, 204, 209
Mitchell, Wesley C., 60–61, 65
Mitchell, William D., 35, 45, 56, 116, 123
Moley, Raymond, 201, 217–18, 224–25, 230, 231; reminisces about Hoover, 226
Monroe Doctrine, 183–84
Moore, John Bassett, 88
Moratorium, 143, 148, 186–87, 191, 209–10
Morrow, Dwight W., 173, 184, 194
Moses, George H., 23, 26, 101
Moton, Robert R., 184
Munro, Dana C., 184
Murray, William H., 198

Muscle Shoals, 134–36
Myers, William Starr, describes Hoover's first year, 85
Myrdal, Gunnar, 79

National Association for the Advancement of Colored People (NAACP), 91
National Civic Federation, 119
National Credit Corporation (NCC), 152–53
National Electrical Manufacture Association, 116
National Recovery Administration, 118
Neagle, Charles, 116
Newberg, Oreg., 2
New Freedom, 149
New Nationalism, 149
New Orleans Banana Co., 185
New Republic, 89
Newton, Walter H., 26, 41, 91, 123, 195, 235
New York Times, its assessments of Hoover, 62, 98–99, 133
Nicaragua, 58, 172, 184, 190
Nine-Power Pact, 176–77, 180–81
Norris, George W., 21, 24, 88, 96, 101, 131, 196, 197–98, 212; on moratorium, 144, 148, 188
Norris–La Guardia Anti-injunction Act, 121, 122, 123
Nye, Gerald P., 101

O'Brian, John Lord, 116
O'Connor, Basil, 230
Oddie, Tasker L., 162
Odum, Howard W., 60–61
Ogburn, William F., 60–61
Ohio River, 228
O'Laughlin, John C., 211, 240
"Open Door," 180–81
Ordered freedom, 4–5, 245
Ordered liberty, 4–5, 40, 115, 245
"Organizational synthesis" revisionist history, 113
Oulahan, Richard V., 48

Page, Arthur W., 140
Palo Alto, Calif., 236
Panama-Pacific exposition, 8
Pan American Union, 185–86
Paraguay, 185–86
Parker, John J., 89–93, 102

Penney, J. C., 34
Pepper, George Wharton, 157
Pershing, Gen. John J., 21
Philippine Islands, 33, 58, 172, 190–91, 221–22
Pinchot, Gifford, 148, 195–96, 212
Pine, William B., 51
Pittman, Key, 217
Pittsburgh, Pa., FDR's economy speech at, 207
Pomerene, Atlee, 25
Pound, Roscoe, 62
Presidency, 42, 43–44, 45, 47, 48, 55, 57, 62, 84, 85, 246; staffs of, 41; as office, 215
President's Committee on Recent Social Trends, 59–60
President's Conference on Unemployment, 120
President's Emergency Committee on Employment (PECE), 99, 149
President's Organization on Unemployment Relief (POUR), 149–50
Press: its views of Hoover, 24, 41; Hoover and, 47, 204–5; Stimson and, 48; in 1932 election, 209
Principles of Mining (Hoover), 8
Progressive Magazine, 86
Progressivism: in Hoover's inaugural address, 40; Hoover on, 46–47
Prohibition, 125–26, 195, 207–8
Prosperity reserve fund, 33, 72
Public works, 97; Hoover's position on, in 1932, 165
Puerto Rico, 138
Pulitzer, Ralph, 13

Quakers (and Quakerism), 4, 12–13, 40, 41; Hoover on, 1, 11–12; Hoover's ancestors and, 2–3; their behavior and thoughts, 3–4; Queries in American Individualism, 18; on prohibition, 127–28; on foreign policy, 167; their ultimate impact on Hoover, 244–45
Queries, Quaker, 18

Rapidan (Hoover's retreat in Maryland), 84, 138, 172, 205
Raskob, John J., 27, 198–99, 204
Reconstruction Finance Corporation (RFC), 145, 154, 162–63, 230–31
Red Cross, 111
Reed, David A., 96, 149, 173, 175

Reed, James A., 12, 24, 86, 233
Reparations, 186, 188
Report of the President's Committee on Recent Social Trends, 241
Report on Recent Economic Changes, 64, 72, 115–16
Republican National Convention of 1932, 195–96
Requa, Mark L., 46
Revenue Act of 1932, 161
Rhoads, Charles J., 57
Richberg, Donald R., 212
Richey, Lawrence, 35, 41, 138, 195, 220, 238
Rickard, Edgar, 212, 236, 241–42
Rinehart, Mary Roberts, 209
Ritchie, Albert C., 142, 198
Roberts, Owen J., 92
Robinson, Henry M., 42, 74, 241–42
Robinson, Joseph T., 44, 74, 101, 129, 139, 173, 198, 233; cooperates with Hoover, 132; favors self-liquidating public works, 165
Rogers, James G., 181
Rogers, Will, 112
Roosevelt, Franklin Delano, 13, 14, 24, 27, 34, 70–71, 74, 112, 149, 157, 185, 193, 196, 197, 198, 200, 209, 211, 216–17, 219, 227–28, 229–30, 234, 235, 236, 239; heads American Construction Council, 118; inaugural address as governor of N.Y., 130–31; on depression in 1931, 142; on Hoover's foreign policy, 191; as "chameleon on plaid," 203; and campaign issues in 1932, 206; economy speech of, in 1932, 207; his Commonwealth Club speech, 208; his victory in 1932, 212; meets with Hoover, in Nov. 1932, 218, Jan. 1933, 224; meets with Stimson in 1933, 221–22; his impasse with Hoover in 1933, 231–32
Roosevelt, Theodore, 184, 211, 215, 204
Roosevelt, Theodore, Jr., 26, 120–21, 196
Root, Elihu, 31, 34, 126, 187
Rosenman, Samuel I., 207, 230
Roy, Eugene, 184
Russell Sage Foundation, 137
Russia, 190, 221–22

Sabath, Adolph J., 151
Sackett, Frederic M., 17, 187

Sandblast, Lawritz B., 196
Sanders, Everett, 196
Sanford, Edward T., 89
Schall, Thomas D., 51
Schlesinger, Arthur M., Jr., 105
Schwartz, Anna Jacobson, 70
Seabury, Samuel, 198
Seasonal Operation in the Construction Industries, 64
Second Industrial Conference, 11–13, 119
Seligman, E. R. A., 159
Shanghai, 180–81, 190
Shankey, Ann, 41
Shaw, Arch W., 232
Shouse, Jouett, 198–99
Simon, Sir John A., 181
Simpson, John A., 144, 188
Slichter, Simon, 137
Smith, Adam, 168
Smith, Alfred E., 24, 25, 121, 130, 157, 164, 204; and Catholicism issue in 1928, 29–30; his candidacy for Democratic nomination in 1932, 198–99. *See also* chap. 2, "Victory"
Smoot, Reed, 23
Smoot-Hawley Tariff, 102, 186; passage of, 196–97; as 1932 campaign issue, 206–8
Snell, Bertrand H., 123, 195
South Manchurian Railway, 178
Stabilization conferences, 75–76
Stein, Herbert, 82, 158
Stimson, Henry L., 9, 33, 45, 48, 58, 84, 92, 101, 102–3, 158, 174, 185–86, 190, 211, 212, 216, 217, 223–24, 231, 234; describes Hoover, 42, 139, 187–88; on prohibition, 126, 129, 195; on moratorium, 143–44, 191; his life style, 169–70; on nonrecognition doctrine, 178–182; on Hoover's Quakerism, 189; on Hoover's defeat in 1932, 215; meets with FDR, 218, 221–22, 228; and cabinet gift to Hoover, 235; his accommodation to New Deal, 242
Stimson Doctrine, 176–80; authorship of, 182
St. James Church (Hyde Park, N.Y.), 232
Stock market, New York, 69–73
Stone, Harlan F., 35, 83, 91, 126, 204; denied chief justiceship, 86; and Hoover, 87–88; supports trade associationalism, 114; differs with Hoover, 242–43

St. Paul, Minn., Hoover's speech at,
in 1932, 200
Straus, Lewis L., 220, 236
Strong, Benjamin, 80–81, 151–57
Strother, French, 55, 60–61
Sugar Institute, 116
Sullivan, Mark, 34, 42, 45, 62
Supreme Court of the United States,
appointments to, 86–93
Swope, Gerard, 99, 117
Swope, Herbert Bayard, 70, 193

Taber, Louis J., 28
Taft, William Howard, 39, 54, 90, 215
Tardieu, André, 174
Tariffs: Hoover on, in 1929, 53; as
issue in 1932, 207–8
Taussig, Frank W., 76
Taxes, in 1932, 160–61
Taylor, Myron C., 76
Tennessee River, 227
Tennessee Valley Authority (TVA),
130, 208
Terkel, Studs, 162
Thomas, Norman M., 30
Thompson, Huston, 25
Tilson, John Q. , 37, 75
Tobin, Daniel J., 121
Tolles, Frederick B., 12–13
Topeka, Kans., FDR's speech at, in
1932, 206–7, 210
Toynbee, Arnold J., 79
Trade associationalism, 64–65, 113, 115
Trade cycles, 80
Trading with the Enemy Act, 233
Tri-City case, 90
Trubee, F. Davison, 37
Tugwell, Rexford G., 156, 224, 233

Underhill, Charles L., 148
Unemployment Conference of 1921,
16–17, 72
United States v. *American Linseed Oil
Company,* 114
Untiedt, Bryan, 138–39

Valley Forge, Pa., Hoover's speech at,
117
Van Buren, Martin, 203, 244
Van Kleeck, Mary, 137
Veblen, Thorstein B., 7
Vernon, Leroy T., 48
Versailles Treaty, 10–11, 189

Veterans Administration, 200
Virgin Islands, 138
Vladivostok, 176

Wagner, Robert F., 30–31, 88–89; his
three bills, 122, 134, 135; his Public
Employment Agency bill, 207
Wallace, Henry C., 15
Walsh, David I., 101, 132
Walsh, Thomas J., 164, 196
Warburg, James P., 241
Warburg, Paul M., 68
War debts, 218, 219
Warm Springs, Ga., 224
Washington Arms Conference, 168,
172, 174
Watson, James E., 21, 24, 91, 96, 129
West Branch, Iowa, 2
Whalen, Grover A., 125
Wheat, stabilization of prices for,
108–10
White, Francis, 185–86
White, William Allen, 29, 46, 130, 153,
165, 194, 209, 212, 226; on Hoover
and western senators, 93, 94, 97,
131, 136; describes Hoover, 111, 205,
239–40; as White House guest,
239–40; favors domestic-allotment
plan, 239–40; as Hoover associate of
high stature, 239–40
Wickersham, George W., 61–62, 126
Wickersham Commission on Law En-
forcement, 59, 123, 195; membership
of, 61–62; report of, 127
Wilbur, Ray Lyman, 36, 45, 83, 138,
162; his role in cabinet, 56–57
Wilkerson injunction, 120
Willebrandt, Mabel Walker, 29, 35, 56,
62
Williams, Ralph F., 34
Williams, W. A., 105
Wilson, Gene, 48
Wilson, M. L., 206
Wilson, William B., 13
Wilson, Woodrow, 9, 10, 184, 215
Wilson Dam, 135–36
Wolman, Leo, 142
Wood, Will R., 98, 131
Woodin, William H., 232, 233
Woods, Arthur, 132; appointed chair-
man of PECE, 99; resigns as chair-
man, 149
Wool Institute, 116
Woollen, Evans, 25
Work, Hubert, 26

World Court, 102, 173
World Disarmament Conference, 171, 181, 186–90

Young, Owen D., 76, 198, 217
Young, Roy A., 98
Young Plan, 186–87